Contact

Down

Under

Contact
Down Under

A century of UFO sightings in Australasia and the Western Pacific

Moira McGhee

Published by INUFOR – Independent Network of UFO Investigators

CONTACT DOWN UNDER: A century of UFO sightings in Australasia and the Western Pacific.

INUFOR books may be purchased for educational, business, or sales promotional use. For information please write: INUFOR, P.O. Box 169, Katoomba NSW 2780, AUSTRALIA.

INUFOR web site: http://www.independentnetuforesearchers.com.au

www.ind.net.ufo.res@bigpond.com

www.FACEBOOK/INUFOR

FIRST INUFOR PAPERBACK EDITION PUBLISHED IN APRIL, 2016

ISBN: 9780646 – 305 – 042

Front Cover: Shows detail of the Orange Ball of Light videoed over Tregear in Western Sydney, on Thursday 24 November 1994 (see page 11).

This book is dedicated to all my departed colleagues who helped and mentored me in the early days:

Rosemary Decker (USA), Millen le-Poer-Trench, Ken Phillips (UK), Betty Wood (UK), Judy Magee, Paul Norman, Colin Norris, Frank Sinclair, Martin Gottschall, David Buching, Fred Phillips.

Contents

Introduction

Australia and New Zealand are no different to other parts of the world. Something is going on in our skies, and has been for many years. *Contact Down Under* details just a small sample of the thousands of sightings reported over the last seventy years and earlier.

Will this book give you any answers to the vast controversy and mystery of the UFO phenomena? Probably not! Most researchers agree they have too many questions and very few answers. In fact I find that for every answer I get, ten more questions come to the fore. UFO investigators all know that UFOs exist – but the definition of their nature and composition is elusive, and their paradoxical behaviour often makes it impossible to determine their origin.

Certainly tangible, solid objects may well be a misidentification, a conventional airplane, or our own secret military technology. In fact, well over 90-percent of reports can either be identified, or have insufficient details to make a determination. Many of the remaining few percent appear too advanced to have come from Earth. However, with each appearance our scientists and boffins start to 'think outside the box' in relation to their own research and innovations.

Some reports seem to indicate an unknown energy form; witnesses describe an opening of the consciousness, and various perceptions of interaction with an alien intelligence or universal energy. Modern quantum physicists now grasp the concept of everything in the universe being interconnected – are we getting tantalising glimpses of parallel realities and other dimensions? Do they emanate from an alien intelligence of incredible complexity? Or have we distorted space-time ourselves, with dangerous experiments which seek to alter or intensify the existing fields and vibrations of Earth's natural energies?

Some areas seem to attract strange anomalies and phenomena more than others. Our Earth generates and is surrounded by a magnetic field, but this magnetism is not uniform, and can fluctuate greatly. Lines of force form strange patterns – often referred to as *Ley Lines*. Ancient civilisations were well aware of electromagnetic energy and utilised Ley Lines and magnetic vortices for sacred sites and rituals.

Many areas of Australia also possess magnetic deviations and changes in energy vibrations which can result in distortions of space and time, and provide a 'window area' to paranormal and inter-dimensional events. Often UFOs are present in these 'hot-spots'.

As our own technology advances beyond our wildest imagination, so it becomes more difficult for researchers to definitively state exactly who or what was responsible for a witness's sighting or experience – earthly, alien, spiritual, time slip, or a combination of these?

While many conservative 'experts' ignore or scoff at contactees' and abductees' reports of interaction with other intelligences, this phenomenon is now so prevalent, the human race ignores it at its peril.

Chapter One

Seeing is believing – or is it?

The investigation of unidentified flying objects is not easy, and far from being an exact science. As far as possible, one has to rule out all conventional explanations for what a witness reports, before the *unidentified* category can be attributed to the object. Once a flying object is classified as being unidentified, it raises more questions than answers – questions all UFO researchers will grapple with and endlessly debate.

In many cases a researcher cannot be sure. If they're honest they will admit this, and file the data away for later scrutiny when further details or information comes to hand. It is, in many ways, a no-win situation. On one side you have the armchair sceptic, who has not spoken to witnesses, or is even aware of all the facts, and often is just seeking publicity by making a pronouncement that the object was a planet, atmospheric inversion, meteorite or some other mundane explanation. Sometimes they will resort to the less likely, but possible, swamp gas, or flights of birds or insects. It is possible, and often suspected, that these critics are the mouthpiece for agencies that need to discredit or suppress information they want hidden from the general public. The fact is, most responsible investigators would usually withhold details if it was genuinely in the national interest.

On the other side, you have many witnesses who are convinced they have seen visitors from outer space. If we could prove this, the objects would no longer be unidentified. If one tries to explain there are either insufficient details to reach a conclusion or a probable explanation, they will accuse the poor investigator of being an amateur or working for the government. Often witnesses will seek a more-acceptable result from a second researcher, and tweak the details in the process. Luckily most witnesses are sane, sensible people, who want to find the answers just as much as UFO investigators do.

The most difficult cases occur when witnesses who have been traumatised by meeting strange beings come forward. There can be physical evidence and a lot of conscious recall, which is difficult to manage. It is still a matter of conjecture, and utmost importance to humanity, as to where these beings originate – their purpose and motivation. It matters not how respectable, honest and reliable these witnesses are, mainstream society – including the political, religious, military and medical sectors – will, for various reasons, actively attempt to discredit or suppress any UFO reports.

Of course I, and all other investigators, have our own beliefs and theories, often vastly different, regarding this entire phenomenon. Wise researchers resist the temptation to pass judgement, and do not let their personal views affect their reports. Where possible, they should just present the witness statements and facts, no matter what their own thoughts are.

In reality, this is easier said than done.

Physical, dimensional or holographic?

As humans we are conditioned to interact with the physical world through what our senses tell us. Can we see it, touch it, hear it, smell it? These are tests our brains automatically use to tell us something is real.

Once our brain has recognised something exists it then usually draws on past experience and knowledge to decide what it is. Often our identification of something is mistaken, and is a more subjective judgement, based on limited physical information and our own personal knowledge and beliefs.

Common misidentifications
Sometimes we can make a mistake when we identify an odd object in the sky. This may be due to an optical illusion created by an otherwise familiar object, or viewing a craft with an advanced technology, giving it an appearance and behaviour we do not recognise.

Possible explanations

Celestial objects
The moon – which can be deceptive in some circumstances.
The planets – especially Venus, Mars, Jupiter and Saturn.
Also, meteors, meteor showers, and (very rarely) comets.

Atmospheric and natural phenomena
Cumulus and lenticular clouds, atmospheric inversions, jet trails (contrails), Laser and other light reflections, aurora australis, ball lightning, earth lights.

Min min lights
These are bright circular or oval lights, which appear to hover anywhere from just above ground level to high in the trees. Min min lights can be quite common in Australia's vast desert areas. They are usually a temperature inversion, caused by a layer of cold air on the ground with a layer of warmer air above. If a beam of light, from a vehicle's headlight for example, passes from the dense cold air up into the less dense warm air, it changes direction, or *refracts*. It can then shine back down on a road, below the horizon, up to 200 kilometres away.

Australian Aboriginals describe *all* unusual lights as "min min", and this is a favourite explanation sceptics use to dismiss many sightings that do not necessarily equate with such phenomenon.

Man-made objects
Satellites, satellite re-entries, space junk, Iridium flare satellites, meteorological and research balloons, airships, Google balloons, model rockets, kites, conventional aircraft and helicopters, hang gliders, microlights, street and other building lights, searchlights, car and other vehicle lights, distress flares, fireworks, drones, and deliberate hoaxes.

Advertising blimps are now joined by new types of dirigibles, which have been reported since the end of the 19th century, and often without conventional explanation. Modern technology has created new breeds of hybrid airships with the advantage of vertical take-off and landing. They include the Vanguard Donut, Havillparawing, Thermo Skyship, and the All-American Aerocrane.

New aircraft and flying contraptions
There is no doubt in my mind that a lot of what is reported is due to our own technology. Some we know about, more still are probably hidden behind official secrecy. While some UFO researchers claim we have developed our own flying saucers by back-engineering them from a disc which crashed in 1947, this is not necessarily correct. Our own boffins were already familiar with the concept of such craft, well before then.

This could still be because there were other UFO crashes, or visiting discs long before 1947. Some reports may well have been that the unconventional craft of radical design were in fact covert military operations. While people concentrate on incidents during 1947, other possible crash events may have gone unnoticed, unreported, unknown.

In 1925 a Russian designer, Tscharanowsky, proposed a rounded aerodynamic shape in his *Parabola* glider, which incorporated semicircular wings.

We know that Hitler's Third Reich had plans for such craft, at least on the drawing board, but did they have some help? An elderly European friend of mine told me how her father was seconded into the German Luftwaffe in World War 2. When I asked what he did, she replied "Oh, he was back-engineering a flying saucer for the Nazis." Interesting! Perhaps more on this in a later book.

At the end of World War 2, the Soviet Army "liberated" some of Germany's most advanced weapons research laboratories, and within a few years had perfected designs for unorthodox aircraft, in secret. While Western Allies had also liberated German technology and scientists, they wanted to know to what extent the Russians had developed Nazi flying saucer-type devices.

John Thomas Jnr discussed a lecture by John Searl where he outlined his development of Searl-effect generators and their use in a "levity disc." Searl claimed he had first built and flown his "flying generator" in 1946. Apparently it flew off at tremendous speed and never came back.

Gravity has always fascinated scientists and in the 1950s physicists were conceptualizing anti-gravity propulsion technologies. Their craft duplicated the aerodynamics of a flying saucer, with high-speed pulsar vehicles, pulsed detonation engines, and electro-gravitational craft. The USAF Aeronautical Systems Division designed a saucer-type VTOL in its *Project 1794*.

Certainly the Americans conducted secret high-altitude reconnaissance flights, and it is quite probable the Russians did the same. From the 1950s the Americans tested and used the A-12 spy-plane. This was faster than the U2 and could travel beyond Mach 2 at 50,000 feet. It could shoot downwards, hover, then soar upwards again at impossible speeds, leaving a glow which occasionally turned green. This may account for some UFO reports.

In 1980 the Polish Journal *Przegląd Techniczny Innowacje* included a treatise by Dr Jan Pająk about a saucer-shaped space vehicle from about 1970, which utilised the attraction and repulsion of magnetic fields. In 1990, his *Magnocraft – earth's version of a UFO*, outlined the mastery and production of oscillatory chambers for two kinds of propulsion – "main" and "side", where the base of such craft would always remain perpendicular to the direction of the earth's magnetic field.

Our own aeronautics industry has progressed in leaps and bounds. We may well query whose high-technology we are observing; our own earth-made UFOs, or something based on back-engineered alien technology? Most of those involved in such technological developments neither confirm nor deny the incorporation of alien technology and concepts.

Drones, remote-controlled, and unmanned craft

The original goal for unmanned vehicles was for secret military technology designed for surveillance or espionage missions. Since that time there has been many unmanned aerial vehicles (UAVs), designed, manufactured, and used for military and commercial purposes. They come in an ever-increasing variety of shapes and sizes, and in the 21st century an unidentified flying object may well be one of these unconventional craft which have become perfectly normal and conventional.

These craft have not suddenly appeared overnight, and prototypes have been tested and used in our skies, long before the turn of this century, making the ufologist's task more difficult. Originally they were tested at night, and required light for retrieval, but that is unlikely to be the case today. In addition to our own craft, there is always the possibility of spying missions by foreign powers. And let us not dismiss those pesky extraterrestrials; if we have UAVs, how technologically advanced will they be?

In 1994, *UFO Afrinews* stated that a previously reported crashed disc was in fact an unmanned aerial vehicle, controlled from a secret base and sent out to evaluate air defence systems. The South African Armscor-Kentcon complex had developed the triangle-shaped UAV, then followed this up in 1997 with *Flowchart 2*, a stealth target drone.

In 1999, in the lead-up to *Exercise Crocodile*, the US-Australian Defence Forces tested out a new surveillance craft, which could travel up to 200km from its ground control station. Each cost about one million dollars, and our military were so excited with their new toy they made proud press releases. It was in fact the CL-227 *Sentinel* with a very unconventional shape – something like a pot-bellied stove with four landing legs and a dome with rotor blades on top, 1.8 metres tall, with a diameter of four metres.

The authorities would have us believe this was the first drone in Australia. This is not necessarily true. Researcher Tim Schwartz reported on 24 June 1996, that a Victorian mother and daughter saw a bright light approach their house and heard the noise of a helicopter. They could see a small black helicopter accompanied by a round shiny metal disc, the size of a car.

The disc came down to land in their relatively small backyard. They were amazed it managed to do so without touching the clothes-line or trees. The helicopter hovered over the other side of the house, as if watching. The disc looked like shiny silver foil in the moonlight, and as it rose back up to eye level, they could see yellow-orange lights swirling over its surface.

It then rose higher, went over the house, and flew off to the west followed by the helicopter. If that wasn't one of the legendary black helicopters monitoring or probably controlling a drone, I don't know where to find a better example.

UAV examples

- Glider-shaped craft include: *Phoenix* RFV, RQ-1A *Predator*, FQM-2A *Pioneer*, FQM-151A *Pointer*, RQ-4A *Global Hawk*, BQM-155A *Hunter*, *Raptor* D-2, the *Gnat* 750, the *Altus*.
- Craft which resemble one long flying wing include the *Centurion* and the *Pathfinder*.
- The Boeing *Hell Wing* UAV, and Bell Helicopter *Eagle Eye* UAV. Both can travel in horizontal flight before switching to vertical hover mode.
- The Canadair CL-227 *Sentinel* (NASA) is identical to that publicised by our Defence Forces in 1999. It is an advanced version of a reconnaissance craft called *Peanut* (due to its shape) produced as early as 1978.
- Remotely piloted craft with a blended wing/body (i.e. slightly triangular) include the McDonnel Douglas (MDC) *Blub*, the BQM-147A *Exdrone*, the STM-5B-1 *Sentry*.
- There are also large, round craft which can easily be mistaken for a flying saucer, including the Micro Air Vehicle, or MAV (smaller versions of this are designed to carry miniature video cameras), the *Cypher*, and Russia's *Sikorsky UAV*.
- Other remotely-controlled craft include the more conventionally shaped *Eagle Eye*, the *Perseus B*, the *Dragonfly*, the BQM-145A *Medium Range*, the *Sender*, the *Outrider*.
- The *TierI-Plus*, and later *TierII-Plus* are glider-shaped, can travel about 3,000 miles and hover at 65,000 feet for up to 24 hours.
- The *TierIII-Minus* (*Darkstar*), and TR-A *Black Manta*, are pilotless reconnaissance planes, produced by Lockheed's Skunk Works. Unveiled by the Pentagon in the 1990s, they are variously described as saucer-shaped or a flying wing that is triangular or manta ray-shaped. At 15 feet long and five feet high, they can travel 500 miles to a particular spot and then operate for over eight hours at heights in excess of 45,000ft. They replace the U-2R; their main role includes data relay and targeting for F-117As.

Uninhabited Combat Air Vehicles

These vehicles, not requiring a pilot, concentrate on stealth and small size, and include Lockheed Martin's *Naval-UCAV* – somewhat of a white triangle, and Northrop Gruman's UCAV designs, essentially triangular, with weird bent wings.

Military cargo planes

The C17 *Globemaster* sometimes ferries goods and supplies to Alice Springs for delivery to the Base at Pine Gap. With a wingspan of nearly 51.76 metres, it can take off and land on runways as short as 27.4 metres.

Experimental planes

The Armstrong Whitworth AW52 Experimental Tail-less Monoplane is a larger, powered prototype version of the AW52G glider, and basically a plane with one wing. (The concept of this plane is interesting, as RAAF files contain a report from Tambar Springs, New South Wales, on 7 December 1956 where the witness heard jet engines and a white disc-shaped object was spinning and coming down. The craft appeared to have just one wing, on one side. It was lost from sight after going straight up until it became a speck in the sky. This appears to be a much more powerful example of this design, but decades earlier!)

In the 1970s, Patent No. GB 1310990 was granted to British Rail for a flying saucer which the British Patent Office stated "was a new invention at the time the application was originally made." The original application was filed on 11 December 1970 followed by final specifications in 1973. This information was discovered by IUFOPRA, who gained permission from the Patents Office to publish the details. I find it hard to believe the Railway Department were the *originators* of this application. Why would British Rail be inventing flying saucers? Were they planning to expand into the aerospace industry? It is unlikely they would indulge in a hoax or practical joke. Make up your own mind as to the true originators, reasons and intent for patenting this new invention.

Lockheed Martin was developing a joint-wing FLA (Future Large Aircraft), with narrow wings extending backwards to join to a narrow extended tail on each side. Russia has produced a very oddly shaped craft, with swept-*forward* wings – the Sukhoi S-37 *Berkut*, nicknamed the Golden Cage.

In 1994 McDonnell Douglas was testing *Diamond*, an unmanned 10x10foot platform, hollowed out like a diamond. Versions 1 and 2 crashed, and in 1999 they were still working on prototypes. In 1996 aerospace engineers were developing a *lightcraft* – a hypersonic flying saucer. In 2013 it was reported the United States Air Force was testing the hypersonic X51A *Wave-Rider*.

In 2014 a new passenger plane was being proposed, the S2. It looks like a glider, has electric motors and a vertical take-off capacity.

Black aircraft

These aircraft are more covert, and it is suggested often responsible for the sightings of black triangles and other unconventional craft. Nobody admits to flying them over another country's airspace, not even that of a friendly state, but they have to test them somewhere!

Aurora was the cover name for the *B-2 Spirit* in its early stages of development as a replacement for the SR-71. McDonnell Douglas designed this type of plane between the 1960s and 80s. It was in operation sometime after 1989, certainly by 1999 at the latest. Constructed using titanium alloys and a special class of propulsion system designed for hypersonic aircraft. It had ramjets, a high-velocity rocket exhaust and an engine with a unique low-frequency high amplitude pulsing sound. It could cruise as fast as 5,300mph and reach any part of the earth in three hours.

Astra – Advanced Stealth Technology Reconnaissance Aircraft – was a supersonic replacement for the SR-71 *Blackbird* strategic spy-plane. The SR-71 itself has Linear Aerospike rocket engine technology, a concept developed and tested in the 1960s and 70s.

The A-17/FB-119A, designed as a replacement for the F-111, has reputedly been in service since the early 1990s. It has been described as a highly swept delta platform with unusual lighting pattern and noise.

We also have the Lockheed Martin F-117A, a covert strike aircraft, almost invisible to radar and an improvement on the A/F-117X. This actually existed in 1975, ten years prior to public knowledge. Also the F-19A *Spector*, a stingray-shaped stealth fighter of supersonic performance, and the F-22 Supersonic Fighter.

Brilliant Buzzard is basically a satellite launcher; the first stage of a Two-Stage-to-Orbit (TSTO) system. Among its functions, it can carry a variety of aerial vehicles to the required altitude for launch or testing purposes. *Hummingbird* (Aero design and development by Israel) is a manned vertical take-off and landing platform which can raise the pilot to an altitude of 250 metres.

PATENT SPECIFICATION (11) 1 310 990

DRAWINGS ATTACHED

(21) Application No. 59083/70 (22) Filed 11 Dec. 1970

(23) Complete Specification filed 10 March 1972

(44) Complete Specification published 21 March 1973

(51) International Classification G21B 1/00; B64G 1/00

(52) Index at acceptance

    G6P 3E1 3E3X

    B7W 2

(72) Inventor CHARLES OSMOND FREDERICK

(54) SPACE VEHICLE

(71) We, BRITISH RAILWAYS BOARD, a public authority established under the provisions of the Transport Act 1962, of 222, Marylebone Road, London, N.W.1, do hereby declare the invention, for which we pray that a patent may be granted to us, and the method by which it is to be performed, to be particularly described in and by the following statement:—

The present invention relates to a space vehicle. More particularly it relates to a power supply for a space vehicle which offers a source of sustained thrust for the loss of a very small mass of fuel. Thus it would enable very high velocities to be attained in a space vehicle and in fact the prolonged acceleration of the vehicle may in some circumstances be used to simulate gravity.

According to the present invention there is provided a space vehicle including a platform, a thermonuclear fusion zone provided at the underside of said platform, means for supplying fusion material to said zone, one or more lasers to provide for ignition of said fusion material at said fusion zone, magnetic means on said platform adapted to deflect charged particles emitted from said fusion zone and a plurality of electrodes on said platform adapted to receive charged particles emitted from said fusion zone to thereby provide a source of electrical power.

A preferred embodiment of the present invention will now be described with reference to the accompanying drawings in which:

Figure 1 is a cross section of a space vehicle,

Figure 2 is an underside view of part of the vehicle shown in Figure 1.

The space vehicle consists of a disk or platform 10 which may have a flat, slightly concave or convex undersurface. A controlled thermonuclear fusion reaction is ignited by one or more pulsed laser beams produced by lasers 11 and reflected or focussed onto a central reaction zone 12 on the underside of the platform.

The thermonuclear fusion will take place in a series of pulses, each pulse being triggered by laser energy, and/or energetic particles reflected from a previous pulse. The system will be arranged so that the fusion process will decay after each pulse so that the stability of the system is maintained. The pulse frequency will generally be greater than 1000Hz to avoid structural vibration within the vehicle.

The fusion zone 12 will be supplied with liquid fuel pumped through a nozzle 13 at high pressure.

The vehicle contains powerful electromagnets 14, possibly superconducting magnets, whose fields will extend into the space below the vehicle. These fields will deflect charged particles produced by the thermonuclear reaction either towards the underside of the vehicle or away from it. The particles deflected towards the underside of the vehicle will be received on insulated electrodes 15 and provide a source of electric power. The particles deflected away from the vehicle will contribute to the vehicle lift by a greater amount than if they had simply ejected from the reaction point (or points).

The electrodes 15 are subdivided radially as shown into a number of sections 16 each separated by an insulating strip 17 from adjacent sections. In this way the voltage on each of the sections 16 can be different, which in certain circumstances can be advantageous as will be described.

The proportion of charged particles generated at the reaction point 12 (or points) may be modified by mixing the material subject to fusion with some other material or placing the two materials adjacent to one another. These means may also be used to increase the opacity of the fuel to the laser radiation and thereby make ignition easier.

Heavy material 18 will shield the upper part of the vehicle from the nuclear radiation emanating from the reaction zone.

In addition cooling tubes 19 absorb excess thermal energy produced by the reaction and carry this to a radiating surface 20 provided on the upper side of the disk 10.

The large burst of power necessary to energise the lasers 11 initially could be provided by a homo-polar generator 21 involving a large spinning disc or two or more contra-rotating disks. This disc generator could be placed directly over the reaction zone 12 to assist in shielding the upperside of the vehicle from radiation. This principle could be used with multiple reaction points also. After initial start up of the device the homo-polar generator 21 could continue to spin and act as an energy storing flywheel. It may also be used as a reference level in a system for stabilizing the vehicle by varying the electrostatic voltages on the electrode sections 16 to apply a correcting couple to the vehicle.

The magnetic fields on the underside of the vehicle will protect some zones of it from charged particles. These zones could be used to situate laser devices or reflectors for laser beams, thereby ensuring a longer life for these components.

By controlling the voltages on the electrode sections 16 and also the magnitude of the magnetic fields from each of the magnets 14, by way of a suitable servo mechanism, the thrust acting on the vehicle can be vectored so that its attitude and direction of movement can be controlled.

A passenger compartment 22 can be positioned on the upper central part of the vehicle.

WHAT WE CLAIM IS:—

1. A space vehicle including a platform, a thermonuclear fusion zone provided at the underside of said platform means for supplying fusion material to said zone, one or more lasers to provide for ignition of said fusion material at said fusion zone, magnetic means on said platform adapted to deflect charged particles emitted from said fusion zone, and a plurality of electrodes on said platform adapted to receive charged particles emitted from said fusion zone to thereby provide a source of electrical power.

2. A space vehicle as claimed in claim 1 wherein the individual electrodes and the magnetic means are arranged alternately in a ring surrounding the fusion zone.

3. A space vehicle as claimed in claim 2 wherein each electrode is subdivided radially into a plurality of sections each insulated from one another.

4. A space vehicle as claimed in any preceding claim wherein an electrical generator is provided for supplying the necessary power to initiate the operation of the lasers.

5. A space vehicle as claimed in claim 4, wherein said generator is a homopolar generator.

6. A space vehicle as claimed in any preceding claim wherein thermal energy absorbing means are provided adjacent said fusion zone the arrangement being such that when the vehicle is in operation the absorbed energy is transmitted to and radiated from the upper surface of the platform.

7. A space vehicle as claimed in any preceding claim wherein servo controlled means are provided for controlling the inclination of the platform by varying the strength of the magnetic field of said magnetic means and/or the voltage on said electrodes.

8. A space vehicle substantially as described herein with reference to the accompanying drawings.

JENSEN & SON,
Agents for the Applicants,
8, Fulwood Place,
London, WC1V 6HG.
Chartered Patent Agents.

Printed for Her Majesty's Stationery Office by the Courier Press, Leamington Spa, 1973.
Published by the Patent Office, 25 Southampton Buildings, London, WC2A 1AY, from which copies may be obtained.

FIG.1

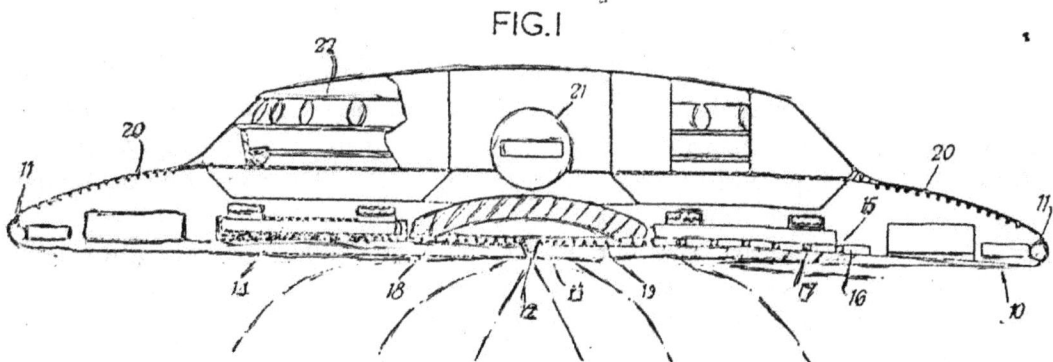

F-121 *Sentinal*: A Vertical/Short Take-Off and Landing (V/STOL) strike reconnaissance vehicle. It is thought this craft has highly-advanced technology with a triangular platform, and emits bright light from what is thought to be its powerplant, part of an exotic propulsion system.

Senior Citizen – STOL: Reputed to be an aircraft with an ogival platform which would be ideal for inserting and supporting special forces.

Aircraft with variable forward swept wing

On 16 November 1999 Northrop Grumman Corporation (USA) were granted Patent Number 5,984,231 for a new prototype aircraft which we must assume has since been developed. Experts have suggested that the YF-23 stealth fighter, the FB-119A, *Astra*, and *Switchblade* may be variations on this theme.

New technologies

This is one area of identification which is extremely difficult for investigators, as the existence of new technologies and innovations are the most closely guarded national secrets, and new toys are rarely made public until many years after their development and use.

In the early 1960s patents 3,713,157 and 4,030,098 were filed for providing a layer of plasma to shield aircraft from radar, among other benefits. However, the weight of the equipment required to generate it was a problem. In the 1990s the Russians revealed much more advanced research in the field of plasma aerodynamics, and in 1996 it was reported that ion propulsion (solar-electric propulsion) was being used in deep space missions.

Modern technologies can include new and powerful sources of energy generation and propulsion, cloaking devices, all kinds of weaponry, mind control, artificial intelligence, teleportation, levitation, the manipulation of time, space and dimensions, and possibly technologies we haven't even envisaged yet. These projects can be so clandestine that accusations are often made regarding the untimely deaths of scientists employed on some top secret projects.

NASA is also at the pinnacle of new technology development. *Popular Mechanics* (November 2000) reported on a Nuclear Flying Saucer which had been declassified in 1999. This LRV (Lenticular Re-entry Vehicle), 40 feet in diameter, housed a small nuclear reactor to provide electricity for flight systems. NASA was also very excited when they launched *Deep Space 1* in 1998 with destinations proposed for Mars, a comet and an asteroid. It was testing a new xenon-ion engine, far more efficient than chemically propelled spacecraft and utilising solar energy and xenon, a heavy inert gas. It gathers speed and can reach 70,200 miles per hour.

The fundamental truth is that rival nations need to maintain military superiority over each other, or at least to remain on an equal footing. Human nature has not altered, and if the other fellow has captured an alien craft to back-engineer, he is not going to share its secrets. His rivals must do likewise to preserve the status quo. It is part of a deadly power struggle humans have engaged in since the beginning of civilisation.

New technologies in Australian skies

IUFOPRA reported that in March 1999 a media release from the Defence Science and Technology Organisation and the Minister of Defence, announced a proposal for the *Global Hawke* – an advanced UAV surveillance system, to fly across the Pacific to Australia in 2001. It was proposed that *Global Hawke* had "the potential to contribute significantly to the monitoring of Australian territory and adjoining maritime areas."

Global Hawke, although it can be programmed to fly itself, can also be tasked by a ground station. It has a wingspan larger than a Boeing 737 airliner, an operating altitude of 65,000 feet, a retractable undercarriage, and can loiter for long periods at high altitude.

Regardless of the sentiments of the general population, these new-fangled inventions – often essential to maintain military superiority, must be tested somewhere, and preferably over friendly territory, away from public view. We should not be at all surprised that some unusual objects are sighted in the skies over the more-remote parts of Australia. While these areas are not only ideal for test flying earthly technology, they would surely attract the attention of visitors interested in our technological advances.

An important development on the home front has been the advent of the domestic drone. Much of the technology first created for military applications has been made readily available for home use – you can buy from a wide range of small, toy helicopters which include a camera. UFO researchers now have to allow for these devices.

Holographic images

Every day we can watch images of people interacting in complex scenarios, and places from all over the world and into the cosmos. These can be at the movies, on our television screens and our computers and digital devices. We can even instantly interact with people thousands of kilometres away. However, we can teach our brains to recognise we are viewing sounds and images which are not physically present. We can distinguish which images have been produced in the past, such as movies, documentaries and replays, and those that occur in the present, such as on video phone calls, the internet and other digital technology.

A holographic image is more difficult for our brain to analyse. We see an image of an object or being and we will usually accept it on face value, because we have no prior knowledge for our brain to analyse or categorise it further.

A hologram is a 3-dimensional image, made using laser light, which recreates life-like images from solid objects. It is a replica in every way to the original object, and it appears to be a physical reality. As one expert described it: "Holography shatters our concept of reality. To view one is to have the weird experience that your senses are deceiving you. In every way the object seems real, yet all a hand reaching out would encounter is pure, radiant pulsating light."

The concept was first explored by Dr. Dennis Gabor in 1947 (funny how that date keeps cropping up!). He was awarded the Nobel Prize in Physics for his discovery in 1971. His research continued in 1962 under Drs. Leith and Upatnieks of the University of Michigan, and later by Dr Benton in 1968. Our own CSIRO helped perfect the process so that fully coloured holograms can be seen in normal light.

By the 1980s the development of laser technology and holography had advanced sufficiently for NASA to envision holographic broadcasting satellites. Thirty years on, the science and application of holograms has exceeded our wildest imaginings. We have holographic data storage, holographic video, and holodisplays – three-dimensional images in the air, without the need for a screen. Just as the military could use this to fool an enemy, UFO witnesses could easily fall for a seeing-is-believing scenario. Are those strange lights in the sky a physical reality? Most people would have no way of knowing.

If we have progressed so far in our manipulation of light, one cannot begin to imagine the capability of a more technologically-advanced species. I am not postulating that all sightings of unidentified lights and craft are holographic images. If some of them are, we still have the unanswered question as to who is projecting them, and why?

Other dimensions?

Can we see or feel something in another dimension, and are there dimensions hidden from our normal perception? Mathematicians and scientists have been exploring the possibility of other dimensions for many years. Given the complexity of this subject, and despite great advances, we are probably still in the infancy of this research. Many science projects have successfully produced 4-dimensional displays in computer-generated form, which are utilised in numerous disciplines in science and medicine. I am quite convinced our military and major corporations have mastered more of this modern technology than we could imagine, including the ability to produce cloaking devices.

Our normal 3-dimensional view of the world comprises height, width, and depth. If you add another right-angled aspect to these, you include a fourth dimension. Physicists consider that space-time definitely constitutes a fourth dimension, and postulate the existence of at least eleven dimensions in all (maybe more), to describe some complex phenomena. These extra dimensions are used to describe the activities of sub-atomic particles and minute energy fields, and suggest they may travel backwards or forwards in time.

9

Research into this field is complex, and combines a variety of disciplines such as mathematics, quantum physics, sub-atomic physics, matter and energies such as electromagnetism, gravity and the strong and weak nuclear forces. All include a quantity called frequency or vibration. *Everything* in the universe vibrates, down to the sub-atomic level and beyond; something the Aboriginal and other indigenous peoples have long appreciated. Frequency/vibration may ultimately determine the dimension in which someone or something exists.

It is thought in some older cultures, that the existence we "know" takes place in a lower vibration (or frequency), three-dimensional world, but sometimes, through meditation and other techniques our consciousness can access further dimensions, and experience space-time. For example, it has been suggested that some religions use meditative techniques to enter a further dimension enabling instant communication, regardless of time and distance. (Similar techniques were effectively used in an experimental program to contact aliens, which I will elaborate on in my next book, *The Alien Gene*.)

It is suggested that our ancient ancestors were aware that certain earth energies present in particular places, (e.g. ley lines and harmonic spots), enable humans and other entities to enter and exit our space-time continuum more easily. It is also postulated by some that the combined particular mathematical structure and positioning of Stone Age megaliths facilitated the interaction with other dimensions.

We should be aware that the world's major governmental, military, corporate, and religious bodies would like to access such presently unknown phenomena.

Therefore we should not rush to judge witnesses who describe objects and beings which first materialise then just as quickly disappear, telepathic communication from alien beings, and other unusual phenomena. They may be experiencing an interaction with a more technically-advanced intelligence. Do they exist in another dimension, or merely utilise it? Until we can better-understand and use these realities ourselves, we cannot fully analyse some of the phenomena reported.

Great balls of fire

During the 1990s, most Australian ufologists were plagued with reports of displays of orange lights. Many of these were hoaxes perpetrated by pranksters, and occasionally, the authorities. Some were definitely unexplained and difficult to determine, from witness testimony alone.

Surry Hills, Sydney, 1992

I and several other witnesses watched one of these objects in 1992. It was about 11 p.m. We were all leaving a UFO Research (New South Wales) committee meeting, and one elderly woman insisted there was something in the sky. At first we all laughed: "You've been talking too much about UFOs!" We turned to see a large ball of fire coming very low (helicopter height) from Sydney Central Station, over Surry Hills.

It wasn't actually round – more of a jagged oval object, about the size of a small plane. It seemed to have something more solid behind the flames, but we couldn't make out what it was. We all stood there gawking, digging each other in the ribs: "Get a load of that! It's just what everyone's been reporting!" It certainly seemed to be under some form of intelligent control. As it moved slowly, silently and steadily towards Victoria Barracks in the northeast, we realised that not one of us had thought to grab a camera to get that all-important photographic evidence we were always expecting from other witnesses!

Extensive inquiries to all authorities and airports determined there was nothing known to be flying in the area at that time.

Marsfield, Sydney, 1995

In 1995 I received a call from a family in Marsfield, Sydney. On two occasions they had witnessed unusual orange-red balls of light in the night sky. At first I thought they might be pranks, prevalent at the time. (In addition, there were the more-sophisticated, official-based orange lights, which I suspected were being used to divert us from other activities by government agencies. One government informant had bragged to a colleague: "We've devised one that flies against the wind. That'll fool those ufologists!")

In May 1995 at 9.25 p.m., Arthur Martin, along with his wife Jeanette, and her five art students, watched a very bright fiery ball, brilliant orange-red in colour, high in the sky. It took ten minutes to travel from the southeast before finally disappearing behind distant trees on the northwest horizon. It was much slower than any aircraft and at times it silently passed under cloud cover.

At its closest point, overhead, they could see there were two vertical, parallel structures with a fiery space in between, giving the object a squarish appearance. They used binoculars, and didn't think to get a camera. However Jeanette and the art students produced some excellent paintings for us.

A second incident occurred two months later at about 10.30 p.m., 12 July. The family spent ten minutes watching three silent, orange-red balls of light, which were at an altitude of about 400 metres. They came from the west and the first object slowed down, allowing the second to catch up. The third light appeared way behind in the west, and travelling much faster, caught up with the other two. All three then moved in a triangular formation, at steady speed and trajectory to the east. This certainly indicated some form of intelligent control, but whose?

Arthur commented, "These objects were very similar to the one we saw in May 1995, and they certainly seemed to be on fire. This time, we did not see any vertical structures, but we did not look through the binoculars. Photography took priority this time, and we got three good shots on 35mm colour slides. It was also interesting that, although we heard no sound, our dog became very agitated, running around in circles, which she hadn't done the first time."

Arthur rang the aviation authorities, without much luck, until they connected him to an INUFOR researcher who was an air traffic controller. Arthur was also given details of two other research organisations and I don't know if they followed up the case. However, Arthur heard a recording made by another witness:

"This chap said he and his wife were at a barbecue when they were shocked to see a fiery red object, resembling a burning aircraft heading straight towards them on a course from the west. A second one appeared and both headed off into the east. They described them as squares 'burning inwards towards the centre'. This was certainly similar to what we saw in May 1995 when we could see vertical internal structures."

These other witnesses, one of whom had been a Department of Civil Aviation Inspector for 31 years, had taken photographs and undertook some comprehensive research of their own, using a magnetic compass, bubble level, protractor and an orthophoto map.

In these cases, it is very hard to determine what these objects are, and who or what is responsible for their mysterious appearance. The question still remains as to whether these objects were extraterrestrial or of a more earthly origin.

A few months earlier, in late 1994, Bryan Dickeson, Glenn Land and I were fortunate enough to receive photographic evidence, along with multiple witness reports, of more than one incident:

Tom Price, Western Australia, 15 October 1994

Tom Price, in northwest Western Australia, is 400 kilometres east and inland from Exmouth Naval Base, alongside the North West Cape Communications Facility. It is situated in an area bounded by bushland and hills, which is sometimes subject to unusual updrafts. The township, a small, isolated, close-knit mining community included about 4,500 people at the time:

This particular night there was no wind, and several witnesses were outdoors having a barbecue. At that stage they had not consumed any alcohol – a friend had not arrived with the beer! At 9.15 p.m. local time, Fred spotted an object coming from the hills to the west.

"It was moving in a straight, steady, purposeful (controlled) trajectory from west to east. It took about five minutes to travel, at a very slow speed, from one range of hills to the other. It was not high up; at treetop level, about the height of a low-flying helicopter.

"It looked like an orange light at first – about five times the size of Venus at its largest. When it came closer it appeared to be a huge round shape of orange flame, about the size of a small plane. It came overhead, was totally silent, and we looked up into a curly chrysanthemum type shape, with flames being drawn up inside. Some thought there seemed to be a black square or rectangular object in the core, with the flames coming from the inside edges burning inwards, and not outside of the square. At one stage, when it was still distant, it almost resembled a white light.

"Just as it moved off into the distance a second one, slightly bigger than the first, appeared and followed the same route. By this time a few of us had grabbed our video cameras and started filming. Someone rang the local police station, but they were already observing this phenomenon. The officer in charge had initially thought that object number one was a meteorite. By the time the second arrived he already had two patrolmen out and reporting back."

They rang the Observatory, Department of Meteorology and local television station; nobody could offer any explanation. The power station at Dampier had a power outage that night and couldn't explain why. There was no sign of teenagers or pranksters, and many other residents had witnessed and filmed the event.

Events after the sighting took a very suspicious turn. Fred's wife Mary, had rung a commercial UFO reporting hotline in Victoria, and when she received no reply, rang me at INUFOR in Sydney. I contacted the owner of the Victorian hotline. He did not administer the tapes, and when he did receive them a week later from his service provider, it appeared that one message had been deleted.

Mary continued, "The next day the town was full of investigators who were busy interviewing witnesses. They also interviewed the police at Halfway Creek, midway between Tom Price and Paraburdoo, where they also spoke to witnesses. Everybody was puzzled as to the real identity of these investigators. Nobody in town believed that residents in Halfway Creek or Paraburdoo would have seen the objects given their flight path over Tom Price.

"A major television channel flew my husband to Perth with his videos and they did interviews and preparations ready to go to air. All of a sudden, at the last minute and with no explanation, they told him they couldn't use the film and flew him back home to Tom Price. All the witnesses that had made their pictures available said they were returned with the videos cleared when they had previously shown the UFO.

"Even our local television station behaved strangely. They had announced the sightings as their major news headline, but never mentioned it when the news was read. Everyone wanted to know what was going on, and we were told that the decision not to broadcast was made by the station owner in Perth, who withdrew the story at the last minute."

Luckily other residents had photographs, including unspoiled video footage. Some of them had thought the objects could be military in nature, possibly associated with the naval base at Exmouth or the North West Cape communications establishment. Why the sudden cover-up? While I considered our military hardware as a valid possibility, my colleague Bryan Dickeson did not agree.

I received a second, similar report from Ryan Fisher of Meekatharra, south of Tom Price. Unfortunately he didn't know the exact date, except it was near the end of 1994. "It was 11 p.m. and I was working a night shift. It was very bright, a huge round white ball with a well-defined outline, and a sort of marbled effect. Some surfaces looked hotter than others. It was much bigger than the moon, and about 1,200 feet up. If it had been on the ground it would have as high as a four-storey building.

"It came very fast from the Pilbara on the northwest horizon, over my head in Meekatharra and disappeared behind the hills in the southeast. It was quicker than a propeller plane, but not faster than a jet. There was some soft, misty cloud, which it did not disturb as it flew silently through."

In 2014, Bryan Dickeson had been talking to a Perth woman, Sheila, who commented she had been living in the northern part of Western Australia in 1994, and had seen an orange UFO during September or October. Bryan was naturally interested, given our earlier investigations into the Tom Price incident at that time, and gave me the following transcript of her report:

"I was on the bus with my boyfriend, whose rugby team were coming home from playing a friendly match in a nearby mining town. It was late afternoon, still daylight. The players and supporters were noisy and in good spirits – a few drinks had been consumed after the game.

"Then, someone called out for us to look out to the right-hand-side, behind the coach. Two very large, orange balls of light were heading, at an angle, straight towards us. They were huge, several stories high, and landed smoothly in a paddock just ahead. They looked like two bright hemispheres of orange light.

"Everyone on the bus panicked and went berserk. Those big, tough rugby types completely lost their cool and were yelling and screaming for the bus driver to speed up to get away from those 'things'.

"Further down the road, when the objects were out of sight, the bus went completely quiet. It was eerie. Everyone just sat down, saying nothing at all, and looked ahead for the rest of the journey. No-one ever mentioned it or talked about the incident again, even when I tried to raise the topic on several occasions."

We will never know if there was more to this incident. In many cases where there is missing time; the witnesses prefer silence and show a great reluctance to recall or discuss the incident later. I must admit to private curiosity and hilarity at the thought of a busload of drunken rugby players being abducted. Quite a handful for their alien captors!

Tregear, Sydney, 24 November 1994

It was just after 11 p.m. when Kevin Cooper heard his son's car pull into the driveway. He turned off the television and headed for the front porch:

"I wanted to ask him, before I went to bed, if he had remembered my shopping when he was at the Plaza. I opened the door, and could see a very large orange light, low on the horizon of the night sky. It was extremely bright, and slowly moving northeast towards us. I shouted to George, 'Hey, look at that – can you see it? What the hell!' My son stared for a few seconds, and was also mystified.

"George had recently bought a brand new video camera (Panasonic VHSC; Model NVR30A). He raced into the house, and grabbed the box, calling out to my wife to come and have a look. Christine, jumped out of bed, and came out to see. It was a warm night and I noticed our neighbours' windows were open and the lights still on. I yelled out to Steve and Maria, and they joined us in the front garden.

West Sussex, England, 31 August 2003
My good friend Margaret Fry, a Welsh researcher for many years, sent me some photographs of an almost identical object, taken at Shoreham with a Kodak digital DX 4330 camera.
This object could not be identified, but except for a more white-blue hue, one cannot disregard its similarity to those seen at Tom Price and Tregear.

"We all watched for about five minutes, and George seemed to take forever getting his camera out of the box, and checking it over. Eventually he was ready and filmed for about two minutes before it disappeared into the city lights on the northern horizon."

Their reports varied slightly, which is normal in a multiple witness event. All agreed that it was round, looked like a ball of fire, and travelled at treetop level, on a smooth, consistent trajectory from south-southwest to north-northeast.

At one stage it had been directly overhead. Kevin and Christine said that it was about two-thirds the size of a full moon. Christine added, "It had a dark centre and haze around. It made no noise at all. I kept thinking it was coming down, but it was just the way it was moving."

Steve and Maria felt it was about "the size of a full moon, and had a dark centre with occasional coloured flashes (blue red and white) emanating from the top."

Maria described it as a "bright white object" but everybody else considered it to be orange. Steve thought it had zig-zagged slightly before disappearing.

Inquiries were made to civilian airports, the RAAF Base, Sydney Observatory, and the Bureau of Meteorology to eliminate any conventional explanation. Glenn Land and Bryan Dickeson conducted an extensive analysis of George's video, which showed the object moving below, and sometimes through, a layer of light cloud, which sometimes glowed orange from the reflected light.

A commercial photographic laboratory also scrutinised the footage and provided fifty-two colour photograph samples. The photographs were shown to the residents of Western Sydney who said the object was the same as two lights seen over nearby Emu Plains on 13 July 1992. Copies were provided to people in Tom Price, West Australia, who confirmed the object was identical to the one seen and videoed by residents some six weeks earlier.

The object was calculated at being 28 metres across, and travelling at 90kph. The video images were fully magnified to show individual pixels, so each rectangular pixel could be treated as a little sample of light from the object. These showed an unusual overall pattern of light and dark concentric circles of pixels, suggesting some light interference pattern was being created.

The extra flashes of colour some witnesses reported were clearly shown as two small, identical intensely blue-white lights moving round the main object and each other. These satellites showed very erratic, complex and fast motion – sometimes in front or behind the orange object.

After in-depth analysis, my colleague Bryan Dickeson came to the conclusion that the light came from a spherical object. The orange light seemed to be *coherent* (laser-type light), generated from a hollow shell, some two metres thick (presumably with something inside).

Unusual Optical effects?
The concentric rings of light were consistent with a known interference light pattern, known as *Newton's Rings*, which have been closely studied by physicists for 250 years. Orange laser light sources were unknown in 1994, and have not been found in nature.

Bryan also noted that laser light produces a series of complex, secondary effects, which affect human eye responses.

The chemical pigments in the eye used to sense light can be triggered so that the brain registers light it wouldn't usually see; an object might appear to scintillate; larger objects might have a surface covered in small flames. Also, eye pigments vary subtly with age and from one person to another. Steve and Maria's description of a "white" object and "coloured flashes" does not necessarily contradict other witness statements or the video footage.

Graham Stewart of UFOtec produced some very complex calculations and submitted the following conclusion: "The evidence here strongly suggests that the Tregear UFO could well be a man-made craft, constructed to resonate in tune with the earth Energy Grid itself. It is quite conceivable that such a craft could use the eddy currents created by the opposing A and B Magnetic fields as a means of propulsion. By generating its own magnetic field and then manipulating its own field strength, it could perform manoeuvres consistent with what is generally observed and reported. This would also explain why the exact Grid Speed of Light Harmonic values, directly associated with electromagnetic transmission and reception, have come up here."

Royal National Park, Sydney, 19 December 1994

Less than a month later we received another report from several fishermen in the Royal National Park, on the coast of Sydney's southern limits. They had wanted to get an early morning start, but two of them were working afternoon shift until 9 p.m.

The park gates are closed from sunset to sunrise, and when they originally arrived, they found two carloads of tourists trapped inside. It took a while for one of them to drive some of the tourists back to Bundeena police so the Park Ranger could be contacted to let them out.

Once reorganised, they decided to forget the camping; they wanted to get an early start fishing, and parked their cars outside at the entry to another track.

(I am very familiar with this area, and this is not something I would recommend. It is easy to get lost in daylight, let alone in the dark and there are snakes and ticks lurking in the undergrowth at that time of year.)

At about 2 a.m. they thought they were approximately halfway to the coast. However, even with torches in the calm moonlit night, they weren't sure exactly where they were. They paid scant attention to a large glowing dome, nestled among and above the trees in a valley some two to three kilometres to the west.

"At first we thought it must be a house," Billy said "and then realised it was nowhere near any settlement, and that area was covered with dense scrub. In hindsight, perhaps we should have paid more attention. We continued on, reaching the coast at about 4 a.m. It took us about 15 minutes to check our bearings before meeting up on a small beach just north of Curracurrong Beach, two kilometres south of Wattamolla."

A small stream joins the sea at the beach, their favourite fishing spot, and is between impressive cliffs and rocks, including Eagle Rock, a well-known landmark.

"My mate suddenly yelled out and was pointing to the south headland. There was this weird thing, an orange-red ball of glowing solid light, coming around the south headland. We all jumped

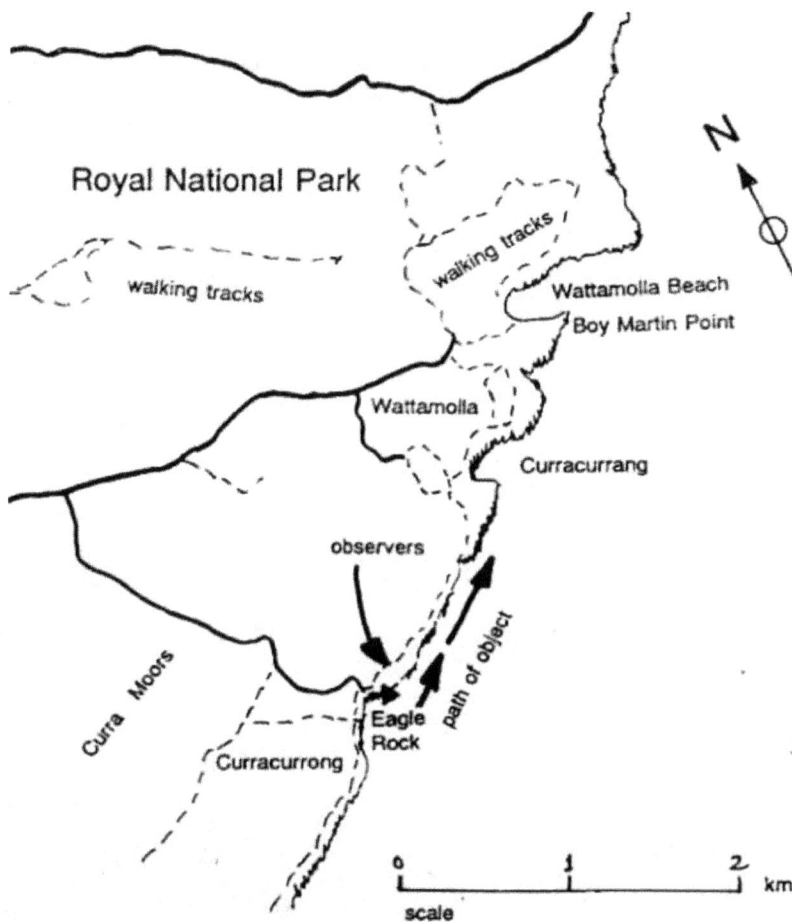

up to look. It was about the size of a full moon, 30 metres above the ocean, and only two hundred metres from the coast.

"It was moving in a very unusual manner, making funny irregular step-like movements up and down. It varied between 50 to 100 feet in altitude, and its speed was slow and steady – easy to see between the two headlands. We started flashing our torches at it, and it deviated and started coming towards us. I reached for my fishing knife, more out of instinct than fear, and it moved back to its original course."

They got their 16x50 binoculars, and were surprised how it actually looked smaller under magnification. It was as if the orange-red glow was minimised to show an underlying object in the centre. One described it as similar to "a bar of a radiant electric heater, with a small dome-like bubble on top." Another said it had more of a diamond shape side-on. Regardless of the actual shape there was a consistency with the other reports of a central object in the middle of the glowing object. One witness thought he saw a beam come from under it, and touch the sea. (It is also possible the orange outer glow had been eliminated or reflected by the anti-glare coating on the binoculars.) "It continued on its course, and I ran to the southern end of the beach, to get a better view. It seemed to be following the curvature of the coastline, and I lost sight of it behind the northern cliffs."

"We checked our watches – 4.24 a.m. We had been watching for eight minutes, so its speed was very slow. We also realised it was dead quiet all around, and there was no sign of the deer and kangaroos we had seen earlier."

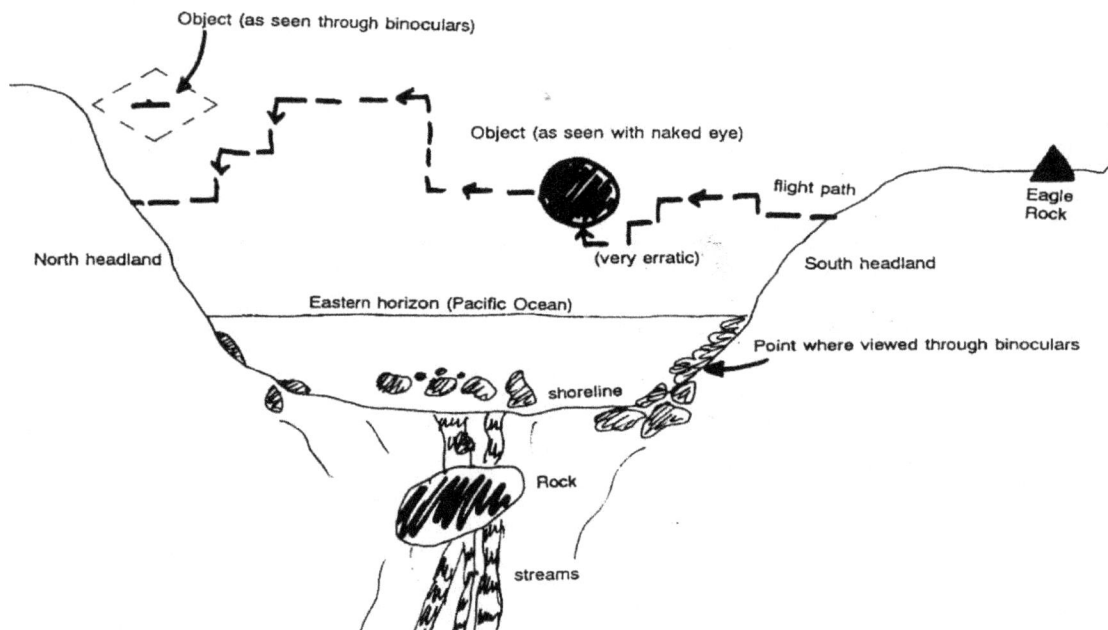

Coffs Harbour, NSW, 26 October 1999

At 3.45 a.m. the three-man crew of *Lochiel*, a fishing boat six miles offshore, spotted a brilliant white-orange ball light just over the southeast horizon.

Their radar observations indicated it would have been about 12 miles away, and the captain estimated it to be "as big as a large block of flats." It hovered for some time, and they filmed it with their camcorder before it moved away to the south, and out of sight.

It was also seen by the captain of fishing boat, *Muff Digger*.

A few days later they were interviewed by researcher Dudley Robb, who viewed the footage and confirmed it appeared to be a similar object to that recorded at Tregear.

Dudley detailed the concentric rings of bright and dark shades of light, and considered that on both occasions the pattern might suggest a laser source.

Dudley's preferred explanation was "a man-made experiment; a weapons test, based on Nikola Tesla's high-power radiated microwave beam ideas he first proposed a hundred years ago."

My own conclusion is that we do not have sufficient evidence to support any individual theory, even if it is correct.

Importantly, there are other *antique* reports which indicate this is actually an old phenomenon. For example, one newspaper report from South Australia, made over 100 years ago, definitely rules out any 'modern' high-technology weapons testing theories:
The following account comes from the *North Coolgardie Herald* (Western Australia) of Tuesday, 29 March 1904 (courtesy, *Xenolog Archive*).

A REMARKABLE PHENOMENON

Sub-inspector Clode informs us that on the night of the [Saturday] 13th February the blacks on Toolachie Run [in South Australia] saw at about 11 o'clock what appeared to be two large balls of fire high up in the heavens. The natives were awe-struck at the sight.

That evening a white man had camped near the place. The blacks rushed down to his camp, aroused him and drew his attention to the unusual spectacle. The white man informed Sub-Inspector Clode the following day that the phenomenon looked like two immense 'red-hot' cannon-balls, thousands of miles in the heavens.

For fifteen minutes the huge globes loomed overhead, and then gradually disappeared. Four of the blacks substantiated the white man's report, and one stated that he had witnessed a similar sight twenty-five years ago [about 1879]. The natives belonged to the Cooper tribe.

Harry Mason is a consultant geologist who assisted the Incorporated Research Institutions for Seismology (IRIS) which was studying, on behalf of officialdom, a fireball and earthquake-like explosion in West Australia on 28 May 1993.

In a series of lectures and a video he suggested that what people had been seeing was an advanced electromagnetic weapons system, utilising Tesla electromagnetic waves being beamed from remote locations, and suggested they may have been responsible for several major events. He considered these were based on original research by Nikola Tesla who had dabbled in seismic weaponry as early as the 1940s.

He went on to propose many theories involving international agencies and our own government conducting seismic weapons and other tests in the West Australian desert, however he does not deny these objects may also be alien

Many of the examples he offered in support, involved a fireball and subsequent explosion, which did not match up with the objects I have detailed here. If they were some form of weapons testing, it would be unlikely that they would be tested over or near heavily-populated areas such as Sydney, or Coffs Harbour in Australia, or West Sussex in the United Kingdom.

Chapter Two

Sydney, NSW

Sydney, the largest city in Australia, and capital of New South Wales, is built around its beautiful harbour, which extends some kilometres inland. Magnificent beaches and coastline border its eastern boundary, and beyond the western suburbs inland, the Blue Mountains rise up from the Plain of Cumberland.

Strathfield 1967

Simon contacted me in 2002, after hearing an interview I gave on a local radio station. His main reason for ringing was to report a strange light over the ocean, which he and his wife had seen from their Cronulla flat. We started chatting, and I sensed he wanted to say more, but was hesitating.

After a while he tentatively broached the subject of a disturbing happening, in 1967, when he was a seven-year-old child, living in Strathfield, a suburb of Sydney.

"I had a little girlfriend, Rebecca, who lived a couple of streets away, and we always walked to and from school together. Rebecca's parents had a much nicer home than ours, with a large swimming pool in the back garden. It was always a great treat to be invited to spend the weekend there. I would go on Saturday after lunch, have dinner and a sleepover at Rebecca's, and walk back home on Sunday afternoon.

"This was one such weekend, during a summer heatwave. Simon, Rebecca, and all her family and friends were out in the back garden, in and around the swimming pool.

"It was dark, about 9.30 p.m. Saturday night. The night was hot and still, the black, starry sky clear of any clouds. All of a sudden, without warning, all the electricity in the street blacked out. We wondered what had happened," Simon said, "because there was no storm activity. Someone suggested perhaps there was a local traffic accident, involving the power lines.

"Up until then Simon, Rebecca and her two older brothers had been skylarking in the pool. They were so noisy, the adults had been trying to quieten them down before bedtime.

"Without warning, a huge, bright white light appeared out of nowhere, and hovered very low over the pool. The entire garden and house was illuminated – whiter than daylight, like a giant Polaire floodlight. It was not flashing at all, just exceptionally bright, and it was impossible to see if there was any craft associated with the light. There was no noise, no wind, nothing disturbed that hot, still garden. It is so clear in my mind, I can think back now and relive the experience."

After a few seconds of stunned silence, total panic erupted. Rebecca's father, Mr. Smithers, started yelling to the children to get out of the pool, and bypassing the ladder, jumped straight out over the side himself. Mrs. Smithers was screaming in terror, telling Rebecca and Simon to get into the house immediately. She grabbed them with both arms, and started dragging them up the path to the back door:

"I was terrified, but curious. I wanted to see what the object was, but every time I looked, it was so bright it dazzled my eyes. When I turned to look, I fell over, but Mrs. Smithers did not loosen her grip on my arm, and dragged me bodily along the ground and up the back steps. Rebecca was calling out to her mother that she was hurting her arm, but she took no notice, and kept screaming at us: 'Come on! Hurry up!' In the meantime her two brothers and Mr. Smithers were still near the pool, looking up, shouting and yelling.

"The electricity was still blacked out, but once inside the back door, we could see light pouring in, illuminating the whole house. It was 'creepy' – there were no shadows anywhere. Mrs. Smithers seemed to be consumed with terror, alternatively yelling at us to go into the bedroom, and then running around all the rooms in an erratic manner."

Rebecca and Simon took the opportunity to try and peek outside again, but Mrs. Smithers slapped Rebecca's face, pushed them into the bedroom, and slammed the door. She was behaving totally out of character, and the children stood in the middle of the bedroom, hugging each other in fear and bewilderment. That room was also bathed in the strange, brilliant white light. They didn't want to be there alone, preferring to be with the rest of the family.

"We heard the voices of the others coming up the back stairs. All of a sudden the house shook, and we could hear them all yelling. There were more noises and voices, and Mrs. Smithers opened the bedroom door again, shouting and swearing at us to stay in there. We had become very distressed, and started crying, as we didn't know what we had done wrong. We crawled under the bed and hid there, together."

Simon's memory was vague as to what happened next, and he couldn't recall details from that point until after the light had gone. I wondered if there were any undisclosed details to this incident. Even under hypnosis, Simon's memory was a blank for the period of time they were in the bedroom. He was also unable to remember the light actually disappearing or the house electricity being restored. "It was strange, like everything was in slow motion."

His next conscious memory is from much later, when Mr. Smithers came into the room. He didn't say much, and seemed subdued and shaken, telling them not to worry and to go to sleep. They lay awake for some time, as everyone was talking in the next room. Rebecca's mother seemed the most upset, crying and then screeching, "What was it?"

"I woke to the commotion of voices shouting about all the fish being dead, and the sound of people running through the house. We went out in our pyjamas and saw that the water in Mr. Smithers' fish tank, in the lounge room, was a milky colour. All the fish were dead and floating, upside-down on top of the water. If the object could kill the fish inside the house, I have often wondered what adverse effect it may have had on the rest of us?"

Mr Smithers went down the backyard in his pyjamas, but when they tried to follow, his wife stopped them with the excuse they had no shoes on.

"I realise now she was only trying to protect us, but at the time we still thought we had done something wrong. Breakfast was very strained. Mrs. Smithers was in a bad mood, and to make matters worse, us kids had developed strange, persistent coughs and kept drinking water all day.

After breakfast they were ordered to stay in the front garden, and not to go down the backyard. They could see an Air Force officer, in his blue uniform, talking to the man next door.

"The neighbour didn't like kids much, so we hid behind some bushes near the fence and eavesdropped. The man was complaining, in a loud voice, that the light the previous night had wrought havoc with his prize pigeons. He had a big race coming up, and the birds were so scared some had already died. Further, his breeding hens were in a terrible state and he would likely lose the expected chicks. We could not hear the officer's replies, as he spoke in a very soft voice."

Soon afterwards the Air Force officer and another man came to Rebecca's front door. "By this time us kids were quite excited, and followed them and the Smithers into the house, only to be sent back to the bedroom, where we tried to listen through the door.

"They were showing him their fish tank, and the officer seemed to be on the defensive and unsure of what to say. He was alternating between apologising for the inconvenience and questioning what could have caused the damage. They insisted the fish were of an expensive tropical variety, which had the best of care, and had been in very good health."

Still arguing about what had killed the fish, Mr Smithers led the officer down the back garden to see even further proof.

"We were curious as to why we had been banned from the back garden, so we slipped out of the front door, around the side of the house, and down the back, hiding behind the shed to get a good vantage point and hear the continuing conversations."

Mr. and Mrs. Smithers were describing the light and what happened, and the officer was politely trying to suggest it was a weather balloon, and they should take it up with the Department of Meteorology. Rebecca's father was becoming quite heated and insisted they knew what they saw! It certainly was no weather balloon! What was interesting was that neither the officer nor his offsider had a clipboard or were writing anything down.

"They inspected the swimming pool, which had a really foul smell, and all the water was now a weird, white colour. They unbolted the joint on the side, and let the water run out onto the grass. The liner was putrid and rotten, and had to be thrown away. Later, all the grass died, and nobody was allowed to go down the back garden for months.

"Rebecca's father caught us behind the bushes, spying, and seemed extremely upset that we were near the pool. Later, while in the front garden, we saw the officer and his companion visit the neighbours on the other side, and across the street, before driving away in a car.

"Normally, I would have lunch with the family before walking the two blocks home by myself. It was different this time. There was no lunch. Rebecca's parents took me to one side, and told me I must not tell anyone what had happened."

Mr. Smithers then walked Simon home, which had never occurred before. "I thought I was in trouble, but he talked to my parents in private. Nothing more was said about the matter again. When I did try to broach the subject with Mum, she refused to discuss it. My father had been an army engineer in New Guinea during the war, and strictly adhered to military security, so I couldn't prise any information out of him!"

Simon didn't think about the incident for years, and rarely mentioned it. In about 1990, Hannah, his older sister, asked him about the sighting, and Simon "went cold" when he remembered that night. Hannah, who was 21 in 1967, said that whatever Mr. Smithers had told their mother, it had really "freaked her out."

"After the incident Rebecca changed. She became introverted, and did not have many friends. We had been best mates, but soon drifted apart. There was talk about her mysteriously 'disappearing' sometimes on the way home from school. I saw very little of her later, as we went to different High Schools. Hannah's questions about that night 23 years ago, brought the entire episode flooding back into my mind. I went to see Rebecca, as I needed to talk about it. By this time we were both in our early thirties, and Rebecca's life had not been easy.

"Her mother had never been the same since that night, and directly after had spent a lot of time in bed. I never knew whether it was an illness, or just nerves. She had been a reasonably pleasant woman before, but changed into a very unstable person, relying upon pills to make it through the day. She no longer welcomed me into the house as she had in the past.

"Rebecca had also experienced a lot of trauma, and was a bundle of nerves due to emotional, drug and alcohol problems. When I asked her what she recalled about that night, so many years ago, she lost her composure and physically threw me out of the house. While she had always been a bit of a tomboy," Simon recalled, "throwing me out was totally out of character.

"What was that object which had such a profound effect on people physically and mentally? It certainly was no weather balloon! Was it one of these alien craft we now hear about, or some more-earthly experiment? What happened while we were hiding in the bedroom, and why can't I remember? I guess I will never know."

In his late teens, Simon went to live with his sister Hannah, in the Snowy Mountains. Except for a few mundane "lights in the sky", he does not remember any other incidents in his life that could relate to, or equate with that night at the Smithers' home.

When I reflected on this case, one detail bothered me. Of the six witnesses present that night so long ago, the four male witnesses appeared to have recovered with no lasting ill-effects. Rebecca and Mrs. Smithers seem to have suffered profound long-term psychological problems. Unfortunately there was no opportunity to investigate this aspect further.

Moorebank, 24 March 1995

Several decades later there was another mystifying incident in a Sydney suburban swimming pool: Pamela Newbury and her husband were sitting outside enjoying the mild evening:

"Just before 10 p.m. David went inside to go to bed, and I said I would stay out a little longer, and let him use the shower first. I sat there for a few more minutes, and as I got up to go inside I noticed two round lights hovering just over the two 20-foot palm trees at the back fence. I walked down the side of the pool to get a better view, and thought they were probably helicopters.

"I thought it unusual I couldn't hear any noise, and noticed there was an indistinct red webbing around the whitish-yellow lights, which seemed to be moving independently of each other. They then began to intermittently beam down four intense blue, laser-like lights; two of which went up into the air, and two into the pool. The dog, which had followed me down the deck, slunk away and hid, without making a noise. I was fascinated and mesmerised by this light display, and for some stupid reason, I don't know why, I beckoned to the lights.

"They descended in unison over the gate and across the yard and hovered about two feet above the ground on the other side of the pool. I felt no menace, even when they beamed their blue lights onto my legs. I didn't feel any sensation and didn't even move. It was like my attention was drawn to the bright lights in the pool itself. They must have moved over the pool, because it suddenly became one huge bluish light, and when I looked back up to where they were situated opposite me, the lights had disappeared.

"I raced into the house to find my husband was already asleep. All excited, I woke him to tell him about these incredible lights, and he wanted to know where I had been all this time. It was now nearly 1 a.m., but I'm sure I only stood watching for a few minutes."

I asked Pamela whether she suffered any side-effects and she said that she had felt very tired, and seemed to be sleeping longer than normal. She didn't believe in UFOs, and didn't think anything untoward had happened. She and her husband were Canadians. He was a geologist, who had studied ancient Indian writings and a hidden valley in Canada. I wondered if there was any connection. She didn't want to pursue the matter any further other than talking to me, and filling in the report form.

Princes Highway, 23 August 1992

Sunday evening, 23 August 1992, was an eventful one for unidentified objects reports. Early on, at 5.30 p.m., Ainslee Brown was driving north, along Highway 1 (the Princes Highway), from Bombaderry on the South Coast to Wollongong, south of Sydney. She thought she saw a plane coming in, and wondered if it might be in trouble, as it went up and down several times, and its lights were fading in and out:

"It tilted on its side, and we could see it was a saucer-shaped object, with a steady white light on each tip. Suddenly it turned red and shot towards Wollongong at incredible speed, halted and hovered again. We stopped a total of four times on the way up the coast, just to look at it, as a couple of members of my family got the silly idea it was following us.

"It would appear, disappear, then reappear again. At Bombaderry it was lower, further up the coast at Kiama it was higher but closer. It was slower than a normal plane, except when it turned red and moved at incredible speed. We lost sight of it at about 6.30 p.m., when we were nearing Wollongong."

Dover Heights, 23 August 1992, 7 p.m.

Jane and Christine lived in Dover Heights, across the water from the naval base at Balmoral, in one of the most affluent suburbs on Sydney Harbour. They were best friends, and lived a few streets apart. Jane's house was two-storey, with wonderful views up and down Sydney Harbour. Jane was interviewed by several researchers, and at times her description and location of the original lights differ and are a little confusing. I will concentrate on what she told me a few days after the incident:

At 7 p.m. she saw what she thought were bright flares over Sydney Cricket Ground: "Two very large, bright yellow lights hovered for about five minutes, and then seemed to get brighter and started moving. I saw a third light over the lower North Shore near Epping, and realised these were not flares. I was startled to see one of the lights had come much closer, near to Watsons Bay and the South Head Army Barracks. It was hovering, stopping, moving backwards and forwards, and eventually disappeared.

"It reappeared a short time later, small at first, then getting bigger and brighter, like an explosion. It remained at this large size for about an hour. It made no noise, and definitely wasn't a helicopter – I see those all the time. I was feeling a little guilty, my young son had said in the past that he saw a 'thing' in the sky ('they come sometimes', he says) and I hadn't believed him. I asked my father to bring my binoculars, and he just ignored me. I found my video camera, only to discover the battery was flat.

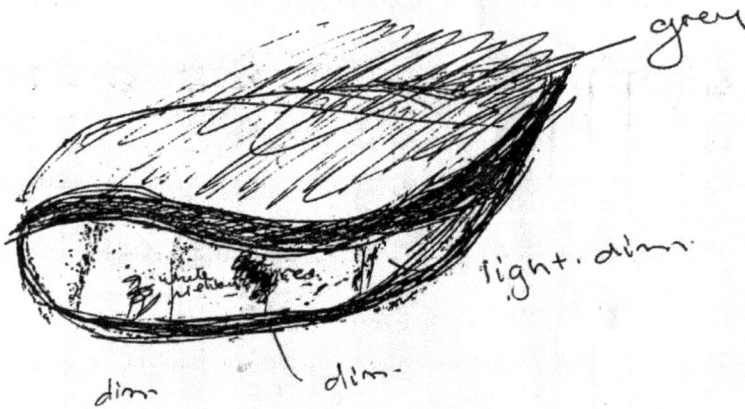

I noticed one of the objects had been moving around and was now over the Bondi Beach area, near the cliffs at the back of my house. I could see it a lot better. It was a dull grey colour. No lights except for a dull red one in front. It was more like there was something I couldn't see surrounding it. I think it was a glass front, or something similar. There was a faint humming noise. I've not heard anything like it. My dog started to bark, then suddenly stopped, which was unusual."

Jane went inside, and when she came back out it had moved to the Rose Bay side and had a strange beam. She rang her friend Christine and asked her to go outside and verify what she was seeing.

Christine said, "I'm afraid I was sceptical, but to humour Jane I went down to the end of the street, taking my cordless phone with me. I saw this big, bright yellow light, at least four to five times bigger than a star. It disappeared for about five minutes than came back again. I was fascinated and confirmed that, while it made a funny noise, it was definitely not an aircraft."

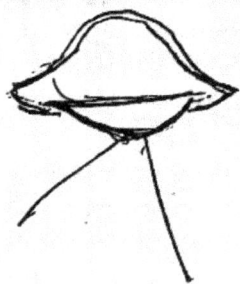

It was below the clouds, would hover or remain stationary for five minutes, then suddenly get brighter and move. Christine drove over to Jane's house and Jane got the video out again and tried using it with the battery-charger plugged in on the wall. One object came across the harbour towards her, and hovered over the top of some houses in Rose Bay. She started filming it, as it hovered for about three minutes, before expanding into a huge light, about half the size of the moon. The light itself was bright yellow, and a whitish-yellow beam come from underneath, like a reflection.

"It was really low," Jane commented, "and we both watched as it did aerobatics. Suddenly it made a swift move upwards and there was a huge beam, like a band of white light. What was strange was that the object then vanished, disappeared! However, the band of light stayed there for another five minutes. We kept watching and were sure we could see another object, much further down the harbour. It was hard to see the details, but we could make out a grey dome on top, and rotating lights around. It moved slowly, at a tilted angle going upwards, and was gone.

Jane and Christine rang the Department of Meteorology which was closed, and the local police, who had gone home. Christine rang a local television station, and the switchboard operator said a lot of reports had come in, and was very interested that they had taken a video. Jane said she did not want to give an interview, but shortly afterwards a television journalist arrived on her doorstep. He said they had another report, but it was different and conflicted with theirs.

"Maybe it was a trick to get the video. I hadn't even seen it myself, and was having trouble getting it out of the camcorder. He virtually ripped it out, saying he would return it later. He later claimed that after four hours of viewing it only showed 'flickers of light' and they had passed it on to another program (I was told by friends that my footage had gone to air). I was furious, I couldn't get my tape back. It was returned several weeks later, with a huge piece blanked out, by whom and why?"

At INUFOR I received a couple of anonymous messages from motorists in the area, reporting strange lights in the sky and Bryan Dickeson was making enquiries. Some months later Bryan spoke to a radio announcer from Gore Hill, who was rostered on the overnight shift at that time. He had been embargoed inside a studio, but when he finished his shift next day at 5.30 a.m. security staff were still talking about the unusual lights that appeared above them the evening before.

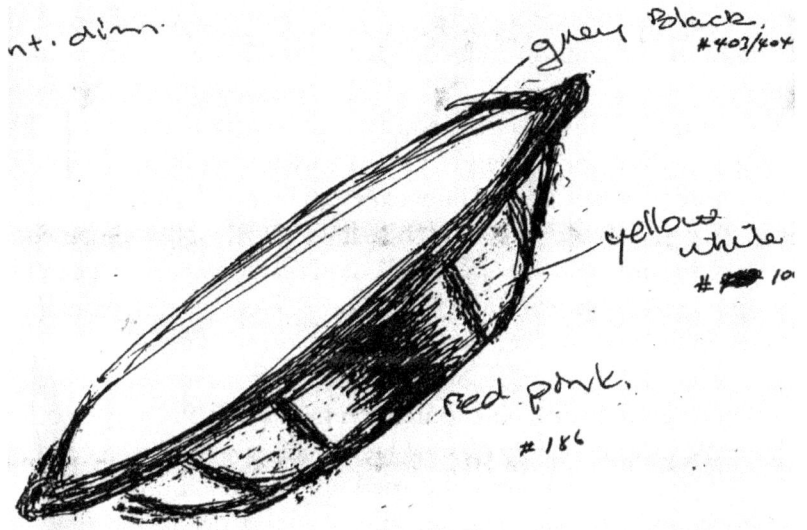

Jane desperately wanted a conventional explanation, but we couldn't give her one.

Dover Heights, 21 October 1992

A couple of months later, at 6.30 p.m. 21 October, I got a call from Ida Michaels of Rose Bay who had seen two big white lights come down the harbour towards her, and over Dover Road. She thought at first they were the headlights of a plane going in to land, but there was no noise, and they were hovering over the ocean area behind her.

I had been liaising with Jane and Christine since their experience on 23 August, and telephoned them and asked if they could take a look for me. They went to the end of Dover Road and the cliffs which overlook the ocean.

"We could see it straight away. A bright white light which was originally circular, then changed to a 'hot dog' shape, with little white lights around the bottom. It wasn't actually over the ocean. It was hovering high overhead, above the cliffs."

They had both brought normal and video cameras. Christine got into Jane's car, which was pointed towards the object, and they started flashing the car headlights hoping to signal it. (When they told me this, I thought to myself, 'Oh no, bad idea!') The craft had dimmed and flashed back, and seemed to be getting bigger and closer.

"I don't know what happened," said Jane. "Suddenly it was gone – no longer there! We drove around a couple of streets looking, but didn't see it again."

The time frames Jane and Christine gave me didn't add up, and in light of later events it is not known what happened after the object signalled back and came closer. They certainly had no photographic record on their equipment.

23

There was another strange anomaly in the details given later to other investigators, who didn't realise that there had been two separate incidents involving the two women. Christine had originally spoken of only going to the end of her street before going to Jane's home on 23 August. She described that object as being a "bright light – four to five times the size of a star", and then went home and drove over to Jane's house to watch the objects over Sydney Harbour.

During later interviews with other researchers, she talked of being at the top of a hill, more consistent with the incident on 21 October. The details she gave also indicated she was describing the craft they encountered on the top of the cliffs that night. She talked about a huge object, only a couple of hundred metres away (estimated at about 250 metres across).

"It had a translucent surface, a bit like creamy-yellowish lampshade parchment, or eggshell. It was lit from within, but did not cast any light or create any shadows around me. It had a distinct rim, with a flattened top and a wider, deeper bottom. It looked a bit like a hot dog shape in cross-section, but had an overall round, or disc-like appearance, and was tilted at about a 45 degree angle."

Some months went by, and I received a call from Jane. Over the last few months "strange things had been happening." She and Christine had been having unusual identical dreams, in which they both participated and interacted, and remembered the next day.

"This is weird," she said. "It's almost like twinned dreams. My main worry is Bruce, my four-year-old son. You remember how I didn't take any notice when he told me 'they come sometimes', recently he's been telling me that 'Peter Pan comes to see him every night and takes him for a ride in his train.' He's never heard of Peter Pan and Wendy – it's not a book we've ever got for him."

Were the visitors resorting to fairy tales with our young, not realising modern kids were watching entirely different content on media? This is not the only case I've come across where the same ploy was used by visitors. One witness was told, as a child, she was going on a trip to "Never Never land." I also was concerned about Jane's reference to "twinned dreams" and a similar connection between a small number of experiencers.

My friend and colleague, researcher Rosemary Decker (PhD) was visiting from the United States, and an expert at dealing with troubled children. When we arrived at the house, Jane whispered to us, "Be careful, Bruce's grandmother, Sylvia, is here. She doesn't even want us to mention unidentified flying objects – says it's all nonsense!"

We all sat down to afternoon tea, and discussed Jane and Christine's "twinned dreams" and a few other phenomena. I was left with a large question mark in my mind. Were the identical dreams more of a flashback memory? Their most vivid dream was of seeing each other being carried down some stairs by unusual beings with greyish skin and large, dark midnight-blue eyes.

The grandmother, Sylvia, was hunched up, with a grim disapproving scowl on her face. As we started talking to Bruce, I noticed there were tears streaming down her cheeks, and her wall of denial came tumbling down. Amid sobs, Sylvia told of how, when she had been a little girl in Eastern Europe, she had gone to play with the other children in the local park one morning. The next thing she knew, she was still in the same place, but it was dark.

"All the villagers and my family came running up: 'Where have you been? We've been looking all day!' All I could tell them was that a lovely, tall, blond angel had been looking after me."

Sylvia then clammed up, and would say no more. Rosemary and I couldn't help thinking about the generational experiences we and other researchers had already encountered.

Ongoing activities

Up until about twenty-five years ago, investigators thought UFO sightings were extremely rare and unusual. For an airline pilot, where UFOs can be something of an occupational hazard, multiple sightings are usually acceptable, but anyone else who saw two or more UFOs in their lifetime was considered to be most probably lying.

However, since then we've become aware many witnesses have a more complicated link to the phenomenon. Some *families* seem to have a long history of sightings – possibly even an ongoing relationship with alien life forms that deserves closer attention.

And this makes investigations much more complicated. The only way to assess any human-alien link effectively, albeit anecdotally, is to collect as much physical detail from as many events as possible and compare these across a much larger number of experiencers. Forget what any aliens may tell a witness (except in passing), because we can demonstrate that aliens often lie. Also, witnesses are usually stressed and confused by their situation, so their assessment of what is really going on is compromised. The devil is always in the detail:

Soon after the two Dover Heights incidents, Jane began experiencing flashes of memory and vivid dreams. However, there were a lot of blank spots that she wanted to clarify. She had trouble comprehending what had actually happened. She seemed to 'know' some things, but didn't know how. There was apparently more than one of these obscured incidents, apart from the extended experience when she and Christine were on the cliffs in October 1992.

"I remembered I was woken up one night and made to go downstairs. A brightly lit white object hovered over my yard, making a funny high-pitched noise in my head. The white light was coming from a dome-shaped top, and underneath the object was a sort of glass-partitioned base with bright red and green lights rotating very quickly. In the middle, above my head, was some sort of a door opening. My dogs remained asleep, and the next thing I knew I was aboard the craft.

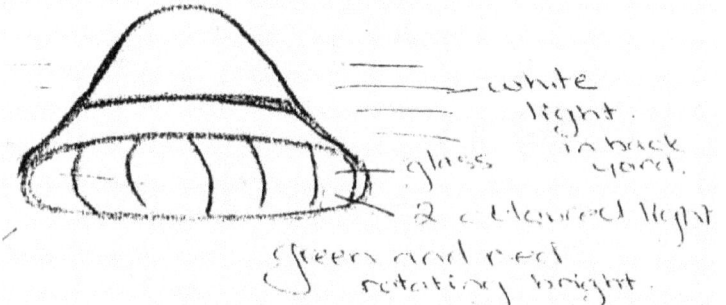

In November 1992, before any chance of an outside influence to affect her recall, Jane had two hypnotherapy sessions with a very reliable and experienced practitioner. She provided me with a transcribed overview of those sessions when Rosemary Decker and I visited her later. Some information was thought-provoking, as the details she provided corresponded with other experiencers' unpublished accounts I had already collected:

The craft

Jane described the craft as being circular, in three or four layers. "The bottom was the landing area, with a metal door which opened and shut in a retractable manner. It seemed to be constructed in a spiral-type fashion leading from one level to another. The walls were a metallic grey colour, with brackets of some kind. The walls curved outwards then back to meet a low ceiling. The floors looked like a type of black glass material with dull lights underneath." (Loretta from Hughenden in Queensland also describes a "frosted glass floor" – see Chapter 8.)

"Around the side of the craft there were grey metal doors, each had a different purpose and they slid into the wall and closed. It had observation domes in the front for close viewing. When travelling at high speed the domes have a protective metal covering. There are two lights inside the craft which are some form of 'defence laser' to attack anyone who threatens them.

"In the centre of the craft was a quite-large, glass-like cylinder, which was making a noise and was bolted to the floor and ceiling. There was a circular hole or opening around it. It seemed to have a thick liquid inside, which was moving in different directions and radiating pink light.

△ ♓ ♃ ≈ ∴ ℳ ‖ = ☉ |ˣⁱ
∀ ⊃ |/\ ⨯ ∵ ᛉ |ˣ‾

"The air was heavy, like a sauna without steam – not as moist. I could breathe it, but it made me feel groggy. There were symbols on the wall plus more dots and funny lines.

The symbols Jane remembers correspond closely to characters Penny from Roma recalled (see Chapter 8) and the automatic writing by Trevor in the Northern Territory (see Chapter 12).

"The walkways were very busy, with humans and aliens walking in and out of rooms. I was shown some of the rooms. One was very different – a nursery of some sort, with balls and square-type objects for children to play with. I could see a human women playing with and nursing babies and a child. A lot of them did not look human, and I didn't really like them. I got a shock when I saw my own child also playing inside.

"Two of the taller aliens took me into another room which had a screen and 3-D images. The screen had dots down the side and showed clusters of stars, not much open space between. I think I was told it was Polaris[1], or something like that. There was also the letter 'Z' – it meant something, I'm not sure but I think it stood for a longer name."

(When Jane told me this, I thought of Lana McDonald from Victoria who initially spoke of the Zs, later saying her contact was called "Zenna" see Chapter 9.)

"This Polaris had beautiful green vegetation, but the buildings were different to ours. The sun was reddish-orange and it had three moons. Then they showed me what an atom bomb could do to a planet. They told me their planet is dying and they have lost the ability to breed like us. They couldn't understand all the fuss about what they are doing, as they don't want to hurt us or cause any pain.

"They showed me an image of the earth, and said they are sick of trying to talk to state heads of government to stop what they are doing to our planet. What we do affects them and others in our galaxy. Unless we get our act together they will show themselves in force to the world, because people don't believe they exist.

"I looked through another open door and saw a sort of dormitory with about fifty tables containing humans, some asleep and some awake, who looked like they were in a state of shock. I can't remember much more, because it was after my examination, and I was feeling sick in the stomach and head, and my eyes were red and sore.

The aliens

Jane gave a very detailed description of three different types of alien she saw during her experience: When she entered the craft, one being was walking ahead of Jane. "He was about five foot, two inches tall, and gold in colour, with a long neck and square shoulders. While his legs were short, with square-back funny heels, his body and arms were long. His arms didn't appear to have joints, and he had four long fingers which had pads on the ends. The spinal cord looked more like deep indents running down his back." He later examined her, and was apparently "the doctor." She noticed he had a large, pear-shaped head with a lot of wrinkles and almond-shaped eyes.

"There were four little grey guys, about three feet tall, with big brown-black cat-like eyes, which were mirror-like, almost glassy, with no white or pupils. There was an extra flap of skin over

---

1. *Polaris* is our name for the northern hemisphere's Pole Star – presently the closest star to earth's celestial North Pole, and the brightest star in the constellation Ursa Minor (the *Little She-Bear* or *Little Dipper*). This is a *white-yellow supergiant*, a triple star, and *unusual* – known to be the closest Cepheid variable star to planet earth, only about 375 light years away. Polaris, and the six other stars in this constellation are presently thought to be very unlikely to harbour any form of life.

the eyes, and they had no ears, just dents. They had small noses and well-shaped mouths, and they walked very strangely, with small steps like rubber men. When I was lying on the table, one looked into my face and he had a very funny smell.

"One was thin, six feet tall, but human in appearance. He was wearing a tightly fitting greeny-gold coloured suit which also covered his feet. On his shoulders were metal badges with something like a bird or animal on the end of it." (Several abductee reports mention the same type and colour apparel, and Penny from Roma described a similar insignia – see Chapter 8.)

"He had white skin and small features," she said, "although his ears looked a little different to ours. His face was perfectly shaped, long black hair to his shoulders, the most beautiful being I have ever seen. His eyes were slightly larger than mine, no whites, just unusually blue, almost violet. I liked him from the moment I saw him; the next best thing to seeing an angel. He seemed to be in charge. Throughout my examination he was there, standing behind me.

The examination

"I was taken to a circular room with a door and in the middle a low table with a light inside. It seemed to be made of the same material as the floor. I felt groggy, as if I was on some sort of medication. They put me on the table, with some sort of hard plastic type head rest, because I felt a jolt. The table itself was not wide, it just fitted my body, and they put brackets on my arms and legs, so I couldn't move, and two metal squares on either side at my temples.

"The four little greys were at my feet, and appeared to be talking to themselves. I could only hear funny noises, and never saw their lips move, but sometimes it seemed they were 'talking in my head'. I wasn't afraid; they said they wouldn't hurt me and I believed them. The good-looking human being was standing behind my head, and the 'doctor' bloke walked in.

"I remember my left shoulder hurting, and the doctor placed a thin needle into my ovary on the left side. I could see liquid and an egg being extracted. Some form of light came down from the low ceiling. It was so bright I told them it was burning my eyes which I couldn't shut – Please Stop! A hand went over the front of my head and temples, something was put into my right ear with a 'pop' and I was told to sleep."

Two days later Jane had to go to the doctor with a very bad infection in both her inner and outer ear. There were several red dots burning under the skin on her leg, which later disappeared, leaving a small brown circle.

The "twinned dreams"

While Christine did not have hypnotic regression, both she and Jane had reported "twinned dreams", some of which Jane detailed. One of which took place at 3 a.m. A being was in her lounge room, which was full of yellow-white light. He told her he had not come to hurt her or her family, but not to come too close as he was not yet 'detoxified'.

"I asked permission to call Christine and she arrived soon after I rang, wearing only her bedtime white sloppy-joe. We asked him questions and he answered telepathically. Basically what he was saying was that the earth and our human race were on course for destruction. There was some suggestion we could go away with them, but we declined when it became obvious our husbands were not included in this offer."

Another memory Jane had was of being in the craft on an examination table, and the aliens asking her where she got two unusual scars from a spinal operation two years earlier. "While they were doing something to my back, I recall telling them not to hurt my friend's head as they were pushing her too hard." It certainly seems possible that Christine also had some interaction with the beings, however, unlike Jane she decided not to pursue the matter.

The experiences Jane recalled under hypnotic regression are very typical of those retrieved from abductees: The free mingling of aliens and humans on-board an alien craft, medical examinations (albeit under a form of medicated control), the presence of children in an educational/assessment environment, a fascination with our nuclear weaponry, frustration with corrupt earth authorities, a home planet a bit like ours but slightly exotic, their present inability to breed, and so on.

Many answers to abductees' questions seem too obvious and formulaic – intended more to induce trust and compliance in the abductee (and just a little bit patronising). They raise far more questions than they answer and sidestep any real discussion.

For example, the last item mentioned: Many aliens seem able to use technology to solve the difficult problems associated with aging and cancer. Our own experiments in the last few decades have greatly advanced biological science. So we have entities who must be familiar with genetic technology over several millennia, yet they still can't reproduce effectively. It's only DNA!

In recent years, my colleague Bryan Dickeson has been undertaking an assessment of 60 years' worth of UFO reports from Australia and New Zealand. He is coming to the view that there must be dozens, possibly hundreds of alien civilisations out there, all more advanced than ours, and more are on the way. Many visitors just take a few samples and carry on to the next star system. (It seems one group of aliens likes to visit earth every 17–18 years just to see if we're still here, and is usually surprised to see we haven't destroyed ourselves in the meantime. Apparently, the transition of a sole-species dominated planet such as ours, into a star-travelling civilisation is not always easy. Failure is common, and while we are quite interesting, it's best for aliens not to get too involved.)

Roseville, 16 April 1994

Mrs. B. was one of those wonderful women from a bygone era; intelligent, independent and resourceful. She didn't scare easily. As for UFOs; up until I knew her, she didn't really know, or want to know about them. During her World War 2 service, nearly five years in the Air Force, and later stints in radar installations, she dealt with realities – balloons, flares and all facets of aircraft. She was familiar with everything aerial, and was very proud of her previous career and acquired knowledge.

Her complacency was shattered in the early hours of Saturday 16 April when she saw her first truly inexplicable object. She telephoned me afterwards, referred on by Directory inquiries:

"It was just after midnight, and I was getting ready for bed. My 16-year-old grand-daughter Wendy was already asleep. (She's staying with me as her parents are diplomats on overseas service).

"My home overlooks the Roseville Golf Club, and as I walked across the room to turn on the lamp, I saw a strange orange light glowing through the window. At first I thought it was the moon, but realised it was moving, and the wrong colour. It was a vivid orange-red and had an eerie glowing aura around it. It was larger than the moon; more the size of a helicopter.

"I scrutinised that object very carefully. It was over the Eighteenth Tee, and was hovering and moving sideways. I wondered if it was a helicopter on fire? But No, it wasn't a helicopter. Even though it moved against the wind in a purposeful manner, and there was no noise whatsoever.

"It appeared to be coming from the east or northeast, and I found myself just staring at it. I felt totally mesmerised at first, to the extent I couldn't move. Then I felt an uncharacteristic surge of fear, and called Wendy to come quickly.

"I was feeling sick, and trembling as I searched for my binoculars. When Wendy came she couldn't believe I had started up the thirty-nine stairs outside, to the garage where the binoculars were kept in my car. She insisted on joining me and we both watched, for about ten minutes, as this object moved and hovered until it eventually descended behind some trees at the edge of the golf course and was obscured from view.

"I immediately rang Chatswood police, who said police radio had received one call, but they had dismissed it as a flare without investigation. So then I rang Civil Aviation, who advised me they had a report of a strange object the previous night at 9 p.m., and then I phoned Meteorology who didn't want to know about it unless it involved the weather."

I asked Mrs. B. how long she had spent on the previous calls – "Not long at all." I had quietly estimated the approximate sighting and subsequent telephone call times at no longer than an hour at most, and gently told her it was now 3.30 a.m.

"No, it couldn't be! I would never ring anyone at that time in the morning!"

It was obvious that there were about two hours unaccounted for. Mrs. B didn't seem to know or understand. I interviewed her again a few days later. She and Wendy both suffered from churned-up tummies and severe headaches the next day, and felt very jittery for most of the following week.

She and Wendy had no memory or symptoms of any missing time, and I thought it unethical to prompt anything extra into the report or to distress a woman of her age. Further, my self-preservation instincts told me it would have been very unwise for me to put any pressure on a senior diplomat's family while he was overseas.

Another case where I was left wondering if there was more to the story.

Milperra, 1968

In the 1960s, the outer suburbs of Western Sydney were not the built-up areas we see today. There was also far less air traffic than today, and our military technology in the air was not so advanced or sophisticated. An ex-serviceman contacted me in 2000, some 32 years after an incident. In 1968 he was attending a barbecue at a small farm in Milperra, on the banks of the Georges River.

"The first thing we saw was a sudden flash of blue-white light. Then an enormous glowing thing appeared over the Milperra Bridge. The light, or lights, turned orange inside and halfway around. It slowly enlarged to a width of two to three semi-trailers, or two lengths of telegraph poles apart. We couldn't see the bottom of the object.

"The light contracted and disappeared with a low muffled explosion. It seems it landed (about half a mile away, as the crow flies) on a nearby golf course, and left a huge cylindrical ground trace (the *Daily Mirror* took photos). About ten minutes later it appeared to rise from the ground, moved back to its original position, then shot off over Condell Park.

"The RAAF spoke to us all later, and I never thought any more about it, and even now don't recall anything untoward happening. Over the last two years I have been having flashback dreams of this incident, which have become stronger during the last three to four months. I couldn't understand why I should even be thinking of it. Maybe it was business stress. I contacted a couple of the friends to see if they had any unusual after-effects from the incident, and was astounded to discover that one friend had refused a request by the RAAF to undergo hypnotherapy. Why?

Glenfield, May 1974

Danielle rang me when she was in her seventies, the first time she had confided what she saw all those years ago:

"I was nursing at the Masonic Homes in Glenfield, situated on a hillside, and had been in a rush to get to the office and store before they closed to get a clean uniform, before I went back in to finish an urgent job. That's how I remember it was just after 3 p.m. I glanced across at the water tower, and heard this voice say: 'Look above the water tower.' I turned around. There was no-one there, and I thought to myself: 'I'm going crackers.' However, I looked above the tower, and there in the brilliant blue, cloudless sky, was this huge silver thing I can only describe as a classic UFO.

"It looked like a big upturned soup plate over an eggcup, with what seemed like oblong viewing windows, and lights underneath. It came closer, but made no sound. By this time I was getting quite excited, but also telling myself this wasn't real, I must be imagining things.' I called to two women coming out of the office but they ignored me and kept going. Then a younger colleague came over, and she went into raptures over the object, so I knew I wasn't stark raving mad. As she ran inside to call the others, the same voice told me to go and do the urgent job. Whether it was my own inner voice, or something more mysterious, I do not know."

"I went back to the ward and saw people watching through the window. I felt a certain sense of satisfaction that they were seeing the same thing. I went home and told my husband and kids and the ridicule was given in roars of laughter. The niggling doubt of what I had seen remained, and I tried to justify it as a plane coming in to land. However, no matter how I tried to explain it, nothing matched the object I had seen."

Leonay, 18 May 1993

UFO Research (New South Wales) was getting a lot of reports of orange or white lights over the west of the city – many were sophisticated pranks; garbage bags with flares or spotlights. I would groan, "Not more of those bloody lights in the sky." Regardless, each case had to be looked into without any preconceptions. This event, and its aftermath were different:

Amy Smith, along with her husband, daughter and three neighbours were chatting in the garden, just after 7 p.m.

"We had noticed three red-orange lights some distance away, and suddenly realised they had moved in a north-easterly direction, towards us. They were hovering over the top of our home and the streetlight outside. The neighbourhood was unusually quiet, except for one dog, barking frantically. We all stared. They were very bright and in a silent, triangular formation. Each was about the size of a half moon and an oval, football shape.

"We watched them for over 20 minutes, until they moved and changed position into a straight line, one above the other. The lowest one, which was at treetop level, shot off very fast towards Sydney in the east. The highest moved north in the direction of Richmond, and the middle one went west towards the Blue Mountains.

"We know a bloke up the hill, in the RAAF station at Glenbrook. He said he went off duty at 7 p.m. As he walked home, across the base, he saw the objects. He agreed they were not garbage bags with flares. Their motion, lack of noise, and low altitude were not consistent with helicopters.

Amy had also rung at least one other investigator, and I wasn't expecting to hear much more until I got a call from her three months later.

"I didn't tell you at the time, but during that sighting I felt mesmerised, almost hypnotised, by those lights. Since then all the clocks in the house aren't working properly. They stop and start for no reason. That is not the main reason I've rung. My four-and-a-half-year-old daughter Tania, who was the first to see the orange lights, keeps saying that 'Peter Pan' comes to see her every night."

I immediately recalled Jane's son Bruce, at Dover Heights, some months before. The reference to "Peter Pan" was rarely mentioned by children who talk about "little people" coming. If, and I must stress *if* – this was alien-related, then it reinforces several researchers' theory that our 'visitors' are way out of date in regards to not only modes of dress, but also the latest in children's reading and viewing material.

Amy continued, "Early this morning (18 May), I woke about one o'clock to see the curtains flapping and moving. Then I noticed a really big orange-red light directly outside. It had a lighter glow all around, which made my eyes sore. I blinked a bit, and it seemed to get smaller. When I went across to the window, it was closed. I couldn't understand it. I thought I was going mad. I went back to sleep, thinking I must have been dreaming. I woke again about three hours later to see the same light, I definitely wasn't dreaming!"

I would like to have delved into this case further, but Amy had contacted a local support network, and was in the process of buying as many books as she could on ufology and abductions.

Sydney's Northern Beaches

North of Sydney's Central Business District and harbour lies a stretch of beautiful beaches and coastal stretching from Manly to Palm Beach. Over the years, we have received numerous reports from this area. Some objects are obviously mistaken identity, some possibly technically-advanced military craft, and others just pranks. Occasionally there are truly inexplicable sightings:

Avalon 1984

Julie Wearne and her husband were walking home around midnight, when they heard a strange sound like a resounding ringing:

"It seemed to be coming from behind Bangalley Head, and the noise seemed to bounce off the ground around us. As it got louder and closer, we were intrigued as to what it was, and stopped. Up over the headland came a dark triangular shape, the size of three house blocks. It had red and white lights underneath, but no headlights or navigation lights. It was very low, and travelling from northeast to the southwest.

"As it passed us, we noticed the rear looked like a rocket. It had no lights as such, but there was a thick column of orange flame coming out of the back. The next day we rang Sydney Airport who tried to say it was a jumbo jet! No way! My husband knows his planes, and other people had seen it at the same time!"

Harbord, 11 April 1996

Paul Cox, a scientific consultant, was fishing from a Harbord headland at about 10.45 p.m., when he saw a bright golden light coming from the eastern horizon, over the sea:

"At first I thought it was a plane coming in to land. The light grew bigger as it neared the coast. By the time it was about two kilometres away it appeared as a golden light about half the size of the moon, emitting rays. I was still thinking it was a jet coming in to land at Sydney Airport.

"I started taking more notice of a small bright red light, just behind it. It wasn't until the craft zoomed in that I realised it was merely the tail light on an enormous object. It travelled on a straight, steady path, at about 250 kilometres per hour, and passed directly overhead. I looked up, and was paralysed with fright.

"From underneath it looked large and formidable, but somehow like something I had seen before. It was dark, and shaped like an equilateral triangle, pointed at the front, and 20 to 30 metres

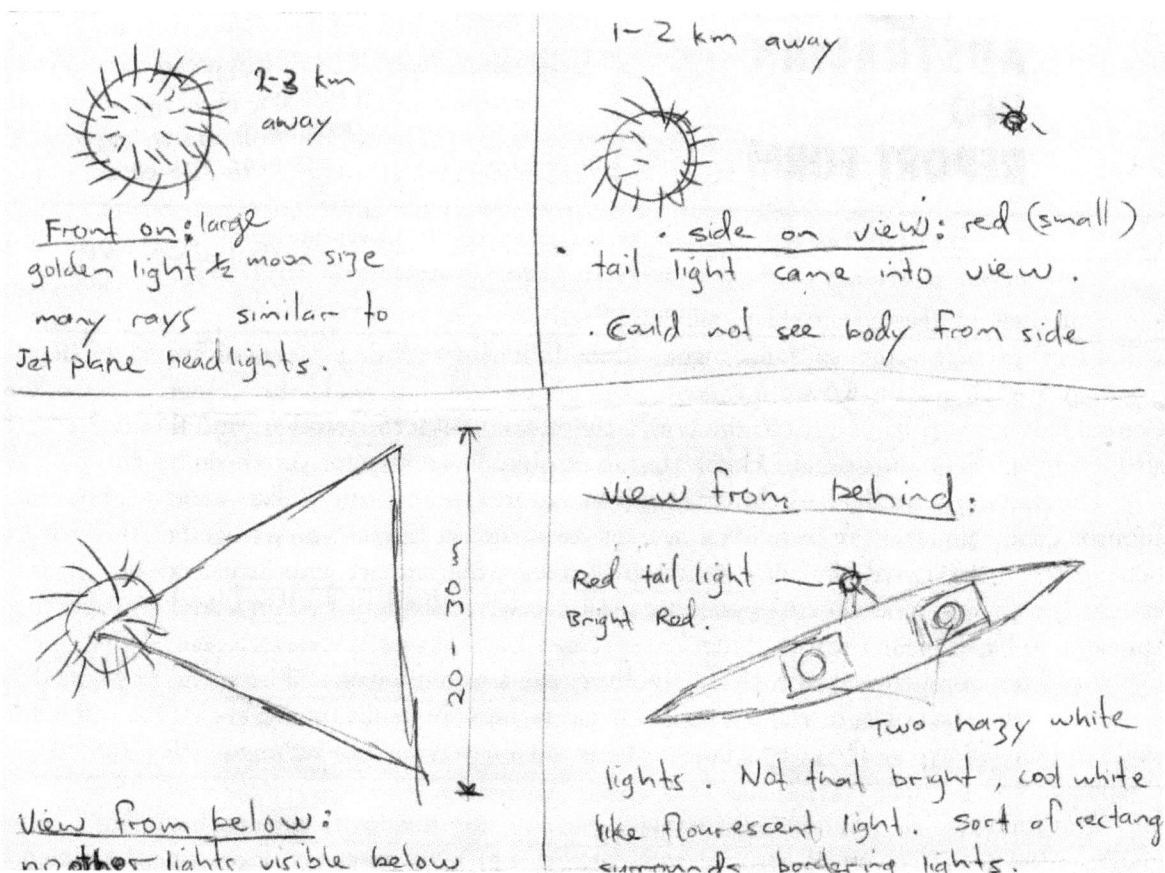

2-3 km away

Front on: large golden light ½ moon size many rays similar to Jet plane headlights.

1-2 km away

side on view: red (small) tail light came into view.
Could not see body from side

50M - 20

View from below: no other lights visible below

view from behind:

Red tail light — Bright Red.

Two hazy white lights. Not that bright, cool white like flourescent light. Sort of rectang surrounds bordering lights.

31

in width at the back. It was unusually quiet, but I could hear a faint sound, similar to that of a jet, like a DC10, but not as loud."

Paul watched it as it continued westward over the land. From the rear, beside the red light, he could see two hazy, "cool fluorescent", white lights with rectangular surrounds. After it had travelled inland a little way, it appeared to slow and hover, then change direction towards the Hawkesbury area, south of Gosford.

Since the object was headed in the general direction of Richmond Air Force Base, it could have been a modern military craft, avoiding public scrutiny as it came in to land. It is also possible this was also the explanation for the 1984 sighting at Avalon.

Collaroy, 23 February 2001

This sighting was reported by several independent witnesses, and resulted in publicity which attracted the media and both experienced and amateur researchers. Just before 11 p.m. this Friday, I received several telephone calls from residents in the area. A few minutes before, at about 10.45 p.m., they had witnessed an extraordinary event:

Bob Brown, my first caller, said "My wife and I were startled to hear this incredible noise approaching our home – like a hundred Harley Davidsons. We rushed outside to see what was happening and noticed several other neighbours were also out on their verandas or in their gardens.

"Down the road, at the local pub, two of the bouncers and a couple of patrons were also staring at the sky in astonishment. There were a few motor bikes parked in front, but their riders were already inside, probably too blotto to even notice the deafening noise. This huge object was hurtling out of the sky from over the hill behind Collaroy. It was coming towards us at a 70 to 80 degree downwards angle, towards the east and the sea. At one stage, when it seemed to slightly change direction, the noise stopped for a few seconds, then came on again. It was moving at a terrific speed, and when it passed low overhead, no higher than 100 feet, there was a physical and audible sensation of a void, into which the air rushed.

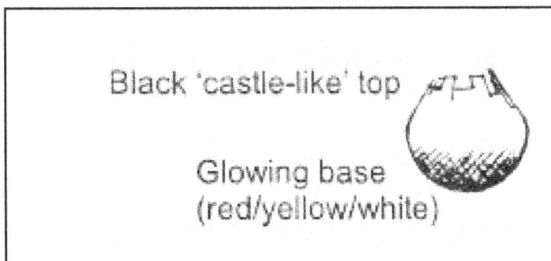

Black 'castle-like' top

Glowing base
(red/yellow/white)

"I am an ex-Army Officer, and in all my years in the military, I have never seen any earthly craft which resembled this. We had a good view of the underside. It was shaped like a half moon, glowing a yellow-white to cherry red, similar to red hot metal. It was hard to discern the upper part. Just a dark, unlit, silhouette which resembled a castle. After it passed over our house, our view of the coast was blocked. If it had continued on that trajectory it would have crashed into the sea."

I received many other calls that night and the following morning. Most confirmed the details reported by Bob and his wife. Some were from people who had heard the strange noise on the Central Coast, many kilometres to the north. By this time other researchers and the media were also receiving telephone calls and emails, and the rush to Collaroy and Narrabeen began.

The next day, Saturday 24 February, I received more reports, from Collaroy and neighbouring suburbs. Many aircraft were being seen over the area, such as a black and orange Naval Recovery helicopter, an Air Force Hercules, and a small fixed wing aircraft with "small round objects" attached, which were assumed to be sonar. All the witnesses and residents thought that they appeared to be "looking for something."

At 10 p.m. residents, already shaken by the events of the previous 24 hours, were stunned to see a huge white ball of light over the ocean. It was not exceptionally bright, but "stood out in the sky", and moved in over the coast from east to west at an incredible speed. Suddenly it turned and disappeared.

The following day, Sunday 25 February, several more planes flew over, including a four-engine naval plane at very low speed and altitude, and with its cargo doors open. Residents commented they had never seen such a large plane so low over a built-up area. Bryan Dickeson was informed, from a usually reliable source, that Monash University (Melbourne) and Phenomena Research Australia (Melbourne) personnel were believed to have been discretely providing technical advice for a Defence Department investigation.

There was a rumour circulating that a plane had crashed. We could not locate any witnesses that had seen any craft enter the sea, or heard any change in noise indicating an impact. In fact, if there had been an accident involving any known or suspected aircraft, a search and recovery operation would have begun immediately, and not been delayed until next day.

By this time there was great excitement and speculation, with researchers and reporters seeking out information. The lack of co-ordination, and different witnesses created understandable confusion, giving rise to some erroneous and incomplete details being prematurely circulated. There was very little, if anything, in the media, despite their time and effort. The local newspaper editor advised Bill Chalker he would not run an article unless the witnesses contacted him, which they advised me they had already done. (In fact more publicity was given to obvious hoax orange lights in the sky, two months later.) It may only be another case of pure coincidence, when Collaroy residents had tried to ring a commercial 1800 National UFO hotline on the Saturday and Sunday, they received a recorded message saying that the service was temporarily unavailable.

One witness had a friend working for the military, and wanting to do the right thing, had immediately advised him of the events. He was told, probably in confidence, that senior Naval Officers were in a flap because of another incident in the Northern Territory earlier that night. There was a second witness with Air Force connections, who had heard similar details. Both witnesses swore they had told nobody, however it is possible other members of their family were also aware of the general gist of it. I would have preferred to verify this further, but unfortunately, the information was conveyed to other residents, and spread like wildfire, both around the suburb, and on the internet. One researcher heard it from a woman on the street, and claimed it was just "the ravings of a drunken old biddy." Other witnesses were not happy that unknown investigators were knocking on their doors, and told me "they had their careers to consider."

Bryan Dickeson provided an interesting, and he stressed unconfirmed, report from Darwin on 23 February, some hours before the Collaroy event, which may explain the media silence.

I quote from his article:

> "An Australian Air Force source reported that four identical UFOs had been seen near Darwin (Northern Territory) earlier that Friday evening. Five Australian Air Force jets from Darwin had given chase, but they had been out-manoeuvred. At one point, when the jets drew level with the craft, the objects had disappeared and reappeared further off and behind the jets.
>
> "The objects had turrets on top, which had swivelled to face the planes, and this had unsettled the pilots. Missiles/weapons had been fired at one object, but these had bounced off while still some distance away. The pursuit had continued across country with RAAF planes having to be replaced for re-fuelling at Pine Gap and Richmond Air Force Bases. The original group had split up inland, and one had been pursued as far as Mt. Gambier, South Australia, before it also disappeared."

After his article appeared, Bryan received an irate, anonymous phone call from, presumably, another young RAAF person, appalled by his report: Apparently RAAF jets in the Northern Territory were NOT armed with missiles, so this *sensational* item had to be untrue! Although suitably red-faced by this rebuke, Bryan was actually delighted to receive such expert feedback!

(Nowadays, with reasonable internet access, this sort of detail can be checked more easily.)

Researchers Bill Chalker and Diane Harrison contacted the RAAF, who did not confirm the Darwin report, and advised that there was only minimal aircraft activity that weekend. They did not specifically deny the reports and did not detail any known activity which would correspond with the multiple witness reports over that weekend.

There is no way of knowing if these craft were from another, less-than-friendly foreign country, invading our air space, or of a more extraterrestrial origin. Neither can we be sure that the craft seen at Collaroy was one of the five craft that had allegedly been pursued from Darwin, although it seems a remarkable coincidence.

Long Reef, 18 April 2005

Larraine Cilla of AUFORN investigated a sighting which occurred at about 11 p.m. when a 15-year-old girl was walking home from the bus stop. She suddenly noticed a huge, luminous disc-shaped object hovering just over 100 feet overhead:

It was very bright, with green, blue, orange and purple lights, and a visible structure. She said it was as large as a car, and while it was silent, she was quite frightened, and ran all the way home, with the disc apparently moving in the same direction until she reached her house.

Several Sydney UFO research groups conduct regular sky-watches from the Long Reef area, and report many unusual lights and objects, often posting their video footage on the internet.

Chapter Three

Central Coast, NSW

The NSW Central Coast is a long, narrow section of ancient sandstone, lying between Sydney in the south and Newcastle in the north. It is bounded by heavily eroded hills, mountains and valleys to the west, and sand dunes, peninsulas and beaches with steep cliffs to the east. The city of Gosford is situated at the end of Brisbane Water, off Broken Bay on the estuary of the Hawkesbury River, part of the southern boundary with Sydney. To the north lies a series of lagoons or "lakes" – Tuggerah Lake, Budgewoi Lake, Lake Munmorah, Colongra Lake, Mannering Lake, and Lake Macquarie.

During the summer of Christmas 1995 and the 1996 New Year, holiday makers were enjoying the sun, surf and beach of the Central Coast. On Saturday evening 29 December, while many residents and visitors were still recovering from Christmas, and preparing for New Year's Eve. Their peaceful evening was shattered by an intense humming noise, a large bright white light, and local dogs going ballistic.

Over Brisbane Water, immediately south of Gosford, a huge metallic disc hovered just metres above the still, dark, surface, beaming columns of bright white light into the inky waters below.

Local police were inundated with more than thirty-five calls from all over the area, and not just about this large craft. Motorists nearby were being paced by smaller, low-flying UFOs, and houses were being shaken by loud vibrations, coming from overhead. The police task of pinpointing the position of these mysterious objects was made more difficult, due to the rugged terrain. Radar installations in Sydney and Newcastle can only detect objects flying more than 300 feet above the beach clifftops, and these craft were keeping well below that altitude.

Shortly afterwards I began investigations in the area, with my colleague Bryan Dickeson. I interviewed hundreds of people who had witnessed unidentified craft that evening, and on many other occasions.

Our book *The Gosford Files* was published in late 1996, and we were soon contacted by more residents, who had been hesitant to come forward until then, for fear of ridicule.

Sometimes we got reports from people with a great sense of humour, who made us laugh and see the funny side of some incidents. Mrs. Douglas was one such witness, still rather angry at her husband, for making her miss out on seeing a UFO, that fateful night:

"We had been to the Christmas holiday sales, and bought a new bedroom suite which we were sleeping in for the first time. I suddenly woke to find our bed vibrating, and the wall pulsating with a slight glow. I raced into the children's bedroom and noticed the same glow, despite thick curtains covering the windows. Frightened of what I might see if I looked or went out, I went back and frantically tried to wake my husband, so he would come outside with me.

"Get up, Get up!" she had wailed, "The bed's shaking!" He had opened a sleepy eye: "Not possible, not possible," he growled, "It's a new bed!", and promptly started snoring again.

With each new report from the Central Coast more questions arose. Who or what controls these craft, and where do they come from? What is their purpose and what are they doing over our installations and waterways? Even though they operate under our radar level, authorities must be aware of their presence and activities. While theories and speculation abound, we do not have any definitive answers to this ongoing mystery:

Norah Head, 1962

George Marsden and his friend Tony had been fishing on the rocks and at about 7 p.m., when the sun was going down, and the light diminishing, decided to pack up:

"We made our way back up to the top of the buff, near the lighthouse, where his car was parked. While we were packing our gear Tony yelled 'Holy shit!' and when I turned, I was dumbstruck. There was this huge orange ball suspended over the water about 500 metres off shore. It just sat there for a minute or so, and then took off at lightning speed in a southeast direction.

"It stopped just above the edge of the horizon for another minute or two, then at the same rate of acceleration went north along the horizon to the east of us, where it hesitated and came straight towards us. It was now stationary in the same position as when we first sighted it.

"After approximately 30 seconds a tubular light came from the bottom of this orange ball onto the water, making everything brighter than daylight. The light stayed on for about two minutes, before going out. Then this huge thing took off at the same rate of speed, and disappeared over the horizon.

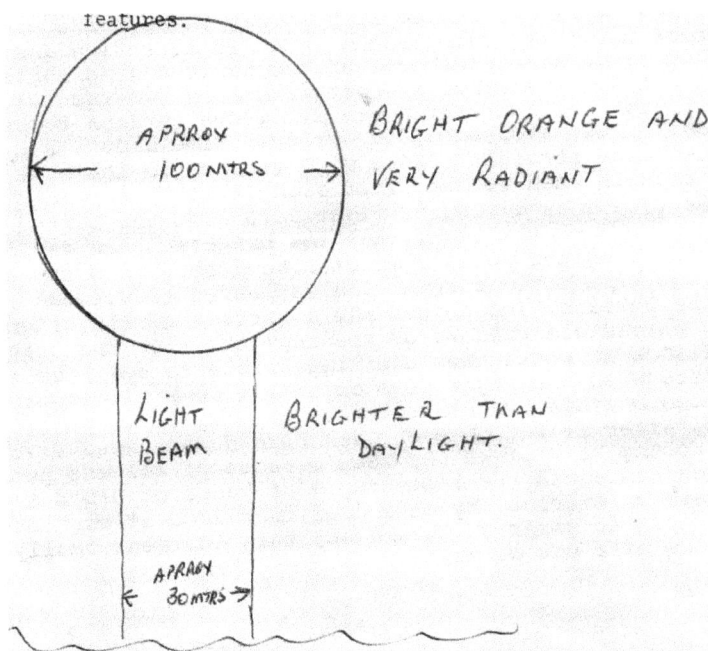

features.

APPROX 100 MTRS

BRIGHT ORANGE AND VERY RADIANT

LIGHT BEAM

BRIGHTER THAN DAYLIGHT.

APPROX 30 MTRS

"The UFO itself was a perfect sphere, a radiant bright orange about 100 metres across. It had no visible windows or doors, but they would have been impossible to see given the brightness of its radiance. When the light came on it illuminated a 30 metre circle below.

"After it had gone we sat there dumbfounded, and vowed we would tell nobody of what we had seen because of all the publicity in the past couple of years about UFOs and abduction cases in America. My mate died in 1976, and it has taken me 34 years to put pen to paper, so I would say this incident really frightened the life out of me."

Doyalson, 1983

Mary Oster was only twelve when she and her family lived in an isolated house which backed onto a power station:

"My brother and I were bouncing on the trampoline when we spotted something in the sky, to the northeast. It was moving slowly, but as it came closer we stopped fooling around and watched, initially out of curiosity. It was big, shaped like an egg, and about the size of a large car. It seemed to be platinum colour – it looked metallic, with alternating red and orange lights pulsating at the bottom.

"When it came over the treetops, and hovered very low, near the Vales Point power station, I got quite scared. I wondered why there was no wind or noise coming from it, everything was so still. I turned to my big brother Les, to find he had deserted me and was running towards the back door. Rusty, our trusted watchdog, had already bolted in terror ahead of him.

"I was about to follow them when the object moved backwards, made a sharp right-angle turn, and shot into the northwest at incredible speed. I don't know if it was the nearby lake (Lake Mannering), or the powerlines and station which attracted it, or whether our watching and obvious terror prompted its speedy departure."

We were fortunate to be able to speak with Les, who remembered the day well. He said that while the craft was hovering he could see it was a spherical shape with a dome top, and when it rose above the trees and sped into the sky, its colour changed to a bright white light.

Brooklyn, 25 October 1997

Carl Roberts is an artist/cartoonist/designer who works on commissioned projects for the media and other professionals, including comic-book companies. He lives on the Hawkesbury River, between Sydney and the New South Wales Central Coast.

He approached me at a UFO seminar, and was still obviously shaken by an experience two weeks earlier. He was quite agitated, and spoke in a very excited manner. It took a while to calm him down and get the details in a logical, chronological manner. On the plus side, due to his artistic abilities he was able to draw some very good pictures of the object:

"It was about 2.30 a.m. I had been working from home, and after several hours of concentration, went for a stroll along the water's edge, near Wobby Beach, to clear my mind. My peaceful evening stroll was suddenly disturbed by a huge, bubbling commotion out on the river. Water was spraying up to 25 feet into the sky. Inside this turbulence was a light, which made the foam look like a city fountain at night."

"Transfixed and speechless, I watched for about 20 minutes. Not knowing what it was, I wanted somebody else to turn up so I could say, 'Hey, look at that! What is that thing?' I left where I was sitting and climbed down onto the rocks at the edge of the water, to get a better look at it. The bubbling and light were about 100 feet away, but too far out in the water to get a better view. At first I thought it was some form of underwater pipe leaking white light; it looked like an underwater spotlight.

"The light underwater began to circle, or rotate, like a glowing football swimming around in circles. I remember feeling glad that I had not run off to find another witness, or I would have missed this underwater movement. I felt I was watching something very special and rare, but hadn't considered a UFO or anything like that.

"It shot up, out of the water, and for about a minute, circled about one to two feet above the river. While the water had stopped thrashing and spraying up, the surface still appeared to be boiling. As it circled it passed to within ten feet of where I was standing on the rocks. I could see it was bigger than what I had first thought, and shaped like a cylinder – big enough to hold two soccer balls, and it made a soft and menacing electrical buzz.

"It was circling faster and higher over the centre of the river. I thought to myself: 'Shit! I've seen my first UFO! Speedy little guy! Why is it getting brighter? What's that light shining off it?'

"It was then I spotted the 'real UFO', the 'Big Momma', hanging there some 30 metres above the water's surface. I could see this global hull. It was huge, as long as three or four cars, and solid metal. The outer rim was turning, not the whole thing, just the one part of its rim, which seemed to fit into the hull somehow, so that it could slowly revolve. It was silent – 'impossible' – and I could not make out any other markings or details. There were no portholes, aerials, lights, symbols, markings, wings, or jets. I wondered what was holding it up. The little guy buzzed with electricity or something, but this big one was totally silent. I got this strange sensation, as if there was some form of lens or force field between us.

"The smaller object was zooming around underneath it, lighting up its lower surfaces. That was how I first saw it. I became a little scared. Was it there all the time? Had it been watching me and my reaction? It still gives me the creeps!

"The fast little object shot into its centre, and was gone. And so was my source of light. The whole area blacked out and I realised that one little object had been lighting up everything. I couldn't see much in the dark, but I could hear the Mothership leave. A huge whoosh and then a really ice cold wind blew all around me for a few minutes. I was scared.

"I sat in that spot for another half hour with the worst case of the shakes. I was amazed as to just how real it all was. I was sober, and couldn't put it out of my mind with an excuse of a dream or hallucination. I was not expecting it, and it was gone.

"The only proof of its existence is that I'll never be the same again. I used to think flying saucers were part of a huge, world-wide myth. I had an all-too-human explanation to the cover-up conspiracies, abductions, and the fruitcakes and celeb-experts, talking on the *Midday Show*. I used to think they were all deluded UFO nuts

"I was wrong! I felt quite ill. Despite the warm night I was sick and freezing cold. I went straight home and crashed, although I think it was more from the fright I received, rather than anything associated with the craft itself.

I didn't sleep for four days and nights. Something went bang in my mind, and

suddenly the universe was a bigger, scarier place.

"To say this thing has left me in a state of Deep Thinker Blues or Extreme Preoccupation is something of an understatement – I can't remember being this confused about the nature of things, ever in my life."

It was interesting and actually made Carl a very credible witness that he did not display the common reaction of a sense of love and peace; they are our friends.

One of his last comments to me was, "Do you get advance warning in case we get invaded? Maybe you could give me a yell, unless you're talking fast about getting the next available comet outa here."

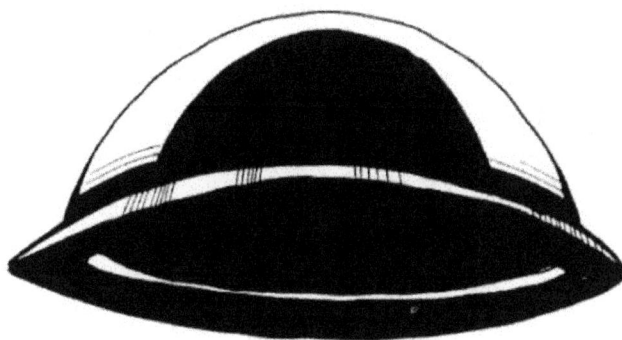

No Portholes. No Symbols or Numbers. No Ariels or Wheels. No Lights or Wings or Jets.
So... What holds it up? The 'Bee' buzzed with 'electricity'. But this big one was totally SILENT.

(This incident was similar to the sighting of a much larger disc-shaped object to the north over Brisbane Waters in December 1995 and Tuggerah Lake in January 1996. There are also notable differences. In December 1995 there were several distinct beams of bright white lights emanating from the craft to below the surface of the lake, which also seemed to boil slightly. Also the earlier objects were very brightly lit with white light, while this mysterious craft was shrouded in darkness. In many of the cases, the water was spraying up into the air, under the craft. Most witnesses felt that the object was affecting something under the surface of the lake, resulting in the disturbance above.)

Gosford, 28 May 2002

Jack Ward had finished work at about 5 p.m. and was making his regular Tuesday night trip to Wamberal. "I was heading in a northerly direction, next to the footy field, and I noticed the most bizarre object I have ever seen in my life – something I have never seen before in the sky. It was something I can only describe as a blob of Mercury, more like half an Aussie Rules Football – tapered off at the tail:

"It was moving at an incredible speed, very fluidly, with much force (my definition of its nature is due to my experience in the automotive industry). Around its tail was an incredible glow of red-orange. It was at least twice the size of a helicopter, and very bright overall, with silver around the outside, a bright inner core, and a red-orange glow around the tail.

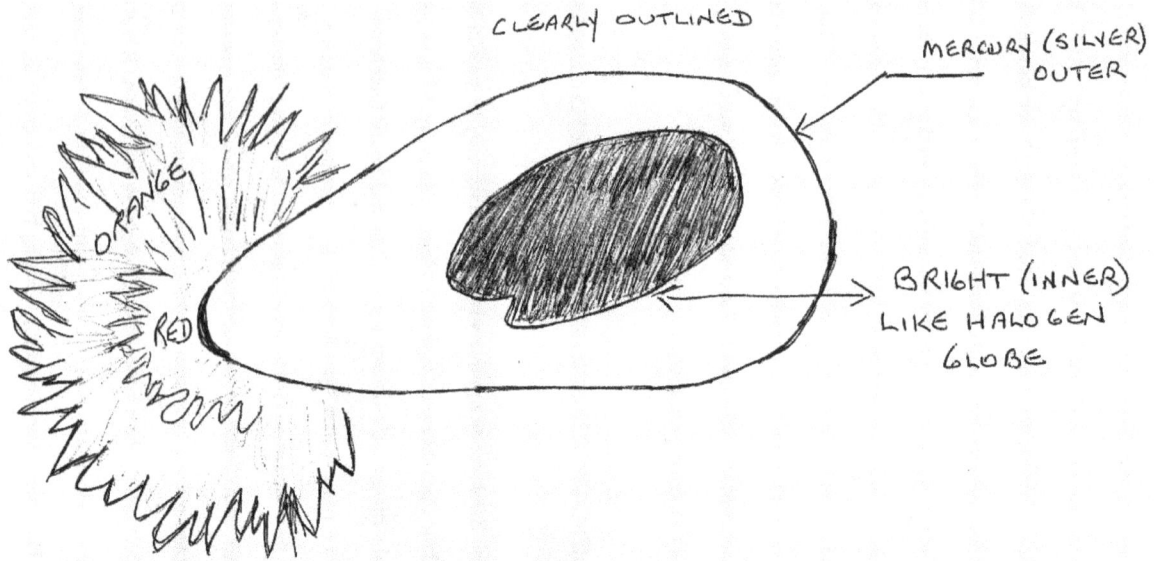

Gosford, 28 May 2002

"I think it was about the height of a small plane, some distance away – maybe a couple of kilometres off, over the more rural/residential area, and I first was it fairly high in the north-western sky at a 90 degree angle to the horizon. It travelled extremely fast to 45 degrees in the east-northeast. As I was approaching the top of a hill, a tree blocked my view. When I was able to fully see the area again, the object was gone, as if it had disappeared into thin air."

Wallsend, 18 March 2012

Louise, and her nine-year-old daughter Sally, were on their way to see her mother at Lambton in Newcastle. They had set off early, and at about 7.30 a.m., were driving past Wallsend. Sally was bored, and started taking pictures out of the passenger window of odd shaped clouds. She had just received a Nintendo 3DS for her birthday.

Louise recalled, "She went quiet for a while and then said, 'Mummy, I think I just took a picture of a UFO!' I just looked at her and laughed, 'Don't be silly Sally – as if you would have taken a picture of a UFO!' She looked back at the photo for a while then said, 'but *look* Mummy.' I glanced at the photo, but as I was driving could not make out what it was.

"When we got to my mother's I took a closer look, and still could not identify the object, but realised it was near a big sports field we had passed. While it only appeared on one of the many photos she had taken, I checked the car window where she had been sitting, but could not find any marks. I checked with the Nintendo manufacturer but there was no malfunction, and they were unaware of any function on this console that could actually put anything remotely like that on the photo."

When we received the picture Bryan Dickeson did an extensive evaluation, including an analysis of the picture's consistency with surrounding background, time of day and positioning of the sun etc.

The 'craft' appeared solid, unreflective, about 12-15 metres across, with a regular 3-dimensional cylindrical symmetry about its vertical axis. The cylindrical sections are a little over half the diameter of the central discus, and slope back to the central axis at about 15 degrees – the upper half is very slightly taller than the bottom half. On both cylinders is a hemispherical cap about half the cylindrical section that each cap mounts.

The edges of the object were rounded or streamlined, suggesting an aerodynamic function, but there does not appear to be any blurring around the edges to suggest it was moving at any speed. It may have been stationary, or hovering or pacing the car. (It was considered unlikely that it was moving towards the car.) The object was surrounded by a light reddish haze, which rapidly falls off into the surrounding atmosphere, indicating some form of coronal discharge or ionic interaction with the surrounding air.

Bryan concluded the object was indeed mysterious and he considered it to be a genuine photograph of an unidentified flying object.

Raymond Terrace, 21 July 1998

Raymond Terrace lies on the coast to the north of Newcastle, and is home to a large RAAF Base. Around the area, and to the north are some very popular lakes (lagoons) and holiday spots.

Several independent witnesses saw delta-shaped craft at about 6.30 p.m. A total of eight craft were described as being wide and chunky, and dark-coloured, with pulsating lights.

Two brothers from New Lambton contacted us: "They were quite large," one said. "They could travel both ways, apex first or base first, and varied in speed from very fast to quite slow. On each point they had a light which pulsated, and sometimes went out then came on again. Occasionally we could see a pulsating red light underneath."

Another witness, who had many years with the RAAF, and constituted a more-expert witness, saw the objects from his back door.

"I jumped into the car and drove closer to a better vantage point. They were about the size of a fixed wing Dakota, but were certainly nothing conventional. I couldn't quite make out their shape. Each craft had two red lights on the right, a blue light on the left and a white flashing light in the centre. When one hovered overhead, I could hear a whirring sound.

"They were at an altitude of 1,500 to 3,000 feet and skimmed back and forth around the sky, like fish in a pond. They would come to a sudden halt, hover, then take off again in another direction. After about fifteen minutes they all zoomed off to the southeast at incredible speed. In all my years around RAAF bases I have never seen anything like it before."

The darker side ...

Not all UFO sightings and experiences are pleasant. Many leave witnesses, contactees and abductees traumatised, some with physical injuries. Other witnesses are just perplexed and confused, trying to make some sense of it all:

Budgewoi, 31 October to 2 November 1997

It was barely a week after Carl the artist's dramatic sighting on the Hawkesbury River at Brooklyn (25 October 1997). Further north, at 8.20 p.m. on Friday 31 August, a Newcastle security officer was outside his home, farewelling relatives:

"I noticed this brilliant blue-white light moving horizontally from southwest to northeast. It was travelling at a phenomenal speed, and sort of egg-shaped. It was only when it passed overhead, that I realised it was much larger than I initially thought. Just the front was illuminated – it also had a large white rear section."

The next day, Saturday 1 November, two mature men, expert sailors, took their five-metre, half-cabin boat onto Budgewoi Lake to do a little fishing. At 5 p.m. they made a routine radio call, with no hint of any problems.

Later that night, at about 11.30 p.m. a family from Windermere Park rang me to report they had been watching six unusual lights over Lake Macquarie for the past 30 minutes. While they were only star size, they were changing colour from red to green, blue, and white as they moved around the sky.

Just after midnight the police patrolled the Budgewoi lakefront following reports of a man screaming for help. The constables heard nothing, and couldn't see anything amiss in the dark. At 10.30 a.m. on Sunday morning the empty boat was found adrift, but intact, on the lake. The craft had a full fuel tank, and there were no problems with the boat or motor. The men's bodies were found floating in the lake a couple of hours later, presumably drowned, although there was little said later about the cause of death.

Nobody seemed to know what happened, but whatever it was, it happened quickly, leaving no time to don lifejackets or send a mayday signal. Was there any connection to the unidentified objects seen that night and over the previous few days?

Again, this is a case where we will never know.

Berkeley Vale, 30 December 1995

On 30 December 1995, and into the early morning of 31 December, a large, humming craft, surrounded by brilliant white light, hovered and manoeuvred over Brisbane Waters for over four hours. The same object, or something similar was also seen over Tuggerah Lake and Mangrove Mountain at least twice during the same night. It was witnessed by countless residents, including the local police, and was the main reason for our book, *The Gosford Files*, and part of the television documentary, *Oz Encounters*.

A local grandmother contacted us in 1997, requesting information and support. Her grandson had been very disturbed ever since that fateful night, when he and his mother had been staying with her over the holiday break.

"We were expecting visitors the next afternoon, and early that evening my 25-year-old grandson, Rory, walked up to the local shopping centre to buy some groceries for me and a carton of beer for himself. Several hours went by, and when he didn't return home his mother and I were becoming very worried. If we had known, at the time, about the UFO being seen in the area, we would have been frantic.

"Late that night there was a knock on the door. It was the police. They had Rory with them, and he seemed very dazed and disorientated. They had found him unconscious in the local park after receiving calls from passers-by, who claimed there was a dead body lying in the grass.

"At first Rory did not seem to know what had happened to him, and the officers could not offer any explanation. He had not been drinking, his wallet was intact, the carton of beer he had purchased was unopened and he had no apparent injuries."

Soon after his return he told his grandmother that he had been walking back through the park, on his way home, when he was suddenly grabbed by some strange little beings who had materialised from behind the trees. He did not remember what happened then, and she did not press him too much, as his mother was in the house.

"He whispered to me, 'Don't tell Mum, I've spoken to you. I tried to explain to her, but she didn't understand.' Not long after, at about 5.15 a.m. we were all woken by a loud humming and throbbing noise which seemed to vibrate the whole house.

"We went outside several times but could see nothing. When I heard about the disc over the Central Coast that night, I was convinced it was connected with my grandson's strange experience and the subsequent noise around our home. My daughter, who didn't believe Rory at first, suddenly insisted that they pack and leave immediately. She gave the ridiculous excuse that there must be a nest of wasps in the house lining. I think it was a mother's protective sixth sense, warning her son must be in danger – had 'they' come back for him?"

While waiting in Berkeley Vale ...

A couple of strange craft seemed to delight in terrorising early morning commuters in Berkeley Vale. Joan Stanley related the sheer terror of her husband early one morning in 1991:

"John set off for work, as usual, at about 5 a.m. I'm not sure how much later it was, but he literally collapsed back through the door, in a terrible state. Apparently he was standing at the Lakeside bus stop when he noticed an orange-yellow light in the sky. Suddenly the object was hovering overhead, and the light was everywhere around him. He confessed that his hair 'stood up on end', and by the time the object shot off, at exceptional speed, he was 'shaking in his shoes.'"

Less than a year later, on 1 June 1992, another Berkeley Vale resident was waiting at a nearby bus stop at 5.15 a.m. As Ben reached into his briefcase to get his cigarette lighter, the entire area was bathed in a soft white light:

"I felt an extraordinary sense of fear,

> **Bringelly, Western Sydney ...**
> A few years earlier, further south, at Bringelly, on the outskirts of Western Sydney, a young woman was running late for work, and in order to catch the 4.45 a.m. bus, her husband ran her up to the bus stop on his motorbike. "We stood there in the freezing winter darkness, peering up the deserted country road to see if the bus was coming.
>
> "Sure enough, something did approach, but we saw it was no bus. It was an immense round object, with red lights flashing around the rim which hovered overhead. It speared a great white searchlight on us for about five seconds, and we felt it was taking an intimate interest in us. Thank God, it suddenly took off at great speed and disappeared."

and the hair on the back of my neck stood up. In fact it is the chilling reaction and feeling of anxiety that remains in my memory more than the sighting itself. I looked up and saw this object to the north, about 50 metres from the shoreline of the lake, and about ten metres above the water.

"I just stared in astonishment. It was hexagonal, with a silver grey dome, a bright orange base, white appendages and a steady white light underneath. After a few moments it moved in a vertical motion for about 25 metres then shot to the northeast at a 45 degree angle. Its speed was unbelievable."

Given Ben's reaction before he even saw the object, I wondered if the physical effects on the witnesses, in both these cases, were caused by the UFO itself, rather than their understandable fright.

West of the Central Coast

I was often contacted by residents of the Mangrove Mountain, Somersby, and Kulnura areas, to the west and inland from the New South Wales Central Coast. It has often been regarded as a possible harmonic place of strange anomalies and earth energies. To the north-west is the mysterious mountain, Big Yengo, held sacred by the indigenous population. There had been vague reports of strange lights in the sky, and tremors like inexplicable underground explosions in the area. Even more ambiguous were the occasional rumours of unidentified objects crashing into the heavily wooded hills nearby.

Kulnura, 1997

INUFOR got its first real breakthrough in 1997, when we were contacted by Vicki, who lived on a property deep in a valley in the tree-covered hills in the Kulnura area:

It was about 1.30 a.m. one Sunday morning at the end of February. The last of her teenagers had arrived home safely from a night on the town and were watching *Rage* on the television, so for a bit of peace and quiet, she took her coffee out onto the veranda to relax in the warm night air.

"It was a crystal clear night, and I was just gazing at the stars when I was jolted from my reverie by a huge ball of golden light. It just plummeted out of the sky at a 45 degree angle, and appeared to crash into the hill ridge above the house. I jumped up in fright as it burst into three pieces which shot in different directions."

"The largest piece appeared to be propelled into the tops of nearby trees. Someone has suggested it may have been ball lightning or some natural phenomena. No way! Yes, we are prone to electrical storm activity, but the weather had been perfectly fine for days before and after. The largest piece was some form of the major definable object, about the size of a Volkswagen car on its nose. It was like a brilliant white oval light, which was spinning in a clockwise direction. In the centre was a red-orange core which appeared to be rotating anticlockwise."

"After it lodged in the tree tops, it seemed to be trying to shake itself free. Eventually it succeeded. There was a massive thud and the ground shook. I fled to the house, but no matter how hard I tried, I couldn't wake Robert, so I peeked out to watch the remains of the two smaller pieces fizzle out."

The following morning she was preoccupied with family matters. As soon as she got the chance, she had a look at the impact area with a pair of binoculars, and soon located a clump of damaged trees, above the valley just down from their property.

"I felt more confident in daylight, but to be on the safe side took my two dogs and walked up the track to the damaged area. As I got closer the dogs freaked and refused to go any further. This was unusual, as they love their walkies."

When she reached the spot, the first thing she noticed was a strange mist or cloud, rising like a column out of the valley floor below, high into the sky above. She walked into the cloud, and was surprised to come back out into the sunshine on the other side. It was only 20 feet across.

"I walked back through the strange mist (it was not smoke), and noticed a distinct smell, like electrical burning. This foul-smelling column of mist persisted for the next three days and nights, despite the fact the weather was clear, dry and warm, and there was no fog in any other part of the valley. I was feeling quite uneasy and nauseated, and the dogs were behaving out of character."

"I could see a distinct track or path of damage across the top of the trees which corresponded to the path followed by the object's fragment I had seen the previous evening. I looked around and could see the tree trunks and lower branches looked normal and healthy. The tops were not burnt, rather baked as if exposed to enormous heat, and totally devoid of moisture. Within two weeks many of the damaged trees had shed their healthy vegetation and appeared totally dead."

Unfortunately, Vicki did not contact us until 27 April, by which time the mist had dispersed and the trees had completely died. A colleague and I visited the area soon after. The heavily-vegetated valley was hard to access, making detection and retrieval of any crash debris difficult.

My male colleague and Vicki's husband Robert, offered to climb down into the valley to search for any evidence. Within a few minutes they came scrambling back up the slope.

"What's wrong?" I asked. "What did you find?" They both looked at me rather sheepishly. "We didn't reach the bottom; there was this big snake in the tree. Maybe it was a python, but we weren't going to chance it. (OK...... I get height sick – what could I say?)"

We took photographs of the obvious damage to the vegetation, almost as if it had been impacted with considerable force. The visible trail of destruction through the tree tops corresponded to Vicki's reported path of the object. Our Geiger counter readings were unexpected. The radiation from the impact site was only half of that from control areas nearby.

Vicki said there are strange phenomena in the vicinity. Their property was situated near an old road used by the Cobb & Co horse and carriages in the early days of settlement. "At night we hear them going by. Sometimes I see and hear the ghosts of the unhappy convicts who built this road, and the Aboriginals who were killed at that time."

This did not concern her as much as the holiday ranch she pointed out further down the valley. "It's not what it seems," she whispered, "There are goats' heads on the wall. Important, well-known people come in the weekends, and there is not much holiday activity going on outside. Maybe it wasn't a UFO – what if they manifested it?"

We could do nothing more than speculate as to the true nature and origin of the object, and as to whether the residue Vicki exposed herself to was harmful. She was only in her late 40s, and less than twelve months later, without warning or prior illness, she collapsed and died.

Near Lake Macquarie, 3 May 1992

While this incident was reported in *The Gosford Files*, there was some thought-provoking follow-up after the book was published:

A newspaper reporter, I'll call her Freda, rang me in 1992 regarding her unusual encounter. Once a sceptic, she was now going to write an article for her publication stating there were definitely UFOs appearing over the Central Coast. We had also received other reports, corroborating Freda's sighting on the expressway that night.

She was driving with her husband along the expressway at about 6 p.m. when they were dazzled by a brilliant flashing white light, which they thought was a plane coming towards them.

"The sky was quite dark, very clear, and the vibrant white light was now hovering, not very far above us, and flashing intermittently. Below it was a faint display of red and green lights, and my immediate thought was that they extended much wider than those on a normal aircraft. It remained in the one position for more than three minutes."

When she later described the hovering light to a RAAF officer he discounted it as an approaching aircraft. I had to agree with her observation that since they were travelling at 110kph they would surely be out of range of something hovering during the three-plus minute interval – unless of course it was pacing them (a thought I kept to myself).

"Anyway, it then began to behave in an even more bizarre fashion. It suddenly turned and flew over in front of us to our left – but, at what a speed! It seemed to descend into the adjoining bushland, but then within seconds, it was back up above us, to the right, exactly as it had been before. This white light was still as strong as ever, the same size, and continuing to flash.

"Two or three minutes later, now completely enthralled, we decided to pull up at the side of the road to take a better look. While it was very large, and at an altitude of about 200 metres, we could not imagine that it was a helicopter because of the speed at which it had travelled. I got out of the car to see if it was making any noise, either that of a chopper or a more unlikely jet.

"Admittedly we were beside the expressway, but it was not busy, and the craft was quite close. I simply could not detect a sound. About 30 seconds later, the lights, still indeterminable in form departed to the north. They moved quite slowly at first, then gathered speed, and while still at a very low altitude, went nowhere near as fast this time."

In 1997 I received a letter from Freda, saying she was encouraged that our book recounted how others had a similar reaction to such inexplicable occurrences. Her main concern was the number of people who had suffered physical trauma subsequent to their encounter. She then added:

"Which is really one of three, your book proved to me that my previous experiences were very real indeed!

"Since that time I have been diagnosed with, (and operated for), an acoustic neuroma, which is a tumour growing at the third cranial nerve that controls hearing and balance. Doctors have no explanation for an acoustic neuroma, but naturally I am anxious to understand what might have caused it. When my husband and I stopped the car to investigate the strange light, which had been locked onto us for such a long time, I was the only one who left the car. I have read that the person who exposes themselves to the UFO was frequently the one to show physical repercussions."

Of course, I couldn't really give Freda an answer, and I wasn't privy to the details of the other two encounters she had alluded to. I began to wonder about the various possibilities including not only exposure to radiation or some other damaging energy transmissions, but also implants etc. One witness whom I'll be discussing in *The Alien Gene* had an implant just behind one ear. It remained in situ for many years, but recently had to be removed as a matter of urgency. The surgeon found that her own immune system had tried to counteract the foreign object by covering it up with a membrane, which was growing out of control.

Copacabana, 1997

Copacabana is a remote beach suburb on the Central Coast. When Katy McKay first rang me in 1997 she was very traumatised, but having read *The Gosford Files*, felt a little more confident at contacting someone who wouldn't think she was crazy. At first she confided three sightings of strange objects over the last five years:

"In 1992, at about 1 a.m., I was alone in the lounge watching television. I heard a strange noise, approaching from the south, which seemed to halt directly over the house. It was a low-frequency throb, sort of overlaid by an ultra-high-tech whirring sound. I've never heard anything like it before or since. I cannot understand why I did not run outside to look, or wake my housemate.

"The sound was beautiful – mesmerising. I was simultaneously enthralled, excited, afraid, but also as if sedated. It lasted a few minutes then faded. I just got up, went to bed and fell asleep as if nothing had happened." (I wondered if there was a little bit more to the event than Katy realised, or was saying, but I said nothing and let her continue with her reports:)

"In 1997 I was driving with a friend, north from Sydney to Gosford at about 4.45 p.m., when we spotted a silver disc-shaped object above the trees, in the clear blue sky, about two kilometres ahead. It was travelling reasonably slowly from northeast to the north, and vanished within a short space of time. Again I felt a connection I can't explain or justify. It seemed beautiful – I felt warm, and kind of touched by whatever mind was controlling it."

It was her third event on 12 October 1997 that prompted her to ring me, and again I wondered if there was a bit more to this than she was saying:

"I had just gone to bed at about 1.30 a.m. when I heard a very low, pulsating, throbbing sound coming over the house from the north. It seemed to be directly over the house for about a minute and then started to fade. I thought it was gone, so I wouldn't alert my housemate. Suddenly it started up again, so I jumped up and raced into his room.

"Touching him lightly on the shoulder, I said 'Hey...there's a ship over the house...can't you hear it?' He woke from a deep sleep and yet seemed to know exactly what I was talking about – 'Yeah, yeah – it sounds just like a big substation generator hum.' I went back to bed after we had listened for a few minutes. Strangely, yet again the thought to go outside and look up didn't even occur to us! That's weird!

"I lay there, trying to stay awake. The sound was throbbing into me, willing me to sleep – forcing me almost. The next morning the sound was gone."

Katy admitted that they had heard that noise a few times in the past. She hesitated for a few moments before deciding to confide her memories and fears:

"One night when I heard the sonic-throb coming in and out I was in the kitchen and had the strange sensation that I wasn't alone. I turned around and before my eyes a strange creature materialised.

"It was blue, and looked something like a praying mantis. It was surrounded by a most beautiful blue light, and I sensed a feeling of love and peace. We just stared at each other for a while, and then it sort of dematerialised and disappeared again. I wondered if it was something inter-dimensional.

"It reminded me of a memory when I was outback, about 11 years old. I was getting my bike out from under a tree and saw a stick insect. I was so inexplicably afraid that I became totally hysterical. When I was fourteen, I was going to a school night at Westmead, when I saw a strange light moving erratically in a cloud. I don't know why, but I felt it was very important.

"I also have memories of a 'being' coming before I went to sleep. Its long fingers were touching and reassuring me. At the end of 1993 I saw this beautiful blue being bending down over my bed. I remember I was traumatised and crying at the time."

Katy also mentioned periods when she could hear a sound from the base of her skull – "like a high-pitched tuning fork." I naturally wondered about the possibility of an implant, but said nothing, as it would have been unethical to add to her obvious confusion and distress. I suggested she see a professional psychologist/hypnotherapist, as I privately felt she might require medical treatment if an implant existed and needed to be removed. I don't know if she ever even made an appointment.

However, Katy did attend INUFOR and other information meetings where we had guest speakers, documentaries and provided an informal support network. I noticed her behaviour was becoming a little overactive and erratic, and after putting a few people off-side she eventually stopped attending our and other meetings etc.

About twelve months later she died of a brain tumour. It was so sad, she was only in her 40s, and I could only speculate as to any connection between the brain tumour and possible UFO-alien experiences, memories or even an implant.

Day-care centres

When writing *The Gosford Files* I included a peculiar incident at a childcare centre "at the edge of the world." A representative, selling children's books and toys, made an unscheduled call at a small establishment, off the main road.

"It was unlike any other I'd visited; the security was like Fort Knox. When I finally got into the foyer a woman walked by. She obviously had not realised a stranger had got in. While she looked normal, a slim brunette about 5 feet 5 inches, her skin was very pale. She had a pair of sunglasses in her hand, and when she turned around I saw her eyes. They were all black – no white anywhere, like the eyes a small child draws.

"As I was quickly ushered out I noticed all the windows were blacked out. I could hear the kiddies, but not see them. I wondered what their eyes looked like. I still do."

Bronwyn couldn't really do anything about it. When she got home she told her partner, who worked for a security agency. He told her not to worry about it – "they already knew."

Following publication of our book, I encountered two cases of harassment by gentlemen who wanted details of the location of the centre and the strange woman with the alien eyes. I did not know much about the children. They could have been special needs children, with conditions requiring darkened windows. I would never expose them to unwarranted scrutiny. During a seminar I attended, one insistent bloke followed me around the dining room, and then outside the venue, abusing me for keeping silent. Not a pleasant moment.

Recently I received a call from Carl Simpson, on the Central Coast, who had visited a second Day-Care Centre', about 30 kilometres from the first. He had read *The Gosford Files*, and felt I would believe his similar experience:

"I worked selling security alarms and called on this centre in the bush, just off the road. The main building was built like a fort – would have cost a fortune. There were even outdoor surveillance cameras. The windows were darkened, and I couldn't see the kids. I got the impression I was being watched from inside. There were no vehicles in sight, and unlike the main building, the few sheds out the back were built to very flimsy standards.

"It was all very odd, and I had a feeling something was not quite right. A small, very pale lady came out. I couldn't see her eyes, as she was wearing glasses. She ordered me to leave immediately, and threatened me if I didn't comply."

These two premises may have nothing to do with extraterrestrials or similar, but they do give rise to curiosity.

Other dimensions?

Many locals and others believe there are energy grids present on the Central Coast, one of which runs up the coastline, touching on Crackneck Lookout, The Skillion, and Norah Head:

Crackneck Lookout

I visited Crackneck Lookout on several occasions, and more than one person in our group sensed some weird energies in the area – something darker, which made me feel uncomfortable, and wary of wandering off on my own. On one occasion we were accompanied by a gentleman who had reported an abduction experience, with an X-ray showing an unusual implant-type object.

Within a few minutes of being at the lookout he developed a headache, and suffered a stroke a couple of hours later. I will never know if it was just coincidence, or if some strange force had interacted with the implant.

Two UFOIC and two ACOS investigators researched a very unusual report from Crackneck Lookout at about 8.15 p.m. on 10 October 1976:

Two couples were in a parked car, and the young men walked over to the edge of the cliff, overlooking the sea. They heard strange noises, "like shuffling and rustling grass." From a small clearing in a little gully, a bit further down, they saw a "thing", off-white in colour, crawling up the hill. They were quite scared, raced back to the girls in the car, and locked themselves in.

They all saw some movements in the trees, and a figure similar to a man approaching them. "He" appeared to be eight to nine feet tall, with no hair, eyes like a fly's and a mouth that was only just round. It was all off-white with huge legs – three-jointed arms, pointy fingers, and shoulders about three feet across. They were all terrified – yelling and screaming, and as they started the car and turned on the lights, the creature momentarily looked away. They drove off as quickly as possible.

The researchers felt that while the witnesses genuinely described what they believed they had seen, they couldn't rule out the remote possibility of an elaborate hoax. However, there were other reports which indicated unexplained events in the vicinity:

At that time a large orange rectangular light was seen on the horizon, out to sea, and had also been seen the night before. Two hours earlier an unusual aerial object was seen hovering over the nearby Tuggerah Lake. It was described as being saucer-shaped, with a dome on top, and four lights, one green and three red.

Over the previous six months there had been reports of sightings of the same or similar creature in this area, and about a week later, cement picnic chairs and tables at the lookout were wrecked. While it obviously took some strength, it may well have been vandals, although I wonder about some researchers overseas who consider the powerful Yowie-type beasts are somehow associated with UFOs. Given the creature did exist, there are varying possibilities including inter-dimensional, extraterrestrial, and possibly several others.

The Skillion

The Skillion is a rocky coastal headland, which many believe is close to the same harmonic grid line. These so-called "hot spots" can attract a higher than usual number of UFO sightings and unusual anomalies:

One elderly resident contacted us with some thought-provoking information. Mrs. C was very alert, both mentally and physically, and fully self-supporting in her own home. She also believed there was a possible grid and anti-gravity in the area, even though I had not made any mention of harmonic spots. "There is something there, especially to the right of The Skillion, looking down at the water over the rocks. I believe it has to do with the grid and weightlessness."

She was raised on a Central Coast property in the early 20th century, when it was still very much a rural community. "Somewhere between October 1931 and mid-January 1932, before I was married, I used to join my future husband, his mother and stepfather, on a Sunday, to go fishing at The Skillion. I think it was her idea, to get the men away from the farm for the day.

"We were lucky Pop had a car; not many people had cars in those days, and Mum took a good picnic. No sandwiches for her, and no shops open on Sunday, even if we could have afforded it. After lunch I helped Mum pack up, and changed into my swimsuit to go down to where the men were fishing and looking for crabs and bait.

"I walked to the hollow in the bank, where the others had gone down to the water, and looked for the best way down. I saw a perfectly plain path, down across the top of the rocks, and took off running from the top of one boulder to another, almost right down to the water. No-one saw me, as I was out of everyone's sight.

"Looking back at those rocks now, remembering the distance between them, and their height, it was not something I could have normally done. I saw the path quite clearly, and there was no sensation of my feet hitting the rocks. There should have been after leaping across gaps sometimes six feet across. It was totally incredible, yet it happened! It was almost as if I were in another place.

"I did not think about it until recently, until I heard about the high number of inexplicable suicides from there. If others experienced something similar from the top of The Skillion, and followed the perceived path, it may have taken them over the edge."

This was not the only strange anomaly reported from The Skillion. On 9 March 1997, residents noticed an unusual dark cloud over the headland. There had been some storm activity earlier in the day, but it had cleared.

"This was different" said Roger. "There appeared to be lightning, not only coming out of the cloud, but also travelling inside it. I watched for a while, then curiosity got the better of me, and I drove up to The Skillion for a better look. I was astounded to find this usually isolated area was full of cars and people. There was a strange, electric atmosphere, and what was even stranger, was that nobody spoke to anyone around them. They were just staring in dead silence.

"No-one seemed concerned about being struck by one of the lightning bolts – in fact, nothing seemed to come to earth. The electrical activity seemed to be confined by some invisible barrier to the centre and perimeter of the cloud."

The cloud and lightning hovered silently in the one spot for more than three hours. Not once did he hear any thunder. At one stage two small planes, similar in size to Cessna aircraft, were circling the cloud and lightning. Roger eventually returned home and was unaware of how or when the cloud departed.

Mullumbimby, 1995

A similar phenomenon was reported two years earlier, in March-April 1995, further up the east coast of Australia, at Mullumbimby:

Katy Green had four children, including a young baby, so she was often up in the middle of the night. She lived on a hill, which was a good vantage point for the surrounding area, and noticed flashes of what seemed like lightning:

"There was no thunder, lightning or rain, and the sky looked clear. I looked out, and there was a large, fluffy white cloud over the ocean, moving south from the north-east. Large bolts of lightning were flashing both up and down from it. It was hard to see if anything was underneath it, and hard to judge the altitude – a bit higher than a chopper, but lower than a passenger plane. This happened several nights that week, always in a clear sky, each time the same, except the last night, when the lightning was only flashing upwards. It was so strange, it didn't affect our electricity, but on the first night Lennox Head, to the south, had a blackout for a while."

There were other witnesses to this strange anomaly. Was it a natural occurrence, some form of experiment or an undercover UFO? I don't think we will ever know, although some Central Coast residents feel these were inter-dimensional.

Toukley and The Entrance

This is an exception to my normal rule to use pseudonyms, as it is not Winifred's real name, which she keeps private and personal. She was an exceptionally gifted psychic, whom I got to know when she was living in a southern suburb of Sydney. She had contact with higher and other intelligences, who had assisted in the development of her many talents. I respected her reticence to discuss any contacts in great detail:

Winifred was born in Wyong and when still a child, the family moved near the lake at Toukley. When she was in bed at night she would see a little creature on the window ledge. She always felt he would look after her and it wasn't until later in life she discovered her sister also saw him, and was terrified. It was not the first time I had heard psychics mention contact with "little people" when they were children. Were their abilities gained from extraterrestrial contact, or a higher interaction on an inter-dimensional or spiritual level? Maybe both. It is sometimes beyond human understanding.

Many years ago she had seen bright lights, from a distance, over the Central Coast at both Toukley and The Entrance. She also admitted to an experience where she was abducted by short beings (about four foot, three inches tall), with slanted eyes.

"They wore silver suits, and took me into a room and sat me down on a metal bed. There were other humans there, almost in a trance, like they were sitting in a waiting room. They treated me like a lab specimen, poking and prodding, and examined me in a very rough manner. I was very sore the next morning. I tried to be friendly, but they ignored me, and seemed to communicate with each other in funny insect-like sounds." Her memory of this event was disjointed and terrifying, and while she preferred to treat it as a dream, felt in her heart it was real.

Winifred also confided the experiences of two of her friends who had lived on the Central Coast. One night she was in a car with Jane and Marcia. A UFO had followed them quite some distance, all the way to their destination at Islington. Both her friends experienced paranormal events at a much later time.

Broadmeadow, Newcastle

Jane and her husband, who lived at Broadmeadow near Newcastle, were disturbed one night when their 14-year-old daughter hurled herself into their bed. She claimed that she had been woken by a bright light. A tall human-looking alien had been beside her bed saying: "Come with me."

Marcia became terminally ill with cancer, and unexpectedly went into remission. She claimed that one day, when her husband had gone up to the chemist, she was beamed up into a craft, and "they worked on" her.

I was privileged to attend a small group Winifred hosted in her own home, where she assisted and encouraged us to develop our psychic and precognitive abilities. She helped us all access our hidden talents and gain better inner peace. She also gave me guidance through a difficult time in my life and I maintained the friendship for many years afterwards.

The Kariong glyphs

Kariong is another area with strange magnetic deviations. It lies on the escarpment just west of Gosford itself. Near here, a series of strange hieroglyphs have been carved on sheltered rock faces.

Kariong's "Egyptian" glyphs cover two sandstone walls about fifteen feet high, and five feet apart which run parallel for about 30 feet. Both walls are inscribed with over 100 individual carvings. They lie within an undeveloped National Park area, and are hard to detect from above or below. You have to walk down into the cleft from the escarpment above, or climb up through a hole in the rock from the slope below. A small cave lies underneath, also hidden from external view, and a large rock cap covers part of the top end of the cleft where the script is carved.

Some geologists have reported that the area has suffered earthquakes and rockslides in the past, and researcher Paul White reported the cleft was originally full of smashed rocks. This may indicate it originally had a full covering of flat rocks overhead, making it more akin to a secret cavern or a crude temple, totally hidden from view and discovery. No matter their origin, and whoever their maker, these carvings were not meant for public display. Regardless of when, or why they were made, the glyphs would have taken a long time to complete – and would require a ladder, or a very tall person to inscribe deeply cut hieroglyphs into the upper portions of the walls. Why would someone regularly travel to a poorly accessible site to carve on a very hard rock face, something hidden from passers-by?

When we wrote *The Gosford Files*, I believed the official line that these carvings were fakes, carved in recent times. Since then I have followed various lines of inquiry and research, and have since revised my opinions. While I cannot reach a definitive conclusion as to the authenticity of the glyphs and other ancient carvings in the area, recent discoveries have shown that ancient Egyptians did indeed have long-distance ocean-going vessels, capable of reaching Australia. There are reports eucalyptus oil was used during their mummification processes, so trade and exploration trips, especially via South-East Asia, seem technically possible.

Travelling back from the Central Coast by train I encountered a Russian Egyptologist returning from Kariong, who considered the carvings to be genuine. More recently, Eric von Daniken made a pilgrimage there, and was reported saying he thought the glyphs were "very old."

I am aware of the political and cultural implications if it were shown these glyphs were carved by ancient Egyptians. When we were assured by local authorities and a university professor that they were not genuine, we were also asked not to disclose their location. (Our discretion did not stop a growing interest and publicity. Today, one enterprising local regularly conducts tours at $50 per head, espousing his own theories.)

Local National Park Rangers claimed that university students had carved them in the 1980s; however, I caught up with one of the students on that particular excursion, and he advised that they had merely cleaned them out so they could properly examine them. Of course the use of acidic cleanser is not helpful for later carbon dating. Another claim was that authorities confiscated a screwdriver from a "demented old codger." It would have been physically impossible for him to have done so, and a geologist told me a screwdriver could not have done the job.

We tried to find witnesses from the earliest date when the hieroglyphs were first seen, and an Aboriginal aunty told me they had been there as long as her people could remember. They had always regarded them as someone else's sacred place (she could not say whose), and to be respected. One gentleman, now dead, told me he had been taken to the glyphs in the 1930s by an elderly man who was first shown them in 1911.

Another, who had lived in Egypt for two years, had seen the glyphs many years ago, and also considered them to be genuine. He pointed out a cartouche, from the same Third or Fourth Dynasty, of one Pharaoh's minor, or insignificant son, whose name and existence was not known until around 1995. A third witness had been with his father, and another gentleman to view them in 1955.

A local historian contacted me regarding a local identity who died in the late 1950s, after spending many years exploring Australia (often with camel trains). This man had been interested in what he considered to be traces of Egyptian visits, and believed they had come here by boat for mining purposes. He recorded his findings in documents and journals, which so far I have been unable to track down.

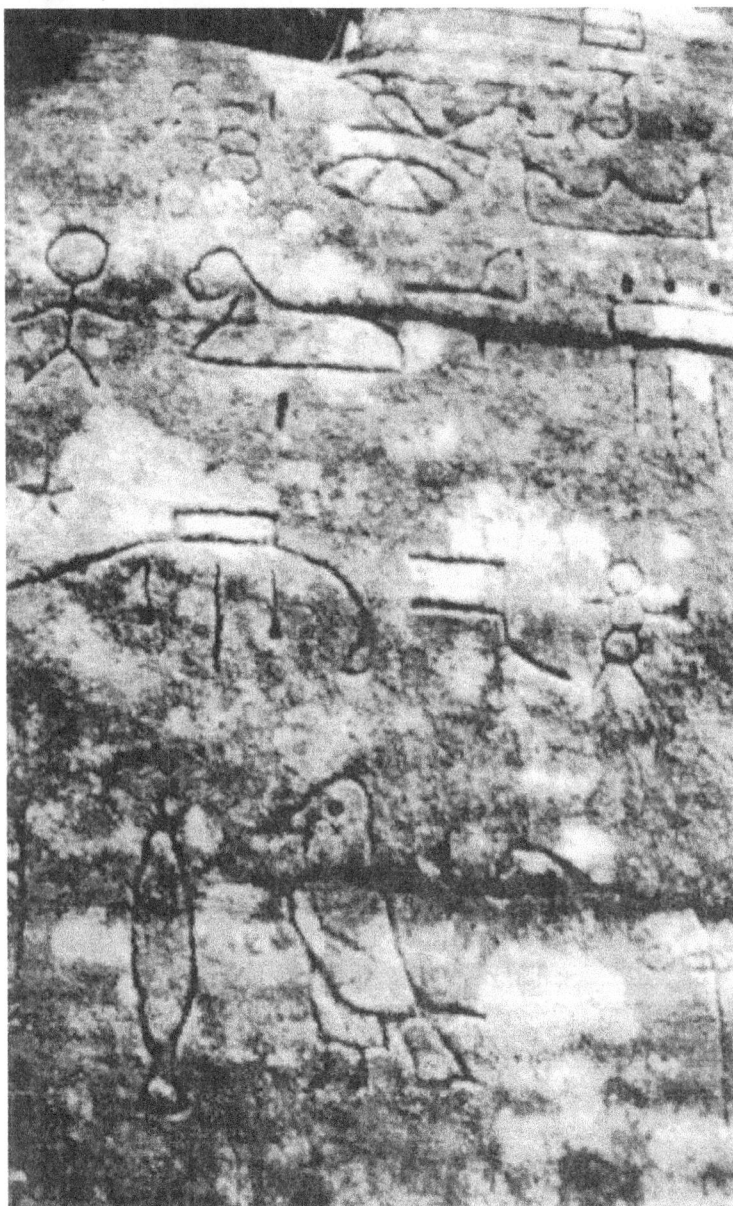

We went out and bought all the recognised textbooks on Egyptian hieroglyphs, and started madly translating, as best we could. About four of us arrived at similar, but differing results, although we agreed they related to the early Third and Fourth Dynasty, both in style and content. I then located the work of Egyptologist Ray Johnson, who specialised in the very ancient form of the language of these early dynasties. He had spent twenty years conducting some admirable research along with several overseas academics. One was a senior director of the Egyptian Department of Antiquities, who asked that he plead with the local Kariong Council to preserve the site.

His research disclosed that the script, dating back to about 2,750BC was archaic, and not as easy to translate from the standard textbooks which relate to a later period in Egyptian history. He also correctly pointed out that a hoaxer, even an academic one, would have used a recognised reference book and not an archaic version which very few scholars have studied. He provided a complete translation, stating that there had been a total of three different semi-literate scribes over those early years.

One international expert told me that these glyphs were so skilled and accurate that he was afraid to say they were genuine. If they were in fact a hoax, it was done on an academic level, and he could not afford to be discredited in the eyes of his peers.

One of our INUFOR members, on an overseas trip, visited a Museum of Antiquities in Egypt and also the British Museum. When she asked the experts, and showed them photographs, she was surprised to learn they were aware of and interested in them, possibly as a result of Ray Johnson's research. They were not prepared to dismiss them as a hoax.

What is the truth behind the Kariong glyphs? We may never know.

Ray Johnson stated that the elders of the Aboriginal Bundjalung tribe claim descent from the people who made these inscriptions, and have placed their own sacred carvings in close proximity, a short distance away.

Paul White also studied the glyphs, their history and proximity to earth power grids. He discovered that ancient peoples knew about the power places on grid intersection points, where many historical sites are located. Local Aboriginals persuaded Paul not to publish a map designating the special spots in Australia, as it would reveal all of their key sacred sites.

While paying homage to Ray Johnson's work at Kariong, Paul had also located other Egyptian carvings in the heart of the Flinders Ranges in South Australia.

An Aboriginal friend also told me of these and more at Wilpeena Pound in South Australia, saying they were even better than those at Kariong, before adding there were more near Mt. Wilson in the Blue Mountains of New South Wales.

A retired gentleman told me of how, over thirty years ago, when working on the new expressway at Cowan, southwest of Gosford, they were constructing an access road and found large carvings on a low cliff, previously hidden by trees.

It was a life-size carving of the Egyptian god Horus holding hands with a man and woman on either side. Work was halted for three days while people, supposedly from the Australian Museum in Sydney, came and removed the entire rock face, breaking one corner in the process. When I asked a colleague who used to work at the Museum, she was not aware of them, "but nobody knows what they've still got in the basement."

A local fishermen has told me that huge cut blocks of stone, which may have formed part of a primitive wharf, exist under the sea off the Central Coast. These were found early in the 20th century and the question remains whether they were constructed by European colonists, or if they have an earlier origin.

The interesting peripheral factors in this research are the reports of unidentified objects and strange phenomena in this area. Many sensitive visitors comment on an unusual atmosphere and earth energies around the glyphs and their location, which some claim is on an energy meridian. Unfortunately, there has been evidence, in the past, of satanic cults meeting nearby.

The Aboriginals have sacred places in the vicinity, and some people are known to go there to sit and meditate. At the bottom of the track, leading up to the glyphs are the foundations of a house long-gone. It took some time to locate one of the previous occupants who had moved up the coast. Peter told me he spent his childhood living there, and confirmed the glyphs were certainly there in the 1970s. He advised of other unusual carvings, which do not appear to be Aboriginal, in hidden locations nearby, and commented that one "resembled a spaceman." He discovered them by accident, as a child, while looking for a lost dog.

He thought the sites held some form of magnetic attraction for the unusual lights and strange objects he had seen there over the years.

One memorable incident came to mind. "I was just married, and had to get up in the dark, at 4.30 in the morning to start early shift at work in Sydney. One morning I was sitting on the outside dunny, still half asleep. I just 'froze' when a huge, bright white light descended from the sky ad hovered low between me and the house. My wife was cooking breakfast in the kitchen, and could see it through the window. She was frightened for me, but there was nothing she could do. I was too scared to move, and just sat there for what seemed to be an eternity until the object shot up and away into the early morning sky."

This was not the only case from the area where a UFO has terrorised a poor helpless local, sitting on their outside toilet in the early hours of the morning. About five years earlier, on the outskirts of Woy Woy, a kilometre below the Kariong site, Pat had gone outside at about 3 a.m. She couldn't understand why their watchdog was whimpering and trying to get into the outhouse with her, until she looked out and saw a cigar-shaped object hovering right outside. It had rows of flashing lights rotating one on top of the other. She was absolutely terrified, slammed the door shut, and didn't venture out until she was sure it was gone.

While I am sure further research will be conducted into the Kariong glyphs in the future, many investigators consider the earth-grid energies in the area have a connection to the carvings, reports of unidentified craft, and other strange phenomena.

Sample of pictograms (not in sequence) found carved in Woy Woy rock face.

There are many more hieroglyphs not illustrated here.

*

Chapter Four

South Coast and Illawarra, NSW

The Illawarra and South Coast of New South Wales stretch from Sydney to the Victorian border. They are bounded on the east by a beautiful craggy coastline of surfing beaches, inlets and lakes, and to the west are the escarpments and forested mountains of the Southern Highlands. The escarpment above includes large coalmines, with deep tunnels and shafts stretching huge distances, both under the sea and on land.

Nearby valleys store much of Sydney's water supply in four large dams; the Cataract, Cordeaux, Avon, Nepean, and in a fifth, smaller, Woronora Dam. Major cities and towns include Wollongong, Port Kembla (the site of Australia's largest steelworks), Kiama (the mouth of the Shoalhaven River at Jervis Bay where *HMAS Albatross* Naval Air Station is located), and nearby Nowra. Also Batemans Bay, the fishing villages of Milton and Ulladulla, Moruya and the dairy centre of Bega, hemmed in on the coast by the Great Dividing Range.

Many sighting reports have a possible conventional explanation. One surprising new identification came from the South Coast when we found out that the Electricity Commission and Telecom test their services in rugged terrain, by running a laser light down an optical fibre along the wire every so often, to check for breakage. This can produce the effect of a bright orange light running along the wires, which can be mistaken for a UFO in the dark.

Top of the Escarpment, 16 June 2004

Above the northern suburbs of the Illawarra are the main Princes Highway and motorway, and the roads leading to the water supply dams and coalmines.

The RACE group (Research of Australian Close Encounters) reported in *The Phenomenon Times* a most interesting account over the South Coast and hinterland at 9 p.m. in 2004. A car driver going to Wilton saw what he thought was a large fireball descend across the sky, and crash with a V-like flash or explosion behind the escarpment near Wollongong, possibly within the catchment area of the dams.

A witness further west at Camden stated the object had flown overhead making a roaring noise. Next day, local radio stations reported an impacting bolide in the Bulli area, and mentioned the presence of the military.

There was a niggling doubt with some people as to the actual identity of the crashed object. Witnesses estimated its size as being anything from the size of a motor vehicle to that of a house – which should have produced large impact effects and ground tremors, and this didn't happen. One witness judged the speed to be comparatively slow – faster than an aircraft, but slower than a meteorite. Furthermore, he described the object as having a cone-like appearance, with a grey-silver sheen, and three tiers, enveloped by a fiery contrail.

A colliery truck driver was stopped by military police, between 11 and 11.30 the next morning, and asked to leave what had apparently become an exclusion zone. He could see at least 100 soldiers combing the area.

With some justification, RACE felt that something other than a meteorite came down that night. They reported the following suspicious factors:

Colliery trucks in the catchment region experienced significant interference with, and in some cases malfunction of electronic equipment. A police officer claimed mine pits had lost power for 30 minutes about the time of impact, and Air Traffic Control (ATC) tracked the object entering the atmosphere from South Queensland. Both the police and ATC later denied these statements. The media made no further comment, except to say a meteorite had exploded mid-air.

Of more concern were the calls received by the original truck driver witness. First he was contacted by someone claiming to be from the Bureau of Meteorology, telling him "it was no use making a big fuss over the event." Even more disturbing was the following, and I quote from the RACE investigator's report:

> "Minutes after my first telephone contact to the witness, he received a threatening phone call, warning him not to talk about the event. The witness then contacted the local police station, where he was informed that his telephone number was given to a government body in Canberra upon demand."

This leaves us with no idea what crashed above the escarpment that night. Given the facts to hand, I would doubt that it was a meteorite or bolide. There is no evidence to say it was extraterrestrial either. It could just as well have been one of our own military prototypes, or perhaps one from a foreign power. We may never know.

Darkes Forest, 2 August 1981

Darkes Forest lies at the top of the escarpment, off the old highway, on the northern tip of the Illawarra. It is mostly native bushland, with the occasional fruit orchard and farming property.

At 6.30 p.m. John, a local coalminer, was driving from Wollongong to Helensburgh to commence his evening shift at the mine, when a strange object passed overhead.

"It was really low, about 600 feet up, and very large. It looked like a house in the sky. An odd shape, like a coffin with angular sides and corners. There was a ring of flashing yellow and white lights in the top section, and a large blue light in the centre of the craft. As it moved along, there was a faint humming sound, and a faint yellow beam was sweeping ahead from side to side."

The unusual object, which had come from the northeast moved away to the southwest. There did not appear to be any effect on John or his radio or vehicle.

Bulli Pass, 1 May 1993

Bulli Pass runs from the top of the Illawarra escarpment, down a very steep winding road to the coast. It was 1.25 in the morning and Bruce Bryant, with his wife and daughter, was coming home from a night out in Sydney:

"I was coming off the expressway, where the road from Appin joins the Princes Highway. I noticed well up ahead, past Bulli Pass, a lot of yellow flashing lights, and commented to my wife: 'Look, there must be an accident up ahead!' She agreed with me, but we thought little more of it.

"When we got further along, after the Bulli Pass turnoff, we saw what I thought was a long wide load coming towards us. It was so big and seemed to be taking up the entire road, so I slowed down and started to pull over to the side. We watched it approach, and my wife said to my daughter, 'Quick Sally, look what's coming up the road.' Sally replied: 'Mum, I can't open my eyes! I don't know why.' I know it sounds stupid, but it's true.

"I could see this vehicle was large and oblong, with lots of yellow flashing and revolving lights. The lights were so bright you could just see that it was a very large oblong shape, with the sides having irregular contours. I did not take that much notice, as my mind accepted that it was a wide load coming along the road. There was no sound that I could hear.

"When it got right in front of us, (about 50 yards away) with its lights illuminating the inside of my car, it shot sideways, so fast, and disappeared inland to the west. I stopped to see where it went, but to our amazement there was no road, only bush! We also realised that we were on the crest of a hill, and yet this object was coming straight at us. It could not have been on the road, and in hindsight we had not seen actual headlights, only the yellow pulsating lights all around it.

"Thank God. After it disappeared, my daughter Sally could open her eyes, but we all felt weird afterwards. We sat there for a while, wondering what it was, before completing our journey. It bugged us all the next day; it still does! I went to Corrimal and then Warilla Police Stations and asked if any wide loads went up the mountain about that time. They rang Bulli Station who confirmed that no wide loads had been up the mountain that night."

Bruce went back and checked the side of the road, there were no tracks going off, and no damage to the bush. He was adamant this was a real object, and not an atmospheric inversion, coal truck, helicopter or plane. He had only just retired from a lifelong career in the RAAF, and admitted that this incident really spooked him.

Wollongong, July 1972

In July 1972, Lydia Reynolds was 18 years old, seven months pregnant, and living with her mother:

"Mum was out, and I was in our Wollongong kitchen, cooking. I can't remember feeling faint. It was daylight then, early afternoon. The next thing I knew it was dark, and I could hear my mother calling, "Lydia, Lydia – come here quick!" I went outside and she pointed to a large disc-shape hovering silently over the backyard. It was round, about the size of a lorry or bus and fairly low. Initially it looked silver, but soon after changed colour to that of a glowing ember. Next it throbbed different colours – blue, orange, purple. We watched it for quite a while, before it shot off over the bushland area, and down behind some power lines. I would never have seen it if Mum hadn't called.

"When we went back in, the custard I had been making hours earlier had just burnt away. I just thought I must have blacked out." Lydia paused, "You know, Mum and I felt very guilty. The week before my brother and his mates told us they had seen a UFO. We didn't believe them, and had teased them because they had been drinking."

Over 20 years later Lydia checked the old *Illawarra Mercury* newspapers, and in the 26 July 1972 issue, found references to the craft they had seen.

Wollongong, 1975

In 1975, Lydia arrived home at 1 a.m. after an evening out with her brother. She retired to her room where Victor, her young son was sleeping, and shut the door. As she got into bed she heard a noise, turned around, and saw the door open. She could see a shadow and felt terrified. "I was shaking, my heart pounding and then the door closed. I rushed into the hall. Nothing! Everyone was asleep. I thought maybe it was a ghost.

"In 1977 my son woke up one morning with an ear print of blood on his pillow. The doctor could find no cause for it. In the late 1970s we were visiting a friend in a third-storey home unit. We left Victor watching television for a few minutes, and came back to find him cowering in a corner, saying he was frightened of the 'man' on the balcony.

"In the early 1980s I had several unusual experiences – waking up to find my bed vibrating and seeing a large light and two beings outside my window. One night I was fully awake. A dark figure, less than five feet tall, wearing a hood, was leaning over me. I felt paralysed, couldn't breathe, and was trying to fight it. By forcing myself to be calm and concentrate, it disappeared. I also experienced several strange visions out of time and place. Whatever this is, it's dark and evil."

She is now a school teacher, but fears for the wellbeing of her son, born soon after the first incident. She worried that her son had an interest in UFOs and hinted that he may have also experienced something paranormal. Her mother and brother had both died, and she was feeling very vulnerable and alone. This case was a difficult one to determine, as most of the subsequent incidents could well have a mundane explanation.

At our suggestion, Lydia consulted a colleague who had not only witnessed a UFO himself, but was also a qualified psychologist and hypnotherapist.

Kangaroo Valley

Kangaroo Valley is hidden between the hills and mountains which separate Nowra on the Illawarra Coast, and Moss Vale on the Southern Highlands. There have been several instances of strange happenings in this beautiful semi-rural valley:

September 1981

The Sydney *Daily Mirror* (16 September 1981) reported that 48-year-old Frank Burke was driving along Cambewarra Mountain Road between Kangaroo Valley and Nowra, when a strong beam of light enveloped his car. He later discovered his tape recorder had melted as a result of the encounter.

Again in 1994 a local doctor and his wife were driving from Jaspers Brush towards Berry, and were astounded when a huge brilliant white light, shaped like a teardrop, descended to treetop level. They were a little apprehensive, but before they could decide whether to stop or speed up, it moved sideways. They lost sight of it when, still at a low altitude, it sped towards Kangaroo Valley "much faster than any military plane."

Sunday 24 May 1992

Donald Gale was driving home, back to the coast, via Kangaroo Valley. It was nearly 11 p.m. when he was coming down the pass from Moss Vale, and as he reached a straight part of the road an enormous object came up from behind at an incredible speed.

"It passed low, about treetop level, over our car. As it moved in front of us its movements were so erratic we feared, at one stage, it was going to nose-dive into the ground. It managed to level off, and went straight into the sky ahead at a shallow upward gradient.

"We were stunned, I've never seen anything like it before! It was the largest, brightest green light, sort of fuzzy or rough at the edges and larger than a helicopter. It was football-shaped and about 60 to 70 feet long. We couldn't see any hard shape underneath it, although it was too bright to see if there was anything solid under the light.

"We didn't notice any noise or vibration. As it moved away it diminished until it became a point of white light and disappeared."

Shellharbour, 22 January 1998

It was a warm summer night, just after 11 p.m. William was in his front garden when he noticed a strange ringing sensation in his ears:

"I felt and heard a very quiet rushing air sound accompanied by a deep, hardly audible energy sound (a quiet rumbling), which I sensed more than heard. I felt it in the ground and my body. I looked up and around, and realised there was something blocking out the sky. A series of stars would disappear from view for a few seconds, as if something were moving across, underneath them.

"As it came closer I could discern a wedge-shaped object, about the size of the moon, 1,000 to 1,500 feet overhead. It looked transparent, almost ghost-like. Occasionally it appeared very slightly illuminated, but basically it had no lighting or exhaust trail. It was travelling fairly slowly, and I can't really explain this, but I saw it from behind and also from the top!"

"It was luminous in the sense of a metal reflecting light, but in the dark, with minimal light, it was more a cloudy-grey colour. I saw what might have been windows; there was a raised area on the top. From the rear, I could see the wings dipped down. While what I saw was definitely well beyond the norm, my intuition tells me it was military and not alien."

William asked for my opinion, concluding: "I would like to know if you have heard of any unusual movements in our skies." (I thought, as a ufologist: "Where do I begin?")

Kiama, 1955

In July 2015 announcements of a new SETI Project prompted Garry Bond, by then in his mid-seventies, to overcome his fear of ridicule and contact me regarding some memorable events witnessed by several generations of his family a long time ago:

Nearly 60 years ago in 1955, when he was about twelve his family were living at Shellharbour on South Coast New South Wales. One night his father became very excited, taking him outside where their dog was barking and agitated. "At first I was a little apprehensive. Was I in trouble? Had I done something wrong? Dad just pointed upwards and there was a huge glowing object hovering about 300 feet above our home. It was so bright I couldn't distinguish all the details, but it had lots of reddish-orange lights all around the edge. It was massive, at least 200 feet across. I thought I heard a slight humming noise, but it was being drowned out by our noisy dog!"

Garry and his father watched in stunned silence for a while. The object then moved slowly to the east, with the dog in hot vocal pursuit, until it disappeared over the coast and out to sea.

"I noticed Dad did not seem to be as afraid as me, but he confided about a similar incident in 1915 when he was about five years old. His father had been killed in an accident, and Dad was sent to live with an Uncle Frank on a dairy farm in Limestone Valley, South Canterbury, in the Southern Island of New Zealand. On several occasions a huge, round traditional UFO had hovered over the milking sheds. The cows would be in a dreadful, distressed state which disrupted their milk production for a few days." While Garry was not aware of any cattle mutilations, he felt his uncle would not have told him anyway, due to his age. (Garry felt privileged that his father had called only him outside, and spoke of the earlier incident in New Zealand. It was their special secret.)

While Garry's siblings were unaware of the UFO hovering over their Shellharbour home in the 1955, in 1963 his brother Patrick had come home and announced "UFOs really exist!" He was then in the navy, serving on the *HMAS Voyager*, to the north of Australia. It was the height of the Cold War, and while operating the radar and he was told "If air contacts disappear from the screen, do not fire. They are alien craft, and not Russians or Indonesians." Another ex-naval officer told Garry that while sailing on a totally flat sea, his ship rolled so violently they thought it would overturn. Many sailors had witnessed a UFO coming out of the water and it had almost collided with their vessel before taking off.

Garry's father had one more encounter before he died. After retiring, he set out with his mate Norm, on a great adventure to explore the Australian outback. One night they had camped beside a creek in the far west of New South Wales. The old blokes were drinking beer and telling yarns by the campfire, when suddenly the darkness was illuminated with a brilliant white light from a large UFO hovering overhead. His father was not forthcoming about what happened next, and Garry was never really sure if he had divulged all of his UFO experiences during his life:

"I always felt there was more he wasn't telling me. My two older brothers are high-degree Masons, and they have remained steadfastly silent on the matter."

Garry's own interest in UFOs was only incidental during the following years. In the mid-1960s he was employed at the steelworks in Port Kembla. One morning when he was clocking-on, just before 7 a.m., he heard a tremendous roar overhead. "A big civilian plane was travelling north to Sydney – it was so low it just missed the higher buildings! We wondered what was going on. Was the plane about to crash; it wasn't on the normal flight path? Then we gasped in disbelief. About 100 metres behind the plane was a huge, round, shiny silver ball. It was about twice the diameter of the plane and seemed to be in hot pursuit."

Garry was living at Kiama at the time, and a couple of years later in 1968, he was putting out the milk bottles one night, when he jumped back in fright. There was a huge cigar-shaped object just above eye level. It was about 500 metres off the end of the headland, travelling from south to north, fifty feet above the water: "It was so low, travelling at about 40 kilometres, and really huge – about three times the size of a jumbo jet. It was dead silent, didn't make any noise! Along the side were windows, brightly lit from the inside, but I couldn't see any occupants." During that summer he was having a quiet beer on the patio when he was startled by a large orange glow which appeared to land behind some trees about eight miles away.

Shortly afterwards, he and thirty other workmates were having lunch outside a machinery factory in Unanderra and were astonished to see a huge craft in the clear blue sky. It was cigar-shaped, bigger than a plane or advertising blimp, and hovered over the BHP site. Garry could not estimate its altitude, but it had a shiny, reflective surface. After a short while it flew off at amazing speed on a 45 degree angle. It gave Garry the courage to tell them about his previous sightings. They had also seen strange lights and objects. "Garry, you live at a great vantage point. You should buy a telescope. We'll show you a great spot to the south to concentrate on."

While Garry's observations were irregular at first, his curiosity was sparked by several instances of more orange and other objects which seemed to go down in the same location. One night his persistence paid off. "I watched this thing land. I could detect it was resting on a tripod. There appeared to be long windows like the first craft I sighted. Suddenly a bright white light appeared. It looked like an opening door with a curved top.

"I was now determined to find out more about these strange visitations. The next day I drove up to the spot. Sure enough, there were the dents in the ground, covering a 70-foot area where the tripod legs had been. I was probably a little obsessed, and from 1968 to 1971 I diligently recorded my observations. While the objects came on an ad hoc basis, there was an emerging pattern every September, when a huge object would appear off the coast."

Garry claimed, even on a conservative estimate, this object was well over a mile long and several stories high. "I'm not mistaken – I watched it through the 'scope for hours. It hovered and a multitude of small discs, glowing orange, came out in a row from the top. They went down over the houses as if they were monitoring or mapping them. After quite a long time they went back to the main object, which then moved further north and hovered. The same small discs emerged again and repeated the previous procedure."

Not long afterwards, Garry was to experience the darker, more insidious aspect of the visitors and our human agencies. He was quietly fishing off the point one night when he saw a disc in the sky. "I was so excited at first I flashed my torch at it, but within a few seconds it moved towards me and hovered overhead. What had I done! In sheer panic I grabbed my gear and fled. It followed me slowly, silently, the whole quarter of a mile to my home and safety.

"It didn't end there. The next morning I was driving my Ford Falcon up Bombo Hill when I noticed pedestrians and other motorists were pointing at me. I thought something must be wrong with the car, so I looked – nothing I could see. I pulled over, checked back, front and sides – nothing wrong. Someone was motioning to the sky. I realised that hovering above me and the car was a 70-foot disc. I can hardly describe my terror. Thank God it took off towards Robertson!

He had two frights within twelve hours, and I thought perhaps ufology was not such a good idea after all! "I arrived at work still shaking. One of my colleagues said he had connections with a UFO group in Sydney and would pass on the details. I don't know who these connections actually were. One night, not long after, there was a knock on the door. Three men, who never identified themselves, marched straight into my lounge room. It was intimidating. They fired questions about my interest in UFOs and my observations. My wife was reduced to tears during the hour-long grilling. They were not amateur ufologists, that's for sure!"

This incident partly prompted them to move twenty miles away, and a decision never to go looking for UFOs again. "I was quite scared when one of the strange men came back, over a year later, this time to our new home! How did he know where we lived? I gave him my assurance I wanted no more to do with it, but I wondered whether what I had seen was human or alien."

Kiama, 1972, "One of Ours"

Garry was not the only Kiama resident to experience strange, inexplicable events. In the early 1990s I received a phone call from Graham, now living in Sydney, regarding some events in Kiama, from the 1970s which still troubled him. After the interview he told me he was going to write it all down, as it would be good therapy to help him to come to grips with it all. He sent me his own well-written report titled *One of Ours, 1972*, which I subsequently published in the *INUFOR Digest*, (minus his surname of course). I will edit it here:

Graham was woken by a light coming into the room, probably through the window, and while still half asleep, thought it might be an intruder. He forced himself up, and looked out – nothing unusual. "I thought I must have been dreaming, as I had remarked on the endless stream of car headlights winding their way down the old highway towards Sydney. I went back to sleep, and when the light came into the room again I jumped up – still nothing unusual outside. Suddenly I spotted a white light beam with a fluorescent blue tinge evaporating from it. Through the luminescence I could see the shape of a flying craft, from which a beam projected at a 75-degree angle to the ground. It was between our headland and the next one across.

"The beam was about thirty feet long, two and a half feet in diameter, and fell like a perfect cylinder of solid light, continuing along the path of its own axis, and not in the direction of gravity. When this solid light hit a caravan it behaved like water, pouring over it. The illumination enveloping every nook and cranny, like fluorescent paint from an electro-, airless spray gun. This only lasted for three seconds before fading away.

"I looked for the craft again, and it appeared slightly to the left with another beam of light slowly descending. When the light beam reached a length a bit longer than the first beam, it began falling as before, this time hitting and completely illuminating an amenities block. Again the light faded. The same light-beam-extrusion sequence was repeated, this time illuminating a 40-foot area of the beach."

"Inside the lighted area two men were standing motionless, looking up at the craft, and were joined by a young woman who had been sitting next to a campfire. A second young woman was running backwards, trying to brush the light off her arms and body, then stopped and stared up at the craft. The light went out, and all I could see was the dimly glowing campfire. I looked, trying to see those people, worried that the craft had taken them, and angry that it had obviously terrorised the young woman.

"I must have fallen asleep on my feet, because when I awoke I was standing on the other side of the window. I looked out. The craft was in front of our house, and moved very close to my window. It was about 40 feet wide and ten feet high, made of one piece of metallic material. Similar to unpolished zinc alloy, no seams, rivets, weld marks or plates visible. It was not a helicopter, there was no noise, or blades and no disturbance, even to small trees. It was not a hovercraft, and had no wings like a plane.

"It began to spin in one direction, stopped, then spun for a shorter time in the opposite direction. It then hovered in a steady position above the skyline. While I was considering the nature and origin of this craft I must have blacked out. When I came to, it was still opposite my window.

"I could see a window shape, about six feet wide, two feet six inches high, with curved corners. The metallic window shield suddenly disappeared and I could see inside the craft – flat, vertical off-white walls and no fittings. A man walked in, looking at something like a thick clipboard, which he was holding in his hands. He stood at the window, and seemed to be absorbed in working on something at bench height below. A second man walked in and appeared to become involved with what the other was doing.

"They were both wearing silver one-piece suits, like wetsuits, with no markings. Just as I was thinking I felt safe (there was no sign of weapons, and they didn't seem to know I was watching), they smiled at each other and then directly at me. I had a physical fright, and my hair literally stood on end. I suddenly realised that in the light, they could control me to feel and think peacefully.

"I dropped to the floor and said, 'Everybody keep down, stay out of the light.' There was a great noise above the roof, and the house vibrated severely. The fridge and washing machine were bumping about. It was like the craft overhead sucked the electricity out of the house and then took off. "I said, 'Quickly, get under the doorways, the house is going to fall!' My father-in-law saw the craft, and thought it had actually taken the roof off, as did the neighbour behind us, who came

62

racing out of his back door. The lady on the other side opened her window and called out 'Where did it crash, do we have to get out?' I reassured her we were safe, it had gone.

"We rang the Nowra Base, and the duty officer tried to say it was a weather balloon, released from Jamberoo, which had failed to inflate properly. The next day, two men in dark suits, with ID tags, came to the door and asked if anyone had seen anything last night. My wife and her mother were scared and said No, later asking me not to speak about it, as they were frightened something might happen to me.

"Some days afterwards my father-in-law read in the newspaper that an expensive navy helicopter flying from Jamberoo over Kiama, had lost its electronics and crashed 40 kilometres out to sea off Kiama. The crew were rescued and the navy were trying to recover it to find what went wrong. I had said, 'Yeah, I know about losing power, the same thing happened to the helicopter as what happened to the fridge and the laundry light, the UFO took its electricity.' After that we ignored the event and nothing further was said."

Graham was no longer living in Kiama when he contacted me, and as is often the case also contacted a couple of other researchers and attended a couple of research group meetings. Bill Chalker documented the sighting in his book *The Oz Files*, and in 2013 reported a further in-depth meeting and investigation with Graham in 2012, when he was collating evidence on light beams behaving as both solid and liquid.

Graham was fairly consistent with the details he provided for both investigations, and admitted he tried to persuade himself it was a dream even though he knew it wasn't. While he provided us both with an identical typed report, in 2012 he advised Bill of some recollections of possibly being aboard the craft, of which I was not aware. On the other hand, during my initial discussions with Graham, he actually gave the date of the event as a long weekend in 1977. He also mentioned 1972, as stated in his typed report, which I had published verbatim. Graham also described the entities, saying that while their faces looked like those of human males, they had a smaller nose and mouth, and no hair or ears. Since these details did not appear in any later reports or interviews, I wonder if he was having a momentary flashback or if there were actually two incidents, in both 1972 and 1977?

Windang, Oasis Caravan Park, 1965

Omar Fowler documented an unusual case involving an English family who migrated to Australia, temporarily staying at the Oasis Caravan Park on the shore of Lake Illawarra: Derek and Dora Hodgson had noticed a few dart-like lights in the sky when they had looked to see what was causing static on their local radio station. They decided to take the matter one step further and attempt to contact these craft, using telepathy and Dora's Ouija board (something I strongly advise against).

They waited until the static started on the radio, and placed their fingers on top of the glass and concentrated. They were startled when it moved to the letters "ZI" – and asked for the meaning. The board told them "We are the Sky People." The Hodgsons claimed there were more questions and answers while the darts were in the sky above, but not when the darts moved on.

They continued this practice twice a week, and noticed their three children always slept very heavily through their secretive activities. At first they were cautious and a little apprehensive, but after prolonged contact with this unseen intelligence, who claimed to be the Guardians of our planet for many thousands of years, they asked for a meeting.

Eventually a rendezvous point and time was arranged for one night, but a small aircraft like a spotter plane, was circling the area and the ZIs didn't materialise. Later in the week they claim they made contact again via the Ouija Board and were told to "go to the agreed place now." They had set off for the specified place, a small clearing at the edge of the woods.

Just after they arrived, Dora spotted a tall human-like figure, dressed in a black one-piece suit, standing under a tree. It was slim, but not thin, and after a few minutes it seemed to touch the middle of its belt and it suddenly disappeared. During the encounter they were transfixed to the spot, but once the entity disappeared could move freely again.

They returned to the spot next day, and worked out that the figure had to be eight feet tall. One night, just before they moved out of the area, there was an enormous thunder storm, and Derek thought he saw a figure standing outside the window. Their power was cut, which would have needed a ladder to restore it on the outside of the cabin. However, it came back on by itself. The next morning, they found a sooty area high up the outside wall. The switch had been reconnected and there was a very large handprint in the soot at the side.

The question remains as to whether the Hodgsons had been in contact with extraterrestrial beings, some form of paranormal or inter-dimensional intelligence, or something else. Who or what was the manifestation under the tree? While I know contactees who claim communication through careful, deep meditation, the use of Ouiji boards is a dangerous practice, leaving the participants open to all forms of intrusion by unknown entities.

Nowra, 31 August 1954 (the *Shamus O'Farrell Case*)

This is one of the best-documented and substantiated cases of an unidentified object, which still defies conventional explanation. Twenty-five-year-old Lieutenant Shamus (James) O'Farrell, a Royal Australian Navy pilot in 723 Squadron, took off from his Nowra base at dusk, for a standard night-navigation exercise.

The base radar was off line, but it was still light, and they were hoping to get it up and running soon. Jim was piloting a British-built Sea Fury fighter aircraft, with an 18-cylinder Bristol Centaurus radial engine, capable of a 400 knots top speed. (The RAAF Meteor plane was the only craft in the country capable of flying faster.)

About two hours into his trip it was dark. The weather was fine, a cloudless sky with no moon. He was at an altitude of just over 12,000 feet, (5,000 feet above any civilian traffic), and "somewhere in the Goulburn area near Canberra" (although he later stated he was also near Yass during the encounter). He spotted two other aircraft, one either side, which he wasn't expecting. They were about the size of a Dakota – dark cigar-shaped objects, with one central bright light on top which clearly defined their outline.

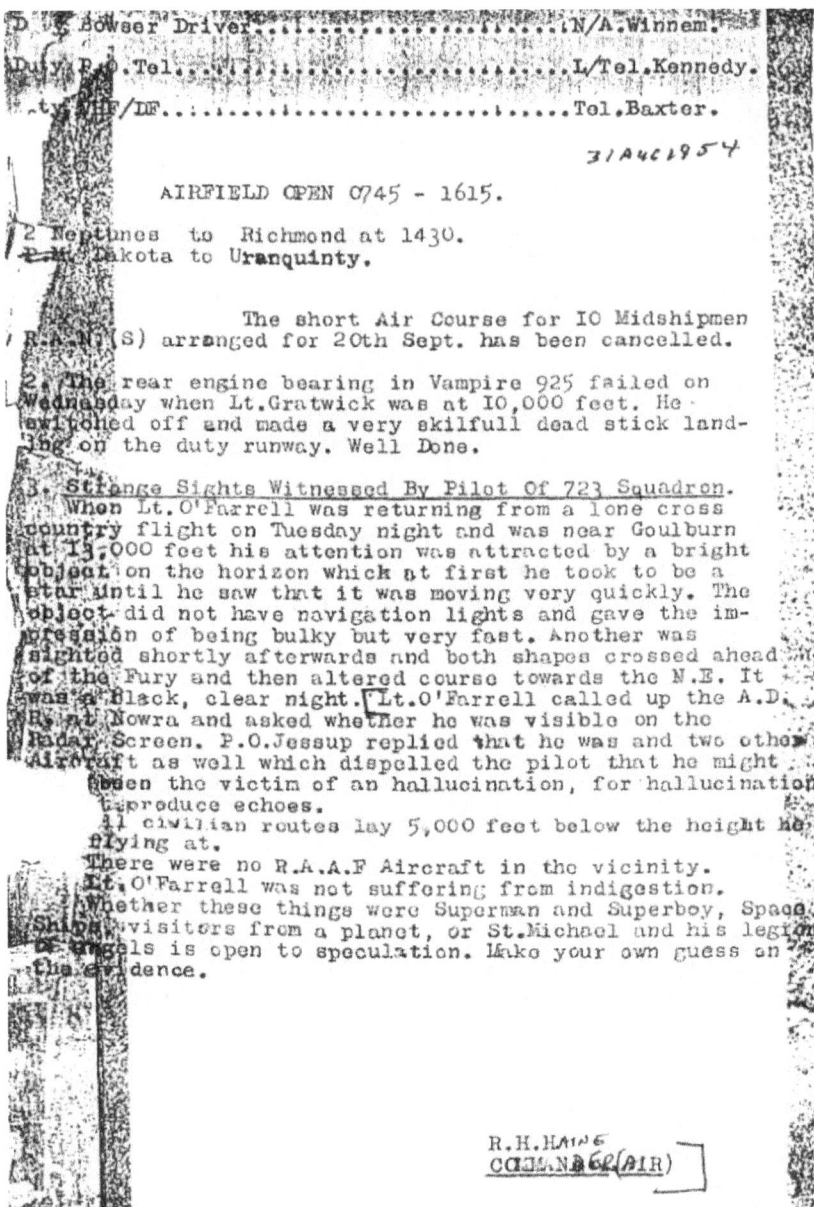

D.S.Bowser Driver...................N/A.Winnem.
Duty R.O.Tel......................L/Tel.Kennedy.
..ty MF/DF..........................Tel.Baxter.

3 AUG 1954

AIRFIELD OPEN 0745 - 1615.

2 Neptunes to Richmond at 1430.
Dakota to Uranquinty.

The short Air Course for IO Midshipmen R.A.N(S) arranged for 20th Sept. has been cancelled.

2. The rear engine bearing in Vampire 925 failed on Wednesday when Lt.Gratwick was at 10,000 feet. He switched off and made a very skillfull dead stick landing on the duty runway. Well Done.

3. Strange Sights Witnessed By Pilot Of 723 Squadron. When Lt.O'Farrell was returning from a lone cross country flight on Tuesday night and was near Goulburn at 13,000 feet his attention was attracted by a bright object on the horizon which at first he took to be a star until he saw that it was moving very quickly. The object did not have navigation lights and gave the impression of being bulky but very fast. Another was sighted shortly afterwards and both shapes crossed ahead of the Fury and then altered course towards the N.E. It was a black, clear night. Lt.O'Farrell called up the A.D. at Nowra and asked whether he was visible on the radar Screen. P.O.Jessup replied that he was and two other Aircraft as well which dispelled the pilot that he might been the victim of an hallucination, for hallucination produce echoes. All civilian routes lay 5,000 feet below the height he flying at. There were no R.A.A.F Aircraft in the vicinity. Lt.O'Farrell was not suffering from indigestion. Whether these things were Superman and Superboy, Space Ships visitors from a planet, or St.Michael and his legion of angels is open to speculation. Make your own guess on the evidence.

R.H.Haine
COMMANDER (AIR)

64

He contacted Nowra, whose radar was now back on-line, and they verified they had three aircraft "coming in from the west – which one was he?" They asked him to "fly a one-eighty for identification." The other two craft were slightly ahead, so he performed the 180 degree turn, and finished with 360 degrees. Nowra confirmed he was the centre object, and the other two craft settled back in formation with him. He knew that since he was travelling at 330 knots, the only other craft capable of staying with him were the RAAF Meteors, and when he was advised that there were no other RAAF or civilian planes in the vicinity, he started getting a little concerned as to who it was flying in immaculate formation with him.

Suddenly, after about ten minutes, they sped off to the northeast at approximately 1,000 miles per hour. This was also tracked on radar. The two objects passed over the Marulan navigation beacon, where a Department of Aviation officer conducting repairs noted them in his log book. An air traffic controller at Mascot also logged the two lights. RAAF boffins plotted and calculated them all as being the same objects.

O'Farrell was not happy with the publicity, which he thought would harm his career. He even tried to concede he might have been hallucinating. But, as the base commander wrote, "hallucinations don't have echoes."

NAVY CONFIRMS 'SAUCER' STORY

CANBERRA, Thurs.—The Minister for the Navy (Mr. Francis) tonight confirmed that a R.A.N. airman had seen two unidentifed objects on his radar.

The Nowra air base had also picked up the objects on their radar, he said.

Reports that Navy radar sets had recorded two "flying saucers" were published this morning.

Mr. Francis said that R.A.A.F. headquarters were investigating the incident.

He said: "On a cross-country flight from the Naval Air Station at Nowra on August 31 a pilot in an aircraft at 13,000 feet observed two lights on his radar with vague shapes underneath.

"The lights passed ahead of him at very fast speed.

"The pilot was flying at 220 knots at the time.

"The pilot immediately contacted Nowra and advised them.

"They confirmed his report on their radar screens.

"It was later ascertained that the only other aircraft in the vicinity was a T.A.A. Convair.

"The report was passed to Naval intelligence

R.A.A.F. intelligence in accordance with usual procedure with reports of this nature.

"These reports are collated and examined by R.A.A.F. headquarters.

Naval pilots and senior naval officers at Nowra today refused to discuss the report.

They said such information was "top secret."

The pilot who made the report—Lieutenant O'Farrell, of Sydney—was not available for comment.

Fellow pilots said tonight that O'Farrell was an experienced airman "not given to halucinations."

They discounted the possibility that the vague shapes he saw were unauthorised aircraft.

Intelligence officers who collate all reports on "flying saucers," irrespective of the source, have noted that:

● More than 90 per cent of reports are made at night.

● Nearly all deal with east coast districts particularly between Brisbane and Melbourne

In his log entry for that day, (Air) Commander R.H. Haine documented the incident, and finalised by saying: "Whether these things were Superman and Superboy, Space Ships, visitors from another planet, or St. Michael and his legion of angels is open to speculation. Make your own guess on the evidence."

When Jim landed he was met by senior officers who placed him under immediate scrutiny. The medical officer not only checked his sobriety and overall health, his quarters were searched, and his record of alcohol consumption in the Officers' Mess reviewed. Luckily, he drank very little at that age. He was also interviewed on several occasions by military intelligence officers.

He is a religious man. Even today he maintains "I still don't know" with regards to UFOs. He was, however, officially interviewed by Professor Allen Hynek from the USA, who told Jim he could not dismiss his encounter with these mysterious objects.

O'Farrell was certainly most-respected and trusted by the military. Two years later, as a qualified helicopter pilot, he was selected to fly the Duke of Edinburgh (who was visiting Australia for the Melbourne Olympic Games) around Sydney. He recalled two incidents at the time, but never alluded there was a connection, although I do wonder:

The day he flew the Duke of Edinburgh, his helicopter emitted two bangs after climbing over the trees at Government House, and another two just before arrival at the E.S. Marks

Field in Centennial Park, central Sydney, forcing him to make a running landing, which concerned Prince Phillip, himself a pilot. The helicopter was subsequently taken back to Nowra on a low loader, but O'Farrell will not say what was wrong with it.

He also detailed an account where Max Holyman, the son of the founder of Australian National Airways (ANA), was flying a helicopter on the west coast of Tasmania, when his engine failed. He and his colleague landed on top of some trees, unhurt, but perched 30 metres above the ground. O'Farrell was sent to rescue them, later receiving a call from then-Prime Minister Robert Menzies, ordering him to stay in Tasmania to help repair the helicopter. He wouldn't comment on any reason for this directive, or any confidential communications, except to say the "cause of the crash was that Holyman's helicopter had been refuelled with water."

James O'Farrell later chalked up over 4,500 hours as a fighter pilot, and continued on to a distinguished career, culminating in his appointment as Naval Attache to Washington, and retiring with the rank of Commodore. I am acquainted with his younger brother Richard, who says James, now in his late eighties, is much frailer, and living in quiet retirement.

Oddly enough, on 9 January 1954, more than seven months before the O'Farrell encounter, the *Melbourne Age* newspaper quoted a high-ranking RAAF officer as saying that during the previous months there had been an increase in UFO reports coming from aircraft in flight.

Jervis Bay 1962

Another ex-RAAF pilot from Jervis Bay recounted how he was night-flying at 20,000 to 30,000 feet with three other aircraft. Each plane had two pilots.

"We sighted an unknown craft in our airspace, and were immediately apprehensive that someone else was there in the dark, at our altitude. One of our planes moved towards the object to intercept and identify it. As the two pilots got within a range of six miles, the target took off at an inconceivable speed, and headed south, still at the same altitude.

"All eight of us filled in reports, and we heard of other sightings at the same time. Later, Canberra told us we had seen an Air Force Neptune on exercise. We all rejected this, although we couldn't argue the point. There was such a quantum difference to a Neptune or any familiar plane and this object – it was just totally unidentifiable!"

Woronora Dam, 1952

An early pilot encounter event on the South Coast, occurred two years before the Shamus O'Farrell case, in 1952. ANA pilot Captain Bob Jackson was flying into Sydney's Mascot Airport at about 11 p.m. one night. When he was over the Woronora Dam area he saw a flash of light, and watched as an object with an orange light at the tail shot past, towards the coast near Wollongong. Mascot Control advised there were no other planes in the vicinity or on radar.

Two minutes later he saw the object again. This time it made a complete circle around his plane and then sped back towards the coast at terrific speed. The *Melbourne Sun* (5 January 1954) quoted Captain Jackson as saying the experience was nerve-wracking, and he, like many other senior pilots, had not officially reported the sighting for fear of ridicule.

I have spoken to several pilots who have told me that if they report the unidentified craft they have seen while flying, no punitive action is taken. However, when they come to renew their endorsements, life can get difficult.

Wallaga Aboriginal Station and Reserve, January 1966

A school headmaster advised that at about 9.30 p.m., in January 1966, he and his wife were leaving the Wallaga Aboriginal Station. His car was full, as the manager of the Reserve together with the local Church of England Minister and his son were also returning to Bermagui.

"We were driving around the shore of Wallaga Lake when the young lad called out 'look at that star!' It didn't take long to see what he was pointing at.

"Hovering about 200 feet above the headland and half a mile away, was 33this hour-glass-shaped, brightly-lit object. It was intensely white, almost having a supernatural quality, and was surrounded by an aura of lesser brilliance.

"We continued driving around the lake, and could see quite well, as it was over the opposite shore. It moved slowly upwards and seemed to vibrate. A beam, like a searchlight, shot out from it. It moved slowly in the other direction, and then came back towards us. We stopped, and got out of the car to get a better look.

"It was just hovering at that time, but almost as if it knew we were watching, it suddenly shot upwards at an angle. It must have gone from zero to 1,000 miles per hour in a few seconds, and when it reached an incredible altitude it became a red dot, as if it changed colour with speed. We all agreed it was not a conventional craft, and were left wondering as to what it was."

Milton–Ulladulla, 15 November 1993

Kevin and Fiona Francis and their two children were prawning on the western side of the Lake Tabourie Bridge, near Ulladulla on the NSW South Coast. It was a clear, pleasant starry night, with a light breeze. Kevin remembers what started off as a pleasant, uneventful family outing:

"It was about 9.30 p.m. and I had just brought in a bucket of prawns. As I waded back out into the lake, Fiona put some more logs on the fire. 'What are those lights?' asked my son Simon, pointing at the mountains to the northwest. We all looked up to see two lights, one white and one yellow, a couple of kilometres across the lake.

"Fiona soon identified the white one as being the caravan park sign, but the yellow light remained a mystery. 'Perhaps it's a car headlight in the pine forest,' she suggested. As it started moving towards us we realised it was flying above the trees, about 50 metres up, and moving slowly to the southeast, towards the caravan park.

"The kids got excited and yelled: 'Maybe it's a helicopter.' The light was travelling slower than the breeze, and as it came closer we realised it was quite large, ten to twelve metres across; about the size of a helicopter, but making no noise whatsoever. It now looked very bright. A red ball of sparkling flame radiating an orange hue around the outside. Its reflection shone clearly on the water below.

"It passed right over our heads, and as it crossed above the bridge and veered to the southeast, we could still see it through the treetops. I ran down the track trying to get a better view, but Fiona got frightened and called me back, so I lost sight of it as it continued on down the South Coast."

The family gathered around the campfire to discuss the incident, and after they had all calmed down, Kevin went back into the lake to net some more prawns. At about 10 p.m. the wind had dropped and Fiona was still thinking about the previous sighting when she yelled out, "Quick, here it comes again!"

Kevin said, "I looked up to see an identical object hurtling towards us. While it travelled exactly the same trajectory and altitude as the first object, it was moving three times as fast, about 60 kilometres an hour. It was scary! The first object moved slower than the prevailing wind, and later, the second one moved really fast when there was no breeze at all! We quickly packed up and went home."

Kevin was a concrete truck driver, and after his workmates laughed at the story, he decided not to report it to anyone. The village shopkeeper was also editor of the local newspaper, and after he heard corroborating reports of other sightings he persuaded Kevin to pursue the matter.

Enquiries to *HMAS Albatross*, 50 to 60 kilometres to the north, disclosed that there were no flares, balloons or aircraft that night, and astronomers at Sydney Observatory ruled out space junk, meteorites or decomposing gases.

Batemans Bay, 4 July 1997

I received a call from a local policeman who was astounded to see, along with other witnesses, a totally unidentified object. Due to his training he provided a very exact description.

Gold or Orange

They turned White, Yellow, Blue, Red

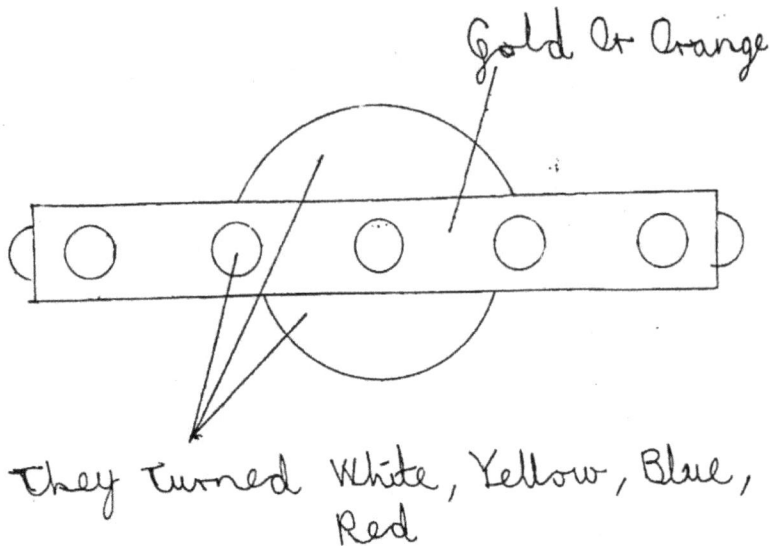

"I was so used to getting reports of those orange lights, which were the result of teenage pranks, that I was shocked and surprised to see a UFO here of all places!

"About 8 p.m. my attention was drawn to an aerial object coming around the point between Sunshine Bay and Caseys Beach. It was clearly outlined, flying slowly, in a level trajectory, at 150 metres altitude.

"It was a rectangular shape, about 30 feet long and 15 feet high. A gold or orange colour with an oblong centre and circular middle.

"There were five circular lights, which turned white, yellow, blue and red, along the middle of the craft. We watched for over 20 minutes as it went over Corrigans Beach, then turned right and disappeared to the northeast."

Bega, 13 June 1994

While this sighting was similar to many others, the later explanation was most interesting and informative. Ron was the first to ring us:

"Just before 7 p.m. I was with five other parents waiting to collect our children from a hockey match. We saw a bright, steady orange light about four kilometres away, at the height of a small plane but travelling much slower. It was about fifteen times the size of a star, round with fuzzy edges, and it was actually more of a burnt red, sodium vapour colour.

"It was moving east, but then stopped and hovered for a short while before heading south until it was out of sight over the horizon. There was no wind that evening, and we never heard any noise at all. During this display all the witnesses were getting very excited, and one raced down to the police station. In the meantime I went to the car and got my camera to take some photos.

"Our local constable came out, took a look, and called one of the detectives who also watched then said, 'The American ships must be exercising off-shore again.' I still kept taking my snaps, but wondered about government involvement when, 30 minutes later, we saw a military plane heading south at a very low altitude, which was very unusual for around here."

When I rang Ron back later his wife spoke to me, and while she also saw the object and testified to the accuracy of the report, was adamant that Ron and I should not follow-up the sighting. I wondered why, but respected her wishes.

A UFO suicide link?

One aspect of *The Gosford Files* which generated feedback from readers was the suggestion we made that an abnormally high level of suicides on the Central Coast in early 1996 might be linked to the increased UFO activity noted at that time. There is no evidence that there is any direct association between unidentified objects and suicides, however we cannot discount that our modern and alien technologies, with their new physics and unknown transmissions might affect vulnerable people.

I received a distressed call from John, a middle-aged family man, living in Queensland, which anecdotally relates directly to this observation. He reported that in about 1968, during school holidays, he and three other teenage friends had gone camping near Wollongong, on the NSW South Coast.

"It was a warm summer night, and we bunked down just below Brokers Nose, which is part of the Illawarra Escarpment Conservation Area. Sometime, during the early hours of the morning, we were woken by a brilliant, large white light hovering directly above us. My memories of that night are hazy, but without even discussing it, we inexplicably packed all our gear, and went home early! It was weird," John said, "none of us even spoke to each other or mentioned the strange light the next morning. Despite completing our education together, we never discussed the incident again."

The years passed by, and the boys went their separate ways. Each moved to a different part of Australia and settled down to normal family life. Then, suddenly, for no apparent reason, three of the four committed suicide between 1994 and 1996.

John was now the only surviving witness to that strange night so many years ago. He had suffered some personal problems over the intervening years, but since 1994 had experienced disturbing flashbacks of strange beings and medical testing procedures, which seemed to come from that incident in 1968.

John wondered, "Did my friends experience the same traumatic recollections, and did these memories contribute to their untimely deaths?"

It is well established that when people undergo events causing critical incident stress, long forgotten or suppressed memories often surface. After all these years, any relationship to the original UFO experience would normally be fairly slight. I cannot accept that it is mere coincidence, after 26-plus years, when three witnesses commit suicide and the fourth is beset with terrifying memories of the incident.

Another report from the same area indicates it may not be a good idea to camp in certain places on the NSW South Coast. A colleague had a heart-rending experience in 1982, on a family holiday, when he was only ten.

"We had camped below the Illawarra Escarpment at Coledale, but there was a cold snap, and we went back to the car to sleep. Dad and I were in the front seat and Mum in the back. Dad and I both woke up simultaneously at about 2 a.m. Our faces and arms felt as if boiling hot water was dripping all over us, it really stung!"

"We jumped out of the car and were astonished to see a brilliant white light, hovering low in the sky, directly overhead. It was huge, but after a short time it zoomed off across the sky and disappeared into a small dot within a few seconds. My father and I looked into the back seat of the car to see Mum sleeping peacefully, apparently undisturbed by the strange happening."

Over the next few days, Robert and his father developed bright red burnt skin on their arms, faces and other parts of their bodies which had been exposed that night. His mother seemed to be totally unaffected by the encounter. When describing the following events Robert became very emotional.

"Two weeks later, to the hour, minute and day, Mum suddenly died. She did not appear to be sick or anything. The doctor said it was a burst artery near the heart, caused by an inexplicable air bubble in the bloodstream.

No-one could understand it, she had not received any injections or medical treatment, or had she?"

Chapter Five

Barrington and New England, NSW

Barrington Tops and surrounds

Barrington Tops is the western wilderness section of the Hunter Valley region; lying north-west of Sydney, and due west of Newcastle. It has long been a source of mystery and speculation. Over the years planes have gone missing between Dorrigo and Barrington, as well as other parts of this rugged area. Despite bad weather conditions, and treacherous mists and terrain, some aircraft losses still remain unexplained.

Several local pilots have told us of strange magnetic anomalies affecting their instruments and navigational equipment. They are reluctant to fly over the area in adverse weather. One veteran pilot won't fly over the area at all. Often, Aboriginals won't go into these mountains. They avoid the surrounding areas – rugged granite country, which includes the Timor Caves and Mt. Yengo.

There have been many crashes and reports of strange lights pacing planes in the area, in a similar manner to reports received from motorists on the road.

Monkerai, 1996

Joan Aston of Monkerai recalled one night in late 1996, when she was standing in front of her farmhouse at about 10 p.m. "I heard the engine of a small plane and looked up into the north-eastern sky. I could see its flashing lights heading southward towards Williamtown and Newcastle. I could also see two constant white lights; one bright, one fainter, moving parallel to, and some distance from the plane. I only heard one engine, but the white lights were moving at exactly the same speed and at a constant distance from the aircraft, almost as if they were pacing it."

Taree

In 1996, a Taree South farmer contacted me. Mark said: "I was unloading my truck the other evening when I saw two distant, dim headlights, which I assumed were two planes heading towards Taree. An extremely fast light came across the sky from behind the aircraft, and when it came close to them, made a quick S-shape diversion behind and above them. I couldn't hear any noise, but kept watching. The object then made a 70-degree U-turn and headed straight back along its original flight path."

Bill Payne, a pilot, told us of a strange experience in 1994, in the mountains behind Taree: "I was about to land my light plane in a fairly remote location when I noticed a strange vibration in the air. At the time I did not pay too much attention to it. Shortly afterwards, while on the ground, an old chap approached me and asked if I had launched any balloons. I hadn't a clue what he was talking about until I turned around and saw a very strange object in the sky. It was certainly no balloon. It was football-shaped, somewhat like a "brilliant airborne submarine." As we just stared in amazement, it suddenly shot to the north and out of sight at incredible speed.

"I often fly from Sydney to Brisbane, and have sometimes seen inexplicable white lights near this general area. These were definitely unconventional. Another night I received a transmission from Sydney: 'Unidentified craft five miles to the south, change track or altitude'."

In the past …

Unusual phenomena and craft have been reported regularly, around Barrington for many years:

One hot summer night in the late 1940s, a Scone family was out on their lawn, cooling off, when they saw a group of about seven flat lights in a strung-out, rounded, triangular-shaped formation. The witnesses thought it could be one enormous object, as all the lights remained constant and moved in unison. It travelled slowly and silently, hovered, then shot up vertically at great speed.

Keith Basterfield of South Australia, documented a 1960 case near Newcastle, when a Belmont mother was woken by a buzzing sound. A bright light was shining through her bedroom window. A large object was sitting on the ground, about 20 metres away, in a paddock near the ocean cliffs. It was about five metres across and 1.3 metres high, shaped like a top. It glowed red and gold through a strange surface pattern. A light strip of panoramic window ran around the object, and on its apex a light, like a car's searchlight, rotated and projected a yellow-white beam.

As she watched through the window she saw a small humanoid figure, about three foot, nine inches tall, walking towards the house, as if looking for something. She shut the window and must have disturbed the entity, as it moved away. She woke her son, and both returned to the window, but the object had gone. All they could see was a large bright glowing spot about a mile away. It was moving slowly across the sky at a low altitude.

In 1964, a Mount George shop owner got the fright of her life. "We lived at the back of the hills. I was at the sink, washing up for the day, and looking out of the kitchen window in an absent-minded way. There was something floating out there. I couldn't believe it – a little man about three feet tall, sort of a grey-green-bluish colour. He was mid-air, I don't know if he was watching me. He just floated past the window and away!"

Barrington Tops

TAFE lecturer, Stephen Tregoar, and three friends were spotlighting for rabbits on his property about 10.20 p.m. one spring night during the mid-1970s. There was a half-moon low in the east over Cockadilly Mountain. Stephen alerted his mates to a second bright object to the south-west.

"It was clearly outlined, a very bright silver-yellow, the size of the full moon. 'If that's the moon in the east,' I said, 'then what the hell is that over there?' It was hovering, at about tree top level between us and the mountain, and making a strange high-pitched noise. We watched for quite a while. Then my mate decided to be brave, and turned the spotlight around to get a better look.

"We got a shock when it reacted! The yellowish glow went out, leaving a line of red dots, like windows, around the perimeter. It wasn't the RAAF, that's for sure. The noise was like a high-pitched whine, similar to the motor of an irrigation pump, and continued for several more minutes.

"Suddenly it moved and within a matter of seconds, travelled first northeast and then south so quickly it looked like a streak of red dots left in the sky. It disappeared behind the mountains towards Copeland, then south towards the Tea Gardens area. I asked a friend in the Air Force about it. He said they track UFOs on a regular basis, but this craft would have been well below radar level."

August 2001

A spate of unusual sightings occurred over ten-days near the Barrington Tops during August 2001:

On Friday 3 August, 2001, Warren Black was driving along the road when he saw a very bright, steady orange light about 500 metres away. It was about six feet in diameter, totally silent and very low. It came slowly from the northeast, as if drifting with the wind. It came over the road, then rose higher and went south.

While this object had some features suggesting a conventional explanation, there was no conclusive evidence either way. It may well be connected with much more spectacular sightings a week later.

The following Friday, 10 August, at about 8 a.m., Mary Locke was driving down a bushland road towards Taree. She lived on a large property in a valley at the foot of Barrington Tops: "I saw something weird, hovering low to the horizon, in the northwest sky. It was higher than the treetops, just above my eye level from the driver's seat. I pulled up to get a better look. It was a very shiny silver, the size of a grapefruit at arm's length, and shaped like an elongated light bulb.

The local school bus arrived, and the driver and all the kids got out and stood gawking in amazement for about ten minutes until it slowly disappeared behind the mountain.

"That evening at 5.45 p.m. I was driving back home from work with three passengers, and we saw a similar object, high above the mountain in the southwest. We all got out of the car and watched for some time. This was a slightly different shape and seemed to emanate flashes of light. To its right-hand side was a red-pink jet stream, which didn't seem to disperse like a normal contrail. It hovered over the mountain then simply vanished." She was unsure if it had just disappeared, out of view, behind the mountain.

Three days later on the following Monday, 13 August, a young boy woke due to a bright light shining through the curtained windows into his room. He got up and went into the lounge and peered out: "I saw a very large glowing ball of steady yellow light. It was hovering in the northeast over a dip in two mountains several kilometres away. I could see a surround of bright light, which flashed regularly over a minute."

Scott said after about ten minutes it either disappeared, or moved away very quickly. The next morning his family rang Williamtown Air Force Base near Newcastle. They could not provide any information, and advised that "the tower was not active at 3 a.m., and we do not give out any information."

Shortly after these events I received a call from Trevor Perry, a 59-year-old farmer, who owns a property in Barrington. He was a quiet, intelligent man, but he could find no rational explanation for what he had seen:

"I went outside to feed the dogs and have a cigarette, when I saw a flash of very bright white light. There was no noise or wind, so I was mystified as to what it might be, and walked around the house. I was stunned to see a 40 to 50 foot-diameter white light shining down on the ground from above. It was as bright as the sun, and only about 150 metres away. I couldn't see if there was any kind of craft or object above the light as I froze for a few seconds. Before I could get it together to investigate further, it moved away very quickly. It took no more than a couple of seconds to flash from west to east, 150 to 200 metres across the paddock."

Trevor assumed the only logical explanation was that the light was coming from some source in the clear night sky above. It all happened so quickly he didn't get a chance to determine what, if anything, was up there.

About that time I gave an interview on the local radio station, and one very irate farmer rang in. He didn't care for UFOs at all. A couple of nights before, one had landed in his vegetable crop. "It left a burnt circle and squashed my prize pumpkins. I was going to win first prize at the Show with the biggest one, and that bloody UFO flattened it!"

He was not a happy man, and while the poor radio host was trying to end the farmer's rants and raves on his live-to-air program, I was trying to suppress my bouts of inappropriate laughter becoming audible to the audience.

Singleton, 1996

Time and time again, unidentified craft show an interest if they detect a spotlight or flashing torch in the bush. Is it that they have realised people are around, or do they assume they are being signalled? Mike Appleton from Singleton shared a similar experience on his accountant's property at the end of the Hunter Valley in 1996.

"Four of us were spotlighting from a ute truck, and as we were driving along the top of the hills, we noticed a red light down in the valley. It was a dark night, and at first we thought it was the eyes of a fox. When it moved down the hill, my accountant decided it must be the back lights of a car, trespassing on his property.

"Just as we were about to give chase, the lights took off from the hill and straight up, on an angle, into the air. We were so astounded we tried to turn the spotlight onto it. It stopped and moved higher and closer, and each time we trained our spotlight onto the object, it would halt and then move closer.

"I don't know about the others, but I was getting scared. It was hard to discern the shape of the 'thing', but I could see two lights on it; one red and one orange. Suddenly, it disappeared upwards into some cloud cover."

Mike thought about it for a while. "We discounted the possibility of it being a helicopter; it didn't make any noise. We wondered about it being some sort of secret aircraft test, but doubted this because of the terrain."

Military connections?

There are times, I am sure, when some unidentified objects have a military origin. The answer was not so clear in 1972, when a group of soldiers were on a night-time training exercise near Singleton Army Base. One told me there was a sudden order yelled out. "Hit the ground, keep your heads down!"

"Something was moving slowly overhead, heading east towards the ocean. A few of us peeked and saw a very large spaceship thing, glowing a brilliant white. We were told quite bluntly that if we ever mentioned the incident, something quite nasty could happen to us."

In the last week of July 1998, residents of Stroud, Tingha, and Raymond Terrace reported an unusual triangle-shaped craft performing unconventional movements across the sky. Were they military tests? According to one witness, with extensive RAAF experience: "I've never seen anything like it before."

Glennies Creek, 1983

In 1983 Brenda Ford was living at Glennies Creek, to the northwest of Singleton, out towards Muswellbrook. One night her young daughter slipped in the bath and dislocated her knees. Brenda had to carry her to the car and rush her to hospital in Singleton.

"I was worried about Anna, who was in severe pain, and trying to concentrate on the dark bush road ahead. Without warning, a huge disc-shaped object rose up ahead, out of the scrub. It was huge, the size of a flattened two-bedroom house, and had a lot of yellow-orange lights all over it. I put my foot on the accelerator and kept going south, and breathed a sigh of relief when I looked in the rear vision mirror and saw it was moving away to the north.

"Suddenly it stopped and returned south, coming up fast behind my car. In sheer terror I sped up to a truck, and sheltered behind it all the way into Singleton. I was in a terrible state, and when we eventually arrived at the hospital, the doctor was more concerned about me than my daughter."

East Maitland, July 1997

On 28 July 1997 an East Maitland mother was taking her dog for a walk at about 8.45 p.m., when she saw a large steady, white light, with slight colour tinge, moving across the sky:

"As I turned for home, the light suddenly did a U-turn and headed back in the opposite direction. At first I was quite fascinated, but after it stopped dead in the sky, I realised it was getting bigger and brighter. The dog didn't take any notice, but I was starting to feel a bit scared as it seemed to be getting nearer. When it was quite close, it stopped and hovered. It was big and bright white, with a hint of blue and yellow around the outer edge.

"I felt a terribly cold, sinking feeling in my chest. Thank God the light receded soon afterwards and moved away on its original course. I got home and inside as quickly as possible, still feeling sick in the chest. The next morning I felt worse, with a burning-ticklish sensation in the same spot. I seemed to get sicker and sicker, and had to take a fortnight off work before I finally recovered."

Wingham, January 1998

It was 10 p.m. on 23 January 1998, and a Taree-based cab driver was taking a mother and her child to Wingham, when they spotted a light in the sky some distance away:

"A short time later my passenger wound down the window, and drew my attention to a strange craft, hovering overhead. I used to be in the Army Reserve, and said it was definitely not a plane or helicopter. It was a quite large square shape, a hollowed out centre at the bottom, with bright flashing red, green and blue lights. On the sides were pipe-like shapes, like rocket launchers, with iridescent lights along them, and it was making suction like sounds. I was excited, and slowed down to a crawl to get a better view. My young female passenger had become hysterical, so I reluctantly sped up and left the area as quickly as possible."

While this case was serious, it brought to mind more light-hearted circumstances from the outskirts of Sydney. A cab driver and his passenger were so excited – they had seen their first UFO hovering low over a sports oval nearby. "It was huge!" There was great publicity; their fifteen minutes of fame. Unfortunately it was not alien visitors. The pilot of an advertising blimp was hungry, and was hauling up his dinner order of pizzas from a colleague down below.

Lochinvar, May 2002

Lochinvar is a small town 50 kilometres south of the Barrington Tops, and we will probably never know what came down or crashed this day, or the origin of the strange lights frequently seen over the area – ours, foreign, or not of this world?

During 2000 and 2001 Karl Oscar had puzzled over the unusual lights he had often seen going overhead, mostly in a northerly direction. While having the appearance of stars or planets, but larger, their behaviour was not consistent with the International Space Station, satellites or normal air traffic. Having some expertise in the aviation industry, his interest was more that of curiosity at the time.

Events became a little closer to home on Tuesday, 21 May 2002 at 5.22 p.m. when he was helping his son fly a kite in the parkland at the bottom of their street.

"A very bright, shiny white burning fireball (with flames), the size of, or larger than the moon, came from out of nowhere. It just appeared. It was on fire, with large, white flames, as long as they were wide, all over the inside, and outside surrounding it. The leading edge seemed to be nearly flat. We both saw it appear in the northern sky at about a 40 degree angle to the horizon. We watched as it moved in a straight trajectory to the south, covering roughly 60 degrees of the sky in about four seconds.

"It disappeared behind a poplar tree, and we are not sure what happened next because the next thing we noticed was two strange, black, pod-shaped objects, flying in the same direction. We assumed they came from the original object, and after a couple of seconds they started to lose altitude and descended at an angle of 5 to 10 degrees. They were large; a sort of squashed-egg shape. We stared at each other in total amazement, then jumped up and down with excitement.

"We looked around, but there was no-one else in the street to verify what we saw. We went home to tell the rest of the family, then sat on the back steps, waiting to see if anything else interesting would appear in the sky. We didn't have to wait long. By this time it was 5.45 p.m., and over the next 20 minutes we noticed several star-like objects – not planes, making unusual movements across the sky.

"At 6.15 p.m. we saw a very large plane with all its lights on – green and red starboard and port landing lights, and a huge spotlight being shone around. It looked like an Air Force plane – possibly a C130, as its tail was swept up high, like those that can load vehicles in the back. It was soon joined by some smaller planes which kept to the south and the east.

"I concluded they must be looking for the pods, but then got the shock of my life. Exactly whose pods were they? Coming low overhead, and then moving to the northeast, at an altitude of 500 to 750 metres, was a silent disc-shaped craft close to 30 metres across.

"The next day my son and I spent several hours driving around in the general area where we thought the pods had landed. We were looking for any evidence of a crash, like burnt tree tops,

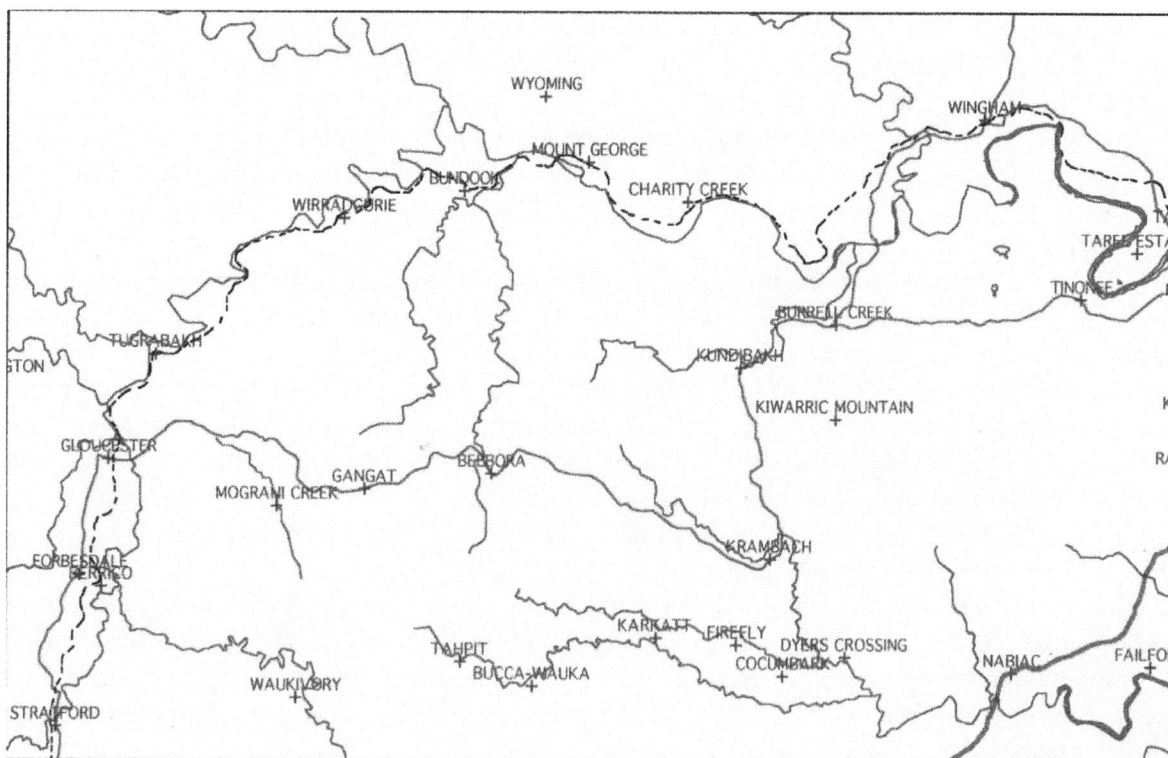

ruts in the ground, or broken fences, etc. The only thing we found out of the ordinary, was at a swamp next to a road on private property. There was a gouge through the top of the trees with freshly broken limbs and some trees snapped off at around 20 to 25 feet above the waterline.

"There was no sign of any debris, burnt areas, furrows in the ground or splashes of mud to support any kind of crash, and we realised that we hadn't actually seen any smoke or explosion when it disappeared from view. My 13-year-old son claims he saw three pods come out of the white fiery object before it definitely exploded, still in mid-air."

This was one case where I couldn't help speculating. I wondered; three pods coming from a large object just before it explodes? Our own planes apparently searching, a large disc later passing overhead. Were they escape pods, and if so, whose?

Krambach

In 1996-1997 Jimmy Martin was a quiet man, employed as caretaker-manager on a remote hobby farm of several thousand acres, in Krambach. He also kept an eye on neighbouring properties, the nearest over two kilometres away, with some sheep and cattle, which also had city owners (*Pitt Street farmers*, as they are locally called). His accommodation comprised a caravan and shed – no electricity, just his trusty generator.

One night, in 1996, Jimmy saw what he thought was a meteor going over Tipperary Mountain. "It didn't go down, it just hovered over the mountain as a huge, bright white light, with smaller gold lights going in, out, and around it." Over the next few weeks Jimmy watched strange objects and lights in the remote night skies. Sometimes they would hover, then take off very fast if a plane came by. Originally he tried to contact them telepathically, with his mind.

"Occasionally they would be high overhead. At that time I had this strange experience. I'm sure I was outside. Maybe it was a dream, because I woke up in my bed, shaking. I went into a golden light, and was floating in the air above my shed. I heard a voice behind me, it said, 'if you go up you will never come back,' and I got frightened.

"Sometimes the dog would run away and hide, or the animals would be spooked. I also noticed unusual military activities in the area – helicopters with detector antennae, planes and jets."

Initially, he took some photos with an instamatic camera, which the film-processing laboratory claimed they had lost. (This particular company has a long history of losing UFO

75

photographs.) He bought a much better camera and over the next few months proceeded to take over 600 photos of strange lights in the sky, some of which he sent to an overseas magazine, and which they featured in their publication.

It became apparent Jimmy had become obsessed, and had sat outside on many nights, taking photos and drinking beer to calm his nerves. To his credit, he kept a comprehensive diary, and records of the dates, times and general direction of the objects. When he contacted me he had literally fled the farm and sobered up.

"I was starting to get really frightened. I found a couple of dead cattle with weird cut marks and injuries. There were others on nearby farms. My dog went missing for good. It was all too much. My family was so concerned, I went back home."

Jimmy had many rolls of negatives, and hundreds of prints, which were totally mixed up and out of order. He didn't trust anyone, and had them developed at the local One-hour laboratory. As a result, some were of bad colour and quality. Further, the leg on his camera tripod had been broken and wobbly, and many shots had been given too much time exposure.

My colleague, Glenn Land, worked for many months analysing the photographs. While about 15 or 20 snaps were not readily identifiable, most appeared to correspond with Jupiter or other astronomical bodies. In order to verify our findings we travelled several hundred kilometres to an observatory to seek the advice of professional astronomers. Our findings were confirmed. However, our advisors were astounded and said that: "Photographs like these, especially of Jupiter, could only be taken from the Hubble Space Telescope, certainly not from the earth's surface, with Jimmy's camera."

While the astronomers were convinced of some strange anomaly which they would like to explore further, one of our colleagues, Mike Lang Davis, offered another possible explanation: He suggested that due to the topography, certain wind conditions could cause a swirling motion in hilly country, theoretically creating an atmospheric lens, kilometres in dimension. This explanation would be highly dependable on weather conditions at the time, and subject to great variance.

We had another meeting with Jimmy, who came to Sydney with his friend Adrian. Adrian told us that he was "going to make sure Jimmy made some money out of the pictures." They were not happy with our findings. At one stage Adrian even suggested we change the accompanying dates and information in the diary.

We tried to explain to them that while a lot of the photos were of Jupiter, they were very special, and we wanted to investigate the phenomenon further. Perhaps there were some strange energies or other unknown factors in the area. Jimmy was not impressed, and told us he had contacted other ufologists, but was only giving partial information to each – creating more problems all around.

He had become quite obsessed with the entire sequence of events, and suggested we were about to use his precious photos for our own benefit.

We therefore returned all of them and suggested he find another researcher. Under the circumstances we felt it was the only ethical course of action. Jimmy's preoccupation with his experiences was bordering on instability, which was concerning to us and his relatives.

Jimmy was a nice man, and we genuinely believed something unusual had happened on that property. We would have liked to continue working on the remaining unidentified photos, and delve further into his reports of unusual dreams and premonitions since his original sighting. He displayed many of the traits that investigators see in contactees and experiencers, which arise from the stress and strangeness associated with such events. It was a sad ending for what could have been a very interesting investigation.

The ufologist's life is not always an easy one!

Animal mutilations

Bizarre incidents have been reported from time to time in the Taree-Barrington area. Reports, such as Jimmy Martin's, of dead cattle in 1994 and 1995, revealed that on some remote properties, shielded by surrounding mountains, animal mutilations had occurred. Local farmers were perplexed; they had never seen a dingo leave such smooth, bloodless incisions:

Looking into the old files, I uncovered an incident from 1972, which was researched by Bill Moser and Michael Guider. Initial reports were of a white light, which experts identified as Venus. Locals were not convinced, and thought it was an object from outer space. After that sighting, reports started coming in of an unknown beast, slaughtering all manner of stock from sheep and lambs to domestic cats and aviary birds.

Intriguingly, while locals did not dispute a commonly held belief that aliens or black ops were abducting or mutilating their livestock, they also insisted that a creature referred to as the *Taree Tiger* or *Taree Terror* had been dropped by a UFO.

By definition, there is a great difference between the frenzied, ragged injuries produced by a wild beast and the precise laser-type cuts found in animal mutilations (usually in cattle), and attributed to something other. And there have been many reports from around the world, that link large, potentially dangerous, hairy creatures with UFOs. Our investigations uncovered both laser-type animal mutilations and more ferocious-type attacks, which suggest more than one species of culprit.

I thought of a report we had recently received from Jack at Stanthorpe, just north of the New South Wales–Queensland border, detailing strange creatures, and how they were similar to the Barrington stories. In 1987, one stockman had seen a UFO while mustering. Some fellow farmers had been hunting dingos or a pack of wild dogs that had been killing young cattle, and he had wondered if aliens might be involved, instead.

The dingo-posse thought they had tracked down the culprits, but were at a loss when they came across a set of unusual footprints in mud. One commented that he had lived on the land all his life, was familiar with all wildlife prints, and had never seen anything like it. The tracks were of a foot or hand, with four long digits, thinner than normal. The distance between each imprint was at least four feet, flat to the ground, and only one-quarter of an inch deep. After 20 feet, they stopped abruptly. Where had this creature gone? Was it earthly or alien? We will never know.

Investigators could not find one eyewitness to actual dingo attacks, but could not refute the evidence of one very credible witness: A Shire Council engineer had recently suffered two attacks on his aviaries, which were so heavily built it took two or three strong people to move them. The unknown beast had moved the cage a distance of two feet, and gone straight through the wire over four feet off the ground.

Is it merely co-incidental that inexplicable attacks on animals have occurred in two periods – 1972 and the mid-nineties, when unusual white lights were also reported hovering in the vicinity?

In his book *Bunyips and Bigfoots*, Malcolm Smith outlined several incidents over the previous 20 years near Krambach. There, witnesses had described a large hairy creature, very tall, which could run very quickly. In many ways it resembled traditional descriptions of the fabled Yowie. However, this creature displayed aggressive tendencies if disturbed.

One woman reported that the creature emitted a high-pitched scream. It was rumoured a local farmer saw the monster disturb his animals one night, but it fled before he could get close. Another creature sighting was reported from Oxley Island on the Manning River in 1977, and a week later the family found their 1500-gallon water tank overturned and huge footprints all around.

A friend recounted to me the experience of his mate Jack, a rough, tough wharfie, who had gone on a shooting trip to Broken Castle Mountain, south of Gosford. After dark he set up his campervan, and was enjoying a bite of supper, when he heard a grunt behind him. He swung around, thinking it might be a wild pig, and saw an eight-foot human shape in trees 60 feet away.

"It takes a lot to scare a bloke like him, but he just fled, leaving everything behind. He showed me the mess that whatever it was had made of his vehicle. The headlights were broken and the bull-bar was all twisted up. It would take enormous strength to do that!"

Two schoolgirls reported a couple of terrifying occasions when they were out riding their horses on a hillside above Krambach. Janice was once startled to see a creature sitting on a rock a few feet away. Her horse reared up and the grey thing stood up and started coming towards her:

"It was bigger than my 14-hands horse. Most of its face was covered by hair and the rest of its body had human-like skin covered with long dark hair." As she rode away she could hear thumping sounds behind her, "like it was chasing me."

Other children claim they've heard it let out a "terrible high-pitched scream," if sighted. When they were swimming in a local creek, it made loud noises and threw heavy rocks at them, before rushing away into the bushes.

Researcher Rex Gilroy has also detailed many sightings of strange Yowie-type creatures, and giant footprints, as far back as 1842 near Wingham, and 1850 near Harrington. Sightings near Taree were reported in 1990-92, with giant footprints found near Wingham in 1993.

New England District, NSW

Llangothlin, 19 October 1975

This case was first investigated by myself and my colleague Bryan Dickeson.

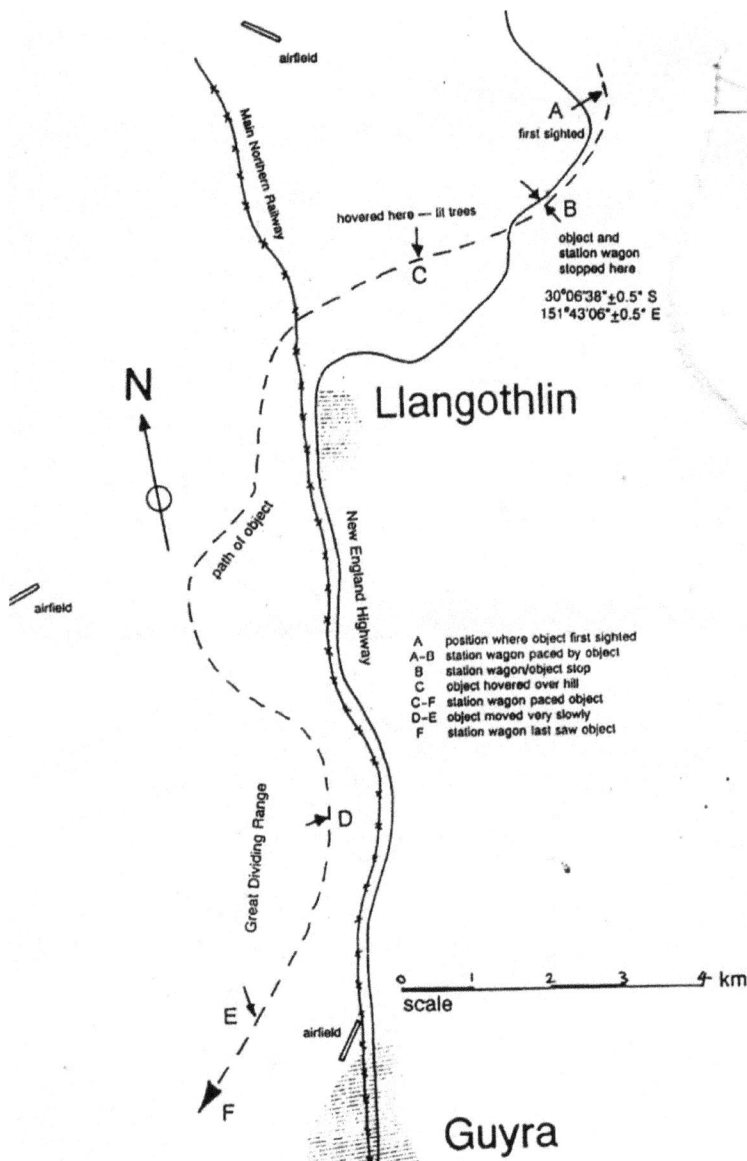

A   position where object first sighted
A-B   station wagon paced by object
B   station wagon/object stop
C   object hovered over hill
C-F   station wagon paced object
D-E   object moved very slowly
F   station wagon last saw object

Adele Morgan and her husband Gerry were motoring home to Armidale after attending a one-day dog show in Inverell. It was around dusk, about 6 p.m., and although it was a fine, clear cloudless evening, the weather was cool. They had wound the windows of the station wagon up, and put on the car heater.

"I had just turned on the headlights," said Gerry. "Adele was napping in the seat next to me, and our young Samoyed dog was asleep on the back seat. We were travelling down the New England Highway. I had just turned on the headlights, and after passing Glen Innes the road went on a fast downhill right-hand turn, four to six kilometres north of Llangothlin. I suppose I was doing between 110 and 120 kilometres per hour.

"I noticed a very bright, creamy-white light rising up over a hill directly to our left. It cleared the hill some 15 to 20 metres above road level, and descended at a slight angle until it was parallel to us between the road and the side of the hill. It was so bright it lit up the inside of our vehicle.

"I yelled out: 'What the bloody hell...!' This and the bright light woke up Adele. The dog yelped and climbed over to the front seat onto her knee. He was going crazy; very hard to control, and was frantically trying to hide, by burying his muzzle in her lap."

Adele continued "I was a little disorientated at first, and thought that a large truck was trying to pass us. Gerry slowed down to about 40kph and we had a good look at the source of the light, which was about 25 to 30 metres away. It came from a long cigar-shaped object, with a bright silvery sheen – like the back of a new, unpainted, aluminium road sign. It was about 50 to 55 metres long, and had short, thick stubby wings and a large front, lighted cockpit window.

"It had lots of brightly-lit windows down the side, behind the cockpit – six large and five smaller above them. We could clearly see into the cockpit, where three figures, visible from the hips up, were standing and looking directly at us. Another two were sitting down, towards the nose of the craft, in white-backed chairs – a bit like lounge chairs. They were clearly humanoid, Caucasian skin colour, pretty normal – faces long in shape, hair light (blond). Human in all respects. All were wearing silver-coloured overalls from the neck down. I couldn't see any gloves or helmets."

Gerry was taking particular note of the craft and the inside of the cockpit cabin. "It was full of 'instrument panels' with dozens of green, blue and red lights, some of them pulsating. There were no visible markings on the object and no apparent landing gear. The two seated figures seemed to be 'operators' or 'pilots' and they kept turning their heads and glancing towards us. Directly in front of them, they had two large red pulsating lights, with a regular period of about five seconds between pulses.

"Between two of the standing figures (about six feet tall), was a shorter 'person' (maybe 5 feet 8 inches) who was pointing at our station wagon, and laughing, possibly at the antics of the dog.

"It appeared to be a female, with shoulder-length brownish, fair hair and 'bumpiness' in the right places. 'She' seemed to be in charge, and there were three horizontal stripes on the left shoulder of her overalls. The three standing figures seemed to be smiling, and the 'woman' waved. They definitely seemed friendly, but amused at our predicament."

The object seemed to be closely pacing the station wagon. Firstly when Gerry slowed to 40kph, then a little later when he sped up to 70 to 80kph. It moved alongside of them, to the left of the road, at the same level for about three kilometres. It floated some 18 to 30 metres above the ground, which sloped steeply away from the road, not unlike an ocean liner trying to overtake the car. There was a faint bluish-red jet coming from the tail, and occasionally a tree passed

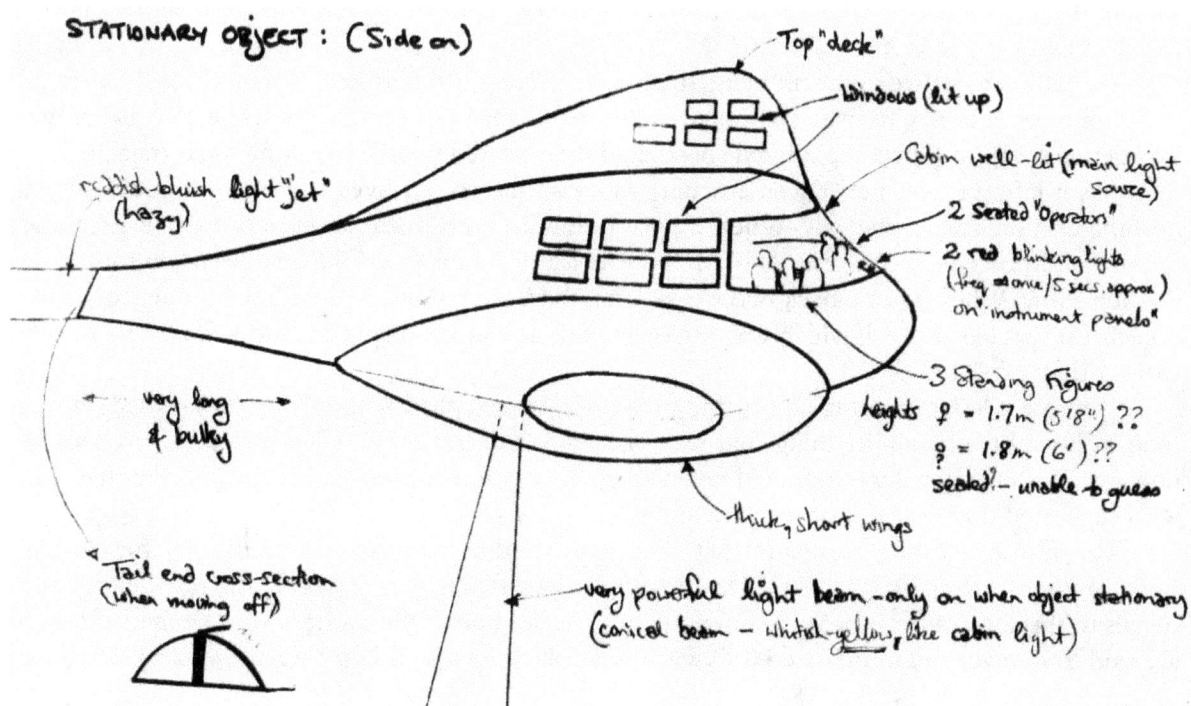

STATIONARY OBJECT: (Side on)

79

PRESUMED 'TOP VIEW' OF OBJECT:

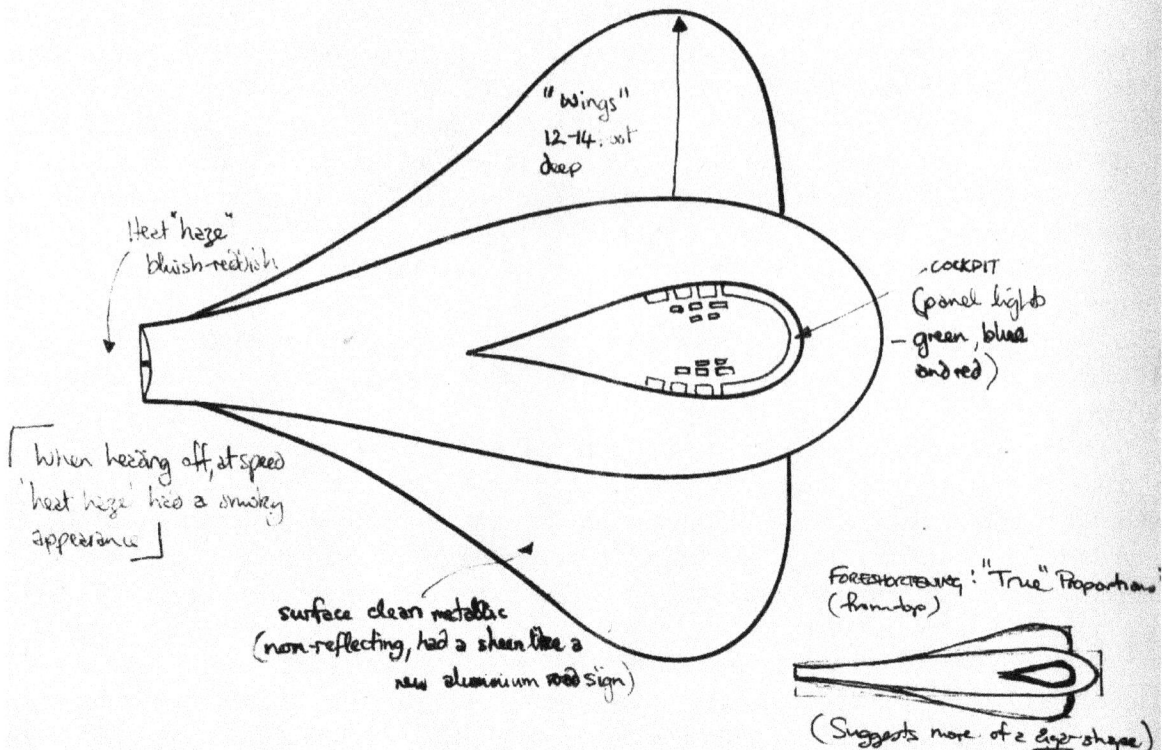

"wings"
12-14. xt
deep

Heat "haze"
bluish-reddish

COCKPIT
(panel lights
- green, blue
and red)

When heading off, at speed
'heat haze' had a smoky
appearance

surface clean metallic
(non-reflecting, had a sheen like a
new aluminium road sign)

FORESHORTENING: "True" Proportions
(from top)

(Suggests more of a egg-shape)

between them and the object. Eventually, Gerry kept slowing the car down until he stopped altogether at the side of the road.

"That object, which had been keeping pace, also stopped and hovered, and when it did, a sharp-edged, cone-shaped light came on halfway along and below the main body. I had never seen anything remotely like this before, so I got out of the car, took my movie camera and shot several sequences of the craft which was hovering almost silently, except for a very faint hissing sound. Adele remained in the car with the dog, which was still a bit upset."

After hovering for about twelve minutes, the craft moved silently down the left-hand-side of the road, then crossed over and climbed west at a steep angle until it was about 600 metres above a hill to the right, less than a kilometre from the road. The cone of light illuminated the trees below "as clear as day."

The Morgans drove home, noticing the object still kept pace, from a distance, for the next 20 to 30 minutes over five to twelve kilometres. It moved ahead of them for a while, and about two kilometres south of Guyra it gathered speed, and disappeared westwards along a flat trajectory.

"As it left, we have never seen anything move so fast in our lives. Adele and I could talk of nothing else the rest of the way. When we got home we both made notes and drew diagrams of the object. I posted my film directly to Melbourne for developing, as I had earlier taken footage at the dog show. When it came back two weeks later, there were none of the filmed sequences of the object. I inspected the reel, which was no longer full. It had been spliced, and it was 14 to 16 feet shorter than expected.

"I wrote a letter of complaint to the processor, who replied with a form letter saying it was their policy not to print anything that was obscene or detrimental. They included two rolls of unexposed film. Several weeks later I received an anonymous phone call from an unknown man who suggested that we had not seen anything!"

The film-processing company that doctored Martin's footage was notorious for 'losing' photographic material showing UFOs and unusual craft. Had they passed on his identity and details to the authorities, or was the unknown male caller one of the mysterious men in black, who are said to contact and intimidate UFO witnesses following a sighting? Given the facts, it is hard to determine whether the craft was extraterrestrial, one of our high-tech vehicles, or one from a foreign nation.

During December 1994, UFO Research (NSW) took part in the sixth Sydney *Mind, Body Spirit Festival* week at Darling Harbour in Sydney. Their display booth included an enlarged, but *untitled* diagram of this Llangothlin craft. One day, while Bryan Dickeson was rostered on the stall, a middle-aged woman stopped, pointed to the Llangothlin diagram and said: "I've seen that one, in northern New South Wales, some years ago." When prompted, she said that it would have been in October, or possibly November in 1975 as she had only migrated to Australia a few weeks beforehand. She wasn't prepared to provide further details as she was on her lunch break, and moved back into the crowd!

Tingha, 29 July 1998

It was after dark, 9.25 p.m., when Dave Smith was in his back garden and an unusual light in the northern sky caught his eye:

"I looked carefully, and at first could make out a long white light with a blue tinge, at about 35,000 feet, travelling slowly from west to east. I realised it was some form of craft, but it was huge, at least six times the size of a jumbo jet, and was not following the usual RAAF or civilian flight paths. Its trajectory became a little erratic when it reached the north-eastern sky, but it straightened up, then banked and turned. I was able to get a much better look.

"I have never seen anything like it! It was a huge white triangle, with four or five big dark areas on each side of the wings. It was travelling apex first, and the sides were shorter than the base, so it wasn't equilateral. It flew towards me, through some cloud, then overhead, but I couldn't hear any noise.

"It went through some more cloud to the southwest, and then was going back to the northwest, at a lower altitude, to its original position. I know the military may have new technology craft, but I doubt if they would be anything as gigantic as this object."

Quirindi, 10 August 1998

This incident attracted a lot of publicity, due to its unusual nature, and involved a co-operative effort by several researchers. While some readers may be aware of the identity of the witnesses, I will adhere to my normal policy of giving them pseudonyms.

At about 1 p.m. on a cool, late-winter's day, Enid Stanton and her daughter Nellie were relaxing in the garden after lunch. Nellie was stretched out on the garden bench looking up at the clear sky.

As Enid returned from taking their empty teacups back to the kitchen, she heard Nellie remark: 'That's going bloody fast!'

"I looked up to where Nellie was pointing," Enid said, "and saw a silvery ball moving quickly across the sky from north to south, disappearing over the roof of the house. It was about the size of a cricket ball to the eye, and bright in the sun's reflection.

"We both went around to the front of the house to see where it had gone. My husband Martin was nailing some shade-cloth to the front veranda and we called out to him to "have a look at the flying ball", but he was busy with his electric saw and didn't take any notice.

We watched the sphere hovering in the sky to the south, and saw two more metallic balls in the southeast, travelling east to west to join the first. Other pewter-coloured balls began to appear and joined the group. They tended to mostly arrive from or depart to the north and east in waves, until there were about twenty craft moving around in the sky.

"One big sphere, about one-and-a-half-times larger than the others, approached the group from the south. As it got closer, it turned slightly on its side. It was actually two spheres connected, or tethered by a dull grey, pewter-coloured horizontal rod – like a dumb-bell shape. In the middle of the connecting rod there was a small cylindrical section, with vertical vanes or struts running to the bright, metallic chrome outer spheres. A second, identical object, later took up a parallel

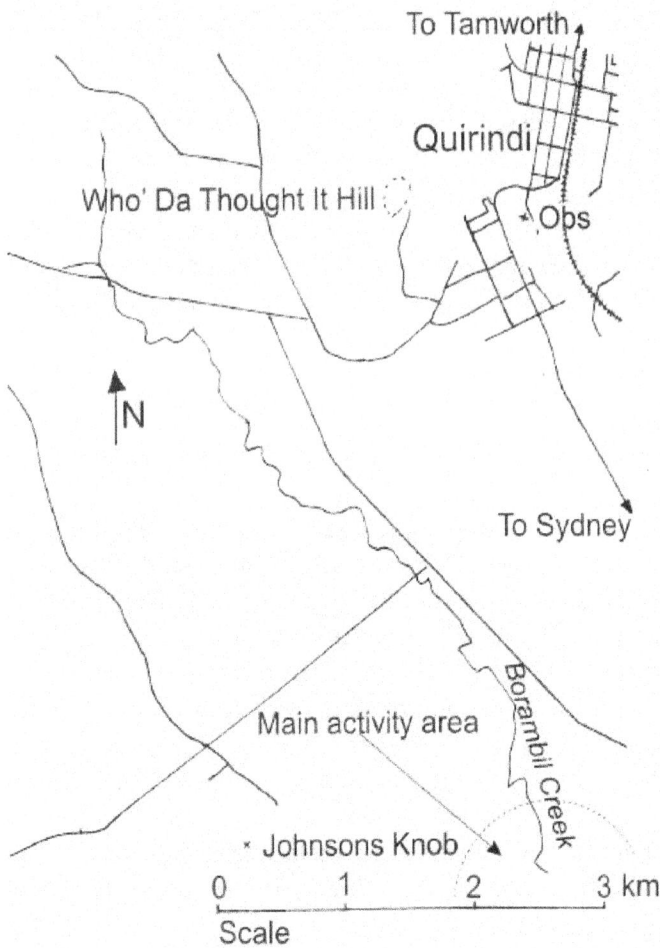

position, behind and slightly above the first. For most of the time they hovered in the same part of the sky, and did not move around as much as the smaller spheres."

By this time Martin had noticed the spheres himself. He turned the saw off and placed it on the veranda floor. It then turned itself back on, and despite surge protectors, after several attempts to turn it off, Martin had to unplug it from the extension cord before it would stay off. (My colleague Bryan Dickeson has suggested this may be due to the flying objects inducing sufficient electrical energy in the electric cord to run the power saw.)

Martin looked closely at the objects. "I am a retired combat pilot, and am familiar with conventional aircraft overflying the area. At first I thought they must be helicopters, but the dumb-bells, 170 metres across, were too big and their movements too different. I watched for about fifty minutes. Up to twenty spheres covered most of the sky with ever-increasing complex manoeuvres, which were highly co-ordinated, and included right-angle turns and slow, even movements abruptly turning to very fast. I saw at least one of the smaller spheres fly at speed up to and into one of the big dumb-bells and just vanish. Another headed directly towards a stationary dumb-bell, on a collision course, executed a right-angle turn, and swerved, passed right through the dumb-bell and came out unchanged on the other side. (Bryan Dickeson comments that, at present, this passing-through phenomenon is only thought to be physically possible for extremely small, quantum or sub-atomic objects and in very special circumstances, not for larger bodies.)

"The smaller spheres began jumping from side to side, fading-out in one location then fading back into view nearby, before eventually they all disappeared. At one stage one of the dumb-bells had taken up position about 500 metres directly overhead. It then flew directly upwards to a height of 50,000 to 60,000 feet, higher than any interstate jets, and vanished."

There are three aspects to this incident which I will explore individually:

Firstly, there were the objects which all three witnesses watched for a total of 90 minutes.

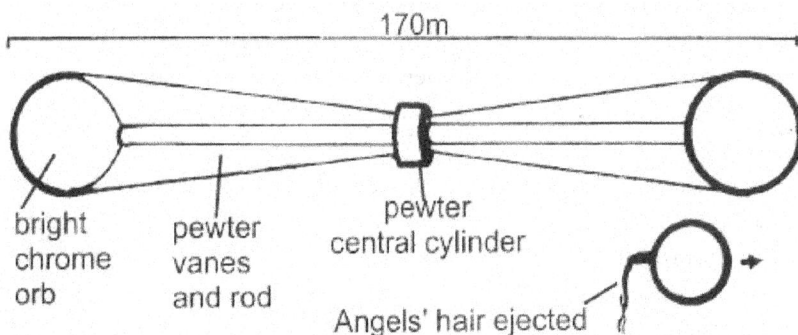

Martin was certainly a qualified witness, he got an excellent view when a dumb-bell was overhead, and his description is very detailed. (Ufologist Barry Taylor, who lived in Grafton at the time, suggested an alternative –

82

that the joining rod and large orbs may not have been one dumb-bell, but three separate objects. Ten months later, in June 1999, he videoed similar objects which were two separate orbs and a cylinder. Regardless, they were certainly nothing conventional and could not be identified.)

Secondly, there was a strange substance being ejected by the objects. While they could not see any exhaust from the spheres when they flew in a straight line, when they were manoeuvring they could see a light, whitish material steaming out of the back of the craft and falling downwards. This phenomenon is often referred to as "angels' hair."

"It appeared to clump in long substantial strands as it fell downwards," said Nellie. "It landed on trees, telephone lines, surrounding areas and a nearby street. There was very little wind to blow it away, and I first retrieved a 30-centimetre strand from a nearby bush. It was whitish, and although very light, also strong – like cotton, requiring a slight tug to break. It soon dissolved away when I handled it, so I found a second piece, about 90 centimetre long, made of two separate strands, which I immediately put into a clean yoghurt container, sealed with plastic film and a rubber band."

A Telstra technician routinely checking the Piallaway telephone exchange, 40 kilometres north of Quirindi reported that at 2 p.m. that day he noticed masses of white cob-web like material falling down around him from a clear blue sky. It landed on the telephone lines, fences, bushes and even his car. He was quite mystified, and could not see anything up in the sky to explain it. He also found it evaporated fairly quickly when handled.

There was a third aspect to this incident. While Enid was watching the display she moved around the outside of the house, following the aerobatics – "I was looking towards the sun, and noticed something strange. The sun itself appeared to be surrounded by an unusual, complicated white and yellow lace-like pattern. It was very beautiful. At first I thought it might be caused by the white substance the spheres were putting out during their manoeuvres, but there were very few strands in that part of the sky, and the lacework pattern, centred on the sun, was very pronounced.

"I also realised that while closely watching the spheres I had inadvertently been looking directly into the sun. I had felt no pain or harm to my eyes – I wasn't even temporarily blinded."

I would like to reproduce Bryan Dickeson's report on the lace-sun pattern:

"This phenomenon has also been associated with BVM (Blessed Virgin Mary) manifestations at places like Fatima, and more recently at Medjugorje (in Croatia). The sun can be looked at and appears to be surrounded by a corona or zone of patterned or coloured light.

"For Quirindi and in scientific terms, this is very probably a three-dimensional Moire pattern caused by the superposition (constructive and destructive interference) of powerful, fluctuating magnetic fields produced by the objects flying and hovering around the area. It provides some extremely interesting insights into how these objects do what they do.

"To my knowledge this effect has never been observed at an entirely ufological event previously, and in some detail. The Stantons did not attach any religious significance to the event, and Enid thought it was just something that was unexpected, which others might find interesting."

During all this weird aerial activity Enid thought she should notify someone in authority, and Telstra's Directory Service advised her to ring a commercial UFO hotline, which she did. After five minutes of speaking to the operator, at $3.20 per minute, she advised him of her phone number, and said he could ring her back if he wanted any further information. Instead of calling back, he immediately sent a general news release to the AAP-Reuters network, with Enid's phone number, and within minutes her phone started ringing non-stop.

Some of the journalists also contacted me at the INUFOR hotline, and because they had been given a misspelt surname for the Stantons, it took me until the next day to locate and speak to the family. I conducted a long initial telephone interview with Enid, and persuaded her to send me Nellie's sample of the angels' hair, intact in the yoghurt container. I only discovered later that when they had checked the sample it had shrunk to something "smaller than a match-head." (This is actually consistent with other genuine angels' hair reports.)

However, Nellie, not realising she was contaminating the original sample, went outside and collected some more similar white fibre she found sticking to a car aerial. She put this into the container and posted it to me on 12 August.

In the meantime I had contacted Bryan Dickeson, and he and researcher Peter Turner, (UFORNSW), also rang Enid and conducted in-depth interviews. (They visited Enid and her family in person some weeks later, and found them to be very hospitable, intelligent and ethical country people, who were a bit overwhelmed by all the attention.) As soon as I received the sample, I placed it in my freezer, and we all agreed that the most suitable researcher to analyse it was Bill Chalker, who collected it on 15 August.

Bill has access to commercial laboratory chemical sampling facilities, and was hoping to analyse the material or the atmosphere inside the container using gas chromatography. Having contacted Enid for details about the incident, he first viewed it with a video-imaging microscope. This showed the sample greatly magnified on a television monitor, and allowed it to be compared with a sample of spider web from Bill's garden. The two were so similar that it seemed Nellie's later addition from the car aerial had been spider's web.

Any further analysis of the sample would have been expensive and inconclusive.

Angels' hair

This is not the only case of angels' hair reported in Australia. In 1961 newspapers carried a report from ten independent witnesses near Meekatharra, 480 miles northeast of Perth.

This involved a total of twelve round, silvery objects, about 9,000 feet in altitude, which flew directly over Mount Hale Station, at regular intervals, between 8.20 and 9.15 one morning. They emitted a "tangible white trail of mesh-like streamers" which floated down to the ground. One witness commented, "They crumbled and disappeared when we picked them up. They just vanished in my hands as they touched my skin."

Angels' hair has some historical significance, having been reported in the

---

An international phenomenon

Good friend and fellow researcher, Sylvie Hoenig, of UFOLINX, kindly made the following reports from France available. One cannot ignore the similarities to the Quirindi incident, in Australia, some 46 years later:

On 17 October, 1952, an unusual object was observed by the local school principal in the village of Orolon, Sainte Marie. It was tilted at an angle of 45 degrees, white, with white smoke or cloud detaching itself from the top. It was travelling at an altitude of about 2-3,000 feet, and about 30 smaller 'domed saucers' were following it, at the same speed and altitude. They seemed to be travelling in pairs, in swift zig-zag movements, and each pair was linked with what was described as an 'electric arc'. These objects left long trails of threadlike substance, which detached itself and floated slowly to the ground, landing on rooftops, trees, street lamps and telephone wires. The threads looked like strands of nylon or finely-spun wool, but when touched became gelatinous, vaporised and disappeared.

The official explanation was 'threads left by spiders, millions of spiders', which angered many residents. The furore had almost died down when ten days later an almost identical event occurred in Gaillac, a little town in the south of France. This time there were only twenty of the smaller objects, which came closer to earth, at an altitude of about 1,500 feet. There were also about 100 witnesses, including two police officers. The threads that had again been left behind were likened to 'glass wool'.

past. During one of the Fatima manifestations of the Blessed Virgin Mary, light white fibrous material was seen to fall on the assembled crowd from a glowing sphere in the sky, (a "second sun"). This sublimated very quickly, and was colourfully referred to afterwards by some as "white rose petals."

Bryan Dickeson and I finally produced a comprehensive report of the Quirindi incident, and included below is his description and analysis of angels' hair and how it differs from spider web:

"Extensive spider web falls (gossamer) are often reported in nature, and have been confused with angels' hair in the past. If you get a population explosion of small spiders in a particular area, during ideal seasonal conditions, the spiders synchronously extrude a long length of web from their abdomen which is lifted on the wind, acting like a parachute, to disperse the spiders to a new area. The web is then discarded and can form a silvery mass on vegetation etc. Spiders' web is a protein which is chemically much more stable than angels' hair.

"Reports of angels' hair are fairly common from the 1950s and 60s, but only rarely reported since then. When fresh, it is white or bluish-white, finely fibrous and breaks easily, a bit like a fine cotton wool. It quickly ages by dissolving back into the atmosphere, (that is, by sublimating from a solid to a gas, without an intermediate liquid stage). The fibres tend to coalesce and a mass of fibres may have a shiny or glossy white surface. Touching it seems to hasten the sublimation process (presumably due to a chemical reaction with the oils and acids on the human skin). It rarely persists longer than one or two hours.

"During the 1950s, investigators proposed that angels' hair was a polymer comprised mostly of an air mixture of nitrogen, oxygen and water vapour, and was created by the unusually high-frequency electromagnetic and plasma effects presumed to exist near some UFOs (especially spinning discs) and under certain atmospheric conditions. Angels' hair was thought to form when rotating magnetic fields near UFOs create highly directed, 180 degree and metastable nitrogen-oxygen bonds. These bonds link up into long polymers or fibres around a quickly rotating body such as a disc or a sphere, or in air squeezed through a magnetic field generated in the central cylindrical section of a bar-magnet-type field. (This is often referred to as the 'fairy floss' model, for obvious reasons.)

"The metastable chemical bonds quickly break down under normal conditions, so that the fibres transform back into air and water vapour. This hypothesis still has to be properly tested in a laboratory.

"At Quirindi, angels' hair was seen to stream out from behind the manoeuvring spheres."

Chapter Six

Canberra, ACT; Southern Highlands and Blue Mountains, NSW

Canberra and the Southern Highlands

North of Bungendore, 1971-72

Late one Friday night, Henrietta and her friend Paula were driving from Sydney to spend a weekend in Canberra. They had taken an alternative route from the highway at Goulburn – a two-lane country back road, which went through the small town of Bungendore.

"There was no other traffic around, but it was late – 11 p.m., and dark. We were only going about 50mph. We still hadn't reached Bungendore, when we saw this huge 'thing' rushing towards us at about 30 feet above the other side of the road. It looked like one object, with six extremely bright white lights, each about four feet apart.

"It was coming so fast, and looked so close," Henrietta said. "I just yelled, 'Shit!' and swung the steering wheel, driving onto the grassy verge, and coming to a screeching halt. There was an enormous rush of swooping air as the object rushed past us at tremendous speed. We sat there staring at each other in stunned silence. The object was gone, but my driver's-side wing mirror was shattered.

"We were really shaken, and proceeded on to Canberra very slowly. The Sunday newspapers reported a burnt-out crater and two dead cows in a farmer's field just beside the road where we encountered that thing.

Federal Highway, Southern Highlands, February 1994

Sometimes people push memories of an incident deep into their subconscious, only to have them resurface years later. Often a new experience triggers recall of something long forgotten.

On 10 February 1994, Linda Brown and friend Joy Blake were driving a late-model Commodore, from Sydney to Queanbeyan to stay with Joy's relatives for a short break.

"We left Sydney at about 5.30 p.m., and stopped for 20 minutes for a bite to eat at a Service Station with a signpost indicating it was 70 kilometres to Yass. We were another fifteen minutes into our trip, probably another 25 kilometres (making it approximately 45 kilometres to Yass), when we saw a very luminous cloud, and sheet lightning. I can also remember somewhere around that time, about 7.30 p.m., commenting on the beautiful sunset, and how I wished I had my camera with me.

"It was about then we noticed trucks behind and in front of us. I realise now they couldn't have been trucks," Joy said. "All we could see were large white lights, which continually flashed on and off. There was no noise, no wheels, and truckies don't behave like that."

Linda continued, "The lights were so bright they hurt our eyes, and I tried to cover the rear vision mirror to help Joy see where she was going. At one time we seemed to be surrounded by these lights, which were all around the 'trucks', not just front and back, as if they were in up to 15 to 20 blinding white 'groups'. Joy tried to outrun them, at one stage speeding to over 145km, but they seemed to keep pace, sometimes to the front of us and sometimes behind. At one stage one 'truck' in front rose up in the air and to the left.

"There was static on the radio, and we couldn't see any other traffic on the highway, which was not normal," Joy said. "The temperature inside the car started alternating from really hot to freezing cold. My feet were burning with the heat at one stage, and later Linda was getting a rug to try to keep warm. Remember, this was summer, and Linda was winding the windows up and down as the temperature changed. I was trying to get away from the 'trucks', crouched over the steering wheel, and having trouble maintaining control of the car."

At this stage their conscious memories were a little confused as to the exact sequence of events. There seemed to be thick heavy rain, like 'tracer bullets' – like a 'vortex' on the front windscreen only. There was none in, or outside the passenger windows. There was a terrible 'stench' around, 'like rotting flesh or vegetation'.

They felt like they were 'going up', and yet there were no hills in the area, they could not see the white lines on the highway, and below them everything was pitch black.

Linda Brown and her friend Joy Blake had been friends most of their lives, but it wasn't until middle-age, and their experience on the Federal Highway, they remembered an event some 18 years previously, which might have been a little more than they realised.

In 1976, they were both young mothers. Linda had driven Joy to pick up their children from school from Sydney's Lower North Shore. On the way home they puzzled at the sight of treetops bending at the side of a street – there was no wind. Looking up they could see a very large object hovering above.

"We could hear a slight whirring sound," Linda recalled. "It was round, with a domed top, a deep pewter colour, and had lights around the base. There seemed to be a 'type of legs' sticking out underneath"

Joy added, "There were portholes – I could see shapes. Some were blacked out."

Both women became vague. They couldn't remember anything more until they were having trouble starting the car. (There was no mention of having stopped it!). Further, they were now some distance away in a local park, without knowing why or how they were there. It was obvious there was a time lapse, but with a car full of children, and having to get home, they did not place any undue importance on the incidence, except to check if any unusual object had been reported to the local media ....

Afterwards they had varying disjointed memories. Linda said; "When we seemed to be going up, and it was just dark below, I saw a huge white 'arrow', as big as a house, either in front or above. Then there was a great flash of light, and a terrible bump, which threw me with great force back in my seat. My seat belt, which I always wear, was not on. I was scared, as Joy was slumped over the wheel, like she was in a trance. I tried to rouse her, scared we would have an accident."

Joy said; "I felt the flashing of these white lights were putting me in a trance. Next thing I knew the cigarette I had been smoking was gone. Linda was carrying on that the road marker said 'Yass 45km', and this had stayed the same for an unusually long time. We weren't going anywhere! I was relieved when the next sign said 'Yass 40km.'"

At one stage Joy recalled seeing many lights, like a huge township in the distance, and was confused. "I had made this trip many times before, and there was nothing like that in the vicinity. Also I could not understand an out-of-place, brightly-lit glowing silo, like a nuclear plant. I pulled into this rundown looking service station, to fill up with petrol, only to discover that I had only used a fraction of what it normally takes for this distance. The only two people there disturbed me for some reason – an 'Asian-looking' man and a 'Caucasian-looking' woman."

There seemed to be some confusion as to which highway they had been on before and after the incident. They had been on the Federal Highway before, and now seemed to be on the Hume Highway. The route to Yass is continuous along the Federal Highway to the west of Canberra where it intersects with the Hume Highway and continues on to Yass. There should be little, if any, discrepancies in the road mileage signs. Given Linda's record of the road markers, it is a mystery as to where the car had been. In addition, there is no explanation as to why they had used much less petrol than normal for the entire trip.

"When we arrived at my relatives they were very upset and worried. We were two hours late. We were due at about 9.30p.m. and it was now 11.35 p.m. We were both so thirsty, and all I wanted to do was have a shower. I had this terrible body odour, like 'chicken poo', and I couldn't get rid of it for days."

Both women suffered side-effects for the next few days, and said they somehow felt 'different'. Both had sore throats and 'bloated', painful stomachs, which they described as being similar to pregnancy or 'first birth contractions'. There was bruising and odd rashes on various parts of their bodies, and Linda suffered nausea for a while.

Joy seemed to suffer the worst: "My eyes were red rimmed, sore and weeping for some days, a terrible thumping headache, and a sort of internal heat in my body causing heavy sweating. The weirdest thing is I wake up about the same time in the middle of the night, and get these vague memories of some form of tests being done – needles being inserted, and big black eyes. No body, just big, black eyes!"

Linda and Joy both felt like there was something more. They were on the verge of remembering things and yet couldn't quite recall. They wanted to find out what happened to them, and whether there was any connection between the incident in 1976 and the horror journey in 1994.

They were referred to an abduction support group and were contemplating regressive hypnotherapy. It was yet another frustrating case of some details and many unanswered questions.

Queanbeyan, 2 June 1999

At 7 p.m. Rhonda, who lived at Googong, just outside and south of Queanbeyan, was driving out of her front gates to go to a meeting:

"I was heading northeast, and in the distance, low over the road, I could see some red and green lights, and wondered what they were. As I drove closer I realised it was a steel-grey coloured craft, hovering a bit higher than the telegraph poles. It was facing me, so I couldn't really see the body or tail. It seemed to be a bit bigger than a Cessna, but nothing like a conventional plane. It did have wings, but whilst similar to a Stealth craft, these were rounded into a point. The green lights were on each point and half way up each wing. There were a series of red lights flashing upwards in the centre.

"God help me, I drove right under that thing! I couldn't hear any noise from it, and there was no-one else on the road. I was really scared! I sped up and away as fast as I could, until I rounded the next corner. I slowed to look back, but it was out of sight, behind the hill and below the tree-line.

"I rang Air Services who had no record of the craft, but the following night someone rang into the local radio station and described exactly the same object. I told my relatives, and was really shaken up to be told they were not surprised. (A couple in the family were in a very distressed state. They were also driving along a country road, had seen very bright lights, and couldn't remember what happened for quite a long while after that.)

The Blue Mountains, New South Wales

The Blue Mountains rise from the Plain of Cumberland, 65 kilometres west of the Sydney CBD. Main towns and villages, include Springwood, Wentworth Falls, Katoomba and Blackheath. All are situated along the top of mountain ridges, the highest point being about 1,100 metres above sea level. These populated ridges, running from east to west, have cliffs that plunge either side into rugged, heavily forested valleys. The wild, uninhabited Grose Valley lies to the north. The sparsely-populated Megalong and Jamieson Valleys lie to the south, and lead to the Burragorang Valley, now flooded to form the Warragamba Dam to supply Sydney's water. The entire area comprises about 215,946 hectares of National Park, and the deep gorges, high cliffs and dense eucalypt forests make much of the terrain inaccessible, except to skilled bushwalkers and mountaineers.

Alien Healings

I was on a solemn promise not to divulge the details of Belinda Davidson's contact until she died. A couple of years ago, well into her nineties, old age took its toll. Belinda belonged to a big animal rescue organisation, and her home in a southern suburb of Sydney, had been made into an animal shelter. I used to volunteer there, two or three times a week, to help care with her little 'waifs'. It was a peaceful suburb, relatively crime-free at the time. I noticed she would never go out at night without her large watch dog, and I once asked her, who or what was she afraid of?

She hesitated for a moment, "I think you'll believe me, many wouldn't. In 1929, when I was twelve, I lived at Blackheath in the Blue Mountains. I had terminal cancer. My father had been a medic in the World War 1, and all the doctors he had served with had become top specialists in the Sydney hospitals. They all examined me, trying to cure 'their mate's little daughter'. All confirmed the diagnosis, there was nothing they could do."

Belinda was silent for a while, "I didn't have to go to school any more. I was quite happy about that, and every day I would accompany my father to his piggery near the Jenolan Caves. When I was fifteen the doctors suddenly realised that not only was I alive and kicking, my cancer had gone!"

She hesitated for a few seconds, "They said I was in 'remission', it must have been all the fresh air and sunshine.

"It wasn't that. One night I was walking home alone from a Girl Guides' meeting. This flying saucer-type thing came overhead and the next thing I knew, I was inside. They were nice people, just like you and me. I don't remember much except lying on some kind of table. Before I found myself back on the street they told me they had cured me of the cancer, but if I told anyone about it, my illness would come back."

Despite her lack of education, Belinda became very gifted and intelligent, contributing to society as a voluntary, qualified veterinary nurse. She was married with three children, and quite healthy until just after she confided in me. Soon afterwards she was diagnosed with bowel cancer, which modern surgery rectified. I did wonder about her disobeying the 'do not tell' condition, and vowed to keep the secret for the remaining 20 years of her life.

North Springwood, 1969

Rex and Heather Gilroy were also told of another cancer case 'healed' by aliens:

In 1969 Janice, who lived at North Springwood, told her friend Ken that her doctor had diagnosed her with incurable cancer, and she only had a few months to live. Five weeks later her doctor could find no trace of the cancer, and she lived for many more years. So, what happened?

She told Ken that a month after the diagnosis she woke-up in her bush-surrounded property to the sound of loud humming, and went outside. The whole area was lit with a silvery glow. She then felt herself being lifted off the ground by some invisible force, and could see nothing beyond the glow except a huge, hexagonal-shaped 'airship' above her.

The next thing she remembered was being in a brightly-lit room. She was terrified as about a dozen strange beings encircled her. They had greyish skin, long five-fingered hands, reptilian-looking eyes and mouths, and were naked! One touched her with a short, metallic-silver rod and she went into a numb, relaxed state.

A silvery oblong block rose up out of the centre of the room and they lifted her onto it. One of the lizard people operated on her, opening and closing her chest with the strange rod – then touched her forehead. She immediately lost consciousness and woke up in her own bed, with no sign of the lifesaving operation.

Air Force concerns?

One January in the early 1950s there was great excitement in the Blue Mountains. Many people had reported unusual lights around the base of Mount Solitary in the Jamison Valley, two kilometres directly south of The Three Sisters rock formation. Mount Solitary has long been attributed with a mystical quality, and was regarded by the aboriginals as part of their magical 'Dreamtime'. They also considered Mt Solitary to be taboo – inhabited by an evil spirit:

Gordon's mother-in-law, Lisa, lived in Leura, her picture-window looking out over the cliffs into the Jamison Valley. She glanced out one night, and noticed lots of little lights 'dancing' in the valley below. She was quite mystified as there were no roads or tracks down there, just dense forest. That Friday night Gordon was having a quiet beer upstairs, above the coffee lounge he owned with his wife.

"Through the trees I could see a red light I had never noticed before, and thought one of the guesthouses must have got a new neon sign. The next day our customers were all gossiping about the strange lights seen from the Three Sisters Lookout the night before. It was all over the radio as well. It was described as being bright red, surrounded by a pink glowing mist."

"On Saturday night the lookout was full of locals, all hoping for a glimpse of the visitors. Not much was seen except for a few lights in the valley below. I was curious, and on Sunday I arranged for someone to help my wife in the restaurant, and together with my two neighbouring shop owners, made my way down to The Lookout."

"A lot of people were there; UFO-fever was well and truly alive. Many, like me, were sceptical – we would believe it when we saw it! We weren't disappointed. At first there was a tiny light at the base of Mount Solitary. It got bigger and bigger, and I jumped out of my seat. The memory is still vivid today. This 'thing' got closer and closer; a brilliant luminous orange 'glow'. There was no mist around it as had been reported before. It is weird, I couldn't judge its speed or altitude, but as it passed overhead it made a 'whish' noise."

"Lots of people were ringing into the radio station. One old fellow at Hartley had an orchard down the hill. There was no electricity on the property, and without a radio he had no knowledge of the excitement up the mountain, in Katoomba. The previous two nights his watch dogs had been howling and barking. One Sunday night he let them out, and followed with a shotgun."

"Half-way down the dogs started yelping, and he could see a man, an ordinary looking man in white overalls, standing under a tree. For some reason he felt scared, and he and the dogs retreated to the house."

"This is where it gets interesting. John Emmet, the radio announcer on 2KA, got a visit from RAAF authorities. John was a good friend of mine, and he told me they said there had definitely been objects on their radar they couldn't account for."

"Then, shortly afterwards, three men arrived in the mountains, claiming they were from *National Geographic*. They visited nearly everyone who had made a report, starting with my mother-in-law, who referred them to me. They even visited the old guy at Hartley. They were all very conservative, wearing black suits. One had slicked-back black hair. Lisa thought they looked more like Mormon missionaries. One man with an American accent, conducted the interview, with the other two more-or-less observing."

"What was puzzling, was nobody saw any vehicle parked outside. They had no cameras, tape recorder or binoculars. Not one of them took any notes, which you would expect. I wondered who they really were – government agents, the CIA, or maybe the often-reported men-in-black."

Katoomba, July 1957

In July 1957, there was further excitement as more lights moving across the night sky were seen over several nights, from Katoomba and within a 100 mile radius around Sydney. Witnesses included policemen from Newcastle, who described "a dazzling bright light moving quickly across the sky". Pilots of two commercial airliners who also reported having seen coloured lights moving across the sky.

Estimates of altitude varied greatly, from 500 to 7,000 feet, but all witnesses insisted they were definitely not a plane, planet or anything conventional. A Manly resident who claimed she saw two brilliant green objects chasing each other across the sky, stated one had come very close: "It was cone-shaped and rotating clockwise."

This is where it gets interesting, and rife for speculation. By the fourth night, the RAAF had sent a 'navigator' to trace the odd objects being seen to the west of Sydney, and placed two of their jet aircraft at Richmond RAAF Base on standby.

At 8.48 p.m. Captain Keith Brown and First Officer Keith Mansfield were flying from Broken Hill to Sydney in a Butler Viscount airliner at 14,500 feet, when they saw a blinding explosion over the Blue Mountains. "We were ten miles from Katoomba when we saw it. It was between five and ten miles ahead on our port side. After the explosion, glowing embers, like those from a rocket, fell from an altitude above the plane. We do not know what caused the explosion, but we do not think it was a rocket."

After that there were no more reports of the mysterious lights, which the authorities insisted had been the planets Venus and Jupiter

Those large glowing golden balls ...

The Blue Mountains has always produced a consistent stream of reports of strange phenomena. Over the years we have received many reports from residents who lived near cliff edges. Often they witnessed up to four large, glowing balls of golden light rising up from a valley below, sometimes accompanied by muffled rumbling noises. One friend's mother used to watch them through her kitchen window, as they rose out of the valley to the south:

Lucy, a waitress in Katoomba, reported a strange incident which occurred sometime during mid-1991. She was working in a two-storey restaurant which overlooked the Jamieson Valley.

One dinner time she was coming up the stairs with several plates of food, when she saw a large glowing object through the window. It appeared to be hovering over the valley, and as she stopped to watch, several kitchen staff gathered to join her.

A man from a table of about ten patrons got up and came over to see what was going on. He took one look and said he was from the RAAF base at Richmond and had to borrow their phone to make an urgent call. When he finished his telephone conversation, all the men at the table left in a hurry, saying they had to report back to base.

Their half-eaten meals were still on the table and their less-than-happy wives and girlfriends had to pay the bill and find their own way home!

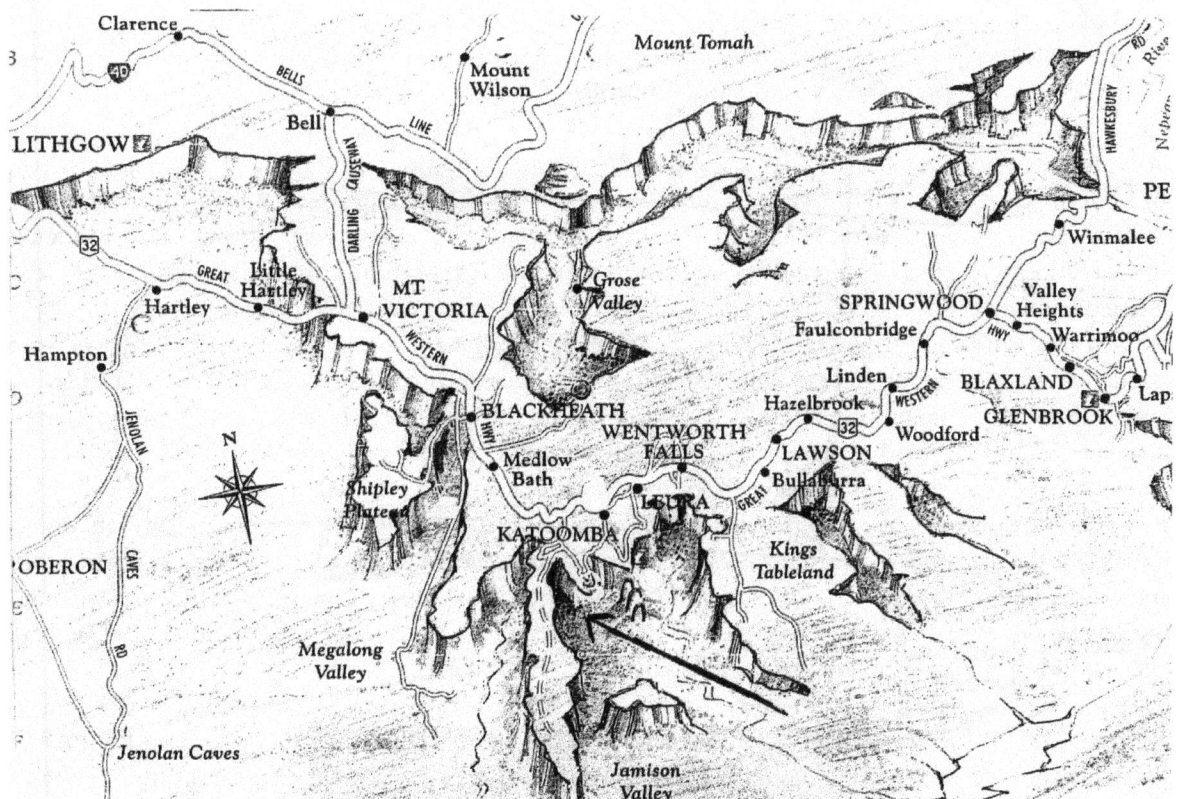

Despite local speculation and theories, we can only wonder as to what the balls of light were, and their strategic significance to cause Air Force personnel to rush back to their base, nearly 40 miles away.

Springwood, 1973

Springwood is a pleasant village, about one-third the way up the mountains. In 1973 a builder was working on a new home on the bushland outskirts of town. He got very frightened, and claimed that for three weeks he had been 'buzzed', often in daylight, by an unknown, aerial disc. He told the family who had contracted him, that unless he could have an assistant, he would not work on the site alone.

The assistant was agreed to, but then both men claimed to have been 'buzzed'. After experiencing several close encounters they fled the site, leaving it unattended. The family did not want their building materials stolen, so the 23-year-old son and his mate camped on the building block. One night, while asleep in the caravan, their son was woken by a blue beam of light, coming through the roof hatch:

He could see it was coming from an overhead disc, and unsuccessfully tried to wake his friend. The next thing he can recall is two hours later, when he was on a track which leads into a valley, about a quarter of a mile away. He had vague memories of some 'Caucasian-type beings' and an 'awareness' of their purpose.

Below that area, to the west, is Sun Valley, a small secluded farming area, from where I have received several reports of strange aerial objects and close encounters. Because it is sparsely populated, residents are reluctant to say much due to the likelihood of being identified.

The Burragorang Valley

The Burragorang Valley runs south of the main ridge and villages straddling the Blue Mountains. It was once a peaceful farming area, with a quaint village, until the mid-20th century when it was flooded to create Warragamba Dam, Sydney's biggest water source. As an important water catchment area, public access is now restricted:

Researchers Rex and Heather Gilroy have long written about unidentified craft in this area, and believe it is the site of an 'underground base'. The valley itself and the surrounding, rugged terrain and cliffs prevents objects being detected by normal radar systems.

The Australian Air Force also shows an unusual interest in the area. On many occasions it flies jet planes through the valley, at low levels. If they wanted to practice flying in difficult terrain there are vast areas of cliffs and valleys free from human habitation. One friend was having a siesta, and fell off the sofa in fright as powerful jets came racing down the valleys and swept up over the cliffs in Katoomba. (I also saw them and personally jumped out of my skin as they suddenly appeared in front of my eyes, roaring up from below The Lookout just ahead of me. I am sure the startled tourists there had to return to their hotels for a change of underwear.)

In late January 2002, a bushwalker on 'The Federal Pass' below the top of the cliffs, was startled to hear a roaring noise coming from the east, between the Skyway and Mount Solitary. A long, black cigar-shaped object came into view below the cliff tops. It momentarily slowed, then with an incredible burst of speed, wove its way through the escarpments of Mount Solitary and Narrow Neck Peninsula, eventually shooting over the Southern Highlands, and out of view.

Another resident has told me that he has seen, from Narrow Neck Lookout, bombers doing circuits under the cliffs towards Warragamba, and one memorable incident reported a few years ago concerned two RAAF Hercules planes on low altitude exercises. It is thought they had entered the south-western network of valleys from the Southern Highlands side at Canyonleigh, where the 'electricity supply was cut' and the 'power off'.

Various contacts and a newspaper article described how radar and radio contact was lost at about 8.40 p.m. and frantic transmissions and calls between the police and Nowra and Richmond Bases ensued regarding the missing aircraft. In advance of any activity from Richmond Air Base, a police helicopter was out looking until 1.15 a.m. Since any crash of two Hercules would have been big news, it is assumed they must have turned up safe and sound. But where had they been all that time, and why fly down such dangerous terrain at night?

Who and what is down some of those valleys, I really don't know, although some hardy researchers have made expeditions into that mountainous wilderness. The topography of the area is honeycombed with caves and massive cliffs, so anything is quite possible, although I would doubt the stability of any secret base under the waters of Warragamba Dam.

Mysterious disappearances

People routinely go missing or get lost in the rugged, densely-forested cliffs and valleys of the Blue Mountains. Besides fatal falls, bushfires and flash floods, there are venomous snakes and other dangers lurking in this vast untamed terrain. Sometimes the list of 'disappearances' gives rise to the thought that perhaps there is more than just a natural explanation. My friends and colleagues Rex and Heather Gilroy have detailed a couple of interesting cases:

It was thought that a wartime aircraft may have crashed in a particular part of the valley, and in 1951 when three soldiers ventured in to locate the wreckage, they vanished without a trace. A subsequent search was called off by senior Army officials. For the next few years many hikers and campers kept a lookout for the plane wreckage or signs of the three soldiers.

In 1953, a lone camper, deep in the valley, and relaxing in solitude under the stars, was startled when a large, dark saucer-shaped craft moved over the tree tops. It made a loud 'crunching' sound when it appeared to land nearby. When daylight broke, he found two areas of trees and bushes that were broken and flattened.

Later that year, Peter Suttor who was hiking in the valley had penetrated an area beneath the cliffs on the south side. It was near where the lone camper had discovered two, similarly-flattened areas. Hidden by the undergrowth, he could see several figures in the distance. He described them as being man-sized, wearing what looked like spacesuits, and they seemed to be collecting rock and soil samples and searching the ground with strange metal devices.

Peter reported the incident to a UFO group in Sydney, and one member told a friend at Liverpool Army Camp. The soldier and two others from Ingleburn decided to use some of their leave for an adventure, and to go camping to check out the area where the mystery 'landings' and Peter's strange beings were seen.

They also vanished, and although searchers ascertained they reached the approximate area Peter had described, there was no further trace of them beyond that point.

Six servicemen missing in two years, yet very little comment was made by authorities. Another case rife for speculation, but no firm answers.

Earthquake faults

Back in the 'good old days', when we weren't so technologically advanced, theories were much more simplistic. In 1957 Fred Stone was the Director of the Australian Flying Saucer Research Society. He postulated a theory that 90% of UFO sightings occur over major fault lines in the Earth's crust. He firmly believed that the intelligence behind flying saucers was concerned about the effects of atomic explosions on the Earth's weak points.

Fred claimed he had seen five flying saucers at Woomera a week before the first atomic test in the Australian desert. Fred also believed that due to an abnormal number of sightings over the Dandenongs in Victoria, a fault line existed in this area.

In the mid-1970s, when I was a young, enthusiastic researcher, one of my older mentors was explaining to me the necessity of gaining people's respect and trust before they would confide their experiences:

He related an incident which had occurred when he had been lecturing to a small group in a country church. "After the meeting, an elderly woman approached me, and confided that many years ago she had lived on the Canterbury Plains on the South Island of New Zealand. She often used to go to the foothills and sit and meditate. One day she met a strange little man, who came out of an even stranger saucer-like craft, which was parked nearby. She asked him where he had come from, and why. He told her he came from another solar system, and his people were monitoring our world because they were concerned about a crack in the Earth's surface. Up until then I was convinced she was genuine and sincere. Due to the close proximity of major earthquake faults in the area, her story was certainly very plausible."

"It was what she said next that rocked me. She had moved to Australia, and lived in the Burragorang Valley, west of Sydney, for some years, until they all had to move out of the village, to make way for the construction of the Warragamba Dam. She used to drive up a nearby hill, and gaze down on the area, full of fond memories, which would soon disappear under the water."

"One day she was surprised to meet that same little man, and asked him why he was now in Australia. He explained that they were also concerned because we were constructing the dam over a crack in the Earth. I was left not knowing whether to believe her or not."

In the late 1950s-early 1960s there had been several reports of UFOs hovering over the valley, but it wasn't until the 1970s that geologists fully realised that an earthquake fault at Robertson, in the Southern Highlands, ran up and under the township of Razorback, in close proximity to the Warragamba Dam, which has since been considerably strengthened.

Perhaps the little old lady really was telling the truth.

Close encounters

In 1986 researcher John Pinkney wrote about a Faulconbridge family who, in 1984, witnessed a huge round structure, glittering with lights, hovering over their house before descending into the Grose Valley, which they overlook. Since then they had been subject to ongoing strange and inexplicable phenomena. A digital clock, which hadn't worked for years, started flashing. Both their, and the neighbour's, video players and recorders were turning themselves on, and flashing impossible numbers on the channel selector.

"The first time it happened we sat there watching the recorder in amazement. Then, in my mind, I clearly heard the words – 'We come on the blue ray.' When the video finally went quiet, we all rushed outside. My three-year-old daughter, Christine, was already out there, pointing up to the empty sky. She kept repeating the word 'spaceship', but when we questioned her she became confused and would say nothing more."

The husband and wife are convinced they have been receiving telepathic messages from the occupants of the craft. This is impossible to verify. However there have been some close encounter events involving other witnesses in the Grose Valley over the years, one of which will be discussed in my next book, *The Alien Gene*.

Grose Valley, February 1930

Researcher Rex Gilroy received a call from one Sydney woman who was still mystified about the unidentified object she saw years ago when visiting the Blue Mountains. She was at Govett's Leap Lookout overlooking the Grose Valley, about midday, with her parents and siblings.

They all saw a big silver object hovering high in the eastern sky above the valley, at about cloud level. It was very large, like a big upright triangle with a flat top and attracted a lot of attention from other tourists during the half hour it hovered there. It then flew off eastwards, towards Sydney.

Blackheath 1958

Blackheath is perched high-up, near the top of the Blue Mountains, with the Grose Valley to the north and the Megalong Valley to the south.

Rex Gilroy reported a huge saucer-shaped craft seen by Blue Mountains City Council workmen at the Blackheath Depot at 6.30 a.m. one cold dark winter's morning. Tony Look and his workmates were startled to see the object hovering about 10,000 feet overhead. After a while it began emitting a blinding white light, which appeared to come from a row of at least ten lights around the side fronting them.

They projected a glow which shone directly down within about 50 feet towards the Council yard, and lit up the surrounding town. They watched in awe for about ten minutes until it suddenly rose up at a phenomenal speed and disappeared into the clouds. When other employees arrived they just laughed. However, a week later a 'monstrous glowing object' was seen to descend from the late night sky in the direction of the Mount Victoria end of the Grose Valley.

Megalong Valley

Western Katoomba 1972: Mr. Edison owned a piggery, on the western side of Katoomba, near cliffs overlooking the Megalong Valley. At about 8 p.m. Mrs. Edison was washing up dishes and noticed an orange light through the kitchen window:

It was moving above nearby trees, and then appeared to descend among the trees behind the pig sheds, about 200 yards away. The pigs and dogs were unusually quiet. She called the family, and her brother went over to see a saucer-shaped object 'of considerable size'. It had a dome with a central blinding light which illuminated the whole area. There were other lights surrounding it, but all the lights and glow rapidly faded away, leaving the whole scene and craft in darkness.

They called the police, but the craft had gone before they arrived. The occurrence was investigated by Rex Gilroy. Motorists had seen the lights from the nearby highway and other witnesses came forward. A farmer, who lived in Megalong Valley, directly below the piggery, had seen a large, dark object descend slowly into the valley and land in a deserted field, some distance from the house. It was about 30 foot across and remained on the ground for about ten minutes before silently rising, gaining speed and disappearing into the darkness. At the site was a circular depression, where no grass would grow.

The official explanation was a malfunctioning RAAF helicopter which had landed for repairs. (Which is totally ridiculous given there were better landing spots close by. Nobody saw any 'figures' doing repairs. Normal airmen would have approached nearby witnesses or been overheard speaking to each other or on the radio. Helicopters are not silent, and do not normally resemble large-domed discs.)

And in 1973 ... Rex Gilroy received another report from the Megalong Valley. A farmer had driven high up the western slopes to check on his cattle. He reached the top of a hill and pulled his Land Rover up to a halt. Just below him, several hundred feet away, on another hilltop straight ahead, was a strange object, a contraption like a giant upturned saucer, with a row of windows around its base. It was sitting on three greyish, tripod-type legs, which had large silver plates at their base.

He drove back to the farmhouse, and phoned his mate and the police. By the time everyone arrived and went back up the hill, over an hour had elapsed, and the craft had disappeared.

I live happily in the Blue Mountains, and am told of unusual events and sightings throughout the area, some of which I may discuss in my next book. Rex Gilroy has investigated Blue Mountains phenomena most of his life, and has written many books. He is very familiar with the ridiculous explanations given by authorities – this is one of his favourites:

"In 1970 Rod Parker, a camper in the Burragorang area, found a circular burnt-out patch of timber that had left a circular depression in the earth about 10 metres across. There was also a strange smell about the place, which he could not identify. Whatever it was, he could see some unknown, large object had rested there only hours before – so heavy that it had crushed big gum trees with trunks 20 to 30 centimetres thick.

"Later Rod contacted the RAAF Base at Richmond, north of Penrith, and reported his eerie discovery. The voice at the other end of the phone had the perfect solution to the mystery:

'About this time of year, Mr. Parker, large flocks of migrating ducks frequent the Warragamba region and rest at night in swamps, where they congregate in large numbers. They leave circular depressions in the crushed reeds when they fly off. So obviously Mr. Parker, what you found was nothing more than a depression left by migrating ducks.'

'Yes,' replied Rod, 'Ninety-ton ducks!' and hung up."

Jamison Valley, 9 April 2000

A friend of mine, Alicia Thomas, had gone for a walk in Katoomba to Echo Point and the Three Sisters Lookout at 10 p.m. one beautiful clear night.

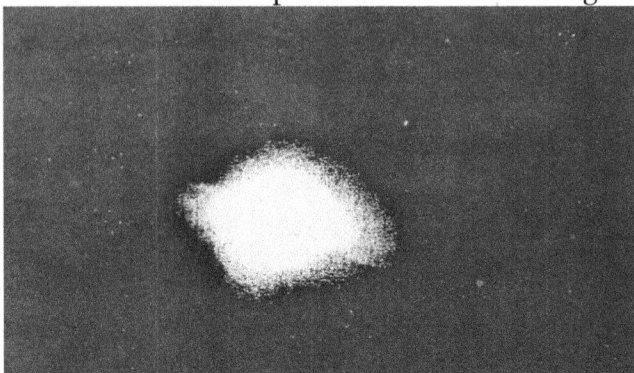

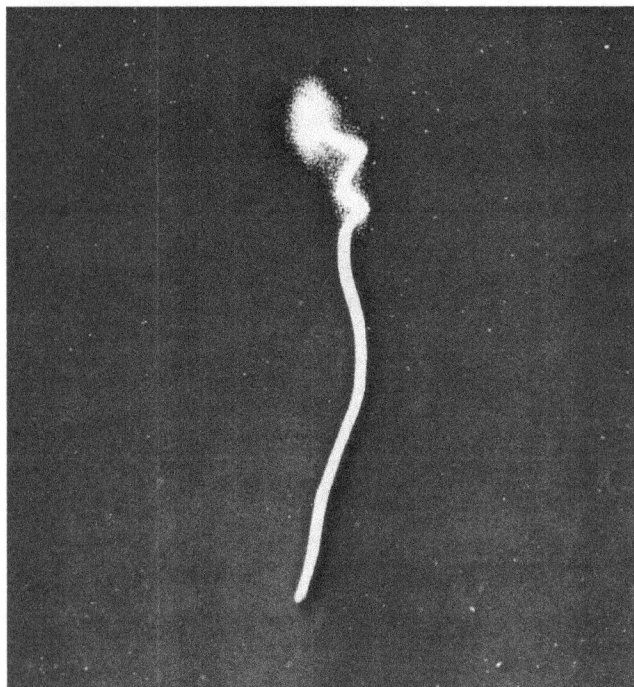

The tourists had all gone, and as an amateur astronomer she had taken her camera, and was looking forward to some peaceful sky-watching:

"I picked a spot on a cliff ledge looking at the Scenic Skyway across the Jamison Valley, about half a kilometre west and about 800 feet above the valley floor."

"At about 10.30 p.m. the clouds began to roll in, and by 11 p.m. I decided to pack up and leave as the sky was completely covered and I couldn't see any stars. Just as I reached the concrete path, back from the cliff top where I had been sitting, something bright caught my eye through the trees."

"It was a small glowing bright white globe, about half the size of a one cent piece at arm's length, coming down through the clouds. It flew across the valley, growing in size as it approached, until it stopped and hovered about 100 feet away. It was glowing white-gold, about 30 foot in diameter, and was lighting up the trees and clouds above."

"While it silently hovered there, I felt a slight sense of vibration, and the distinct feeling I was being watched, so I watched back, and got off three shots with my camera. It only stayed there a couple of minutes before it backed away, took off at incredible speed and winked out and was gone just before it reached the clouds".

Chapter Seven

Western New South Wales

Mid-Western New South Wales

On the other side of the Great Dividing Range, and on its western slopes is a mixture of pasture, plains, forests and dense bushland. Country towns include Bathurst, Dubbo, Griffith and Wagga.

Days gone by ....

There are many cases of unidentified flying objects being seen long before the modern surge of reports which began in 1947. Some years ago, an elderly man, Ian Rogers, rang me about an incident when he was a boy in 1924: One morning he was checking their rabbit traps in the Lysterfield State Forest, south of Coolamon. He has lived on the family farm there all his life, and in those days rabbits and other game formed a regular part of their diet.

"I was behind a tree, when I heard a humming noise, looked up and saw this flying object which landed in a clearing about 100 yards away. I have never forgotten it, and as best as I can remember, it was a long cylindrical shape, rounded at both ends, with four square windows along the side. It was at least 30 feet long, and I remember lights of some kind.

"I hid behind the tree, and watched it for about an hour. At one stage some people got out, they just looked like 'people', and I don't know where they went – they didn't come my way. After about an hour it flew off the ground and away into the sky."

I noted there were no helicopters in 1924, and asked him if anything else happened:

"The ground was all burnt black where it had been, and the trees were singed. There were dead birds all around, and nothing grew in that small area for a long time. After it had gone I saw something glinting on the ground. It was a small piece of metal. I kept it for a long time, as it was like magic. When I rubbed it with my hands it would move off of its own accord. I raced home to tell my mother, she scolded me for getting back so late. I don't remember being gone so long, and she said not to tell anyone else about what happened."

Ian had mislaid his magic piece of metal, and it was pointless even looking for the landing site so many years later. As for any missing time, given his age, that was also futile.

Trangie, 1976–77

John was working with heavy machinery one night, levelling some cotton fields, when a huge bright white light appeared overhead. "That damn thing was pacing me, following me as I went along.

"I was so scared, instead of taking my machine back to the shed, where my car was parked, I just jumped off and started running. I took off across the fields, crashing through fences and any other obstacles in my way, in an effort to escape that thing.

"Needless to say, I did get away, but I don't talk about it much. Not only would people laugh, but I'm a bit ashamed of the fact I was so scared."

Mudgee, May 1982

In 1982, John Cook had retired from the RAF, migrated to Australia with his wife, and was starting to build his dream home.

"It was about 11 a.m., a beautiful clear day. We were having a coffee and waiting until the concrete was ready to pour out of the mixer. I looked up and saw a silvery object, just in front of us, about 3,000 feet up in the sky. Julie said it must be a helicopter. I know my aircraft, and told her there was no helicopter in existence that conformed to the shape and size of that particular object. In fact this was no ordinary aircraft, military or otherwise.

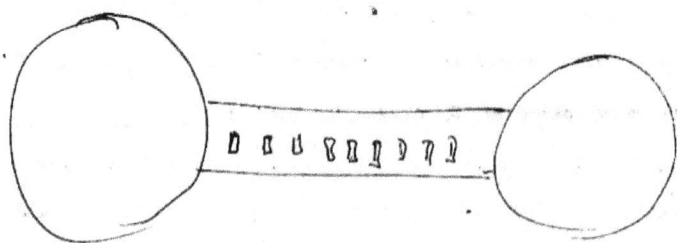

Silvery in colour

John's sketch

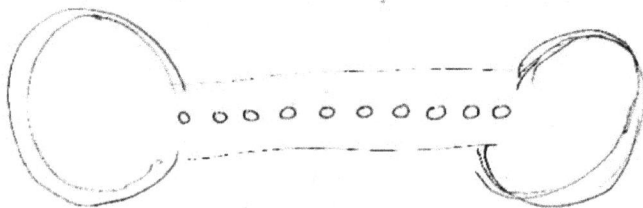

I'M NOT SURE HOW MANY PORTHOLES IT HAD BUT IT WAS SILVERY TO DARK GREY IN COLOU

"Julie wanted me to turn off the concrete mixer, to hear if it was making any noise. I couldn't do that – it was full of concrete, and I may not have got it started again. I told her that since the object was much bigger than a Jumbo 747, and now very close and low, if it had a conventional engine we would be deafened by the noise.

It was clearly outlined, silvery-grey, and shaped like a dumb-bell of all things! Along the middle part, which joined the two rounded ends, were nine or ten portholes or windows. It travelled in a straight, steady trajectory, from north to south, and we eventually lost sight of it behind the hills."

Alien influences

Sometimes I am contacted by an eccentric witness. It is unwise to dismiss them out of hand. Often an in-depth investigation into their individual claims and their family history can prove very interesting.

One such case was Roy Wallace, who privately approached me in 2010, when I was managing a charity bookshop. He came in looking for science and technical books, saw the UFO books I had donated and we got talking. I also became acquainted with his wife, Lorna, a professional psychologist who was concerned about his behaviour and compulsions. She confirmed he was definitely a quite sane and intelligent scientist and that she believed his UFO experiences. She was a little out of her depth when it came to the alien influence on him, and the possible harassment, or worse, by unknown persons to both Roy and previous contacts.

Lorna said: "He has this weird idea that he has certain objectives in life, but doesn't know why. One is a compulsion to build a library. He has been acquiring books, mostly scientific and technical, and has literally ended up with a warehouse full. He joined forces with another man, Peter Roach, who is a biomedical engineer specialising in cryogenics. Roy and Peter discuss very little with me except that they are working in tandem."

Lorna sighed, "Between them they have purchased over 350 technical and scientific libraries. Then they bought two mountain properties in the country to house the collection, insisting they had to be more than 600 metres elevation, a reasonable distance from Sydney and the coast, and away from any main road. And then, after all that, the structures have to be partially underground and covered with earth and concrete."

My interest was aroused by his wish to house a multitude of reference books in an area and manner reasonably safe from natural disasters or modern warfare. Was he expecting some form of cataclysm where there would be no more electricity or digital technology?

Roy and Lorna had moved inland in the1990s, away from the coast. He had a dread of being in Sydney. He commented that he was not alone in this. One of his workmates, a physicist designing electronics, computers, etcetera, was quite manic, saying he had a feeling or intuition, and moved his family to an elevated area up the north coast. (Quite a lot of witnesses and contactees develop a similar impulse and move away from coastal areas.)

Roy confided he had seen unexplained craft several times in the past. One event really interested me. When he was a young biologist in the 1960s, he was conducting surveys with two other colleagues in a bushland area near Wauchope, New South Wales.

"We had been spotlighting wildlife, and at about 7.30 p.m. decided to pack up and head to town for a meal. We were driving back down the winding dirt road when a bright light came up fast behind us. Thinking it was another car, that couldn't pass, we sped up. After another ten kilometres, it was still there. The light shining in our back window and rear vision mirror was starting to affect our eyes. We managed to pull over into the verge so it could get by.

"We checked the dashboard clock – 8.30 p.m., still time for dinner. Things were a little hazy. I suddenly jumped up, as if I'd been asleep, but I didn't remember anything about going to sleep!

"My mate said, 'Those headlights are gone! I don't remember that car overtaking us.' We got out of the car and looked – nothing. It was weird, the dirt road was wet, but there were no other tyre tracks besides ours. We thought maybe the other vehicle had broken down, and did a U-turn to go back and check. No-one there. Better get back for dinner!

"We continued on our way, and as we were going down the hill towards Wauchope we saw another light. This one was up in the air, not at road level, so we knew it wasn't a car. We got to the bottom of the hill, had dismissed the light, and were talking about other things.

"Everything was closed in town. We were dumbfounded when we saw that it was now 4.30 a.m. on the dashboard clock!

"It was afterwards that I started to get ideas – a sort of telepathic communication. An intuition to start beneficial, worthwhile activities."

I could not contact the two other witnesses who had been in the vehicle. One has moved to Darwin, and the other was killed in New Caledonia. Naturally a missing-time scenario came to mind. Lorna was a qualified psychologist, if she had conducted regressive hypnotherapy, she was not prepared to admit it or discuss any details.

Lorna herself, is now not so sceptical about unidentified craft, although she is undecided about their origin (as alien or terrestrial). They had never told their daughter about UFOs, but in 2006, when the daughter was fifteen, she and Lorna were together in Cowra one night and saw a black triangular craft which hovered overhead. It was silent and had a hexagonal back, which looked like a crystal.

"This frightened me," Lorna said, "especially with regards to my daughter's wellbeing. I often wonder about her in relation to her father's experience. She is super-bright, almost a genius. I was driving from Bathurst home to Cowra late one night, between 2 a.m. and 4 a.m., and there were strange lights in the sky. I had seen them before, and was scared. A friend who lives on a rural property, near Grenfell says he sees them quite often."

Lorna was also uneasy because of the unknown fate of a colleague, Alan, which had made Roy very wary of the authorities.

Dr Miran Lindtner

Dr Lindtner was a respected scientist, a fighter pilot in World War 2, and President of UFO Investigation Centre in Sydney (UFOIC). In the late 1960s he 'fell' under a train in Germany. Colin Norris, veteran South Australian researcher once wrote to me: "The sad ending of his life was not necessary – an accident when he fell under a train in Munich. Was he pushed, as he was going to a conference back in his original country?"

I was friends with his daughter, and she told me her mother always blamed his death, along with that of many others, on ufology. There was a lot of bad feeling, accusations and counter-accusations over the fate of the files and data in his possession. It was said that Mrs. Lindtner burnt them, others accused another researcher of hijacking them. Alan did locate some of the missing paperwork in a university basement, where he found letters and magazines dating back to the 1950s in a couple of dusty bins.

"Alan told us that, in the 1960s, he once saw a UFO and contacted the Department of Defence. After the sighting he went in search of information on alien craft. He also sent a report to Dr. Lindtner of UFOIC in Sydney. On following up, and hearing of Dr. Lindtner's untimely death, he wanted to access Lindtner's files, for some reason."

Lorna said, "I don't know what Alan was looking for, or why, but he took a lot of the letters. Alan said that he 'should have kept quiet', and claimed he was being followed by cars and his credit card was blackened. He was really frightened. A short while later he moved to South Australia and then just disappeared. I don't want something like that happening to my family."

Sometimes ufology can be a dangerous business. We will never know what it was Alan witnessed or reported to UFOIC, or what was in the paperwork he smuggled out of the University, and whether it had any connection to his disappearance or Dr Lindtner's death.

Orange, 27 January 1986

Four youngsters in their late teens and early twenties were concerned when they heard the horses in the adjacent paddock "going crazy" at about 11.30 p.m.

"They were making an awful noise" Robert said, "and then I saw 'the thing' hovering about 50 metres away, and 50 metres off the ground.

"It was oval-shaped, about the size of a small car, with a flat bottom and dome on top. On the bottom was a bright red revolving light, about 22 centimetres in diameter, which was surrounded by about twenty other fixed red lights. It was making a very quiet noise and sounded a little like an old grader."

He called his sister and their two friends who also came out from the veranda, and all got quite a scare when it started to move towards them. It flew around the house, and out of sight, only to "do a big circle" and come back around. It had dropped in altitude to about 30 metres and took off at a fast speed in a southerly direction.

"I got my Mum's car and we all drove after it, as it had seemed to stop and hover over a vacant block near the Channel 8 television tower. But then we lost sight of it, and were in a bit of a state, so we went into the television station and told the girl on duty, who called the police."

The police told the press that they believed the witnesses who were highly excited, almost hysterical, and they had to calm them down. They confirmed none of them were affected by drugs or alcohol, and that there was a flattened area of grass two metres by four metres on the block where Robert thought he saw the object land.

Dubbo

Dubbo is situated on the Macquarie River, 420 kilometres northwest of Sydney and includes the Western Plains Zoo, a large open-range wildlife park. The surrounding area produces wheat, wool, fat lambs and some fruit and vegetables.

Herveys Range, late 1980s

Sheryl McDonald and her husband owned a farm 25 kilometres south-west of Dubbo, in hills bordering Herveys Range, near the Parkes radio telescope. Sheryl worked with a shearing team which travelled all over the place, and her husband Tim had a job in Dubbo. They were fairly isolated; the nearest house was to the northwest, over five kilometres away.

"It was often quite late when my boss took us back to Dubbo, and Tim would wait to drive me home. This particular night it was dark by the time we got back to the farm, and I helped him unload the utility. We still had our own animals to feed, and my husband went inside to change before looking after the pigs.

"It was a very dark night, no clouds, a few stars, and I had to use the torch to see what I was doing. I fed and watered the horses, about 100 yards away, and went back to the house and looked after the rabbits next. I was just starting on the cats when I heard a humming sound. It was similar to a constant droning, which hurt my ears and got louder as it came closer. The cats and the dogs all went silly, and the horses were making a noise, and getting hyperactive, as if something had scared them. They had never been frightened of planes before.

"I looked up, and could just make out this dark shape, coming over a hill in the west, from the direction of Narromine. It was moving very slowly, and when it got close to the house it stopped, and just sat in the sky, about 25 feet above the trees. It was on the other side of the house and paddock, about 200 yards away.

"It was at least three times the size of a Hercules Air Force plane. (We had seen a few of these on exercise several weeks before, which was unusual.) It was black or dark grey, an odd shape, almost like a triangle with a rounded nose. It had an orange-red glow, but it didn't reflect, and seemed to blend like lights, or fuel burning underneath. There were a lot of lights, flashing on and off, underneath, up and down, and in the middle, but not on the edges.

"It just sat there for a few minutes. I was frozen with fear, and stood staring and thinking, 'Oh my God, what is it?' Suddenly it took off in a straight line over the trees, east towards Dubbo, and was gone in a flash. I sort of snapped out of it to the sound of the pigs squealing, and blindly

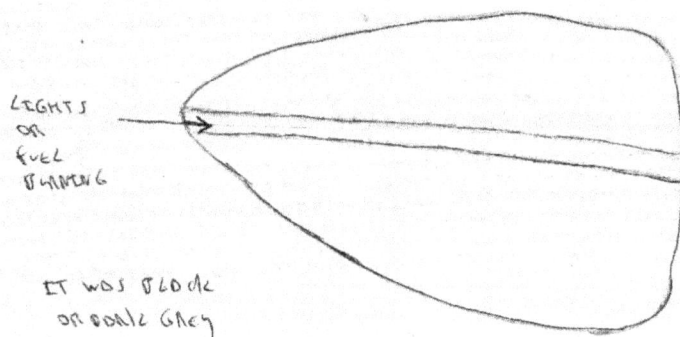

raced to the shed out the back where my husband was feeding them. He walked back to the house with me, and helped pick up all the dog biscuits I had dropped in fright.

"I was still shaking all over, and my husband, who had only heard the noise from inside the shed, tried to calm me down by suggesting it must have been a new experimental plane. He had once told me about seeing a UFO when he was young, but would never talk about it. My friends and family just laughed and said I was probably overtired, imagining it, or had I been drinking? It was none of those things, and I had hoped there may be something on the radio, or in the newspaper, but not a word."

Newell Highway, 8–9 September 1994

Charlotte Kilpatrick, a nurse, and her brother were on an overnight coach trip from Victoria to Queensland, and were on the Newell Highway, south of Dubbo:

"It was just after midnight, and unlike the other passengers, I just couldn't sleep, and was waiting for the coming coffee break. George and I were sitting in the front left-hand seat, just across the aisle from the driver, with a good view out of the front windscreen.

"My brother is eccentric at the best of times, and at first I felt like throttling him when he started asking the coach captain if he believed in flying saucers. The driver replied that he was sceptical of all that baloney, so George told him he was about to see one because there were a whole lot of small lights flying through the air in front, and they weren't stars.

"I told him to shut-up and stop embarrassing me, so he turned away, shut his eyes, and must have gone to sleep. We were about ten minutes out of Dubbo, when ahead of the coach I could see this huge dark shape to the sky on our left. I was aghast, and said out loud: 'That's not a plane.' I was looking at this huge object – it would have been as big as Safeways Store. It was high- up, and moving very slowly, something like a bulldozer in the sky.

"It was the shape of a horseshoe, and had literally hundreds of small yellow lights all around the exterior. It was almost like there were lights within lights, or one on top of each other, to form a pattern around the horseshoe. They reflected clearly on the underneath, which looked an aluminium colour, blocked out in squares. There was a mist around the whole craft. The front was in complete darkness, and I can't accurately describe it, except that it was large enough for a small plane to fly in. The same goes for the upper part, although it looked sort of flat, it was hard to see if there was anything above.

"The coach driver asked me, 'Are you looking at that? It must be a plane.' A truckie who had just passed us called him on the CB radio: 'Can you see it mate – that's no plane!' After we passed it I raced to the back of the coach and watched it through the back window. There was a man at the side of the road with what looked like a video camera filming it.

"I had been so intent on the strange craft, I had forgotten about George, and when I woke him, he was furious that he had missed it. Soon after we reached the Dubbo coach terminal and the booking clerk raced out saying 'You will never believe what I have just seen!' – Oh yes we would! The bus was delayed for a short time at the depot, as the driver said the wiring on 'certain electrical equipment was burning' and he had to fix it."

One local wrote in advising it might have been an atmospheric illusion. However an unusual cloud they reported was not evident until 4.30 p.m. the next afternoon in Millthorpe and 6 p.m. near Cowra.

Wednesday 9 March 2005

There was a vague report from Dubbo in 2005, when a housewife saw an object "as large as a house", moving and changing colours and hovering only 500 metres off the ground.

Dubbo housewife Sally Fulton commented, "I've never seen anything like it," when she, with her husband and three daughters, first noticed the hovering craft in the southeast at about 7 p.m., when it was still daylight. It was many miles away, but still appeared to be the size of a car, a black triangular shape with a flat top and a deeper shape at the bottom.

"In some ways it looked like a stationary helicopter," Harry Fulton said, "and once the sun set, there was a light flashing on and off every couple of seconds, just like a lighthouse. Every so often it would move to the left and then silently return to its original position. It was so unusual we filmed quite a bit of it, before and after dark."

"At about 8 p.m. we notified the police who came out and also watched. They saw our video footage and took it for an official report to the federal airways monitoring bureau, Air Services Australia (ASA), who told the police inspector there were 'numerous reports of objects flying in the southern regions of Australia.'

"We kept watching it until after 11 p.m. when it speared off out of sight behind the trees."

Thursday 17 December 2009

Grant Charlton lives on a rural property outside of Dubbo. About 9.30 p.m. Grant went outside to check on their old dog, before going to bed, and saw something odd in the eastern sky. It had been raining, and was very dark, with no stars visible in the sky.

"I stood for at least five minutes, just staring at it, before I called my wife. She came out of the house, and we both just looked in amazement at this thing. It was perfectly still, and so low it seemed to be just above the tree tops. It was the size of a full moon, shaped like a six-sided Star of David. By the time Louise went inside to get the camera, it would have been hovering for around ten minutes."

Louise recalled, "It was extremely bright, a golden colour, very low in the eastern sky, and not moving. I came back out with the camera, and took four shots, one after the other. I don't know if it was the flashes from the camera, but after a minute or so it started moving very slowly towards us. It came in low, and straight over the top of the house, the glow reflecting off our roof."

"As it passed overhead, its shape seemed to be perfectly round and glowing, with flashing (or more like pulsating) lights all over it. It couldn't have been going more than 30 kph. It made a strange motor noise, a low humming sort of sound, and slowly disappeared to the north-west."

Griffith, 1961

Out in mid-west NSW are countless remote properties, and country folk do not confide easily. In 1996 I was conducting a seminar on the South Coast when I was approached by a retired couple, who said this was the first time they had confided in anyone.

Nigel told me that in the 1960s they owned the isolated Kywong Homestead Property. "At the time we were concerned that something was killing our lambs, we thought it might be foxes and had never heard of these animal mutilations back then."

"My wife and I drove out one night, and sat in the car in the middle of a 100-acre paddock, with a spotlight and a rifle. We were there for a short while when suddenly, without a sound, the whole car lit up with an orange light. It extended around the car for about fifty feet."

"I don't know how long we sat there. Quite a while, the car was becoming very hot." At this stage Nigel became a little confused as to the actual time, or when they got out of the car. "We were outside the car and there was no sign of the light and the car cooled down."

"We both served in the RAAF during World War 2, and do not imagine things. I have flown for 38 years, and owned four aircraft. As a pilot I studied meteorology, and looking around later could not find any explanation for the light and heat. It was a clear night with moon and stars. I wrote out a report at the time but didn't send it."

I suspected there was more to the incident than what Nigel either remembered or wanted to tell me. He had put on his official report form that there was an object "directly above" the car, and it wasn't until afterwards that he read a couple of books about unidentified objects.

Binya, 15 April 1995

Henry Doggert and his wife and son were on their way home from Griffith to Wagga, and had just passed through Yenda onto the Ardlethan Road, heading for Binya. It was just after 9 p.m., on a clear night, with no clouds and a full moon.

"About five minutes after we left Yenda," Henry said, "there was a brilliant light behind me. At first I thought it was the floodlights from the football field at the end of town. Five minutes later I realised that it was not; it must be another car with all lights on full beam, even though he seemed quite a distance away. Within five seconds he was on my tail." I said to my wife, 'God, that fellow's coming up really fast, and his lights are blinding.' She looked behind and said she could see it too. I got a shock when she told me it couldn't be a car, because it had just risen to treetop level.

"My wife was fascinated and quite excited, giving a running commentary. My son, who was sitting alone in the back seat, could also see the object and was getting upset. I was concentrating on driving, feeling stressed and tight in the chest, afraid of crashing the car."

Margaret continued with the details. "It was about the size of a garbage bin lid to the eye. It was very bright, not really an orange-yellow glowing light, more like a ball of fire. It followed us, directly behind the car, for nearly ten minutes, very low to the road, except for a short period when it literally jumped over the trees and along the adjacent railway line, only to come back to tail us again."

There were no other cars on the road, until they got to Binya, where there are a few houses and a shop. They felt safe to stop, and Henry pulled up the car where they got out. "By the time I had turned off the engine, put on the handbrake, and opened the door it just shot vertically straight up into the sky and hovered, and seemed to move even higher until out of sight."

Insidious encounters

About three hours drive west from Sydney, on the other side of the Blue Mountains, are the thriving country towns of Bathurst, Millthorpe, Blayney, Lithgow, Portland and Mudgee. Nestled on the slopes of the Great Dividing Range this pleasant area includes pine forests, hobby farms and properties, fruit orchards and vineyards.

Trunkey Creek, 1997

Early 1997 began with second-hand reports of strange white lights being seen by farmers in the Trunkey Creek area. Our initial investigations proved fruitless. While we could confirm that several sightings were reported to local authorities and media, we were unable to locate any of the original witnesses.

Portland, 12 March 1997

Linda and her two children, Lucy and Peter, were living on a recently rented property just outside Portland. Linda was a university graduate, working in a respected profession at the time; Lucy (11) and Peter (9) were both intelligent and mature for their age.

"It started as a normal night," Linda said, "much like any other. At about 9.30 I was on the phone to my friend Donna. My daughter had gone to the toilet before bed. This was located outside at the end of the veranda, and as Lucy was spooked by the dark and the quiet, Peter kept watch by the door to the veranda. My conversation was interrupted by their excited voices yelling 'Mummy, mummy, come and see the UFO!' Thinking it was a fuss about nothing, I asked Donna to wait a minute, and put the phone down.

"I went outside to see what all the commotion was about. The entire back of the property was lit up like day. Hovering over the far side of the garden some 50 feet away, was this huge oval ball, about 30-40 feet high and 20 feet across, of silver-blue sparkling light.

"On later reflection, I behaved totally out of character – as if mesmerised. I casually went back to the phone and said: 'It's OK, they're just watching a UFO in the back garden.' Donna

thought the object might be affecting me strangely.' I kept talking for about another fifteen minutes, and just left my children out on the veranda watching that thing!"

Suddenly the phone cut out. Donna told us that she had became very concerned, as the family lived in a very remote place, and was worried that someone may have cut the phone lines, as Linda was living incognito to avoid a violent domestic situation. She considered calling the police, but didn't know how to explain the UFO. (When checked later, we found the phone cable to the house is an underground one, buried about a metre deep!)

Linda had also thought there might be an intruder. "There was no dial tone or anything, so I loaded my gun kept under my bed, went outside, and checked around the house. I ignored the UFO and remember thinking – all clear, no need to worry, there must be a logical explanation for it'. I was only concerned about the phone being out of order. Looking back now, my behaviour then seems very odd."

"For some inexplicable reason I felt very tired, and just walked back right past the kids, into the house and went to my bedroom. I lay down fully clothed on the bed. It must have been about 10.30 p.m., and I just blacked out. At about midnight I woke up, had a shower, and went to bed. It was as if I was in a trance. I had not even thought about Lucy and Peter, let alone gone to check on them.

"The next morning I woke at daybreak, in sheer terror. Memories flooded back and my first thoughts were for the children: 'My God, I left the kids out there with that thing!' I breathed a thankful sigh of relief when I checked and found them peacefully asleep in their beds.

"I ventured outside. The morning was quiet and peaceful; nothing amiss or strange in the sky. I crossed over to the fence beyond the garden, where the 'thing' had been hovering, and stopped at an odd eight-foot patch of swirled grass. The grass seed heads were bent over and flattened some 40 centimetres above the ground, but the plants were otherwise unaffected.

"Over breakfast I tentatively asked the children about the previous night. Lucy described the object as being similar to what I had seen – a large blue light, hovering over the ground, with air and light emanating from all sides. She noted the entire back area was lit up, and went on to say the grass underneath the object was moving and swirling. I was taken aback when she mentioned a door in the middle of the craft.

"Peter's recollections were essentially similar, but far more detailed. He said he first saw a star sized light in the sky, which seemed to get bigger and come close very quickly.

His description indicated that it was a more traditional type saucer object with claws around the circumference, which descended after hovering just over 100 feet from the ground.

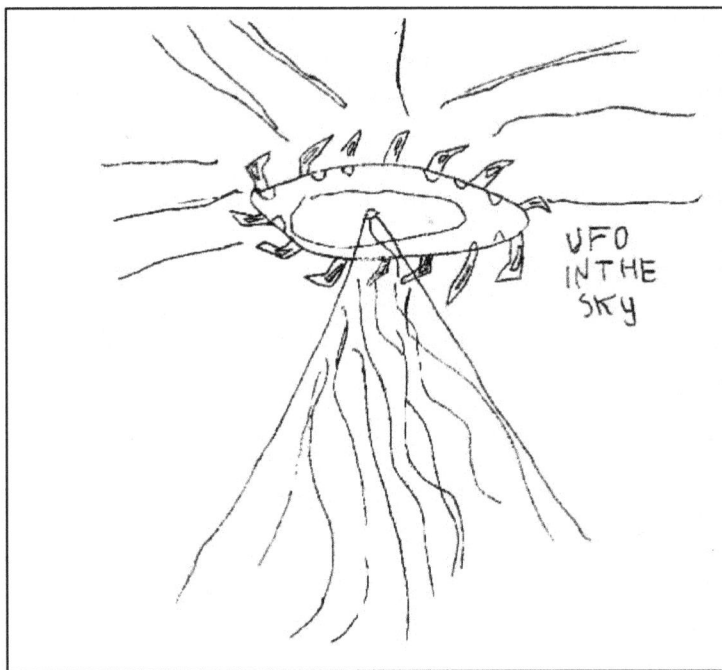

Both mentioned that the object bobbed around when hovering, and travelled at incredible speed when moving.

"I felt a growing concern as I began to realise that Lucy and Peter did not seem to have any immediate recollection of what happened later that night. They could not say when or how they got to bed, but both mentioned a beautiful blue light and a floating sensation. I was as if their memories had been blanked out, with just odd flashes of something else."

(A few days later, Linda rang me, and my colleague Bryan Dickeson visited the property a week later, to sight the strange ground traces and gather other evidence.)

"My sense of trepidation worsened two weeks afterwards when I had what appeared to be a dream, in bed one night. There was a loud humming sound, and the whole house seemed to be vibrating. I was petrified and calling out 'Go away – don't touch us!' and asking God to help me."

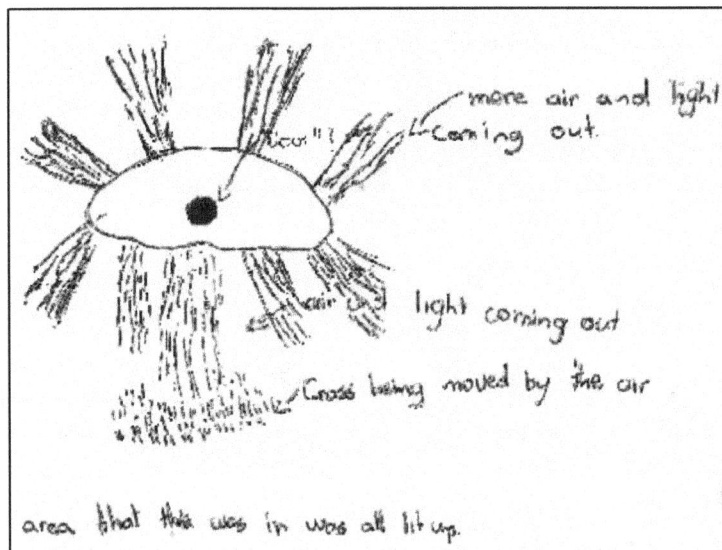

Before Bryan could follow-up on his preliminary interview, and conduct more tests on site, Linda had moved out, and we could not gain access to the property. Linda and the children moved in with her mother down on the New South Wales South Coast: Linda said: "It is not so remote; I feel safer with another adult in the house and neighbours all around."

During the next three months other disturbing factors were becoming apparent. The children, especially Peter, were starting to recall more and more on a conscious level, including entities. (They had no exposure or access to alien or ufology literature at any time.)

Neither of the children seemed to have further conscious recollections – the next thing they recalled is when they woke up in their beds the next morning. They did not remember leaving the craft or indeed any other details of that night. They both agreed they did not like the strange beings, and did not want to see them again.

Linda said, "I don't recall any of this at all, and more than what may have been done to me, I am indignant and angry that some unknown force or entity should interfere with my children.

"Both children had three strange red spots on their inside ankles, forming a triangle, and Lucy mentioned someone 'doing something' to the back of her neck. I knew she had never had any

106

operation or accident involving the back of her neck, and felt a sinking sense of disbelief when I lifted her hair to see a small scar, complete with 'stitch marks'. She also claimed there had been a strange 'person' outside her window one night."

I visited the family in their new home, and the children seemed to be regaining some of their memories of that unusual night at Portland. In order to prevent any cross-contamination of details I separated Lucy and Peter during interviews. I sat in the garden with each one, playing with the rabbit, and only inserting crucial questions into normal conversation.

Both had consistent memories of the craft having some form of door in the middle, and being floated into the UFO without their feet touching the ground. They both drew pictures of the beings they had seen, and had clearer memories of what happened inside the craft.

Peter said there were creamy-blue walls inside. He described bright white lights on the ceiling, and a table in the middle. He described the beings as being quite tall, whitish in colour, with big round black eyes and no mouth.

Lucy's memories were slightly different. She drew a picture of what she initially saw "after the UFO came." It resembled a window, with a side-on figure, and she has written "side-facing thing like a ghost." Lucy recalled a continual electric buzz and said that the middle door to the craft looked like a black hole in which five beings were standing – looking out at them.

She described "skittle-shaped" entities (she didn't notice any arms); they seemed to be wearing some form of silver-green strap around the lower half of their faces. She also detailed them as being creamy-white with large black eyes. Their heads seemed too large for their bodies.

Lucy recalled that while nothing was said and they made no gestures, there was some communication "in her mind."

She spoke of "a needle on a cord which was attached to a wall." It gave her an "electric zap", and said the beings were doing something to the back of her neck, like an operation. She also saw her mother, Lynda, lying on a table. One entity was

These things I saw after the UFO came.

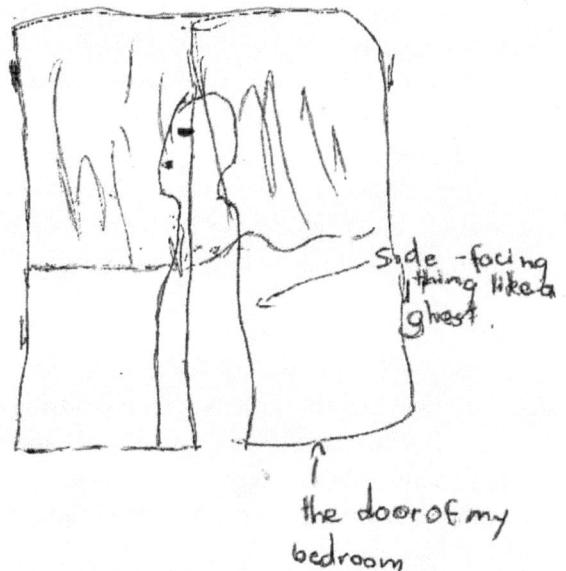

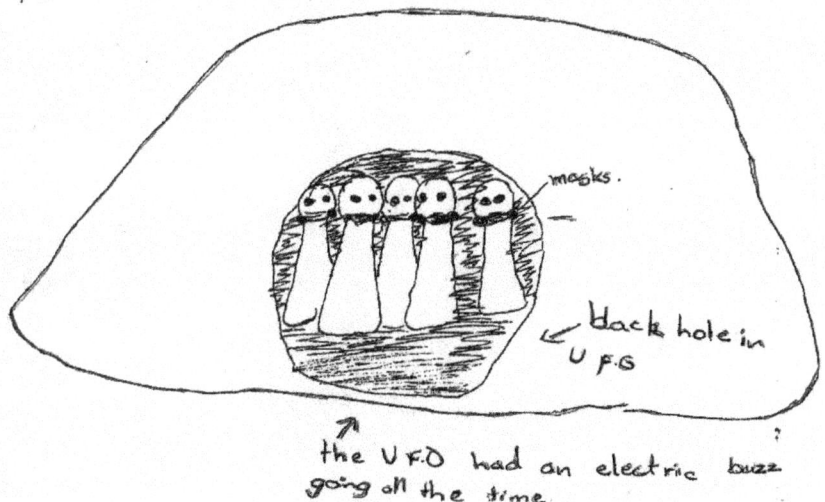

Side-facing thing like a ghost.

the door of my bedroom

masks.

Black hole in UFO

the UFO had an electric buzz going all the time

standing next to her "with something metallic in its hand, like a clipboard – which it appeared to be looking at."

The children were seeing a fully-qualified psychiatrist for counselling about the family break-up, and he was quite satisfied that they have had a genuine experience. I also found them to be a very credible, well-balanced family, and have remained in contact ever since. While Linda and Lucy have adjusted well to their unfortunate experience, Peter (now 27) has become more distant and refuses to discuss it.

Bathurst, 20 March 1997

Only two weeks after Linda and her family's experience, a farmer, 15 kilometres north of Bathurst, was taking his regular walk at 11.20 p.m. He was startled to see a ball of bright, iridescent-blue light about a quarter the size of a full moon.

It seemed to be in the east, near the Trunkey Creek–Blayney area, and travelling fairly fast to the south. "It was not a meteorite," he said. "Not only was it slower, I've seen meteorites on many occasions and this was completely different."

Newcastle, 6 April 1997

Residents of the Newcastle area also reported large balls of silver-blue light descending from the night sky. Coastal residents advised military type aircraft or helicopters were seen overflying the area a short time later, and appeared to be searching for something.

The mystery deepened when the Air Force denied any activity at the time, and we could find no official record of space junk deterioration or re-entry.

Astronomical advice indicated that the objects were most likely a bolide. However, there were some unusual aspects to the incidents, and in conjunction with the occurrences out west, they added to a memorable two months of inexplicable, possibly connected events.

Rylstone–Mudgee, 9 April 1997

This was not a good month for the residents of the Central West, especially single women, who began to wonder who or what was terrorising them:

On Wednesday 9 April, Christopher and Gloria Dixon were north of Mudgee, driving home from a friend's coffee evening. It was a clear night, with no wind, and their relaxed mood was interrupted by the sight of something bright red and orange flashing on the right-hand side, about 100 metres ahead.

It seemed to be coming over the grass paddocks from the Rylstone area, and veered over to the left-hand-side of the road they were on.

"It was much lower than local planes and seemed to be descending at an angle, and when it changed direction it seemed to rotate, rather than move," Gloria said. "We were astounded as we did not know of any plane that resembled this craft. It was round, huge, about five or six times bigger than the moon. It was much larger than a house it passed over! It was very low, just above tree top level, about 30 metres up, and so slow, no more than 30 km per hour.

"As we passed by, we got a much better view. It had a dark flat base, with two huge white neon lights identical in size, which covered most of the underside. Although they were very bright, they seemed to be recessed in some way, as they did not illuminate the house underneath.

Above the flat base were two short wings, covered with steady orange and red lights, which is what we must have seen in the first place. They were such funny little wings. They seemed too small to hold up such a large body. We couldn't hear an engine or any noise at all.

"Christopher wanted to stop to get a better look, but we live in an isolated area, right at the edge of town. I'd heard all about UFO abductions on the television. No way! We got home and from the safety of the front porch, watched the orange and red lights, now flashing, slowly disappear into the distance in the west."

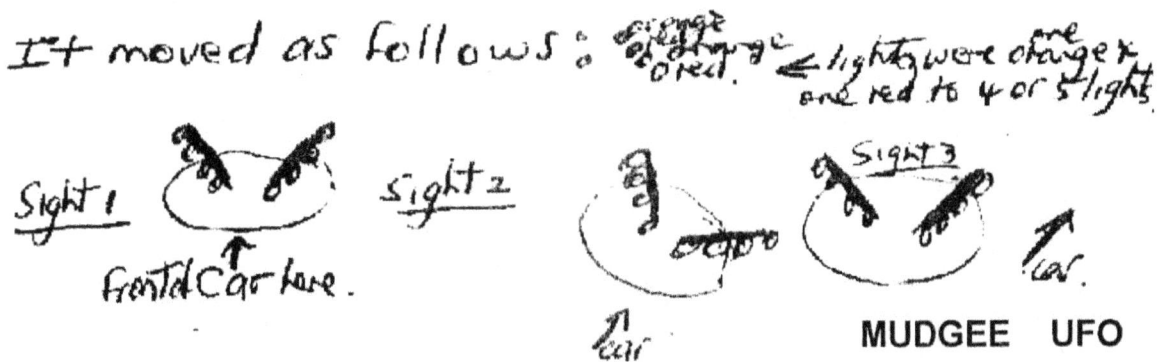

MUDGEE UFO

Bathurst, 14 April 1997

On Monday 14 April a Bathurst mother was driving home with her two children aged eight and sixteen. "Look at the big plane," called the eight-year-old, and her older sister ducked her head to look. "Mum, what is that? It's not a plane."

Donna glanced to the side of the road, and was startled to see a huge bright, gold-coloured object moving slowly in an unusual zig-zag fashion at sharp angles. It was pulsating strangely, and didn't seem to be making any noise.

"It definitely wasn't an 'advertising blimp'. In fact, I had never seen anything like it. We watched it move slowly across the paddocks, but my little girls' excitement soon turned to fear, and they started to cry. I must admit I was starting to feel uneasy, and breathed a sigh of relief when it took off across the sky at incredible speed. It vanished over the horizon in seconds. I don't know if it was an optical illusion, but it seemed to turn blue as it sped off over the horizon."

Blayney, 19 April 1997

A few days later, at 10.30 p.m. on Saturday, 19 April, Kerry Pine was driving through Millthorpe on her way to Blayney. "I noticed a bright red, round light, about half the size of a full moon, heading east towards Bathurst.

"It definitely wasn't a blimp, balloon or ultralight, and I thought I could hear a light humming noise. I was a bit scared, being all alone, so I pulled up at the side of the road, and watched for about five minutes, until it disappeared from view."

Daisy Smith, a professional career woman, was less fortunate. About an hour and a half after Kerry Pine's sighting, she was driving home from work, following her normal route through

Bent headlights phenomenon

One aspect of Daisy's report which got my attention, being the unexpected fatal car crash of a local resident at the same place she encountered difficulties.

Nearly forty years earlier, in October, 1959 a businessman was driving home, about 30 miles from Maryborough in Queensland, when his headlights suddenly turned sharply to the right, for absolutely no reason. "Instead of lighting up the road," he said, "they lit up the fence, as if they were being dragged by a giant magnet, hidden somewhere in the paddock.

"I braked as hard as I could, and as I did so, I glanced to the right. In the middle of the paddock was a great column of brilliant white light about 25 feet high, and shaped like an ice-cream cone.

"It was sort of tapered, about three feet at the bottom, resting on the ground, and 10 feet at the top. Looking into the light, I could see all colours of the rainbow. It silently rose into the air, and flew off at tremendous speed.

His headlights returned to normal, and were not found to be faulty when tested the next day. At 10 p.m., only a few days before, a man travelling along the same straight empty road, had a fatal accident at exactly the same location.

He seemed to have swerved sharply, for no reason, and crashed head-on into a tree.

The authorities were interested in a connection between the two incidents, and found a 'saucer shape' depression, three foot in diameter, in the paddock, 150 feet from the accident spot.

Millthorpe back to Blayney. As she reached the top of a hill, which leads down into Blayney, she noticed a vast, brightly-lit white disc hovering over the township. It extended the full length of the town on her eastern horizon – some two kilometres across. It lit up the countryside all around about Daisy, as if it was day time – she could clearly see every tree, every rocky outcrop.

"Before I even had a chance to identify it, the light seemed to rush towards me at unbelievable speed. My entire windscreen was flooded with brilliant white light, so bright it temporarily blinded me. I came to a screeching halt, dazzled by the brilliance.

"After what seemed like a few moments, the light moved away and I went to drive on. I hadn't remembered turning off the engine, but I must have, as I had to turn the key to restart the motor.

"When I reached the house, I realised I was over 20 minutes late. The clock in my car had inexplicably stopped at the same time as I was on the hill and had slammed my brakes on." Daisy and her husband Gary are both university graduates, no-nonsense professionals, and did not place undue importance on the incident at the time.

One week later, at 11 p.m. on Saturday 26 April, Daisy was again travelling home from work, having finished her shift a little earlier than usual. She had put the white light of the previous week out of her mind.

"After I passed through Millthorpe I glanced through the window, and spotted a bright white light travelling across the sky to the side of my car. For the next 30 minutes I drove the rest of the way home, terrified there would be a recurrence of the previous weekend. That damn light stayed with me, but I don't have any recollection of it coming closer.

"I got home, and the light was still there. I was so spooked by then, I raced in and got Gary. By the time he came outside it was gone, and I wondered if he really believed me. He asked me why I didn't leave work early, as intended. I had! This time I was about an hour and a half later than I should have been. I couldn't understand it. I hadn't stopped the car at all this time. I checked my watch; it had stopped at 11 p.m.!"

(Earlier that same evening, 26 April, a strange white light was seen by several independent witnesses. At about 5.30 p.m. a local family told us a bright white object followed them for about 30 minutes, as they returned to Blayney after attending a meeting several miles to the north. At about 7.20 p.m. a second family was travelling from Neville into Blayney for a Saturday night dinner. They noticed a very strong white light mass moving low in the sky over Blayney, going in the direction of Millthorpe. Pauline Ward said the light was very brilliant, about the size of a golf ball at arm's length, and travelling at medium speed just above street light altitude. She was starting to feel a little nervous, even though she had her husband with her. It was fairly close at times, and while she tried to dismiss the thought that it was following them, she breathed a sigh of relief when they lost sight of it after turning a corner into town.)

Daisy Smith was now quite frightened, and has not worked evening shifts since. Gary was concerned, did believe her and contacted us. We suggested he keep an eye on her, but not to dwell on the events. At that stage we all hoped she would get over the incidents without any lasting effects. We kept in contact, and for the next few weeks everything went back to normal, except for Daisy's bad dreams, but it became apparent that Gary also had residual problems himself.

"She starts crying out in her sleep, 'No! Don't! Leave me alone! Get away,' and appears to be sobbing. When I am finally able to wake her she can't remember the dreams but says she feels upset about something."

Gary was the one who had contacted me first, and at that stage he certainly had no memory of any strange lights or phenomena himself, but that all changed three months later. "I woke one night to see an incredible white light shining through the bedroom window. I thought perhaps my neighbour had left his car headlights on, but it was too bright, and I couldn't hear any engine noise. It was odd, my heart was pounding from waking up with a start, and yet I went back to sleep almost immediately."

Daisy also woke, and has since told me the light was so intense it created a white-out, and she could not even distinguish the curtains or doors in the room. She also fell asleep almost instantly.

"After that I noticed Daisy and I seemed to become much more psychic and in-tune with each other," Gary reflected. "Sometimes I will think of asking Daisy something and she will answer me before I've said a word. What is really weird is the shared experience of having exactly the same dream simultaneously, but each from our own perspective. One of them – was it a dream or a vision? – involved a triangular shape craft and several strange planes with large wings which turned down at the ends."

While Gary had not been in the car when Daisy saw the unusual object, the white light had shone through the bedroom window affecting both of them. "I do recall, a couple of years ago, about 1995, we had been driving south from Bathurst to Blayney one night. We puzzled over a large black triangular object travelling across the sky from west to east. I never even thought about it until after all these current happenings."

Bryan Dickeson visited Daisy and Gary at the end of April 1997 to get more details. While revisiting the hill top on Millthorpe Road, exactly where Daisy had first seen the enormous disc, he noticed a set of car tyre-skid marks on the tar seal and a roadside memorial with a wooden cross and fresh flowers. On checking local papers he found there had been a fatal accident, a few weeks before Daisy's first encounter, at exactly the same place. A young local man, had crashed into a tree on the roadside late one Saturday night.

The police said he had apparently braked suddenly, lost control, and skidded on loose gravel. They couldn't understand why he had to brake suddenly on a dark, but familiar country road. He wasn't drunk and was due to join the army. We wondered if he had also been blinded by a strange object, and if Daisy had made a lucky escape.

Twinned dreams

Daisy and Gary also appeared to experience twinned dreams, a phenomenon which has occasionally been described by witnesses who have shared the same experience – was there more to their 1995 sighting? Gary will be thinking of asking Daisy something, and she will answer before he has said a word, like a form of telepathy. These phenomena are occasionally evident in identical twins. Gary was also quite spooked by a vision he had one night while lying in bed.

"It was like a very vivid picture which flashed into my mind, a setting with some people whom I didn't recognise. I turned to Daisy and asked if she knew anyone who looked like that? It turned out that I had just described her workplace and two colleagues, none of which I had seen. I told her that I had a really bad feeling from this, and on that basis she swapped shifts for the next night with another worker.

"Two days later she came home from work and said: 'Remember those blokes you described? Well, the night I should have been working, they got into a terrible physical fight in the kitchen'.

Scientist Michael Jouvet has instigated research into such shared subconscious phenomena, but concentrating on genetic factors. This gives rise to many more questions and speculation with regards to people like Gary and Daisy.

Far West of New South Wales

Way out west is getting into frontier territory, an enormous area – sparsely populated and arid, with fearsome dry summers. Broken Hill, a major outback city was created as an artificial oasis and is basically a mining town. Wilcannia, which is just down the road by Australian standards, is also close to the opal fields at White Cliffs and was once a key inland port in the days of paddle steamers on the Darling River. The area round Broken Hill and Wilcannia is relatively close to the border with South Australia and a possible testing ground for all manner of things unknown.

Australian authorities apparently needed to keep some incidents under wraps in the years following World War 2. One cannot discount their paranoia, in confiscating all photographic evidence, as an indication they may have been testing a new prototype craft. The *Australian Saucer Record*, (Vol. 3, page 13), reported a case from Eucla, West Australia on 3rd April 1954, when three young men were followed for 80 kilometres by a saucer-shaped object with portholes. They had five cameras and took 92 pictures before reporting the incident to local police. The authorities confiscated their cameras and returned them, minus all film.

A senior police officer told me of an elderly country woman, now deceased, who saw a traditional flying saucer during daylight hours, near Wilcannia, in Western New South Wales, in the 1940s, just after World War 2. She claimed that after reporting the sighting to the authorities, she received a letter from the Australian Air Force confirming the report, and warning her not to tell anyone about the craft. The police officer attested to having seen the letter, which appeared to be genuine.

Wilcannia, 1953 and 1956

In 1953, John and Kevin were driving on the road leading into Wilcannia, when they suddenly became aware that something was hovering above them.

"We got quite a start," John said. "We were travelling in an open jeep and looked up. We were astonished to see a 20-foot saucer-type craft directly above our heads! The hull appeared to be metallic, like satin-finish stainless steel.

"We could see, from an angle, that there was a turret with round portholes on top, and four ball-like objects suspended underneath."

"We pulled up and jumped out. It was still motionless and Kevin was able to photograph it. Maybe it knew what we were doing, I don't know. Suddenly it streaked off across the sky at unbelievable speed and was out of sight within about three seconds"

When the roll of film was developed it showed a really clear image of the strange object they saw. Kevin was so excited he wrote to the army about the incident, but never received a reply. He then, in hindsight, made the mistake of sending a second letter to the RAAF. Without warning he received a visit from an Air Force officer, who promptly confiscated the film, leaving Kevin with only one print.

Another resident of Broken Hill had seen a similar object during daylight hours. He had drawn a sketch which John confirmed as being almost identical to the saucer he and Kevin had seen.

A husband and wife were also near Wilcannia in 1956 when they saw an object like those reported in 1953. It was hovering stationary in the sky. The witness grabbed his box camera, and despite his shaking hands and the low shutter speed, the snaps developed quite well, albeit not

A "BDT" artist's impression of the flying saucer seen by John Gregory and Kevin Power on the Wilcannia Road.

Reader's Secret Snap Of Wilcannia Saucer

Our feature story yesterday – "Flying Saucers Have Landed Here And Locals Have Photographed Them" – brought a prompt reaction from a reader.

very clearly. This couple also received a visit from an RAAF officer who confiscated both the negatives and the prints. Country folks are not silly! They had heard what happened to Kevin's photos, and did not tell the Air Force they had a second film. They kept it a secret for ten years before allowing the local newspaper, *The Barrier Daily Truth*, to publish it.

Wilcannia, 1954

This case is very interesting if considered along with our 1953 and 1956 reports. *Disclosure Australia* unearthed an interesting case from the Department of Civil Aviation files. Mr. Keith Weston of Mena Murtee Station, 18 miles northwest of Wilcannia, claimed that in late 1954 he saw a large, saucer-shaped object, and took three photographs which were developed at the homestead.

He claimed the object, which was 80-90 yards across, came from the direction of Netalia Station, hovered over the woolshed at an altitude of about 500 feet, and departed with a loud clanking-explosion sound.

The matter was investigated by the Department of Civil Aviation. However, a couple of weeks later an internal memo, dated 10 November, was placed on the file claiming: "a Mrs. Weston, asks your department to drop the matter, as it is a faked snapshot, which was taken to have a joke with someone in Wilcannia, and the matter has gone too far."

However, adding a little mystery and speculation to this report, is a further internal memo, some two weeks later, dated 23 November, from their head office: "If the photographs are genuine, they will be of considerable interest, and a request has been received from American Service source for copies."

Now why did Mrs. Weston want to drop the matter, and not Keith? Was she being truthful, and what did she mean by it had "gone too far"? If there was no pressure on her, and they had been faked as claimed, why were they still considered genuine, and why did the American Service source want them?

Cobb Highway chase, 1959

The sighting of strange objects in the area continued throughout the 1950s: Eddy is now a 76-year-old grandfather, and a respected citizen of his country town in Western New South Wales. He contacted us after we had broadcast a segment on his local regional radio station.

It was about 8.30 p.m. on a pleasant Saturday evening in 1959. Eddy was only 20, and he was driving down the Cobb Highway from Ivanhoe to Wilcannia, in western NSW.

"I was about 40 miles from Wilcannia when, suddenly, through the open window of my ute, I saw a light ahead at the right hand side of the road. As I approached, I was astonished to see a strange craft on the ground, near the telegraph lines. It was round, about 30 feet long and 20 feet in diameter, and was supported by short, two-foot legs. It was a silver colour, with at least four brightly lit portholes, with rounded corners, down the side.

113

"As I neared this thing, it rose about six feet above the ground and hovered motionless. A multitude of sparks was spurting from the base to the ground. I recall being amazed that they did not ignite the dry grass underneath."

Fear overcame curiosity, and Eddy decided to "get the hell out of there", but when he tried to accelerate, his vehicle would not respond. Terrified he continued slowly down the highway with the object following by his side.

"It was as if it had some magnetic hold on my ute," he recalled. The nightmare continued for the next half mile, when suddenly the object broke away and sped off to the horizon. Once the strange craft had departed; Eddy regained complete control of his vehicle and sped into Wilcannia, still in a state of shock.

"My mates wouldn't believe me, and said I must have been drinking before I left Ivanhoe. I insisted I hadn't touched a drop but they still laughed despite the fact that other Wilcannia residents had reported a strange daylight object only a few hours earlier."

When Eddy returned home on Sunday, he was sure his relatives would be more supportive. "Maybe they were scared of unwanted attention from the authorities, but they refused to listen to me, and insisted that I mention it to no-one, saying it would give people a bad impression of me, and could reflect unfavourably on other members of the family."

Eddy commented to me, "It's a long time to remain silent about something like this, but now I'm older, and I feel I have, at last, found someone who may believe me."

Broken Hill, 1962
Bryson Brown was 16-years-old when he and a mate had just left Broken Hill to drive to Menindee.

"We saw this unusual object hovering beside the road, and stopped to look. It didn't make any noise, but we could hear a very slight whistling sound. It was disc-shaped, a purple and green colour. It was rather creepy. My friend said he had seen the same thing another night, and we should get out of there. It didn't take me long to understand why he was nervous; that damn disc followed us for nearly 70 miles!"

Wilcannia, 1968
Artist Pro Hart, along with some friends, watched four or five dish shaped objects fly over a dry lake bed at Wilcannia in 1968. Both he and a colleague took photos. His mate was silly enough to show it to RAAF officers, who promptly confiscated it for security reasons, something they had done with quite a few UFO photos taken in the area. Pro Hart had lost his, but he had studied it closely, and was able to paint his *Saucerscape* from memory and committed the sighting to canvas. He later donated the painting to the tourist information centre as it was getting too much attention in his Broken Hill gallery.

Pro Hart later told journalist Gregg Kerr, "Several years before, when I was an army corporal at the Broken Hill camp, I along with several soldiers saw several unidentified objects fly over. They did a U-turn over the drive-in, where some people blew their horns, and then went back over the town. They weren't rockets – no wings.

"They follow cars, my sister used to cop it. It's a bit frightening. I don't believe they are extraterrestrial, rather they are secret surveillance flights by aircraft so sophisticated that our government won't tell us about them."

The RAAF and Woomera denied all knowledge and responsibility, and local police, although they receive sighting reports from time-to-time said there was no evidence of secret aircraft on clandestine missions.

Springs Creek, mid-1970s
In the mid-1970s Jill and Derek, friends of mine, with their two children were diving south through the isolated area of Springs Creek, heading towards Broken Hill. He was an expert witness, having

worked as a nuclear physicist for 30 years, and not quick to put his reputation on the line to pronounce something an unidentified object.

"At 3 p.m. (I checked my watch), we saw this object, motionless to the left and just above the top of a clump of trees about one kilometre away. It was a fat grey cigar-shape, about 50 metres across. It could have been a saucer on edge. It had red, yellow and green pulsating lights at the right end. I got my wife, son and daughter to verify what I was seeing, as their long-distance vision is better than mine."

"I stopped the car, got out and took a photo with my 35mm SLR camera. Using the car odometer as an accurate measure, I drove point two of a kilometre down the straight road. I stopped and took another photo using the car roof as a steady, the idea being that with trigonometry, I could work out the angles, distances and thus the size of the object. (There was no discernible noise.)"

"It was as clear as could be, with sharply defined edges, and we watched for 30 minutes until suddenly, like a switch it was gone. It was a clear sunny day, and I was quite excited at the photos I had taken – they should be good! As soon as we got home, on the north coast, I put them into the photo processing agent in town, where they were on-forwarded to the main laboratory."

"A week later I eagerly picked them up to find the photographs of the object were missing. Two frames had been removed from the cut film sections and replaced with blank frames. Microscopic examinations showed the edges did not match at all!"

This was the same notorious company that was responsible for all the other instances of negatives being removed from films and photographs. When asked on his report form if there was any photographic evidence, Derek wrote "Yes, the Government has it!"

Ivanhoe, Summer 1991

Robert Quinlan was on a camping holiday. When he reached Hay, the sun was going down: "Usually I put up my tent about that time. However I really wanted to be in Ivanhoe before morning. I normally avoid driving alone in the dark. Perhaps I should have stuck to that rule."

"About 50 kilometres before Ivanhoe I noticed a very bright light in the south-west behind me. I thought it might be a helicopter as two bright search lights were switched on. Maybe it was searching for something, perhaps I could help. I stopped, got out of the car, and signalled it with my nine volt torch. That's unusual; not a sound to be heard – perhaps high winds carrying the sound away."

"Without warning, a huge bright white, moon-sized object, was there to my right, about 500 metres behind me. It followed me, for about an hour, all the way to Ivanhoe. When I got into town it made a strange crackling sound, and took off straight up into the sky. Within 30 seconds it disappeared in the south-east, zigzagging as it got smaller."

(At this stage I realised Robert's accounting for the timing of his trip from Hay to Ivanhoe was a little confused, and didn't add up, but I let him continue:)

"I continued my camping trip without event. A few weeks later, when I was back home on the South Coast, I started hearing a high-pitch frequency sound in my right ear. Over the next few months it got worse, and became unbearable."

"I went to my local doctor, and somewhere deep in or around my ear he found a piece of electrical wire. He asked me how on earth it got there, and I couldn't tell him, although I did remember the crackling sound as that 'thing' flew away."

I did contact his doctor, who confirmed what Robert said about the wire. Unfortunately, he had not kept it.

Chapter Eight

North Coast NSW and Queensland

North Coast NSW

The northern coast of New South Wales runs north of Newcastle to the Queensland border. A long stretch of golden beaches is interspersed with some coastal rainforest, rocky headlands and country towns: Taree, Port Macquarie, Kempsey, Coffs Harbour, Grafton, and Lismore. The hinterlands to the west are heavily forested, leading up to the Great Dividing Range and the New England area. The main industries are timber, bananas, market gardening, dairy products and fisheries.

Grafton, 1982

Jackie Hayes rang me mid-2003, and while traumatised by her own experiences, was more concerned about three generations of her own family, especially her young children. Her father, a quiet man, was born in 1949, married early and became a father at 21. He worked as a farm manager, and the family lived on various properties over time:

"In 1982 we were living near Grafton on the New South Wales North Coast. Dad went missing for three weeks, and when he came home, genuinely believed he had only been away for a week. He had no memory of the other fortnight. Around about the same time, he also used to talk about several occasions when he met a six-foot, blond-haired man with blue eyes. Once he had his wife with him, who looked almost identical – except she was female. They had weird powers. One night the horses went missing, and the man told him where to find them, several valleys away!"

(As a researcher, this interested me. Jackie was not aware I had heard of a similar case, Kasey Cook in Bunyip, Victoria, where the family's father had gone missing for three weeks and could only remember one week; there had also been mention of a "strange, fair-haired man.")

The next year her father and his mate were in the truck with the dog and noticed unusual noises and strange lights. They got out of the truck, saw a UFO, and remember nothing else until they found themselves back in the truck. An hour had passed!

Jackie continued. "In later years, Dad confided in me that when he was nineteen, he was on his motorbike, just out of Sydney. It was a very cold day, and he pulled over into an area where it felt quite warm – a hot spot. He didn't remember anything else until he woke up feeling groggy. Locals who helped him had said: 'It must have been the UFOs in the area – we all saw them.' He admitted to dreaming about strange things after that. I was rather disturbed when he told me that he thought my mother had also been abducted, but felt the beings were telling him to tell her not to worry.

"In 1998 we had moved near Port Macquarie, where my father had a new manager position. One night there were unusual lights and noises. The next day we found cattle with their anus surgically cut out, as well as flesh cut from their faces. What upset Dad the most was his favourite horse Toby, was similarly mutilated. It was horrible!"

Jackie reflected on her own childhood. When she was young, she would have dreams of flying, (not so unusual), but also precognitive dreams which were always accurate. On these occasions she would always wake with a start at 5 a.m.

"In about 1978 we had a Christmas Evening get-together, and looked out to see lots of coloured lights in the sky. My aunty told me they were 'Santa Claus with his sleigh and reindeer'. A couple of years later, around midnight, I saw an object hovering over the neighbour's homestead. It was bigger than the house; round on the bottom, with a dome on the top and red, blue and yellow lights all around. It was totally silent when it moved away, and I tried to tell myself it must have been a dream."

Jackie then discussed her adult life. She married her first husband in 1988, when she was eighteen. Just after having her first baby, she woke to see tall figures at the end of her bed. She admits it may have just been a dream, but she was very frightened at the time. They were like ghosts, and had "grim reaper-type" hoods.

Everything was fine until 2001. She was 31, had divorced and remarried. Her age at the time interested me, as I have known of several female childhood experiencers to experience follow-up visitations in their early thirties. In July-August 2001 she saw an unusual blue light in the sky on a few nights. It would hover for quite a long period then suddenly go, leaving an aura around the house. The neighbours also noticed this.

"Around about the same time I went to sleep in a sarong one night, and woke up to find blood on the front and back. I was really scared, couldn't think of a logical explanation, and got my mother to come over and stay. In September I heard an explosion and saw a light overhead in the sky. Suddenly my one-year-old son was floating in the air next to my shoulder! I grabbed him, terrified, and held him tight. What was happening, and who would believe me?"

In 2003 more abnormal events started affecting the whole family. Early in the year, her sister and brother-in-law, who lived at Peakhurst in Sydney, woke to find their bedroom bathed with red light. At first they thought there was a fire outside, but when they looked, there was what could only be described as a fireball, hovering nearby. Her sister recalled a similar incident in Picton, south-west of Sydney, two years earlier.

By March, Jackie was feeling so much discomfort in one ear she went to the doctor. The specialist couldn't see anything blocking it, but a catscan showed, deep down, a five-centimetre object. It was split into two halves, like a miniature brain. She has a terror of needles, and didn't get it removed.

"In June, my father and his girlfriend heard a beeping and a noise like a revving truck. By 3 a.m. they opened the window to look. The noise was still there, but they could see nothing except a blue light some distance away."

While this is consistent with many other reports, it may have had a logical explanation. Jackie, however, had further unusual happenings to contend with.

"My 14-year-old daughter has recently told me that when she was eleven, she had a dream that a little man, with black eyes, like an owl, had put something in her. She said that later she picked the roof of her mouth, and something came out. Now, at fourteen, she is getting nose bleeds and had a similar dream. The 'little man was there, with the stars behind him', and he told her not to be afraid."

Jackie fears for her children. She and her sister discussed a shared feeling that they were sexually interfered with, as children. Not only was there no known culprit within the family, but neither woman has any memory of any abuse. They concluded that it must have happened in their sleep, but both knew in their hearts, that it was the strange, elusive beings which had haunted them.

Harwood and Palmer Islands

In June 1995, Christine and Darryl were going on holiday. UFOs were the last thing on their minds as they set off for Palmer Island off New South Wales' north coast. It was to be a quiet break, staying at the local caravan park, with Christine's dog, Pebbles, along as part of the family.

At about 8 p.m., on Saturday 3 June, they decided to go fishing on the Clarence River, about 400 metres down the road. At about that time Darryl glimpsed a bright whitish-orange ball of light, but didn't pay much attention to it. They spent some time unpacking the rods and fishing gear from the seat of the car, and then Darryl busied himself preparing sinkers, hooks and bait. "Christine doesn't touch fish or bait" he joked, "she just holds the line and catches them!"

117

Christine was sitting on the bank enjoying the night sky. "It was so tranquil – really clear with a few clouds and the moon and stars quite visible." Darryl was also very pleased with a new krypton globe in his torch, which he was waving up and down towards both sky and earth. (When Darryl told me this I thought – "Oh my, waving torches and spotlights is not a good idea if there is a UFO nearby.")

"Suddenly Christine pointed out a long, thin, white cigar-shaped, luminescent light," he said. "I told her it might be the moon behind a cloud, but privately I thought it was a little strange, and remembered the light I had seen a few minutes earlier. I was still preoccupied with a few fishing problems as there was a fast current and the lines were getting snagged on the rocks below. I did not pay too much attention to Christine's 'light in the sky', and after clearing several snags while juggling the torch, decided to stick to one rod."

Christine watched the strange light for about fifteen minutes: "Suddenly, for a twenty-second period, it started diminishing in size, then zig-zagged upwards into an orange dot. I didn't say anything to Darryl as I wasn't concerned at the time, and he would have made me feel silly with a logical explanation."

For the next five minutes or so, they were distracted by the fishing line becoming firmly entangled about ten metres down the river bank. While Darryl was struggling with the rod, and trying to cut the line, Christine called out: "Are you all right?" As they both looked up, they were astonished by what they saw emerging from the other side of the river. As Darryl raised his head to answer Christine, he realised the light he had previously ignored, had expanded from five centimetres to over a metre wide in the sky.

"A large oval object seemed to be rising upwards from the ground, behind the trees, and moving towards us." Christine recalled. "It was huge, like the size of a caravan close up. I was starting to panic, and was telling Darryl I wanted to get out of there, and quick!"

Darryl, for some inexplicable reason, was also feeling worried, but tried to keep calm for Christine's sake. "She was screaming 'Get the f... out of here' and I swore back and said 'Shut up! Relax!' With a deliberate display of outward calm, I started packing the gear back into the car."

Christine, now in a very agitated state, kept her eye firmly on the strange object which was moving closer. Darryl kept methodically loading things into the boot. "I was packing shit," he admitted, "but I tried to keep calm, and hoped Christine hadn't realised the closeness of that thing"

As the object reached the river, and started to move over towards them, it appeared to tilt on its side, exposing a vast under-section. It had two concentric circles of intensely bright orange light, one inside the other. "Can't you see that Darryl?" Christine shrieked. Darryl could see it well enough, but felt scared and confused, concentrating on getting everything into the car to get away.

"Darryl didn't look up again, but that 'thing' was just about overhead. I was shaking with fright," Christine continued, "and praying for it to go away and not hurt Darryl or Pebbles. Strangely enough, the dog was lying on the back seat, totally oblivious to the mayhem around him!"

With one eye on the object, they jumped into the car, and started up, first muffing a U-turn, and then managing a three-point turn in their frantic efforts to flee the area.

"It was almost as if the object recognised our fear," Christine reflected, "at this stage it veered back over to the other side of the river. As we left, it seemed to be moving slowly and smoothly towards the hills in the other direction.

"We got back to the caravan park at 9.20 p.m. We wanted to ask if people there had seen anything, but we were still scared and in shock; we didn't want anyone thinking we were nutters. Darryl was asleep within an hour! I lay awake for another six hours, just thinking about what had happened. I remembered that as a child I had read about aliens, and always hoped to see a real one. I thought that it was ironic that when I eventually encountered a UFO, I forgot this wish, and prayed for it to go away!"

Despite his outward calm, Darryl experienced the worst side-effects from the sighting. At 3 a.m. that night, and on several occasions since, he had suffered bad nightmares, which he won't

118

discuss. Christine noticed that before he wakes in fright, Darryl starts screaming in his sleep, and his body temperature alternates from feverish to freezing cold. "I have never known him to have bad dreams before, and his scream is the most bone-chilling noise, a sort of 'Wooooo' – like nothing I've heard before. Sometimes his body goes momentarily rigid, and when he wakes, he just clings to me, burying his head."

"Pebbles, who seemed completely oblivious to the object on the Saturday night, became quite ill, began vomiting, and we had to take him to the vet the following Wednesday."

Strangely, Christine and Darryl did not discuss the incident for about ten days, when Christine became concerned about Darryl's nightmares. "It was almost as if we were in a state of denial or amnesia." They contacted the local newspaper, who in turn referred them to INUFOR. Their story was corroborated, in part, by other witnesses who reported seeing strange orange lights in the area that weekend.

About two weeks later, Christine's father was visiting from Sydney. He suggested they take a day trip back to Harwood Island, on the other side of the river, from where the craft seemed to rise. Harwood Island, on the Clarence River, consists of sugar cane fields, a refinery and a few scattered houses. They all went to the approximate spot where they thought the object had been.

"We were astounded to find a large area of depressed cane. The outside walls were intact all the way around, and there were no signs of footprints or tyre tracks. It was as if something from above had just plummeted down, just onto that area. I don't know if a freak wind could have created that effect," Christine said. "Dad and Darryl are both sceptics and neither could offer an explanation for the damaged cane, let alone its being where we'd seen the object."

They took some photographs of the damaged cane. However, it was on private property, and some time had elapsed since the incident, making further investigation of the area uncertain.

Of greater concern to me was the psychological wellbeing of Christine, and especially Darryl. While Christine commented to me that she was sure they were only there for about half an hour or so, (not one-and-a-half hours), "time went funny" and she was sure they started packing up long before 8.30 p.m. There was only a bit of fishing gear to put in the boot. While Darryl was moving in a calm, methodical manner, he wasn't wasting time, and they should have got back down the road by 8.35 p.m. at the latest.

There was no real evidence of missing time, (if there was, it was for a relatively brief 45 minutes). The after-effects on the couple suggested more may have occurred on that riverbank than they remembered. The object was overhead, yet when they jumped in the car it was moving away.

Then there were Darryl's nightmares, plus their not discussing it for ten days! All classic signs for lost time! We decided it was better to let the matter rest. While it is tempting for a researcher to gain as much information as possible, ethics dictate the wellbeing of the witness is paramount.

Researcher Bill Chalker has conducted a lot of investigations in this part of New South Wales, and was very interested in this case because of a startling coincidence with an event he had recollected exactly 20 years before on 3 June 1975. That evening, at 7.30 p.m. a group of young men saw a bright, green and red object hovering nearby after approaching from the west. It moved in the direction of Palmers Island and they followed it in their car. The UFO approached to within 200 yards of their vehicle and hovered. Its lights had dimmed and they could see it was disc-shaped and about 30 feet in diameter.

After shooting off down the road, it hovered at the end, before zigzagging across the tarmac, crossing the Clarence River, and hovering over the cane fields on Harwood Island. It moved to the side and was either fading or landing behind the sugar cane sheds. At about the same time other witnesses had seen a fast-moving light in the area and farmers reported disturbances among their dogs and other animals. Unfortunately, a landing site could not be found afterwards.

I have wondered about that particular area and paranormal events. In about 1991 I received a call from a very disturbed lady who claimed she was in constant contact with aliens. She claimed there were three golden beings, who looked like cocoons, on nearby Palmers Island, where she and her husband lived. They would come to help her whenever she called. However, small grey lizard-beings had arrived both in Yamba and Palmers Island. She had memories of a white, metallic, curved hospital-type bed, and images of a wide red circle and a red beam being directed to her mind. She was terrified of the dark and needles, and her husband left her after he woke to a blue light in the bedroom which temporarily paralysed them.

She also talked of a beacon on Palmers Island, and mentioned a circle, behind a corn patch, where a huge black triangular UFO landed. She said her life was in danger as she "knew too much." I was curious about the similarity of her "wide red circle" to Christine's "concentric orange rings." It would have been unethical for me to push this poor woman for further details. It was obvious something had happened to her, and the best thing I could do was guide her into seeking professional medical help.

New South Wales northern border

Kingscliffe, 1993

Sub-tropical Kingscliffe lies on the Pacific coast, just on the New South Wales side of the Queensland border. Pastoral rolling hills, rainforest, banana palms and other fruit plantations frame the western side of this beautiful coastline and beaches.

Occasionally I receive a report which leaves me wondering as to the origin, nature and purpose of an unidentified craft. One such case occurred after midnight in 1993.

Tony Walker and his 16-year-old son, Rob, were fishing at Cabarita, facing north to Kingscliffe. There was a large rock on their left and the ocean to their right. They often see military helicopters, Hornets and F111s on exercise, flying low, up and down the coast. Tony explained what they saw this night was very different:

"A massive, brilliant, white light came in fairly low from the mountains and Mount Warning area in the west. It was heading east towards the sea, at a speed faster than a small plane, but slower and lower than the military jets. It came past us, lighting up the large rock, and hovered out over the sea.

"There were five or six smaller, coloured balls on either side of this white light. They moved out and shot up vertically with incredible speed and precision, indicating some degree of control and guidance. The main object moved further out over the sea, and emitted a long series of precise dots and dashes from the rear, before taking off at tremendous speed.

"The next day Rob's school mates said they had also seen bright lights the previous night. A farmer in the back hills of Murwillumbah had found crop circles on his property, but was not prepared to confirm this publicly.

"I am an ex-radio operator. What astonished me, was that while the craft was like nothing I had ever seen before, it was most definitely morse-code signals flashing from it. Unfortunately, I was not quick enough to decipher the fairly long display. I rang Amberley Air Force Base (quite close by, in Queensland) and was connected to a senior officer, very interested in the details."

I was definitely tempted to confine this report to the too-hard basket. I thought of several possibilities without reaching any satisfactory conclusion. Could this unusual craft be a new toy the Australian military have kept top secret, or could it belong to a foreign power, using morse-code to avoid electronic signals being detected?

On the other hand, if it was not terrestrial, why use a primitive signalling morse-code system when they would have advanced technology at their disposal? Further, no matter what the origin or purpose, who were they signalling to on the shore, and why? Another mystery to which I don't have answers!

Lightning Ridge, 12 December 1991

Lightning Ridge is a remote, inland, opal-mining town near the New South Wales–Queensland border. It is here that the valuable black opal is mined; fossickers come from all over the world to try their luck. Its residents are hardy, self-sufficient, and very community-minded.

Just before 11 p.m. the power and lights started going on and off in cycles of about one minute at a time, plunging the town into light and darkness alternately. Puzzled residents went out to see what was happening, and spotted a huge black disc above the town.

"It was hovering, slightly tilted, about 500 feet above the ground, and seemed to be silently positioned above the water tower. It had two dull red, neon-type lights along the bottom ring and a dome on top. Our power went back to normal later and I don't know if it caused our power to go on and off, whether it was attracted by the fluctuating lights, or if it was taking some water on board. I never thought to check."

Queensland

Stanthorpe

Stanthorpe is situated in the mountain range immediately north of the border with New South Wales, and 225 kilometres southwest of Brisbane. It is the main town in what is known as the Granite Belt, where large silver and lead deposits were mined in the late-nineteenth century. Today it is primarily agricultural – a fruit growing area with some sheep and wool production. According to one of our witnesses, numerous copper, gold, silver and tin deposits are known in the area.

Joe Whitney wrote in *UFO Encounter* about "The Highway Stalker" on a stretch of the New England Highway, along two long sections of road between the mountains near Stanthorpe. In one case, a large, bright white light followed two young women just after 8 p.m., along both stretches of road. It was about 20 metres behind them. At first they thought it was as motorbike, then realised it was something unknown and sped to the safety of the next town.

Another couple told of a similar experience on the same part of the highway just after 9 p.m. on another night. The husband, who was driving, initially thought the bright white light, 20 metres behind his vehicle was a motorbike, possibly even a traffic cop, but then realised the light was twice the height off the roadway compared to that of a regular motorbike. Again, as with the young women, the light just disappeared at the end of the same section of road.

A third witness told Whitney of an identical experience, but this time the light was to the right of the highway, just above the tree tops. It was too big to be a star, and definitely not the moon. When he first saw it the witness thought it might be a plane, but there were no flickering lights, and its behaviour was not consistent with a plane.

Inexplicable phenomena

Country people usually prefer to keep things to themselves, and are reluctant to discuss or report unexplained events. They don't need to be exposed to ridicule or gossip within their close-knit, remote communities. Sometimes, locals will break this silence to confide strange events which have disturbed both them and their close neighbours.

A few years ago I received a call from Jack, a gentleman who, while intelligent and articulate, wasn't so young any more. He lived in his homestead 70 kilometres out of Stanthorpe, and was traumatised by UFO activity over his property, during the previous three nights in particular. Talking to someone who was distant and non-judgemental must have been therapeutic, because it all came pouring out:

His 16,000-acre property, and those of his neighbours, is in hilly terrain, mostly covered by scrub. Two lights, mainly a red-orange colour, would usually appear between 7 and 8.30 p.m. They would hover, then flash across the sky at incredible speed, only to reappear and repeat the same behaviour a short time later. The first night they had been very close, but on the second they were further away, in front of one of the nearby hills. (These hills are 300-400 feet high, indicating the objects were fairly low.)

The third night, when Jack saw them appear and disappear at least twelve or thirteen times, he noticed they also turned slightly, and he could see a flashing light. His neighbour Kevin had already telephoned, nervously gabbling on about something silently hovering at tree top level over his dams, but "couldn't get it on camera." Kevin's camera, which worked perfectly well inside the house, just wouldn't work there.

Jack said the night before, his ten dogs had been going crazy. He was also curious, because on the fourth day two military jets flew very low over his property, as if searching for something.

A third neighbour, Sally, and her son also saw the unusual lights. When they shot across the sky, they moved faster than any military craft they had ever seen.

Two to three months previously, all three neighbours had seen four solid lights in formation, two above and two below, which travelled in a straight line across the sky and took about 60 seconds to cover about 40 kilometres. At first they thought they might be helicopters, but there were no flashing lights, and they suddenly disappeared, only to reappear later, still in formation. Were they four separate objects, or one large craft?

Jack's house was situated on a hill, overlooking ten kilometres of his own cattle property. He often sat on the veranda where he could see the road, to keep an eye out for poachers. He had only seen lights over the previous three months, and at first had dismissed them as helicopters.

Before he contacted me, Jack had rung an old friend who had risen to a very high rank in the Australian Navy (I cannot divulge whom). He had told Jack that he knew of nothing conventional that could move at that speed, stop, hover, then switch off: "We have nothing that can do that."

Jack started to confide in me. "I had an even stranger experience you may not believe. Three years ago I bought another property for the cattle, closer to the hills where we saw the lights. My legs aren't the best, so I'd driven around to lock some of the gates. I got to one gate, about 100 metres up a slight rise, and I got this inexplicable sense of fear. There was no reason, just a sort of instinct. I went back to my vehicle and got the gun."

"When I walked back up to the area surrounding the gate; it had grass so green and lush, the like of which I'd never seen before. Grass clumps were up to two feet tall and ten inches round; I had to brush it aside to lock the gate. Three days later I went back. There was no sign of the grass, no gate, and I walked to the boundary through short brown stubble. The good thing is there wasn't that sense of fear. No, I'm not mistaken and it wasn't the wrong location. I've never seen all that grass or the gate again."

I wondered about elusive inter-dimensional and time-slip factors investigators sometimes come across, and my interest was further aroused when Jack continued confiding in me. (Perhaps he had, at long last, found someone who would actually believe him, or at least listen without laughing.)

"There is another property down the road, owned by my friend Allan, and the people living there are really spooked. All six of them have seen this six-foot-high, bright fluoro-colour apparition – it's too big to be a person. It's happened four or five times, around 8 p.m., when there's a full moon, which makes visibility easier. They see it on the bank of the dam, and it sort of floats across the dam into this ball of smoky-green mist, which has a bright light in the middle.

"Allan went down to the shed one night to fill the generator. He didn't see anything unusual in the sky or anywhere, but as he came back out he turned and saw two tennis-ball-sized lights sitting in the gutter by the side of the drive. They were a whitish colour – not quite fluoro. He got quite a start, and in a split second they took off at incredible speed across the gutter – one went to the left and the other right." Allan has also seen UFOs; one night an unusual object lit up the ground all around him.

"We have a dam in the area nicknamed the Graveyard Dam." Bulldozers and other heavy equipment always have a problem there – their turbos blow and they get all other kinds of machinery malfunctions. It was also unusual what happened with the fish."

This was becoming more intriguing as Jack was opening-up, so I asked him what happened to the fish? "It's a 100 square metre dam, and I sometimes put fish in there. I put 2,000 yellowbelly and silver perch in it once, all originally about two inches long. Over the next six months the dam went dry, and I used the opportunity to scrape out the bottom, as it used to leak. Now those fish can usually bury themselves in mud during a drought, but I was upset as I thought all the fish would now surely be dead.

"Twelve more months went by, and there was ten inches of water in the dam. All the fish were there – the yellowbellies, half a kilo, and the silver perch three kilo and more. The next day there were so many I had to move some to another dam. I couldn't even get into the water without stepping on some; I don't know how this could be?"

I wondered about the unusual phenomena of the incredible, almost impossible growth of the fish, and the lush grass around his gate. What kind of energies were at play here? I asked him about his electricity supply.

"That's very strange too; I've been here three years and my electricity bills are always very low. It was the same with the previous owner. I use a lot more electricity than my neighbours, and yet their power bills are much higher than mine." This wasn't the answer I was expecting, and I thought of Sophie Gardner in Western Australia and others who experience odd phenomena and who receive astronomically high bills – Jack was just the opposite!

It was in my next interview with Jack that I realised he was not really thinking that these unusual events might be associated with extraterrestrials, but perhaps something of a more earthly origin. While I was starting to form a few theories in my own mind, it is not wise for an investigator to prompt a witness or suggest any explanation, so I just let Jack continue relating the strange happenings in the area:

"One day I shot a feral pig, but as it was late afternoon. I went back the following day for the carcass and got a shock! This was a 40-50 kilogram animal and its head was gone. I was really puzzled. You cannot take a pig's head off that way – it wasn't trophy hunters, and it wasn't eaten, so it wasn't your normal predator."

"It was severed at the base of the neck behind the shoulder blades with the shoulders still intact – a clean cut. No nicks or cuts on the flesh and no blood around anywhere. It appeared to have been surgically removed and was so well done that an expert couldn't have been so precise. A local brush-cutter told me he has seen kangaroos literally snapped in half with a clean cut. The front half and head are gone, leaving the liver and back half – even the tail is intact. They were not shot, there were no scratch or claw marks, nor crush marks to the bones. In fact, except for being cut in half, there was no obvious cause of death.

"A few months ago I found a wiener calf – just dead. Occasionally I find cattle that are dead for no reason. Some are intact and some have obviously been eaten by predators after death, but there is nothing to show a predator actually killed them."

"I have seen foxes and feral pigs, also a couple of big cats. At one time what I'm sure was a black panther was near a mob of panting sheep. It was six feet long, and before I had time to get my rifle it covered 500 metres in a flash. Three years ago I came across what looked like a four-to-five-foot chocolate brown cougar. I chased it for about 100 metres until we met two rather large, angry bulls; both the cougar and I took off in different directions."

Jack was convinced that there were Yowies (called Bunyips or Bigfoot in some cultures) in the area, and they may be responsible for some of the deaths. (I did not tell him that the precise mutilation of the pig, or unexplained death of the cattle were sometimes attributed to unidentified objects, and that some researchers had connected so-called Yowies with UFOs.)

Jack elaborated on the existence of the big, hairy, humanoid creature. "My family have farmed properties in the area for over a hundred years. My grandfather, who used to call it a Bunyip, said he thought it lived in a cave at the top of a large hill or mountain, and left that part of the property and the Bunyip alone. Difficulties arose when the deer rutting season occurred, and the Bunyip came much closer."

"In the mid-1950s there were some problems. A neighbour bought a rifle and went to the local authorities to apply for a permit to shoot it. Next thing he was contacted by a Government Minister who said he was doing research on these creatures, and spent over an hour asking questions. He offered to give him a camera, but said if he shot it he would be hit with a very hefty fine and six months jail. He said three months later he actually saw it. The sun was in his eyes, but he caught a glimpse of a seven to eight-foot silhouette walking in the scrub.

"Allan has five sites up the back of his property. These are 'dead' areas, where the grass has been pulled out and woven through a rough roof and walls, made of woven branches. The biggest is about seven feet and the smallest four feet. Allan says he found them two years ago. They are still there but he leaves them alone. He is sure they are from Yowies, not local Aboriginals, who won't go near the area." (I found this interesting as Jack couldn't know about similar nests being found in 1983, deep in the bush near Canning Dam in Western Australia, after several Yowie sightings.)

"The brush-cutter who found the dead kangaroos also swears that Yowies exist. He used to hunt, and said that when there is a full moon in the colder months they are around. Seven or eight years ago he was camped near a creek at Kilroy. About midnight, he heard a massive roar coming from behind a Moreton Bay Fig tree, vibrating the car and rattling the tent. He froze in fright, and spent a sleepless night hiding in the tent.

"Two months later he was in the same area, cooking some deer meat for supper. He heard a gurgling-humming noise. He picked up his rifle and walked towards it, some 200-300 metres away, down the steep hill. He didn't see anything, but when he turned around, he saw Yowie footprints going uphill behind him. The ground was soft; his own footprints were quarter of an inch deep, the other prints were two inches deep and eight inches across. He walked back to his camp the long way round.

"The UFOs are not causing us any harm, and as far as the Yowies are concerned, I don't think anyone has ever shot or captured one. I wonder if they are from another dimension, popping in and out, only seen occasionally. Maybe they are more scared of us than we are of them!"

(I didn't tell Jack about less-friendly encounters with a Yowie at Krambach, near Barrington in New South Wales; no need to spook him!)

Brisbane

A sub-tropical area, north of the New South Wales border, Brisbane is the capital city of the State of Queensland, and situated on the Brisbane River, which flows into Moreton Bay. The city itself, sprawls over small hills around the river, and up to Mount Coot-tha, eight kilometres from the city centre.

Sunnybank, March 1987

People have long dreamt of being able to make themselves invisible. Recent fiction has popularised this idea; from Harry Potter to *Star Trek*. The military implications would also be enormous.

Jack Carpenter and two friends were lying on a blanket on the back lawn, just relaxing and watching the stars come out in the early evening sky, when a huge black shape glided slowly overhead.

"It was hard to gauge its size, but I would approximate it to be about a football field across and at an altitude of a couple of hundred feet. This object was not the commonly-described 'saucer shape'. Instead it looked like a boomerang or triangle. It was black, with no lights whatsoever, and moved very slowly and silently. All three of us watched in amazement as it passed over.

"Stranger than that, to this day another aspect of this phantom craft intrigues me. I've studied the sciences, and as I watched I could see this shape was solid, and appeared to have edges where the plates of its under-girth met, like that of an aircraft wing. However, as it moved it also seemed to possess translucent qualities. We could see stars dimly through the body of the object as it moved under them. Solid, yet not solid? Strange indeed!

"The shape passed over the house, and we in turn pursued it until we lost sight of it as it continued over the rooftops. All of this took place over a populated area. I had thought to myself, 'Great, I had two witnesses and God knows how many other people saw it.' But there were no reports of it in the newspapers. Could we have been the only ones to see it? Surely not!

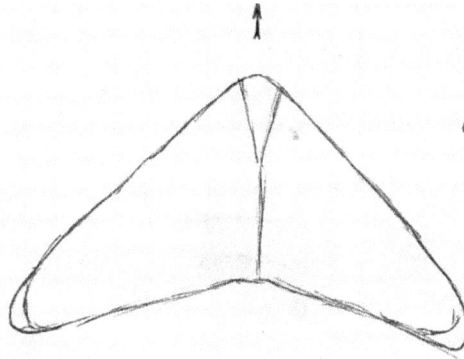

COVERED WITH A PLATE OR LINED / SEAMED TEXTURE.

TRANSLUCENT YET I'M AM SURE IT WAS SOLID.

LARGE AND MOVED LIKE A SILENT SHADOW.

"I only wish I had a camera that night. It most definitely wasn't the traditional disc or cigar-shaped object people talk about. And it was silent, not brightly lit; it didn't emit any sound, and was in a heavily populated area rather than some isolated location."

The *ACUFOS Reports Digest No.38* reported a similar case which occurred at Babinda, North Queensland, after 8 p.m. on 15 August 1990:

> "Two people driving along the Bruce Highway, watched an unusual craft for about three minutes. It was a large, bright oval moon-sized object with smaller lights along its circumference. Although brightly lit, the witnesses could still see the stars as pinpricks of light through it."

Central Queensland

Hughenden, 1956

My colleagues in VUFORS documented an occurrence which happened 60 years ago, in late 1956. To observe her wish for anonymity, they called her "Miss L", so I'll use the pseudonym "Loretta."

Loretta was only twelve years old when she lived on a farm near Hughenden. It was a fine day, and as she was walking across the flat open paddock at about 4.30 p.m., she heard what sounded like "the soft hum of a vacuum cleaner."

"I felt some kind of force across my shoulders and down my back, and realised I was being lifted from the ground. As I tried to see what was above me, I must have fainted, and when I came to, found myself in a large room. There were two men, with their backs to me, dressed in silver-white ski suits.

"They seemed to be operating a panel which faced a wall upon which was a screen showing what looked like a full colour-outline of a galaxy. I looked around the room which was unfurnished. On one side was a three-metre-high arched doorway which led into a corridor. Along another wall were porthole-type windows, which appeared to be made of dark, highly-polished glass.

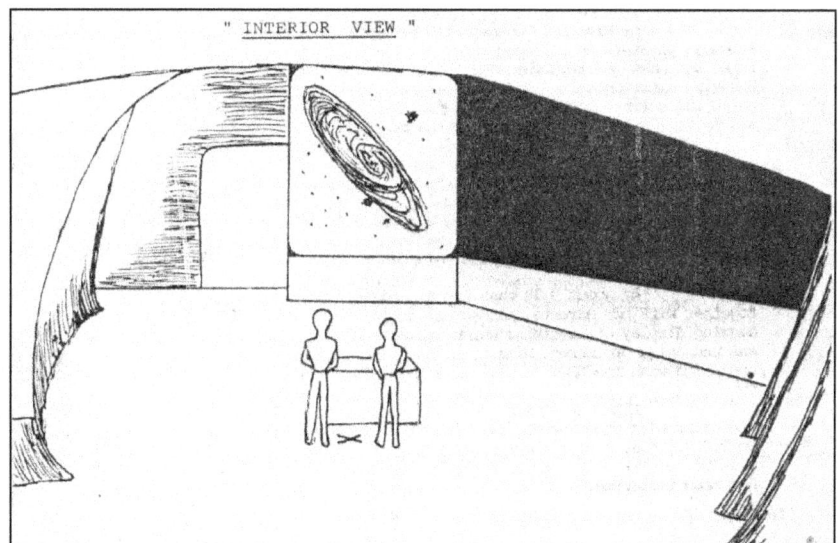

" INTERIOR VIEW "

"The floor looked like thick frosted glass, and the whole room varied between light-tan and mauve-white, except for one wall which was jet black. The floor, ceiling and walls seemed to be moulded together, as there were no apparent joins. The two men had not communicated with me at all, and as I was still looking around the room, I felt an enormous pressure on my head and neck, and lost consciousness again.

"Next thing I knew I was back on the farm, but in a different paddock. Hovering about six metres above me was a huge, saucer-shaped craft, about 80 metres in diameter. It moved slowly at first, with a bouncing movement, as if on a cushion of air. As I tried to get back to the farmhouse, a violent, ringing sound nearly deafened me, and I turned back to see the craft rapidly ascending

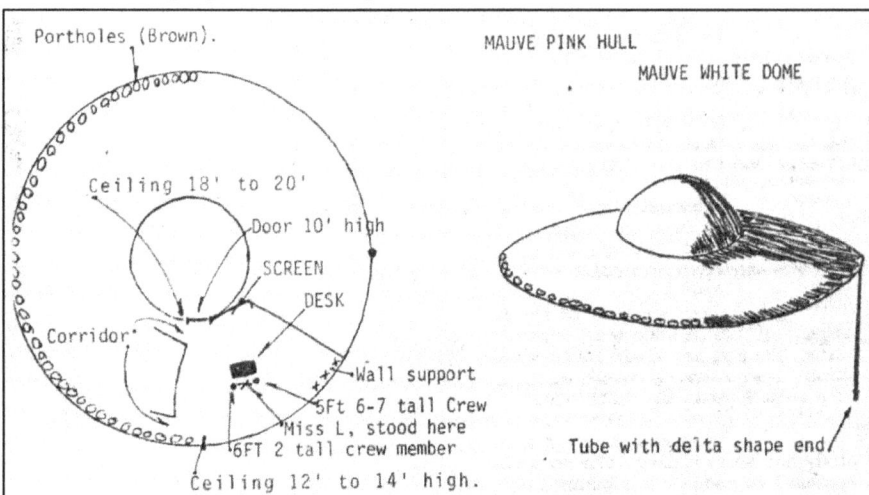

towards a bank of clouds in the west."

When Loretta got back she realised two hours had passed since she first started across the paddock. She was a very shaken 12-year-old, but there were no witnesses, and she didn't tell her family or anyone else. Later in life she was hesitant for fear of ridicule.

Tell me more!

Often, a researcher receives a communication which has the potential to develop into a very interesting investigation, and then hits the proverbial, frustrating stone wall.

One such instance occurred after an interview on *Good Morning Australia* in 1989. I received a letter from James, who lived in the outback. The only address he gave was c/o a Post Office near Hervey Bay, on the central Queensland coast. He was obviously intelligent and articulate, and seemed genuine. I was unable to track him down without a telephone number or adequate address.

His letter certainly got my attention, but he had not specified exact dates and locations. While I would have preferred to check and verify the incidents he recounted, I can only relate parts of his report as received:

"In June 1984, I lived out in the bush, some 180 miles from the nearest town, in a caravan with my family. We were on top of an ironstone ridge, but right on top of the incline was a rocky outcrop. There was another family in the vicinity, and often, late at night, we would play chess. Sometimes it was nearly midnight before I went back to my van.

"It was during this period that I occasionally noticed a very bright light. I thought it might be a helicopter, maybe two miles away, with a searchlight going from side to side. Just for fun, I'd got my torch out, and flashed it on and off at it. (This sounds crazy – I know!) If I mention it to anyone they think I am a bit touched, especially when I told them that the light would flash back.

"This went on nearly every night, for about three weeks. Then one night, at about 10.30 p.m., there was this fantastic bright fluorescent light, and everyone came out to have a look. There was this huge object hovering just above the trees. It was close enough to see windows on the side and a sort of pink pulsating glow.

"I was stunned, to say the least, and there I was, standing in front of everyone with my torch. I still believe if I had shone my torch in that direction, it might have landed, (but that's even crazier than the next incident.) It hovered for what seemed like minutes, then took off, straight up and off.

"A few weeks later, one old chap passed through, and stopped for a talk. He mentioned that some sort of UFO had crashed into the side of a mountain about 20 miles away. There were all these Armed Forces fellows over there, and no-one was allowed within five miles of the area.

"I haven't mentioned this to many people, simply because they look at you like you're having them on."

I was left thinking – "A UFO crash into a mountain? Military retrieval? Tell me more! James, where are you? I need to talk to you."

North Queensland

Tropical Far North Queensland is an area which is often overlooked for UFO phenomena – there are so few investigators there. Black Mountain is a short drive north of Cairns, near Kuranda.

Black Mountain

Yvonne, whose brother is a pilot, is a registered nurse in charge of a local hospital ward. Her husband Geoff is a mathematics teacher. They married in early 1978, and travelled by train to Cairns for their long-awaited honeymoon.

When they arrived in Cairns they did not book into a motel, and decided to hire a vehicle and head north. Perhaps later, they would book in elsewhere. The road went up the coast – on the left-hand-side was the cliff face, with the ocean to their right. It was some 45 kilometres north of Cairns, near Black Mountain, when the couple decided that maybe they would sleep in the station wagon.

They stopped the car, and turned off the lights. Geoff got out to go to the toilet around the back, and left the car door open and the interior light on. Other than that it was pitch black. Yvonne got out of the car and also went to the rear.

"Suddenly we saw a bright light over the ocean," she said. "It came in an arc towards us, and stopped 200 feet over our heads. It was like an inverted lightshade, with rows of coloured lights around. I cannot remember colour, details etc., but I clearly recall a cluster of blue bulbous lights underneath. It was rocking from side to side, and seemed to hover for a short while, still rocking."

"I stood there, mesmerised, as if in a trance. It was like this object was sort of, watching us! The next thing I knew Geoff was pushing me, telling me loudly to get back in the car and shut the door. He said the 'thing' may have been attracted by the shining interior light."

After a while it moved behind a nearby hill, and for some time they could see a large pulsating light coming from behind the rise, as if it had landed. They were in the car, and Yvonne was smoking a cigarette to calm her nerves. Geoff didn't smoke, but he was so distraught that he grabbed it and tried to have a puff anyway.

"Suddenly we noticed a pinpoint of light from the road, outside the car. It was blinking through the window and was similar in some ways to the lighted end of a cigarette. (Not a reflection of mine, which I had put out.) We were scared, and thought it might be the eyes of some small animal. Geoff started the car, spun it around, and turned the headlights full on. We could see nothing but the rhythmic pulsating of the light source. It was hypnotic."

Since the road was even more isolated further north, they drove straight back to Cairns, and parked outside the hospital. Too agitated to sleep, they went to the 24-hour truck-stop garage and drank coffee until dawn. Once it was daylight, they decided to go back to Black Mountain and look for any evidence of something landing. They drove back in the early morning, parked, and walked off the side of the road.

"We started walking through the bush to the rear of the hill where the object had landed. We suddenly came across a huge, barbed-wire fence, with some kind of sign on it, warning about trespass. I don't know if it was something commercial, or a military type area. It was totally obscured from the road. Behind the fence was something Geoff told me looked like a huge microwave tower. I cannot remember what happened or how long we stood there. It was weird, as if I had suddenly lost my memory and my mind was being controlled. I can't explain it. We were like zombies or robots, staring at the bush and each other, and not remembering why we had come. We didn't even check for a landing site, as we had intended."

They just got into the car and rushed back to Cairns, arriving in the late morning. It was summer, and they had left at dawn. "The return trip normally takes 90 minutes, leaving at least three hours we couldn't account for. We are not aware of any facility in this area, except for an animal sanctuary, so what was that place and where were we during those missing hours?"

They caught the first train back that afternoon. It was only when they were on the journey, returning to Brisbane, that they recovered their equilibrium and realised that they were supposed to be on their honeymoon.

"We didn't really know why they were returning after one day, and when we arrived back in Brisbane, Geoff's family said we were like a pair of jabbering idiots."

Since then Yvonne has suffered strange gynaecological problems, and is almost scared to find out the reason why. She has experienced heightened psychic and clairvoyant abilities, and some strange dreams, which always include a UFO with human-sized beings who have pointy heads, "sharp" faces and big eyes.

"They look like mice, standing up erect, and they point at me saying, 'We – you. We are going to get/take you.' In my dreams I am always very scared. In one I imagined I turned myself into a cat to combat them."

Geoff has also reported some strange dreams, including one where little creatures were sitting on his legs in bed.

Two years later, (at the end of 1980), their daughter was born. She is also quite psychic, very talented and creative. She has excelled in academic pursuits plus dancing and athletics. She has always drawn pictures of "little people", which, to some extent, disturbs Yvonne and Geoff. They considered some hypnotherapy to find out what, if anything, happened, but are still hesitating a little, and will progress slowly at their own pace.

Sugar cane farmers – not happy!

About 30 years ago in 1985 a sugar cane farmer had complained to his friend George about some mysterious crop circles he had discovered in his cane fields. This was no longer a novelty up there, and growers were not happy to lose considerable income as a result. Farmer John invited George to come up and look for himself. George and his girlfriend, Janice, were curious and excited; this was something they had to see!

"We went up on my motorbike, and took a shortcut we knew down a back track. We did not know at the time that we had bypassed military security or special services, who had cordoned off the entire area. We left the bike at the edge of the cane, and worked our way through to the flattened circle.

"It wasn't long before we heard the sound of someone approaching, and we thought it was my friend John. It was a shock to see a very angry fellow who wanted to know what we were doing inside the circle. While his overalls looked military, they had no insignia. He wore a balaclava, but we could see his face was covered with scar tissue, as if he had been burnt at some time. He was rather intimidating, and scanned us both with some form of device before ordering us back to the homestead.

"When we went to John's farm on the motorbike, the whole place was crawling with military personnel. They ushered us into a caravan to be questioned as if we were criminals. It was scary! God only knows what was in that caravan; it was full of all kinds of electrical equipment – I assume communications gear, radar and other high-tech stuff. Before we could fully assess the purpose of this mobile centre, another bloke, obviously senior, rushed in. We were not supposed to be there!

"We were taken back to the house for further interview, and told to stay there and not to leave without permission. These guys really meant business. They never identified who they were or what they represented."

The couple had intended staying with John for the night, but fearing for their safety, managed to sneak out to their motorbike and get away. "It was getting dark, and we were shaken by our experience, so we found a motel in a nearby town. We thought we should be safe, but took the precaution of locking the motorbike in a shed, out of sight. We had a quick meal, and went straight to our room.

"The next morning the motel owner told us that later in the evening a bunch of military types had been looking through the window, obviously searching for someone. They had not come inside, and I was glad I'd had the foresight to hide the motorbike."

Needless to say, the couple left the area that morning. George asked me not to publish his name or occupation, as he is still concerned about evading the military. What was so important about the crop circle? Was it extraterrestrial or some more earthly experiment or technology gone wrong? George will never know, and John is too scared to say anything.

I am sure there were more intriguing events to our far north which we know nothing about. Another researcher asked me if I knew about an incident reported in the media in June or July 1947, where a photo was published of an unidentified object that crashed in a cane field. It was located at the end of long path it had cut through the cane. About a week later it was reported that the object was taken away by an American warship.

Torres Strait, 1959

The Torres Strait and its islands lie between northern Australia and Papua New Guinea, and are under Australian jurisdiction.

While rarely mentioned, they have strategic importance to Australia. I have always made it crystal clear to witnesses that I will immediately advise the RAAF of any lights or sightings, no matter how insignificant, from this region.

In July 1959, just after the Father Gill Sightings, a series of reports came in from this area:

Prince of Wales Island is just ten miles off the tip of Australia's Cape York Peninsula and an isolated place. Its twelve terrified inhabitants sent a report to Thursday Island police, twelve miles to the north, that they were scared of a "huge red glowing object" which had landed on a hilltop on Port Lihou Island, on the island's southern edge.

The object apparently could not be seen in daylight, but gave off a reddish glow in the dark. (We do not know if that witness was colour-blind). Other reports stated that the object was definitely giving off a "huge, bright green light."

On the 11 July 1959, five separate Trans-Pacific airline pilots reported seeing unidentified objects or lights flying to the south. Thursday Island residents reported seeing a "green object" flying low, and Mrs. Gwen Maloney of Thursday Island said that the object was also seen from Mappoon Mission on the west coast of Cape York.

Four prominent businessmen and doctors had gone crocodile shooting. When they returned to Cairns they reported that on the same night (11 July) they had seen an unidentified flying object over the Norman River, about twenty miles south of Karumba. They described it as a "round patch of yellow, red and green iridescent light, travelling at about twice the speed of a Canberra jet bomber." It silently travelled to the north-west in a flat trajectory, at an altitude of 2,000ft.

Chapter Nine

Victoria and Tasmania

Victoria

Victoria in southeast Australia is noted for its rich pastoral landscape, spectacular coastline and rugged mountain country. Melbourne, the capital, is situated on Port Phillip Bay, a sophisticated cultural centre and Australia's second-largest city.

Stawell, 1958

Stawell is located 123km northwest of Ballarat on the Western Highway, near the northern end of the Grampian Mountains.

Ben was only ten years old in 1958. At about midday he opened the front door and noticed a

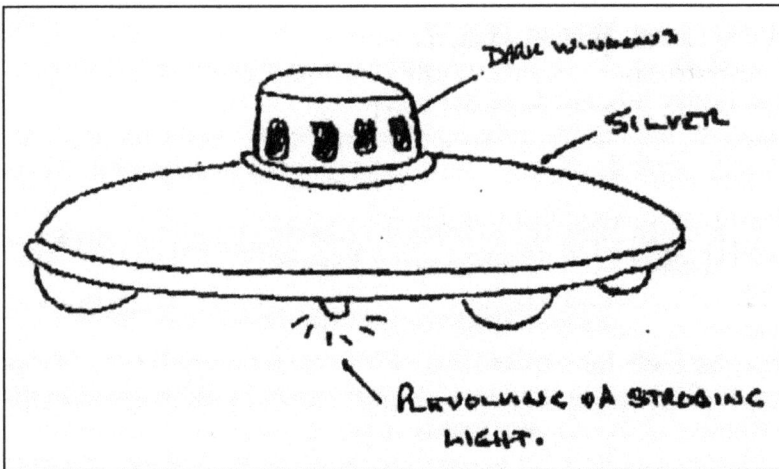

silver craft high in the clear western sky.

"I watched for about five to ten minutes, as it was stationary, and not moving like a plane should. I couldn't quite make out the shape, but there were lights – blue, white, green and red, coming from underneath it. I called my parents and we all watched for another fifteen minutes.

"They called our neighbours, the Millers, who

brought over their tripod and telescope, and we could then see an easily recognisable, Adamski-type UFO. It had a revolving or strobing coloured light from a central point beneath, and darkened windows in the dome section. Everybody took turns in watching through the telescope, and there was great discussion until 2.30 p.m. when we had to leave. It had gone by the time we got back."

Bunyip, 1960s

Many reports of sightings and encounters occur in country areas, well away from mainstream civilisation. Not far from Warragul and the Latrobe Valley, Bunyip is an area with a large amount of granite, often a common factor in areas of paranormal phenomena I've investigated:

Margaret and her family had a property in Bunyip, in southern Victoria, and were friends and neighbours with our later witnesses, the Cook family: "In the 1960s we saw strange lights in the sky. One was really bright. As it came closer, it increased in intensity, with lights underneath. Another time we saw this orange ball, which took off at a 90 degree angle towards the Cook's farm. The Tupperware lady was driving along a local road when that same object came over her vehicle. The engine stopped and the lights went out. When it disappeared her car started again."

Margaret said many "paranormal" phenomena happened in the area. "We used to see a strange man, and when you would look back where he was, he had disappeared! This happened on several occasions. He had such a beautiful face, and fair hair. Once he was with a woman who looked almost identical. Several times I wanted to stop and talk to him, but something prevented me. He once came into the shop where my sister and I worked. He never spoke a word and was looking around as if studying the place. I was about to go up to him, but turned away for a split second, and he was gone! Just vanished into thin air!"

Margaret paused. "Something happened to those four children on the Cook farm – but it's all right, we were protected here." Was she referring to the strange 'fair-haired people'?

The Cook family

Kasey Cook and her family bought a remote property near Bunyip in 1962. The house itself has a long and colourful history – an important part of the small, close-knit, community. It was originally built in 1898, and was a mansion compared to the modest dwellings in the area.

The first time they saw the house, Mrs. Cook was with her husband and father. When they opened the front gate, she felt some unknown force, and slipped and miscarried. She remembered, "I was never fully relaxed in that house. Sometimes I felt an unseen presence was watching me and thought it might be a ghost!" Their neighbour's daughter, Jane, was best friends with Kasey's sister Julie, and often used to stay over. Jane told her mother, Margaret, she also felt that while the Cooks were very hospitable, something about the house always made her feel uneasy.

Mrs. Cook continued, "I often saw strange lights in the sky – what you would call UFOs. Once there was this big light hovering, and a small light came out, followed by three little ones. They sat underneath for a short time, and then took off. I often saw UFOs, especially on clear nights with a full moon. Young Kasey used to say: 'Where, where?'

"Once one was right over the hayshed. I got Mary to climb onto the roof, but it disappeared. It wasn't just us, in approximately 1966, the same year as our big event, the *Warrugul Gazette* reported that a cigar-shaped UFO went in front of a car driving between Bunyip and Drouin."

Kasey's younger brother, Carl, independently told us of a recurring theme. He cannot know for sure was it a repetitious dream or a reality. "I would hear a strange sound, which I cannot describe but I would recognise again. Whenever I heard it I would know the little people were around. There were three locations in the house – the spare room, the lounge opposite (where we were watching television), and the cellar underneath. On the tip of my mind is the image of small humans wearing white, grey or silver coveralls."

Carl also recalled strange events while he was a child on the property. "I used to see a round, bright face looking through the bedroom window. I would hide under the blankets! Once we were all outside the back of the house and the whole family saw a huge, bright white light fly over. In the same period Dad just went missing a couple of times. It was a mystery, he wasn't in the small local town or anywhere to be found. Once he was gone for three weeks and thought it was a few days; he had no memory of the rest.

"For some inexplicable reason I was terrified of walking along the road to get the school bus. I think this happened after I heard a sound in the nearby bush. I don't know why it scared me so much, I wouldn't go along there by myself again. From then on I would detour through an adjacent property."

Kasey also had vivid memories of her childhood at the farm. Her shared recollection of a face looking through the bedroom window was more of "a big metal clock face, but there was something else there – I could not distinguish what it was I really saw, and always passed it off as a bad dream."

"I also saw the UFOs, but my older brother would reassure me, 'It was just a plane'. I, like Carl, was also frightened of that same stretch of road on the way home from school, but only when it was windy. I felt scared looking up at the trees blowing, and would sit on the channel gate until either Mum or Dad came to get me.

"There was a track behind the milking shed, and it was further down in the scrub where the UFO landing occurred. Whenever Carl and I went down to that area, we would both feel uneasy and run back out." Kasey and Mrs. Cook both remember on many occasions hearing buzzing noises, which started off like a small, slow chainsaw, then increased in intensity to jet engine higher pitch – only to suddenly stop. This happened towards the back paddocks. When they walked towards the area, the noise would stop at the channel, only to start up again after they returned to the house. They would check and check, no-one around – no intruders, and no neighbours living out there to account for the noise.

"Dad had two fairly old coopers, bolted together, hidden in the tea-tree scrub in those back paddocks," said Kasey. "He got upset one time and said 'they' had moved them. This may have nothing to do with it, but it would have taken a small truck to shift them. About this time he saw a huge green oval object, with an orange-purple tail hovering over the dirt road, and despite the limitations of his small Volkswagen car, Dad gave chase to the unwelcome visitor."

(As a researcher, I do not normally resort to speculation, however since I had determined these were not water tanks, I silently wondered if what Mr. Cook had in the scrub was an illicit still? We have many cases of UFOs accessing water – had they found a source of free alcohol? Drunken aliens? The mind boggles!)

"In 1966, when I was about six years old, we children helped around the farm, and every morning my 14-year-old sister, Mary, used to milk the cows. It was about 4.30 a.m. one morning when Mary came rushing into the house screaming that there was 'a huge green light out there, and something had landed behind the milking shed'. The cows and dogs had run away in opposite directions."

Mrs. Cook, now in her eighties, still remembers that day: "Mary's face was a strange grey colour, and she was shaking like a leaf. When my husband and I went out to investigate the cows were frantically running around in circles. (They never went near the landing site again.). We got no milk production for several days. One little dog threw himself into my husband's arms, and the others had disappeared. Lady, one of our favourites, didn't come back until the afternoon. I didn't know what to make of it!"

A bit later on they ventured further out the back. There was a circular area of depressed grass (about 20 feet in diameter) and several strange footprints, which seemed to go sideways. Kasey's father contacted a local UFO society, who came out to have a look. After that a few men in suits came to the farm and investigated an area behind the paddocks at the back perimeter of the property. They took plaster casts and other samples and used some form of counter, declaring something had been there! Kasey didn't know if they were from the military or government. While they were led to believe these investigators were from the university, Mrs. Cook commented that there was a tall, strange woman with them. She had fair, curly shoulder-length hair, which brought to mind the man and woman her neighbour, Margaret, had described. For a short period members of the UFO Society visited a few times.

An interesting aspect of this case was a possible generational factor, and the startling similarity to the Jackie Hayes case, hundreds of miles away near Grafton in New South Wales. In both, the father of the family had been missing, without recollection, for at least one three-week period, and there was mention of the "fair-haired" people.

In 1971 they sold the property and moved. Despite living hundreds of miles away from the farm they have still experienced strange phenomena.

Carl has never been able to sleep in a room without the light on. When he was in his teens he felt his bed move and woke up. He felt a presence pinning him down by his shoulders, and successfully called upon the name of Jesus for it to go away. Julie still keeps talking about the UFOs of their childhood, and continually moves house. She has trouble with her reproductive system, and efforts to fall pregnant.

Kasey contacted me after she experienced more strange phenomena in 1998. She had been beset by recurring dreams, mostly of the farm, which had continued to the present day. She was living in Wollongong, on the NSW South Coast, and worked in Sydney.

"I was on the early shift, driving to work, and had turned onto the entry road to the expressway. I have no memory, just a blank, until about 20 kilometres further on. I got a shock and didn't know where I was! I had missed over fifteen minutes, but was still driving the car!

"In June this year I was sitting in the lounge room, when my partner went out with a torch to get wood. I saw the light of the torch and for a split second didn't know where I was and felt a heart-pounding fear. I wanted to run, and didn't know where to go. I came back to reality and calmed down, but it left me wondering what I couldn't remember from Bunyip."

This case was quite intriguing. There was the matter of the old house and possible paranormal events and haunting. We had the UFO phenomena and landing traces. Many experiencers refer to little people who came to their bedrooms during childhood. Also of interest was the reference to high-pitched, humming, chainsaw-type noises, frequently described by witnesses.

We did arrange hypnotic regression for Kasey; apparently there were ongoing abduction episodes. She requested all details be kept confidential.

White Acres, near Sale, 30 September 1980

When we investigated the Central Coast sightings before writing *The Gosford Files*, many witnesses could not really be sure if the strange craft over the lakes were actually taking up water, however Australian researchers have documented cases where there was no doubt UFOs were draining wells and dams. The *White Acres* case is probably one of the most famous:

White Acres is a property 19 kilometres west of Sale, which is the main administrative city in Gippsland. Situated 200 kilometres east of Melbourne, and close to the Bass Strait, it is near to the Gippsland Lakes area, which stretches from Wilson's Promontory to Lakes Entrance and is bordered most of the way by Ninety Mile Beach.

George Blackwell, one of the property's station hands woke at about 1 a.m. to the sounds of an unusual whistling, cattle bellowing and his horse galloping around the paddock. He went onto the back porch, and stood on the rail to see what was going on. About six feet above the ground and 550 feet away was a low-flying object, dome-shaped and about 26 feet long and ten feet high. It was emitting a blue and orange light, and was responsible for the low whistling sound. On closer examination he noted it was more of an orange coloured bell shape, with a white dome on top, and a circular ring at the bottom – much like a hovercraft tube, which later receded in width when he saw the craft rise.

He watched as it flew over the fences hovered over their concrete water tank, a short distance from the house, and landed about fifty feet away. George hastily got dressed and rode his motorbike over to the site, where the object was stationary on the ground, still making the whistling noise. He could now see the orange and blue lights were seven inches in diameter, ten feet apart and slowly revolving.

After about ten minutes it started to lift off and George got back on his bike and rode directly towards it. The whistling increased to the pitch of a jet engine and it slowly rose in the air, emitting a blast of heat, and flew off to the east, gaining height as it went.

Later investigation found that the 10,000 gallon water tank was nearly empty, having lost all of its water overnight. George thought it had over 2,000 litres in it, but the owners said it had been full. A 30-foot diameter circular brown ring was found on the ground, with six evenly spaced half-spokes pointing towards the centre of the circle, which had not turned brown.

None of the animals would go near the circle, or the paddock it was in. Around the outer edge of the circle was a fourteen-inch rim, which seemed to correspond with the bottom of the tube that George had described.

George later told the *Australasian Post* that he first thought he was dealing with rustlers, "but as I got down to the paddock I was stunned. What's more, when I put my hand on the gate to open it, I got a hefty electric shock. Maybe it was their way of telling me to stay back."

Two years later, in 1982, a North Queensland family was amazed when they went out at 1 a.m. to see a huge disc, ringed with red and green lights, hovering over the creek at the bottom of the garden. For thirty minutes they watched as it drained the creek to the extent it seemed to be standing 'mid-air' on a wall of water. Finally it started to spin, and shot away at high speed towards Cairns.

Corowa (NSW)

Robyn Colson and her neighbours also witnessed a classic saucer over Berrigan:

"Only two years earlier in September 1976, at Corowa, on our previous farm in New South Wales. It was about 6 p.m., we were standing at the western gate when an object, I think you would call it 'cigar-shaped', came out of the sunset. It was the size of seven semi-trailers with decks on it, each lit up with smaller, mostly white, lights plus windows. It was incredible, at low altitude, travelling at about 15 miles per hour.

"We just stood and stared, mesmerised. It looked like a small compact town, moving above tree top level in front of the hills. There was no misidentification or optical illusion – it passed over a semi-trailer on the road (the craft was far longer!). Next thing a small saucer-type object, about 22 feet in diameter, flew out of the sky into this large object, which immediately took off at a 45 degree angle up into the sky. The speed was unbelievable – we have nothing that could do that!"

Robyn paused, "In 1958, when I was a girl in Corowa, our neighbours found an indentation in the paddock, which must have happened overnight. It was 22 feet in diameter and six inches deep. They notified the police who laughed. Two years later they found a traditional crop circle with similar dimensions, but did not report it for fear of further ridicule."

Robyn recalled that in 1964-1965 in an area north of Corowa and west of Albury, on the NSW border, there were several reports of 'white discs' following cars. "My girlfriend and her parents were followed by one when they were driving from Culcairn to Henty. They were very fundamental, religious people, and were very angry, and kept insisting the only explanation could be someone playing a prank."

"It was strange, only two weeks later, one cold clear night (no storms or anything), there was a huge explosion, heard for 30 or 40 miles, followed by a blue-white flash. One car on the road was thrown in the air and landed on its roof. Nobody ever found out what happened. We expected the police, but it was the RAAF who came out to investigate, and they were very 'tight lipped'.

Mallee country

These are not the only cases of unidentified craft stealing water, which is a precious commodity for Australian farmers. Researcher Paul Norman commented he had investigated similar cases, many in northern Victoria:

The Jolly family lived at their 9,000 hectare farm, *West Park*, in the western Victoria Mallee wheat-belt. In November 1987, following sightings of "eerie aerial lights in the sky", they found their 4,000 litre water tank had been totally drained overnight. In 1989 Nancy Jolly told a newspaper reporter "We haven't a clue what happened. All we know is that someone, or something, took every drop of our water."

In December 1988 the Jolly's son Stuart, was woken by an ear-splitting sound, like a jet engine revving up and down. When he looked out he could see nothing but an empty sky.

I wondered about the similar sound described by George at *White Acres* when the mysterious craft was taking off.

At about 9 p.m. in May 1989, Stuart was home alone when he heard a commotion in the sheep paddock. The entire flock of 700 sheep was totally in panic – bleating and dashing around. Overhead was a large, yellow pulsating light, making a weird, high-pitched noise. At first he thought it was someone spotlighting his sheep, but realised the light was far too big for that. He could see his neighbour's flock were also distraught, trying to get away by scrambling over the fence.

"After a few more minutes of chaos," Stuart said, "the light started to move. Foolishly perhaps, I got into the car to chase it, but before I could start up it vanished behind the pine trees. When my parents arrived home over an hour later, the sheep were still distressed. They weren't the only victims; we went out with our torches and found a large wedge-tail eagle stumbling around the paddock, seemingly in shock and totally disorientated. Although it kept flapping its wings in a slow drunken way, it seemed incapable of taking off.

"Something associated with the yellow light seemed to have destroyed its sense of balance, but happily the effect must have worn off, because it was gone the next morning. Several days later a mysterious light hovered over our neighbour's dam, and she watched it for fifteen minutes before running in to her husband, but it had gone by the time he came out."

In December 1989, while harvesting the wheat, the Jollys found a pattern of five perfectly swirled circles in their crop – two large circles about three metres in diameter, surrounded by three smaller circles, each about one metre across.

Geelong, 1996

Lana McDonald rang me in late August, 1996, not knowing quite where to turn. In mid-July 1996 she and her husband Mark were travelling from Ballarat to Geelong. They had dropped Mark's two children at Ballarat at 9 p.m. and were driving back to Geelong, a trip which takes one hour, so they were due to arrive home about 10 p.m.

Lana said, "We were driving our station wagon along a two-lane highway, one lane in each direction, and we thought there was a car behind us, zapping its high beam. Other cars were overtaking us in a hurry, and the light behind us was affecting my glasses. Suddenly this bright, sparkling silvery light shot over the top of our car, over the bonnet, and then shot up into the clouds on the other side of the sky. It looked something like one of those modelling or photographers' spotlights', and it was big – about the size of a room, much bigger to the eye than a car or full moon.

"Mark looked at his watch and neither of us could believe it was 11.30 p.m.! We were concerned as we had left my two children with my mother, and as expected, she was very angry that we were late getting back. After we got home, every time I shut my eyes all I could see were silver lights and dark black eyes, like cat's eyes with no eye whites or pupils. There were little bruises all over my buttocks and thighs, and I couldn't understand where they had come from. They were so bad I couldn't wear a short skirt.

"I had epilepsy as a child, but it has been under control for many years. I even have a driving license. Since this happened a few weeks ago, I have been getting blackouts three or four times a week. These blackouts are weird, they come with dreams of future events, like some type of psychic prediction. I am getting headaches, which I never had before, and I have to take pain killers to get any relief. Two weeks ago I got an infection in the reproductive area, requiring antibiotics."

She was also worried about Mark. "He has developed nose bleeds, and gets occasional bad dreams he cannot remember. We both get very lethargic, and suffered a strange two-day flu with high temperatures. I get sick if I go near radios or television sets, and there is static if I sit in the car. I get dizzy quite often, and the doctors want to attach an EEG monitor to test for a leak, but I'm a little hesitant about this.

"A few weeks after the encounter the whole house seemed to become hot and then very cold. We used to go to bed at 9.30 p.m., but now stay up until 1 a.m., often going out onto the balcony to look at the stars like dick-heads."

"A couple of weeks later, something flew over our house, and a whole lot of metal stuff came down, like short, fat silver chips. There was one large piece, like a half-egg shape. I picked them up, but something made me throw them away.

"I didn't normally dream before, and when my dreamt predictions came true I told a personal friend, who was a paranormal researcher and journalist. He told me to write them down in advance, and if they came true he may write an article. He also put me in touch with two women who ran a support group, and I was led to believe everything was strictly confidential. I couldn't believe it when a couple of weeks later there was an article in a women's magazine which duplicated my report and attributed it to one of these women. When I rang them up, they just brushed me off."

At this stage I thought just how stupid and unethical both the journalist and these two women were. One does not play silly buggers with this kind of situation. Twenty years later they have all certainly dropped off the grid – I just hope nothing untoward happened to them.

Lana was getting some memory flashbacks; of lying on a table, surrounded by white light. She could see beings about 5 foot, 8 inches tall, with white skin, heads that look human, no hair and totally black eyes. She was wearing a pendant,)0(, with an amethyst centre, which she thought she once found, and could see a similar symbol around the being's neck.

The only other memory she had was the being reaching out and touching the pendant and saying in English (with no accent) "You're one." (I can't remember where I got the pendant, but the jeweller couldn't get the stone out, and he said he hadn't ever seen the symbol before.)"

I asked Lana questions about her psychic dreams and asked if she was getting more recall of what had happened during the apparent 90-minutes of missing time. It seemed to me as if some of what she considered dreams, were in fact flashes of memory.

"I asked the being on the road who *she* was? She said her name was Zenna, and they were visiting me. They had a base in Peru, and it took them an hour to get to Australia. They are in a glass ball on their ship, and must sit in the glass ball to contact earth people. They work through people's minds."

The reference to a base in Peru interested me, as it corresponded with the terrain Penny had described when she was taken on her space ride after being abducted at Roma, Queensland (see Chapter 16, *The Agony of the Abductee*). It also matches a place described by two other contactees during a possible inter-dimensional experience.

"I was told when I understood how to contact them, I could call them anytime, and they would send me a message. I asked if they believed in God, and they said he was 'the Master of all' and that they prayed. They also said that they would teach me how to use modern medicine and cure people, and I was to keep notes."

She said they told her they are here to take our uranium as there was none anywhere else. (Lana couldn't even pronounce "uranium" correctly, and didn't seem to know what it was.)

Given her history and all the information, I felt that Lana may well have had more than one encounter, possibly long before this recent incident.

She had mentioned a subsequent reproductive infection was in her only remaining ovary, the other having been removed due to a cyst.

(It is common for quite young abductees to have ova removed from one only ovary, causing a cyst to develop. I did not suggest any of this to her, as it would only distress her and contaminate any later investigation.)

Having counselled her regarding the careful consideration of any hypnotherapy, I referred her to a very qualified colleague, with the comment: "I think Lana needs help urgently, regardless of authenticity."

During our long interviews Lana had given me some prophecies which have come true during the intervening twenty years, one of the reasons I have decided to relate this story. I had also asked her three trick questions, relating to a different, totally unrecorded UFO event, to which she could not possibly know the answers, or my reason for asking. I was floored when each answer was correct.

How much of what Lana said was actually communicated from aliens (who are known to lie)? How much may be psychic communication with another reality? How much may be the product of some form of mind control or even the distinct possibility of an implant? And how much may be delusional ravings or an elaborate hoax? I really don't know. In some ways I wondered if Lana was the victim of some form of possession, a conduit for channelled messages

Communicating with Aliens?

Lana said that she had been directed to telephone me. – 'Me, why me, I thought?' It was after this that things got really interesting. Given *her obvious naivety, I later asked her if she could get her aliens to answer some questions for me. At times she obviously didn't have a clue as to the implications or meaning of my questions, and yet the answers provided were logical:*

Is the genetic 'collection' for their benefit or ours? – Both.

"Are they the only ETs here?" – No not the only ones, but the others will not reveal themselves, our world is too violent. They are very angry as we have tortured some of their people. (This complaint kept surfacing – we tortured their people alive!) Further, the United States had two of <u>their</u> bodies, and they wanted them back <u>now</u>!

They 'reprogram' human minds and test abductees, but never harm them. It is other humans who hurt abductees, and this also makes them very angry.

"Why are they here?" (This is an overview of a lot of answers) – They don't eat food, but need a clear atmosphere to live in. Their planet is dying. They come in peace, but need our planet for all their people to emigrate to.

At this stage I was becoming aware that Lana may had been 'implanted' with messages and beliefs, and as I appealed to her logic, she realised some of the information was misleading, and not as peaceful as she had thought.

After that the communications became more aggressive. Lana herself was not aggressive, just the content of her messages. They said there was another planet – many years of travelling, to which they would move the Earth's population, but then as they added the chilling comment: *"Two of everything"* (I couldn't help but wonder about *Noah's Ark*!) The messages became quite adamant that will move wholesale onto the Earth very soon, and all humans will have to go.

It all became a little garbled but essentially I understood what some of the messages were about. In one part it got mixed with what were essentially predictions. Keeping in mind that these discussions with Lana occurred in 1996, some predictions have proven correct. In hindsight I suspect that at one stage, she was referring to Assange, Snowden and others when she mentioned London and America and said: *"Those that tell what they know, won't come back."*

By this time I was beginning to doubt my own sanity. Was I talking to Lana or some alien or entity channelling through her? Often her answers would contradict her own opinions and reasoning. I decided to go along with this, even though both of us might be crazy. I had to speak-up even if there was the remotest possibility that somehow I was providing feedback to her alien contacts.

I advised that the aggressive takeover of another planet and relocation of its population was not peaceful and something akin to an intergalactic Hitler. Further, if they couldn't retrieve two bodies from the United States, how could they expect to take a whole planet? Thirdly; according to other prophecies, they would be defeated. I suggested their course of action would be disastrous for all, and suggested that another alternative be sought, such as a different planet, suitable for their people.

Schools and children

It is a little disturbing that sometimes UFOs show an interest in vulnerable children and our schools:

Westall, East Melbourne, 6 April 1966

This is probably one of the best-known cases, which still has many unanswered questions. The entire incident, and many of the details would never have come to the public's attention, except for dedicated investigations by VUFORS and PRA, plus George Simpson, Keith Basterfield, Bill

Chalker and others (including Shane Ryan, whose diligent research led to a documentary *Westall 66 – A Suburban UFO Mystery*).

The incident occurred near two schools; Westall High School (now Westall Secondary School) and the adjacent Westall State School (a primary school). It began just before mid-morning recess, when most students were inside, and some were playing football on the oval. The older, high school students who were outside, claimed there were several flying saucers buzzing the area between the schools and pine trees in The Grange reserve, to the south of both schools. Some witnesses described one saucer with several small planes following it. (Another student, in a school at Clayton, two kilometres away also saw a flying saucer.) Many said they saw the craft go over, descend behind the pine trees and rise again some time later. They ran across the playing field to the fence to get a better view.

One student recounted how everyone rushed to the classroom window to watch a strange object, a couple of hundred metres away, between the two schools. She described it as being metallic, with a clear dome on top, "exactly like a flying saucer." Inside the dome were what looked like people doing "things." They seemed to have large heads, and when they raised their arms up their fingers looked very long and thin. (An older student, from another classroom, remembered that some creatures got out and "did something" to the ground before returning to the craft, which then ascended.) She did not get a chance to see much more, as their teacher ordered them back to their desks, and when they were able to look later, it had already flown away.

Teachers and students came running out of the school, and over to the fence to watch. (Some teachers claimed they were only there to stop students from going any further.) After recess the excited students were ordered back to class, but many did not comply until much later, and climbed the fence to view the large circular landing mark on the other side. The grass was swirled, with possible scorch marks.

Bill Chalker documented his interview with former student Victor Zagruzny, who claimed he climbed over the fence and stood close enough to one landed object "to touch it", except it appeared to be radiating heat. Three other students were in close proximity to a second, landed object. Victor's description indicated the craft were 5.4 metres wide and 1.5 metres high, and they left behind two circles of burnt grass when they took off. One went west, and the other circled a small plane before going southwest.

High school science teacher Andrew Greenwood is reported to have first seen an object rising from behind pine trees during morning recess. It was like a "thin beam of light" which seemed at times to thicken, similar to a disc. It tilted to show its underside.

One witness stated: "Scores of students and staff watched enthralled for 20 minutes as five light aircraft chased a saucer darting around the sky. These Cessna-type planes and their pilots proved to be as unidentified as the object itself."

The primary school headmaster returned at lunchtime to find the students (who would all normally be actively scattered around), "huddled together in groups, and wide-eyed with fear."

The high school held a special assembly, during which all students were told not to talk about the incident to the press or anyone else. (I wonder if "anyone else" included parents?) Of course some disobeyed, being kids, and three were given detentions for talking to the media. Their media interview was cut short by "some unknown person, off-camera."

Another landing site in Glenmorgan Close behind a factory, was in the paddock part of The Grange reserve and close to pine trees. Military vehicles arrived soon afterwards, and when a witness, who saw a craft touch down there, took VUFORS investigators to the site, RAAF officers instructed them to "divulge nothing about the case."

A local man who went into the paddock to see the circular patches, backed off when he saw the place "swarming with military." When he returned shortly afterwards, the whole paddock area had been burnt. Government vehicles, including a bulldozer, came in and removed all the soil and grass, taking it away in trucks.

After hearing of the incident, the father of one student went to a landing site near the pine trees where he saw a clearly visible circular impression, and scorch marks on the ground. Maybe the officials were not aware of its existence, as it was never cleaned up like the other trace areas.

Some of the official explanations included *Project Crowflight* which involved flying USAF aircraft from Victorian RAAF bases to measure radioactivity in the upper atmosphere. This did not equate with witness details, and the project had been wound-up two months previously, in February 1966. Another suggested the Mildura Highball balloon tests, but again "this did not equate."

There are certainly many unanswered questions to this entire incident. The two we may never get answered are why did the authorities arrive so quickly? (Some have suggested they could not have arrived in such a short time from the nearest base.) The second is why did they go to extraordinary attempts to hush it all up?

Personally, I would want to know more about the unidentified craft. Where did they originate and was anybody able to intercept them? Were they one of our own prototypes, and if so was their landing at Westall an accident? One totally unprovable, and probably unlikely, theory is that if you wanted to gauge public reaction, then test something on school children who can be more easily silenced.

Parramatta, Sydney (NSW), 1963

I discussed this incident in *The Gosford Files*. However it should be briefly mentioned again to show that uninvited visitors displayed an interest in our youngsters during the 1960s. It is not known if they were alien, or perhaps a more worldly experiment to test the reaction of children whose innocent perceptions would be different to adult, more-questioning responses.

Allan was living in a Boys' Home in Parramatta, in Western Sydney. At about 8 p.m. he and his room-mate heard a humming sound outside their second floor bedroom.

After about ten minutes they gathered enough courage to look out the open window. For 30 minutes they watched a pink cigar-shaped object, with a red light on top, hovering low in the north-east.

Without warning the brightness and humming increased as the object moved with incredible speed. It stopped abruptly behind the home, and descended behind some nearby trees.

The next day Allan and his friends went down to the area. The trees had broken branches, as if something had been 'pushed down from the top'. The grass underneath was flattened in a thirty foot diameter circle, with a smaller burnt circle in the middle. The 'patch' was still warm, while the surrounding grass was covered in frost.

There was considerable excitement in the Home, and when reporters wanted to interview the boys, a housemaster accompanied by a uniformed policeman, pressured them into remaining silent.

Ballarat, 1968

An elderly nun, Sister Maria, told me of a confronting incident in 1968, when she was supervising about fifty children at a local swimming pool in Ballarat, Victoria. It was about 5.30 p.m. on a Friday night, and she was trying to round up all the youngsters back into the dressing shed to get dry and dressed ready for 6 p.m. dinner time.

"I was walking in front, holding two toddlers by the hand, when the children behind me called out: 'Sister, what is that?' I turned and saw a cigar-shaped craft, hovering very low, at tree top level, over nearby houses. I had a clear view, as there was only a grass playground in between. It was gold in colour, appeared to be about the size of a tram, and had windows along the side.

"At first, in order to avoid alarm, I encouraged the children to wave at it, but after a while some of the kiddies became quite terrified, and I was feeling quite frightened myself. I ushered the youngsters into the dressing sheds, trying to make a joke of it.

"I told them we might be getting visitors, and they would have to save some cordial for them. This seemed to calm them down; the prospect of visitors was a novelty. After that I avoided mentioning anything about it to them again.

"By the time we returned to the convent the object had gone, but I told Sister Angelica who just smiled and made no comment. During the night I was awakened by a bright, pinkish-red light, shining in my room from the sky outside. At that time, although I didn't connect it with the previous evening, I felt very nervous. I tried to show the other nun who shared my room, but she wouldn't wake up, no matter how hard I tried.

"About 10 a.m. the next morning I went outside to clean some windows, when an identical object moved slowly and silently overhead. I dropped everything and ran inside, calling out to Sister Angelica, 'There it is again! Now can you tell me what that is?' She just stared, then went back inside without saying a word."

Sister Maria is familiar with airships, advertising blimps and most conventional aircraft – it was none of these. She was rightfully concerned that, whatever it was, it was showing some interest in the children under her care.

Hanging Rock

Hanging Rock rises dramatically to 718 metres above sea-level and is situated 70 kilometres northwest of Melbourne, a few kilometres from Mount Macedon which is an extinct volcano. The fields on the plain surrounding it are fully 105 metres lower, adding to its majesty. Part of it is made up of a solvsbergite-form of trachyte, a volcanic mineral only known in two or three other parts of the world, which slowly weathers into spectacular formations. Hanging Rock is reputed to have caves and tunnels within, and along with Mount Macedon a gravity anomaly and natural springs.

This prehistoric rock, with its strange eeriness, was originally named Mount Diogenes in 1836 by Sir Thomas Mitchell. It is held sacred by the Wurundjera Aboriginal people, and has been the focus for many paranormal stories over the years. However, it has provided surprisingly few reports of unidentified objects.

In 1954 the *Melbourne Age* and *Sun* reported a metal craft, four times the size of a DC4 aeroplane, with a smoky colour transparent dome, (a "mushroom-shaped head"). This was seen travelling at high speed by Convair pilot Captain Barker. On 1 January 1954 witnesses at the Hanging Rock races, reported seeing the same, or an identical object. They said it hovered silently in the sky, then turned on its side and disappeared.

In 1974 a witnesses saw a huge object over the mountain behind the Mount Macedon Hotel, where they were staying. It was shining enormous yellow and orange spotlights on the slopes as it passed over.

Joan Lindsay's novel, *Picnic at Hanging Rock* was written in 1967, followed by the movie in 1976. Set in 1900, it details the disappearance of three schoolgirls and their maths teacher from the mysterious landmark. One girl, Irma, returns days later with very little recall of events. Joan Lindsay was never forthcoming about the factual or fictional basis for her novel. Joan Lindsay herself was reputed to have an interest in time travel and parallel universes, and some people claim that there was always the unspoken suggestion that the girls were abducted by a UFO.

The mystery deepens when police records from 1900 were destroyed, possibly in a fire. However, if the events actually occurred Lindsay may have deliberately altered the date and year. Some people who had old family members from Woodend claim the story is essentially based on fact.

In 1975 the *Herald* newspaper quoted Joan Lindsay as saying, "A lot of very strange things have happened around the area of Hanging Rock; things that have no logical explanation." Two years later, she admitted to a *Melbourne Age* reporter that: "A great deal of the book is based on things I've done and seen and know."

While the final chapter divulging the secret was supposedly written and published after her death, its authenticity is contentious. Her housekeeper of 25 years, Rae Clements, does not believe she wrote a final chapter.

On three occasions I attended a government college at Mount Macedon, close to Hanging Rock. There were strange anomalies in the area. Once I witnessed an electrical display, with spectacular lightning all night, but no storm and not a cloud in the sky. While I felt energised by this, and even stood in the grounds taking it in, other adult students (some of them police officers) were quite spooked.

One recreation day we decided to have a picnic at Hanging Rock. The director of the college was a very senior military officer, and not happy about the idea. He asked all the men on the excursion to keep an eye on us three female students and not let us out of their sight. Was he just superstitious, or was there more to the mystique of the location of the college and Hanging Rock than this officer would disclose?

I climbed the steep dirt tracks, and quietly relaxed against some boulders near the top. I could feel and sense strange forces, with which Joan Lindsay was obviously familiar, and started to absorb them. All too soon, three male students located me, and despite my protestations, protectively ushered me down the Rock.

It only added to my curiosity when two of the male students (also police officers), detoured to the local town on the way back to the college. The director paced the floor for two hours until their return. Why was he so relieved?

The Bass Strait Triangle

Bass Strait is a mystery-shrouded stretch of water, separating Victoria and Tasmania, 300 kilometres wide east to west, and 200 kilometres north to south. It was at one time a land bridge between Tasmania and the mainland, and is relatively shallow, with an average depth of only 30 metres. These waters are considered quite treacherous, with tidal flows, unpredictable currents, rips, freak waves, and gale-force winds. While these factors have certainly played a major role in many disasters, they cannot explain all strange anomalies, such as the countless mysterious disappearances of ships and aircraft within the area.

Ivan Sanderson and several other researchers with scientific and technical expertise have investigated areas around the world which could have similar anomalies to the Bermuda Triangle. They located three in the Southern Hemisphere, one of which was Bass Strait, west of the Tasman Sea. One of their crucial measurements was at 72 degree intervals, indicating a correlation to the earth's rotation and energy grids etc.

While an enormous amount of shipping has been lost there over the past two centuries, here I shall concentrate mostly on some of the missing aircraft:

Frederick Valentich, 21 October 1978

One of the most discussed aircraft disappearances has been that of 20-year-old pilot Frederick Valentich. He was making an evening flight to King Island with the dual purpose of picking up some lobsters, and to increase his night-time flying hours.

The official Accident Report stated that Valentich attended a meteorological briefing at 5.23 p.m and submitted flight plans for his VMC return flight, at an altitude less than 5,000 feet, from Moorabbin to King Island. It confirmed he was a qualified pilot with approximately 150 flying hours experience, and a Class 4 Instrument Rating. He left Moorabbin at 6.19 p.m., taking four lifejackets in the plane with him. He established radio communication with Melbourne Flight Service Unit (FSU) after take-off, and estimated a timeframe of 41 minutes to Cape Otway and another 28 minutes to King Island, where the aerodrome lights were to be illuminated for his landing. The weather was clear with excellent visibility and light winds.

He reported to Cape Otway right on time at 7 p.m.

His next transmission, six minutes later, was to ask if there was any known traffic below 5,000 feet, as there seemed to be a large aircraft below that altitude, which looked like four bright landing lights. FSU advised there were no known aircraft in the area, and asked for further information.

Valentich reported that the large aircraft had passed at least 1,000 feet over him at a speed which made him ask if there were any military craft in the area. Apparently there were not. For the next four minutes Valentich transmitted the following messages to Melbourne:

"It's approaching now from due east towards me... It seems to me that he's playing some sort of game; he's flying over me two-three times at a time at speeds I could not identify... It's not an aircraft....As it's flying past, it's a long shape.... Cannot identify more than that... Has such speed... Before me right now Melbourne.

"It seems like it's stationary; what I'm doing right now is orbiting and the thing is just orbiting on top of me also... It's got a green light and sort of metallic .... It's all shiny on the outside.... It's just vanished.... Melbourne, would you know what kind of aircraft I've got? ... Is it a military aircraft?

"It's now approaching from the southwest.... The engine is rough idling; I've got it set at 23, 24 and the thing is coughing.... My intentions are to go to King Island.... Melbourne that strange aircraft is hovering on top of me again.... It is hovering and it's not an aircraft..."

No further transmissions were received, and an unsuccessful extensive air, sea and land search was undertaken until 25 October. The official report could not determine the reason for the disappearance of the aircraft, and Frederick Valentich's fate was presumed fatal.

No trace has ever been found of Valentich or his aircraft. The public may never have known the full circumstances, except other pilots heard the radio transmissions, and the story leaked out. Further details became public, and it seems there was a sound of metal screeching or impact after his last transmission. The *News Weekly* reported that during the crucial last six minutes of radio contact there was no sign of his Cessna182 on radar screens.

Paul Norman of VUFORS was on the scene fairly quickly, and received reports from fifteen witnesses who had seen a green light over Bass Strait at the same time as the incident. There had been many reports coming from the area over the previous six weeks, with more than fifty people advising they saw bright lights at Portsea, Frankston, Baxter, along the road to Geelong, and near Cape Otway. At 11.30 p.m., three nights before the loss of Frederick Valentich, a Tasmanian man at Queenstown saw a long, vivid green object in the sky. He claimed it corresponded exactly to what the missing pilot had reported.

At 3 p.m. on the afternoon of 21 October, 37 witnesses at Cape Otway had watched two silver cigar-shaped objects moving from east to west, and other independent witnesses reported seeing them an hour later. At 6.45 p.m. Roy Manifold photographed an unidentified object in the same area, and despite intensive analysis, there are still conflicting opinions regarding the pictures. The RAAF immediately pronounced that it was merely cloud, while intense analysis undertaken in Australia and the United States concluded it was a bona fide unidentified metallic object, apparently surrounded by a cloud-like exhaust or vapour residue.

At 6.50 p.m., just minutes later, a bank manager and his wife observed an object with green beams of light over Bass Strait. At 7.10 p.m. yet more witnesses noticed an unidentified craft with a green flickering light at one end over the same area. Another man and his two nieces all saw the lights of a small aircraft, and a large green light travelling directly above it.

On the same afternoon, further afield in Sydney, several witnesses saw a silvery cylindrical craft moving very quickly across the sky. It glittered and flashed occasionally, as if slowly rotating. One witness claimed that as it passed over she felt the hairs on the back of her neck standing on end. At 9.30 p.m. a man reported a huge metallic object with a triangular green light at the front. He said it made a strange noise, and looked like something out of *Star Wars*.

Rumours and speculation were rife, many casting doubt on Valentich himself, making blatantly erroneous claims. Paul Norman was able to disprove them all. It did seem like there was a concerted and orchestrated effort by the media to detract from the true facts of the case, especially any connection with a UFO. One has to ask why?

There was further speculation regarding the official transcript of the flight tapes recorded that night. Michael Fields claimed in a 1979 article that he had access to an uncensored flight tape, and in 2012 Jon Wyatt claimed, in an article in the *Ufologist* magazine that in 1996, when the television show *Sightings* broadcast a segment about the incident it used the uncensored version in the script.

If this is correct, one must ask why was the original transmission censored in the first place? The description of the object is much more detailed, and the following additional transmissions by the pilot include:

> "Nearest in likeness to a massive cylinder and approximately twice the size of a standard 707 or a B-52 … Long wingless metallic tube spouting flame … Torpedo type shape but so distended it appears to have outline of immense four-pointed star … Outer projection appears to be aluminium or some other light metal … The windows are unmistakable and I see four other lights from the interior. No windows, some other observational area … Able to become stationary while at height of unmeasurable high velocity …"

His engine only stalled when the object passed him, and was then resumed okay, only to start failing again when the craft came up fast behind him, followed by the screeching metallic crunch. It must be noted that while there is still controversy over the existence of an uncensored transmission, Jon Wyatt stated that John Pinkney rang a New York magazine publisher, who claimed he had the tape. If this is true, it indicates most details, describing the UFO were edited out.

The Valentich family have always sought the answer as to what happened to their son. There have even been instances of consultations with psychics and clairvoyants. His mother claimed that famed oceanographer Jacques Cousteau sought government permission several times to look for the aircraft, but was refused. Why?

Despite intense speculation and disagreement, I doubt if there will ever be any certainty as to the cause of the disappearance without trace, of Frederick Valentich and his plane. Only two months later journalist Quentin Fogarty was a passenger in the famous New Zealand plane-Kaikoura-UFO incident documented in his book *Let's Hope They're Friendly*.

Other missing vessels and planes

July 1920

A schooner went missing, with no wreckage ever found. During the intense search huge hovering flares were seen in the sky by the crews of rescue vessels. During the search, two schooners, the *Amelia J* and *Southern Cross*, plus a De Havilland plane piloted by Army officers, also went missing.

October 10, 1934

A new four-engine mail plane, the *Miss Hobart*, a De Havilland Express, took off in fine weather, with two pilots and ten passengers on board. It was about eight miles from the coast when it disappeared without a trace. The last known transmission from pilot Gilbert Jenkins was "Everything OK." That morning two government surveyors heard the drone of *Miss Hobart's* engines when suddenly it stopped, "as if it had vanished in thin air." Another witness, Mr. Millington, came forward saying he had seen a huge white flare in the sky from his vessel off Cape Liptrap. Holymans Airways said the plane had four Gypsy V1 engines, and even if two failed, it should have maintained altitude until landing.

October 2, 1935

In a similar bizarre incident the airliner *Lorna* had left Essendon airport for Tasmania, and was about to land at Flinders Island. The pilot's transmission that he was "on course-136 degrees and closing down" was cut short. No more was seen or heard of the *Lorna*!

May 1942

During World War 2, RAAF aircraft used to do training flights, usually from their Sale Base in Victoria, over Bass Strait. Several Beaufort Bombers were lost, some due to low-flying, the cause for others, unknown. In May 1942 the crew of a Beaufort reported their radio and direction-finding equipment had failed for five minutes while a "silvery globe" pursued them. It had hovered and darted all around the plane.

December 24, 1969

A Fuji light aircraft was going from King Island to Moorabbin when the pilot radioed that he was losing height. No more was heard and no wreckage found.

September 8, 1972

Brenda Hean and Max Price, two prominent Tasmanians involved in a campaign to prevent the drowning of Lake Pedder, were flying a De Havilland Tiger Moth from Tasmania to Canberra. They went missing between the east coast and Flinders Island.

Whyalla, late 1964

The *News Weekly* reported that Colin and two other crew members of the *Foremost Prince*, an ocean-going dredger, saw a 'blue lattice light' in the sky. It was hovering over the old Whyalla loading jetty, halfway down the Spencer Gulf.

"My colleague John came down from the bridge. His face was as white as a ghost, and he handed me a pair of powerful binoculars. I took a look and certainly got a shock. It was a large disc-like object, curved top and bottom, with three huge antennae on top, and two blue jets. This was probably what we could see as the lattice work of bluish light."

For about twenty minutes the craft would hover, moving to either side from time to time. Without altering its altitude, it took off down the Gulf at amazing speed, and after about ten minutes, briefly returned. Colin used to scoff at UFO reports, "But now, as far as I'm concerned, they're for real."

Tasmania

Tasmania, the "Apple Isle", is situated off the southern tip of the continent. The incomparable wilderness of the west coast, and towering mountains of the central district are tempered by gentle pastoral areas and orchards further east, where there are spectacular beaches and wild coastline.

Oyster Cove, Summer 1954

It seems that during the 1950s the RAAF was very diligent in confiscating UFO photographs. TUFOIC reported on an incident from a dairy farm:

"A man and his young daughter were bringing in the cows for milking at 5.30 a.m. when the area became illuminated and they could hear a low whining noise. She looked up, and saw a silver oval shape, with a dome above, red and white lights, and a beam shining down below. Her father rushed into the house, grabbed his camera, and went further down the road to get closer.

"As he took a few photographs his daughter opened the gate to the cattle pen. The cows had been making quite a noise, trying to get out. As the cows took off across the paddock, the noise from the craft increased, and in a second it shot off over the sea."

When the photos were developed he contacted "an authority" to report the matter. Not long after three men arrived. They were wearing dark blue serge jackets, and demanded the negatives, becoming very threatening when he refused. They eventually left with five prints, and he was not really sure of who they were or where they were from.

Years later the father was involved with training German shepherd dogs for the Air Force. One day some RAAF personnel were visiting and mentioned the photographs, leading him to believe the original investigators were also from the Air Force.

Lake Sorrel, Central Tasmania, 26 February, 1975

The *Saturday Evening Mercury* of 29 March 1975 contained an interesting report of a Mr. Smith who was camped at Shepherd's Shore on Lake Sorrell for a week's fishing with his mate. They had set up a big tent together with cover for the car. Smith was an intelligent professional, and an ex-RAAF tail gunner.

"At 8.45 p.m., with little daylight left, I saw through the broken cloud cover, three objects, two big and one small, flying from the northeast. I lost sight of them for a few minutes, and later noticed two travelling southwest towards Sorrell. They stopped over Dogs Head Point, and I lost sight due to the cloud, later spotting them heading towards Mt. Penny.

"Except for mild curiosity, I hadn't paid too much attention. Suddenly one of them moved out of the broken cloud straight towards us. In less than a second it travelled a distance of two miles to only 1,000 yards away and 500 feet above the lake. I've never seen anything like it! Without seeing it for myself, I would not have believed any craft could have such performance.

"I felt very apprehensive; the object was at least 200 feet in diameter – it was fantastic. From one side of the underneath came a monstrous well-defined light, half its diameter, which it directed towards the lake. It was so bright, like a welding torch, that it hurt my eyes. It illuminated a distance of one-and-a-half miles around the lake.

"I am sure it was intelligently controlled. That beam of light swung back and forth in an arc, as if it were making a careful search of the Robinsons Swamp area. We were listening to the radio in the car, and as soon as the craft came close there was nothing but loud static on all the stations on the band.

"At 9.30 p.m. it had been 45 minutes since we first saw the lights in the sky, and the UFO switched off its gigantic beam, leaving a blue-white phosphorescence hanging about 30 feet above the lake. We were then better able to see a good definition of the shape of this mysterious craft. It departed in a flash, at phenomenal speed, joining the other light which was still hovering over Mount Penny. They both shot away together – like tracer bullets going across the sky."

The next day Mr. Smith spoke to some other fishermen who were camped a mile away at Silver Plains: "They told me they were in their tent, and all of a sudden it lit up like daylight inside. There were other people in the area who also saw the same thing."

The object did not appear to show any interest in the witnesses, and I wondered what, if anything, it was looking for.

Black Bobs (Wayatinah), 17 February 1976

Tasmanian newspapers reported a hair-raising experience when a strange object paced two truck drivers for three hours when they were taking a load of abalone along the Lyell Highway from Strahan to Dover:

Ron Wilson said, "I was driving down Nive Hill when we first saw the object over the logging township of Black Bobs. It had a brilliant yellow-white light in the shape of a dome, and there seemed to be a body part underneath. It appeared to be about 50 feet in diameter, and looked something like a sausage bent down at each end.

"It started keeping pace with our truck, staying slightly in front and to the left of us. We stopped the truck 40 kilometres further on, near the old Plenty Bridge, on the Lyell Highway, and the craft flew across the Derwent River, hovering on the opposite side. As soon as we started the truck it came back, and resumed its position, about 600 yards away.

"We tried to use the truck radio, but all we got was static. After we passed through New Norfolk a second light appeared further away, and kept pace with both us and the first object. Between New Norfolk and Granton we could see the original craft clearly outlined as it flew, lower than the hilltops, between us and the Dromedary Hills. We watched it until we reached Berriedale, when it started to climb, and eventually disappeared. After that our radio worked normally again."

Ron said, "I didn't want to report it, but our boss insisted as there had been other sightings in Maydena. People don't believe you. I wouldn't have believed it myself if I hadn't seen it."

Hobart, 1985–86

George and his family had lived on their property, 55 kilometres north of Hobart, for fifteen years without incident. Their farm consisted of rolling paddocks backed by sandstone hills with steep rocks and gullies. TUFOIC detailed this series of events in a 1994 report, after George had sold his "UFO-haunted" property. It had me wondering, animal mutilations aside, if some species of visitors do not like us killing our wildlife.

It all started in about July 1985, when George and his 16-year-old son Peter were shooting possums at the base of a hill on an adjoining property, about 2.5 kilometres away. Possums are a protected species in most parts of Australia, and George already had some carcasses, so Peter called to him to turn off the spotlight, (powered by a backpack battery), as he thought someone was coming.

George looked to see a bright blue object about five kilometres away in the sky. It came closer, and within a few minutes was only 200 metres away, not far above the ground. Some seven to eleven round blue lights were emitted from the top of the object, and they hung in a line about six to seven metres above it. It silently dropped vertically down and landed. It was surrounded by a bright blue glow which illuminated the whole area, including where George and Peter were standing.

The craft was about 20 to 25 metres tall and 6 to 7 metres wide. It was bullet-shaped with a rounded top and a straight base. Halfway around the object was a ring, or ledge. After it touched down George felt something warm on his back; the twelve-volt battery in his backpack was starting to warm up and bubble. He grabbed the dead possums and told Peter they had to get back to the car one kilometre away. As they started to move the object began to make a noise. It was like a type of singing but unintelligible, like a foreign language.

They dropped the possums and left behind the rifle and battery (now cooled off) when they reached the car, and drove slowly home in the dark, without headlights. There was no sign of burning on his skin, shirt or jumper, but the singlet underneath had a 15 centimetre burn hole.

Then one evening in January 1986, at about 10 p.m. he was outside with his daughter Sally, at the edge of a bush-backed paddock, some two kilometres from home, to shoot some kangaroo for dog meat. George noticed a bright light in the northern sky, which was heading their way, and getting bigger, brighter and lower as it neared.

George and Sally lay on the ground as the enormous object, about 150 to 200 metres across passed overhead. It was oval, with numerous white lights around the edge, other lights in the centre, and what seemed to be a dome on top. After it passed above their car and out of sight over the bank, they made a dash for the vehicle, and drove off down a track towards the road. The craft reappeared behind them and moved over the car before swinging away back over the bank.

George had seen distant UFOs from near the farmhouse in the time period between these two events. After the second incident, the same (or a similar) craft was seen, usually at a distance, on many occasions by the whole family. George nicknamed it *Charlie*, and he often noticed it when he was out feeding the dogs just after dark.

It came a bit closer on a couple of occasions. One night around 10 p.m. it came from the south and hovered about 300 metres over the house for two or three minutes. It let off two star-like lights; one went at a steady speed to the southeast, and the other to the north. The main object then moved away over the hills to the east.

The last time he saw it, George thought *Charlie* was giving a farewell performance. It was then March 1986, and he was closing the gate at about 10.30 p.m. The brightly lit craft came past just north of the farmhouse, and swung past a shed about 100 metres away. As it passed over, darts of light were shining down, illuminating everything it passed over. It continued with its circular trajectory and then went up high in the sky until it disappeared in the northeast.

Chapter Ten

South Australia and the Nullarbor Plain

We often see South Australia and the Nullarbor Plain as one vast geographical entity. Together they form the hot, dry southern fringe of the continent. For many, it is both a physical and psychological barrier that separates Australia's populous eastern states and its remote west

From the wine regions of eastern South Australia, you move west to the state capital, Adelaide, to connect up with the Eyre Highway. This runs northwards from Adelaide, skirts the Spencer Gulf to Port Augusta, before turning west out across the Nullarbor Plain well inland from the cliffs that edge the Great Australian Bight. A largely unexplored network of caves beneath the plain's surface, contains many underground water sources.

The plain itself is a wide treeless expanse, and includes one of the world's longest stretches of straight road. You pass through Ceduna and Yalata, then cross the state border into Western Australia, and on to Eucla, Mundrabilla, Caiguna, Balladonia, and finally Norseman. Here, where the Eyre Highway also ends; the way splits north to Kalgoorlie, and south to Esperance.

The Great Victoria Desert lies north of the Nullarbor, and mostly in South Australia. This is Australia's largest desert region, and includes Maralinga, a remote mid-20th century British nuclear bomb test site. Woomera, once a weapons-testing site, lies 500 kilometres further east.

South Australia has a long history of UFO incidents, as indicated by the Toolachie Run event of February 1904, widely reported by Australian newspapers at the time, and reprinted here at the end of my Chapter 1. The Eyre Highway has its own distinct UFO lore with many tales of lost time and strange night lights from truckies on the long haul between Port Augusta and Norseman:

Meningie (SA), 1975

The four witnesses to this event lived on three adjoining farms in Meningie. Victor was a bachelor living in the bottom farm:

"It was 10.30 p.m., and I had been raking lucerne hay. It can be hot out there. I was farming 11,000 acres and some jobs are better done at night and in the early morning. I had just come back to the house on the tractor, and something in the sand hills caught my eye. There were four small objects – literally playing hopscotch along the sand dunes.

"They were small metallic craft, each about three feet high. They had three legs, and a round cylindrical type cabin on top. They were leaping over each other, as if playing. I was terrified, and raced to the garage, jumped into my car and drove like mad to the middle farmhouse, where my brother and sister-in-law lived.

"On the way up the road I met up with these little guys, and they leap-frogged all around and over my car. When I got to my brother's home I was in quite a state. Jack and Gloria came outside and watched with me as these *things* hopped around the sand dunes. Then they went across Lake Albert to the sand hills on the other side. After a while they progressed to Lake Alexandra and disappeared due to the terrain."

A neighbour later advised he had also seen the little craft, and reports of strange objects were received from Victor Harbour and the mouth of the Murray River the same night.

Gloria advised that about the same time in 1975 they saw a different unidentified object. "I had guests staying with me at the house, and suddenly the television lost its power, and roared with static. We all went outside to see if we could spot the cause, and there, near the shed, was a small red light. We suddenly realised it was on a large dark disc-type craft, which moved away over the lucerne paddock. Later we found some round cylindrical patches in the crops."

I had considered that the small craft Victor encountered may have been drones given their size and behaviour – but whose drones were they? Researcher John Auchettl had been investigating a case for VUFORS, and established that in even in 1982, seven years later, there was only one drone in Australian air space, being the Woomera *Jindivik* target aircraft.

So were they drones of unknown origin and purpose – or given their size, were they unidentified craft with very small pilots behaving like teenage alien hoodlums doing wheelies over the countryside and frightening the locals?

Remote encounters, South Australia

Valerie Maxwell lives in a caravan in a fairly isolated part of South Australia, north-east of Adelaide, where the terrain is mostly flat limestone country.

People in caravans and tents seem to be more prone to encounters, perhaps because they are more accessible, not that solid houses prevent a second or subsequent event.

During the 1980s and 1990s Valerie had several encounters over a 15-year period, and until she finally contacted me, had tried to persuade herself that it was all in her mind. She sought help from a psychologist, but this did not prevent the phenomena re-occurring. She just needed to talk to someone as she felt it could be therapeutic.

While she had several encounters and interactions, she only discussed the two most significant. I wondered if this particular intelligence had utilised some form of inter-dimensional technology in their visitations.

"It's happened on several occasions – the animals get restless and the atmosphere takes on a strange quality. If it's dark or twilight there's a clear blue glow, and looking up I see almost the whole sky filled with a blue, glowing UFO. It is faint, but cannot be ignored, and seems to be associated with my unnaturally tranquilised condition and usually short episodes of missing time.

"It was round and domed overhead. The dome looked to be high, but the base seemed to be all around me, and no higher than treetop level above the ground. It did not move, merely hovered, but stars, clouds, trees, distant ridge etc. were visible through it and distorted, as if through a lens. The ridge appeared to be about one kilometre away instead of three kilometres, and the horizon, all around, appeared much closer than it really is.

"After the missing time I would seem to experience another abrupt shift in consciousness, and continue on with what I had been doing. It simply wasn't there anymore, although the blue light persisted. I would have a temporary feeling of being unwell, and changes in my apparent gravity. Sometimes there would be metallic and other substances in my mouth. They seemed benign except for the telepathy and implants."

The second incident was the first time she feels she was fully conscious when she saw an "alien being." "I was lying on the bed reading, when I glanced up from my book – distracted by flashes of clear blue flame-like light to my left side. Although the wall was only a foot or so away from me, it appeared to have dissolved, and I was looking into a dark space. The lights were actually a couple of metres away, about the size of tennis balls, and they silently exploded, as if to get my attention.

"On my right instead of, (and as well as) the body of my caravan was a large room. It was round, with a high ceiling which curved down to meet the floor, which curved up. There were a few geometric shapes in it. The clear blue light became stronger and filled the room, which I now saw was bigger than my caravan. There were lines indicating structure, and every so often a vivid yellow-white flash. There was no atmospheric change as there had been on previous occasions."

"Beside my pillow was a man; human, average build, and dark hair. He was wearing quite ordinary street clothes, and had an almost humorous expression on his face. Thoughts were passing through my mind, although I felt tranquilised to an unnatural degree. I was thinking 'maybe it is space people', and the man replied, as if I had spoken out aloud: 'They're not all *that* alien looking,' and pointed to the end of my bed. Standing there was a being who answered the description of the tall 'greys' in the abduction reports I've read.

"I was aware of being given some injections, and being assured that an implant would be removed from my head. Apparently it was responsible for intense, intermittent irritation I'd been suffering for some months. I then went (was put) to sleep and woke up at the usual time the next morning. The irritation was somewhat relieved, although a trace remains even now.

"Up until this fully conscious experience, the previous incidents seemed to be submerged and only vaguely remembered, so I was inclined to be sceptical, and even self-ridiculing."

The Nullarbor Plain

Many Australians think of the Eyre Highway as being the Nullarbor Plain. There have been many reports of strange craft and occurrences over this vast area, including people reporting strange lights had followed their cars when travelling between Perth and Adelaide, especially during the 1960s. It is only intended to relate a few, however they must be analysed in conjunction with sightings and events at Woomera and other surrounding areas.

10 October 1970

In *Australian Abductions – Catalogue of Cases*, Keith Basterfield reported a case of two people travelling across the Nullarbor who were unable to control the speed of their panel van after seeing a bright white light overhead. At one stage they felt that they were "up in the air", and when finally back on the road, their watches had stopped, and they had lost 32 hours!

Ivy Tank (SA), September 1973

In 1980 the Australian Centre of UFO Studies (ACUFOS), published a report by Keith Basterfield of an incident which occurred in September, 1973. It was about 3 a.m. and a 32-year-old single woman had been asleep, for about an hour, in the passenger seat of a semi-trailer. (Truck drivers have always given travellers and hitch-hikers rides across the desert to and from Western Australia, as they like the company, and a second person, on long, lonely trips.)

She claimed that when they were near Ivy Tank, on the Old Eyre Highway in South Australia, she heard a voice calling her name, telling her to "wake up", and to "look out the window." She then saw an object on the ground. It was about ten feet high and 30 feet long, and resembled a stationary egg. It glowed, looked semi-transparent, and appeared to have some kind of force field around it. The illuminating surround seemed to diminish in intensity until the glow disappeared, leaving a single white light coming from the object.

She spotted two "humans" – one walking in the direction of the craft, and one sitting near a window inside. The person outside was wearing a white or silver "all-in-one", puffed up at the ankles and wrists.

This case is contentious as they were travelling at about 75 kilometres per hour, giving her a very short timeframe to view the object. Researcher Bill Chalker also examined the case in *UFOs, the Psychic Connection*, where he compared not only sightings of similar objects, but also the fact that there are other cases of a precognitive factor, where people hear a voice or have a compulsion to look in the direction of a UFO.

West Australia, Mid-December 1976

Barry was a 28-year-old fun-loving truck driver, and he had broken down halfway between Norseman and Esperance. The local garage had to change motors, so he went to stay with friends in a nearby caravan park:

"It was a weekend, and we all went to their equivalent of a drive-in to watch *Blazing Saddles*. It was such a hot night, we agreed to take some of the other families' teenagers for a swim at a local dam near the side of the road. About ten of us crammed into a couple of cars, and off we went.

"Everybody ditched their clothes and went skinny-dipping. This was the age of peace, love and harmony after all. At about 2 a.m., we noticed that the tall trees nearby were shiny, lit-up and dipping, but there was no breeze! A huge white light appeared, about 30 feet up, just above the treetops. It was dead silent, about 40 feet across, and so bright it just illuminated everything and everyone. It didn't even cast any shadows.

"Sheer terror broke out, with everyone scrambling for the cars. I swear I was doing over 120 kilometres per hour as we took off. We had gone quite a distance before we realised we were driving down the main road, all stark naked and dripping wet. Some had grabbed their clothes as they fled, others forgot in the ensuing panic. Since I was the responsible adult I was trying to figure out how I was going to explain this to their parents.

"Luckily, the people in the caravan park were listening to the Kalgoorlie radio station. There had been problems with the transmission, and the announcer said they had received lots of reports of UFOs. The people I was staying with had been sitting outside in deckchairs and watched a white light move slowly across the sky from east to west, and then come back again."

Barry reflected for a minute, and commented that in future he would always pack a pair of swimming trunks.

The Nullarbor Goods Train, 16 January 1985

The Trans-Australia Railway Line runs from Adelaide to Perth. This incident occurred 740 kilometres north-west of Adelaide near a remote railway siding at Ooldea, only a short distance from Maralinga testing site.

An Australian National goods train was crossing the Nullarbor Plain when the driver and his offsider saw a bright light descending from the sky, to the ground, and then disappear from sight. Their first thought was that it was an aircraft crash, but 15 minutes later they saw the same light very close to their engine, which suddenly started to lose power. They turned off the train's headlights so they could better observe the object in front of the engine. Whatever it was, the craft possibly thought better of trying to take on a fully laden goods train (not so easy as a sedan car!), and departed.

They were forced to detach/unload most of the cargo to get up a steep incline, and left half of the wagons at a siding. They continued west to Cook, where they handed over to a new crew. The engine had only malfunctioned while the strange light was present, and no fault was found when it was checked out at Port Augusta.

The driver was most upset that the station clerk, not present during the incident, had told the media that the object was just a reflection of the engine's headlights on a sand dune. He contacted VUFORS researcher, Paul Norman, who felt this was just another case of debunking a genuine sighting. The driver, who had been a South Australian police officer for seven years before becoming a train driver, said he and his offsider were scared when the engine had started to lose power. A man of his experience and employment history is a trained observer and does not scare easily.

This was not the only case of trains being accosted by mysterious craft. John Pinkney reported that four trains, hundreds of kilometres apart, were buzzed at exactly the same time, 9 p.m. on 9 September 1989. This was confirmed by the Port Augusta Rail Control Centre, whose memo of 14 September logged reports from Zanthus (WA) and, Hesso, Watson and Manguri in South Australia. All the drivers and witnesses described essentially the same experience. The Perth Observatory dismissed it all as "probably space junk re-entering the atmosphere," which the witnesses hotly disputed.

"It's easy to sit at a desk and make pronouncements like that. We were on the spot and we know what happened."

Transline express driver Lou Becarrelli, and his offsider Mick Yuryevitch were about 14 kilometres east of Zanthus when they noticed a vertical pencil-shaped light in the western sky.

They realised it was just the exhaust trail of an enormous contraption which was travelling at incredible speed and was 'swooping' the train within 20 seconds.

"In 25 years on the railways, I've never seen anything like it. It was totally silent and ringed with six white lights – each of them pouring white smoke which made me cough, and blacked out passenger windows for several minutes. It was obviously intelligently controlled, because it kept pace with the train. I got on the two-way to the guard, Greg Bourne, and we stopped the train to report what was happening."

The moment the train came to a halt the intruder vanished leaving a vast cloud of exhaust smoke which dissipated into thin mist which was evident all the way to Zanthus.

Salt Creek (SA), 1986

A colleague's husband Fred, who has since died, told me of a hair-raising experience at 11 p.m. one winter's night on the Highway southeast of Adelaide, between Salt Creek and Tillie Swamp, and Mount Gambier near the Victoria border.

"I was driving along and my mate Tony was following behind, both of us in our diesel trucks. We could see a massive array of blinding white lights coming in the other direction. I spoke to him on the two-way radio and we reckoned that it must be two semi-trailers racing each other. And that they didn't give a shit about anybody else who was on the road that time of night.

"We pulled up on the side, and ran up an embankment across the road. The lights kept coming, only it was not trucks at all – but an enormous silent craft, about the size of several semi-trailers, perhaps about 300 metres in diameter. In addition to the obvious lights in front, it was round, with an apparently smooth surface, and had two back lights with static blue lights moving around the side or outer rim. The lights lifted as it passed low overhead and we were not able to see what the top looked like.

"As it moved overhead, we noticed our truck engines, which we had left running, stopped, and our headlights went out. Once it had left the headlights came back on, and we were able to start our engines."

Tony does not want his identity known, and this has affected him so much he is no longer capable of driving.

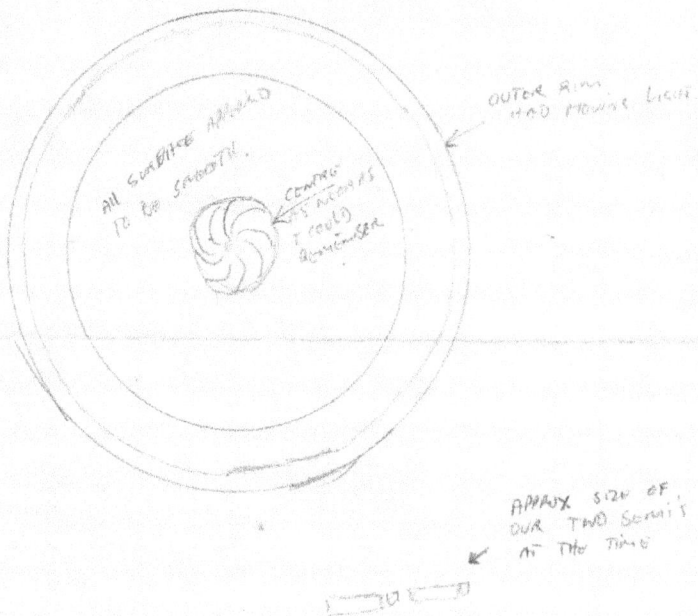

Mundrabilla (WA), 20 January 1988 (*The Knowles incident*)

This event caused massive disagreements among UFO researchers, and since I respect the integrity of the research of all my colleagues, it is intended to relate the various conclusions as presented

On the night of 20 January the Knowles family, Faye and her three sons – Wayne, Pat and Sean, were on a 3,500 kilometre journey, from Perth Western Australia, to Melbourne Victoria, which entailed crossing the Nullarbor. At 1.10 a.m. they had stopped at a Caiguna (WA) roadhouse to refuel and have a quick meal. While it may have no bearing on the case, Faye commented on seeing a "blond-haired lady" who smiled at Wayne, who also remarked on noticing a "blond lady" and a "bearded man."

It was a dark moonless night, with Sean driving, and not long after they had started off again, all experienced a period of confusion, disorientation and a mutual sense of fear.

After a while their awareness of their thoughts and surroundings returned to normal, and they recalled travelling down the Eyre Highway, at about 110kph. Soon after, they noticed a curved-shaped light pacing the car from a distance. Sometime later, they encountered what they think was the same light obstructing the centre of the road. It was extremely bright, shaped like an egg sitting in an eggcup – white with a yellow core, and a brighter light at top and bottom. It was bouncing on the road, backwards and forwards, coming towards them. Sean swerved to the right to avoid it, and nearly collided with an oncoming car and caravan as he went back to the left-hand side of the highway.

The family stated that the object pursued them down the highway for the next hour and a half, despite Sean's attempts at evasive action. A truck driver, travelling west, in the opposite direction, later reported to Eucla (WA) police that he had seen a car, travelling east, being followed by a light.

The light had been some distance behind, just over a kilometre, when suddenly without warning it jumped on top of the car. Everything, including the car, seemed to slow down – and yet the instruments indicated that they were travelling at 200kph (something not possible on the ground). The car was filled with an extremely bright light, which at first made them think it was on fire. The vehicle appeared to be vibrating with a combination of three sounds – hissing, whirring and humming, and when Faye touched the inside of the roof, she could feel these vibrations

Pat opened a window a little way, and the inside of the car was darkened by a fog of black dust which smelt like burnt Bakelite. Breathing became difficult in the foul, strong choking atmosphere, and the vehicle, dogs and family were covered with a fine grey-black dust.

Everyone independently reported a feeling of pressure or force, and their voices assuming a robotic quality. (Some reports say "deeper and in slow motion", which equates with other similar incidents.) Wayne's hair was standing on end, and Pat said he saw Sean slumped over the steering wheel, as if unconscious – head down and arms and hands hanging loose at his side. Faye partially opened her rear window, and as more dust "sshhhed" in, she stuck her head out and placed her hand on the roof. She saw and felt something round black and spongy – warm to the touch, which she thought was some form of "suction thing" trying to lift the car up.

"Oh my God!" she shouted, "It's on top of the roof. I'm burnt, I've touched it!" Almost immediately her hand began to redden and swell-up and has ached ever since. Pat said that as soon as Faye touched the roof, and pulled back her hand, the car was dropped to the road, and the right-hand rear tyre burst with a bang.

It was about 3.55 a.m. when they came to a halt at right angles to the road, 50 kilometres before Mundrabilla Roadhouse (and 210 km from Caiguna). The bright white, glowing UFO was up the road and at a very low altitude of about 30 metres. After the family fled the car, and took shelter in some low bush 180 metres to the south, they could see the object had a spotlight which appeared to be searching the terrain below. Another truck driver had witnessed the car, at the side of the road, but he did not stop fearing danger from strangers in such a deserted place.

Just before twilight the UFO mysteriously disappeared, and at 4.15 a.m. the family returned to the car, changed the tyre, and travelled in great haste to Mundrabilla (WA). They were still in a state of shock when they told the station owners and three truck drivers (one of whom had seen an unusual yellow-white light in his rear vision mirror) what had happened. One driver said Faye was hysterical, the boys were terrified and the dogs still cowering.

At the beginning of the entire incident the two dogs had been really crazy, jumping around the car and barking. Due to all the confusion and blank periods, the family cannot be sure when the change occurred, but later they were "quiet, stiff, cowering and frightened." Later examinations showed both dogs to be covered with black dust, and they subsequently suffered a lot of hair loss, which was similar to that caused by radiation. "Blood haematology, coagulation and immunology showed biochemistry abnormality."

They then headed towards Ceduna (SA) and later the Victorian border; to the subsequent police and researchers' interviews and the media frenzy. The newspapers, anxious to go to press as soon as possible, often got the details wrong. There were so many experts giving their points of view, often without the benefit of all the facts. Several varying theories came from sceptics – dry lightning or thunderstorm, ball lightning, meteorite, Jupiter, and a distorted view of the rising sun! (One expert even altered the time of the incident to fit his theory!)

Hang-on fellows, you can't all be right! In fact, there was such a concerted effort to discredit the Knowles, the poor family went into hiding. I began to wonder what it was these experts were trying to cover-up.

Several investigators have researched this incident in some detail, including John Auchettl and Paul Norman from VUFORS. Later Paul Norman stated: "There is reason to believe this was an abduction attempt that failed."

Dust, ash and residues

Following the event, the Knowles found a grey-black dust covering the roof, bonnet, boot and parts of the interior of the vehicle. This substance has been reported before. (In her book, *Skycrash*, Jenny Randles mentions a case in Taos, New Mexico. On 5 July 1978, many witnesses saw a huge saucer shape object buzzing a sedan, and a similar glittering powder was recovered.)

Truck driver Graham Henley was the first to see the family after the encounter. He said "I felt the sooty material on the roof and it was not brake dust, which I know well. This stuff was a fine silicon type material. It was like powdered glass, and had an incredible feel to it. There were four dents, as if the car had been picked up by a magnet."

Paul Norman also met with a local resident who said on the day of the incident he noticed a short fibre-like substance, scattered in spots along the bitumen, about a kilometre from where the Knowles family had stopped. The fibres crumbled between his fingers, "like graphite but only lighter", and soon blew away. A few days later this man began to suffer symptoms similar, but much worse, to those of Faye Knowles, and was later admitted to hospital.

When analysing the conflicting forensic reports one has to consider when the samples were taken (i.e. how long after the incident), and from what part of the vehicle. It is submitted that on the basis of the evidence there were most probably two main sources of dust and residue – one from the UFO reported on top of the car, and one from the burst tyre

Police collected samples of the substance deposited on the car as soon as the family reported the incident. Adelaide Forensic Squad said the dust found on and inside the vehicle was not ash. Their laboratories had done extensive tests and had failed to identify the substance.

John Auchettl of VUFORS instigated comprehensive research by scientists from Monash University into the dust/ash. As much as possible had been vacuumed from the car, and even Faye's pocket, soon after it reached Adelaide, and before Channel 7 hooked the car up for transportation. (Therefore scant, if any, dust or powder was left for Channel 7 to collect for AMDEL (Australian Mineral Developments Laboratory in Adelaide). Full details are given in the *Australian UFO Bulletin*, of March 1989.

Their conclusions were double-checked by two other laboratories. The final analysis was that the particles were unusual and made of potassium chloride. Instead of being a crystal formation, which is normal, they were velocity particles, which indicates they must have been forced out of something with great force. Scientists said that under enlargement the dust molecule looked as if it may have come from a space shuttle blast. Most known possibilities were ruled out including brake lining dust and car tyre residue.

Researcher Paul Norman of VUFORS wrote a very interesting article in *Flying Saucer Review* – (December 1988 – this entire issue is well worth reading, and gives an insight into the development and testing of advanced technology craft in the area.) He discusses tests conducted by Dr. Richard Haines and two other laboratories, on samples provided by VUFORS. He mentions the possibility of atomic element 85 (Astatine) being present. This is a radio-active chemical element which was first produced, synthetically, in 1940, at the University of California. It has a half-life of 7-8 hours. (Another report states that USA tests done by NASA's Ames Research Laboratory show that the dust was not from the brake system.). Paul concluded, with good reason, that there was a massive debunking campaign against the Knowles report. One wonders why?

The *Skeptical Inquirer*, (Vol XII) featured an article by a Ben Harris (a magician and investigator, from Brisbane) who claimed that only two sticky tape samples of powder could be lifted from the car for analysis by AMDEL in Adelaide. He went on to state the AMDEL results were a carbonaceous material and iron oxide (rust), consistent with residue from worn brake linings. (While Harris conveniently did not state how long after the encounter these tiny particles were taken, other reports state these samples were taken from the left front wheel, quite some time after the incident, when it had been driven many miles from the scene and was being held by Channel 7 in Wudinna.) It is known that Channel 7 intercepted the family en-route to Adelaide, after they had concluded interviews at Ceduna (SA) police station. The journalists persuaded the family to let them have the vehicle, and Channel 7, who instigated the AMDEL testing, kept it locked up away from researchers for quite some time.

Who does one believe – the police forensic experts, the Monash University and others, or AMDEL? I will leave it to the reader.

There was one other test conducted and filmed. The family had claimed they travelled at 200 kph when trying to escape. The 1984 Ford Telstar could not travel at this speed on the ground, however the wheels, if suspended in the air, could rotate at a reading of 200kph.

Other sightings at the same time

The October 1988 edition of the *TUFOIC Newsletter* detailed two simultaneous events. A Tasmanian man and his girlfriend were on holiday and travelling the 73 kilometres from Penong (SA) to Ceduna (SA) on the Eyre Highway on the night of 20-21 January:

"It was about 2.40 a.m. when I heard a loud thump coming from above the vehicle. I couldn't believe it was the gas bottle on top of the car – it was screwed down, and hadn't come off in 450,000 miles, but there was stuff coming off that roof I still haven't found.

"Then we saw a series of flashing lights in the sky, which lasted about 15 minutes. They looked like a row of bright white steady beams, covering a wide area of the sky, and coming towards earth. I don't know what they were, but it was funny that the wind picked up at that time. As it buffeted the car, things were flying off the roof. It moved the vehicle about across the road, and during this period the car would not go over 70kph."

What was interesting about this report was a 45-minute time anomaly. He said that as soon as the light beams finally disappeared the car regained power, and the one-hour wind-buffeting stopped. He said originally he only saw the lights for 15 minutes.

The same night, a Tasmanian yacht was participating in the Tall Ships Race from Hobart to Sydney, and was in rough seas near the Beecroft Peninsula (South Coast, NSW). Over a period of several hours a total of five lights came and went low over the sea around them. They were either red or white. One appeared to have a perimeter of small white lights, which changed to red and dropped into the water. Another shone a beam of light into the water. The lights were present until 3 a.m., and during that time the crew and vessel were full of static electricity.

The tuna boat *Empress Lady*, from the Australian Southern Bluefin fleet, was just off the South Australian coast, and had seen a bright light hovering overhead around the same time the Knowles' encounter occurred. Its crew had made a radio call that while the object was hovering overhead they found themselves unable to speak. A tuna-spotting plane also witnessed the object hovering above the trawler. It also appears that a second boat, the *Monika*, also witnessed strange lights, but the captain did not file a report, as requested, due to the media frenzy elsewhere.

Sargent Jim Furnell of Ceduna (SA) police was quoted as saying they had received two other reports of a strange light in the previous week, and two weeks later a bus driver sighted an unidentified metallic craft in the sky. Another woman motorist had seen a bright light, in the shape of an electric light bulb, near Mundrabilla (WA) and the Eyre Highway a week before.

The owner of a motel on the West Australian–South Australian border reported that two weeks earlier, on 5 January, she and her husband saw an unidentified craft coming from the west. "It was about 9 p.m., a clear night, and the craft had red and white flashing lights. It was very close to the ground, and it turned and stood still. There was no noise, and when we rang Air Traffic Control in Perth, they said there were no planes in the area."

While investigating the case Paul Norman was contacted by a gentleman who advised that a year earlier he stopped at a location in the same area near Mundrabilla, where a car had gone off the road and overturned. The driver told him the accident happened when he tried to avoid a UFO.

Similar car-lifts

It is not known whether the incidents of cars being lifted off the road are deliberate, or an accident due to some unknown magnetic or similar force. Many sceptics doubt that this has in fact occurred, however there are many cases documented in both Australia and other countries. Some indicate it may not have been an intentional act, with the vehicle accidentally being caught beneath a craft – on other occasions the capture may well have been intended (see box).

Launceston, Tasmania, 14th December 1987

About six weeks before the Knowles encounter, on December 14th 1987, sometime after 9.30 p.m., an executive was driving home from an isolated area 30 kilometres from Launceston. Mr. A, who worked for a car dealership, was driving his employer's expensive Mercedes car, and about two miles before the junction with the main road, noticed some lights behind, which he assumed were from a helicopter or plane. About a kilometre further on, the lights passed overhead, and as his car lights and motor all stopped. A mass of light landed, blocking the road, about 15 metres ahead.

He got out of the car. The lights were so brilliant, it was hard to distinguish the object above and behind them. He thought it was a grey colour cigar-shape, about five to six metres wide and two metres high. He ran and took cover behind some bushes, so scared, he vomited. The situation worsened when he saw his employer's car being dragged about ten metres down the road towards the object.

He thought he was only in hiding for a few minutes. However, subsequent investigation into the timeline indicate there may be an unaccounted period for up to two hours. A man in another vehicle, whose lights had also failed, pulled up behind him, and left his motor running. Mr. A ventured out and explained what was happening.

They heard a high-pitched whining sound and the object rose into the sky and curved off, disappearing to the south. There were rubber marks on the road where the car had been dragged, and the bitumen had melted – -some of it splashed on the front. While TUFOIC said there was no soot, Mr. A told a VUFORS investigator that there was a "sooty sort of carbon" covering the car, which also needed electrical repairs before it was sold. When he got home it was midnight – he should have arrived about 10 p.m. The incident was also thoroughly investigated by Keith Roberts of TUFOIC.

Coonabarrabran, NSW

In our book *The Gosford Files*' we published the case of Jack Ulster, a country farmer who had a memorable experience just before moving to the New South Wales Central Coast in 1988:

He was returning home, along a dark tarmac road at about 8 p.m. His utility truck was suddenly flooded with brilliant white light, and he pulled over and looked up. There was a huge object, no more than eight or nine feet overhead. The dark, round underside was about six feet in diameter. A large round white light in the middle, shone down upon him and the road below.

"I could hear a faint whirring sound, and felt a sense of awe, rather than fear. There was some kind of intangible, almost benevolent quality about it. I stretched my hand out to touch it, but before I could reach it the craft rose slightly and glided a few feet backwards. I could see it much more clearly – a large black saucer shape, no windows or lights except for the searchlight on the bottom."

After a few minutes it moved smoothly and quietly back down the road, and Jack got back in the car and continued his trip home. He had only travelled a short distance when his vehicle was flooded with white light again. The whole area was illuminated, and he realised he was no longer on the road or in control of his little truck. Out of the windscreen and side windows he could see he was now at treetop level.

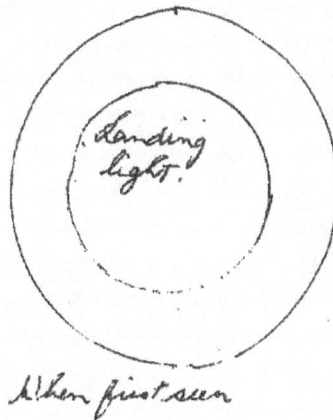

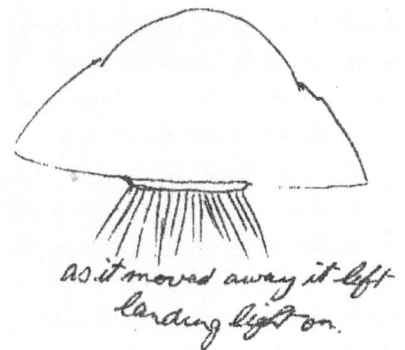

Landing light.

When first seen

as it moved away it left landing light on.

"I travelled mid-air for several hundred metres. I wasn't really scared, for some reason I trusted them, whoever they were, but I did wonder what was going to happen. I was put back on the road again, and the craft departed to the south. When I got home I just wandered around, looking at the sky, thinking if it was all real. Could I have just imagined it?"

Jack had not imagined it. A neighbour had been driving along in the opposite direction, and passed under the bright white light with Jack's vehicle hanging from it. He rushed home to tell his sceptical wife: "It's a big one and it's got Jack!" He had wondered what to do at the time – if his wife didn't believe him, the police certainly would not.

There is an addendum to this incident which left a very bad impression on Jack and my more ethical colleagues. Sometime after the publication of *The Gosford Files*, Jack, distressed and angry, contacted me. I had promised him anonymity and used a pseudonym. A prominent Australian researcher, unable to obtain details, had gone to Coonabarrabran and inquired among all the local population. He had gone to the estate agents to discover who had sold their property and moved to the Central Coast at that time. He eventually tracked down Jack, leaving a trail of gossip with his friends and relatives in Coonabarrabran.

Unfortunately ufology has its share of participants, who consider an unidentified object report and the witnesses, to be a commodity or possession to further their own quest for either the ever elusive answers or their own recognition. The witness or contactee – their confidence, privacy and psychological concerns must always have priority, they should not be tracked down like some prize trophy.

Blue Mountains, NSW

Rex Gilroy reported three incidents in the Blue Mountains. The first on 15th June 1978 when a couple were driving along Tablelands Rd, in Wentworth Falls, and a "green glowing saucer" appeared from nowhere, hovering overhead.

It was emitting some form of force field which lifted their car about four feet off the road then dropped them again. This happened three times in succession before it zoomed off over the valley.

The second incident was at about 2 a.m. one morning in June 2000. A car containing four people driving from Bell to Bilpin was surrounded by an ionised blue glow.

As the terrified occupants tried to speed away they felt the car being lifted at least two feet off the road. After being carried for some few hundred feet, the glow vanished and the vehicle hit the road.

A third, more disturbing encounter happened in Kurrajong, at the base of the Blue Mountains one September night in 1986. Leticia Martin was driving along Richmond Road towards Kurrajong when a blue glow totally enveloped her car, and her engine and lights died. She felt as if the car had been lifted off the road, and felt as if she was weightless.

"Suddenly I felt the car come to rest, and the blue glow faded away. I was terrified, and opened the door and found myself in a paddock, which I later discovered was on the outskirts of Penrith, miles away from Kurrajong. About fifty feet ahead of me was a large, pulsating, yellow, glowing egg-shaped craft. A round opening appeared and I could see a pink glow, but nothing else.

"I was dumbfounded at first, but regained my senses and was about to run for help to a nearby house, when I felt my arms being held by some invisible force, drawing me towards that opening. When I was only a few feet away I tried with all my might to break free, but felt magnetised, drawn inside. The opening vanished behind me. In my terrified state I found my whole body frozen of movement as the feeling of unseen fingers prodded and pressed into my body.

"I must have blacked out, and when I came to I was lying on the ground, and the family came out of the house nearby. I ran over, crying and sobbing, and asked if they had seen what had just happened. The couple could not understand what I was raving about. I was on their property, and wanted to know how I had driven my car into their paddock, when it was all fenced off?

"I told them what had happened, but they had been watching through the window, and said all they saw was me leaping out of the car, and making funny movements before standing still and collapsing on the ground. I was so embarrassed; they were laughing at me. I got back into the car, and after one of the sons opened a side driveway gate, I was off as quickly as possible."

Kununarra, West Australia

Wayne Trembath of the *Northern Star* reported that a man returning to Kununurra from Derby, had parked his landrover-ute next to the old Mary River crossing to have a short sleep. He had rolled his vehicle earlier at a washaway near Halls Creek, and was still feeling a little shaken up. He was woken by lights flashing and a strong wind rocking his vehicle. Thinking a storm was coming, he wound the window down to discover the lights were only around his vehicle, which was illuminated as bright as daylight.

As he was sitting there he had the sensation he was being lifted up, and put his hands down and found a space between himself and the seat. He didn't fall back down until the lights and wind stopped. He drove straight to Halls Creek, and stayed under the street lamp in front of the police station for the rest of the night.

This reminded me of the Tasmanian man and his girlfriend on the Nullarbor, the same night as the Knowles encounter.

North Ballarat, Victoria

The Daily Mirror, of 22 January 1988, noted an incident which occurred the same day pilot Frederick Valentich went missing. Evonne Hall, a 44-year-old farmer's wife, was driving along a country road with her two children, seven-year-old Jenny and David, aged four. A cigar-shaped object, about half the size of a single-engine light aircraft, hovered over her car. It made a loud whirring noise, and she felt it was actually on her car, which was lifted at least a metre off the road then dropped with a thud. The craft disappeared, and Evonne was left with an injured back.

Black Creek, NSW

People magazine published an interview with a motorist from Yass, who was travelling from Gulgong to Gunning on 13 June, 1993. He had stopped just before dark, at Black Creek, to have his sandwiches and coffee. As he drove on again, his glasses seemed to be covered with some kind of substance, and he stopped to clean them so he could see the road ahead.

"As I sat there alone on that desert road, I heard a sound like wire scratching against metal. And then I felt something grip the rear of the car and lift it up. I could see nothing through the rear vision window, but this invisible force, whatever it was, lifted the car's rear four times before dropping it back onto the road."

He drove away as fast as possible, still shivering as he felt he was being observed. When the road curved to the right he could see a small, bright, brilliant-green object hovering about 45 centimetres off the ground. He could not see anything else in the darkness, and as he kept driving it kept pace with him to the left of his car.

"It seemed to be relating closely to me, and vanished after a few kilometres. I'm sure it had something to do with my car being lifted from the ground."

Other encounters

Murray River, Morgan (SA), 1974

The Murray River in South Australia runs through some uninhabited areas, which have often been the haunt of unusual aerial objects. While some may be associated with Woomera and similar military bases, others are of a more mysterious origin.

The Captain of the Morgan-Cadell ferry, with fourteen passengers on board, first noticed the light in the sky. It rapidly descended and hovered about sixty yards upstream, shining a brilliant blue beam of light onto the surface of the water. It was reported as being "as big as a double-decker bus", and one passenger became so hysterical they had to call an ambulance. She was hospitalised for the next two days.

At least the ambulance officers were not sceptical. A few days earlier they were on the way to an accident when a huge cigar-shaped object appeared above them. The engine and lights died and the siren cut out.

Mundrabilla (WA), October 1988

The *Canberra Times* reported that Peter Chapman, a Pioneer Express coach driver, and seven passengers were travelling along the Eyre Highway, near Mundrabilla, about 100 kilometres from the South Australia border, not far from where the Knowles family had their unfortunate experience, the previous January.

A bright light came up behind the bus, and flew alongside. It was low, only about 100 metres up, at a distance of no more than 50 metres. A second light appeared to be revolving around it. Before the object disappeared it lit the side of the bus with a couple of beams of light, which made Peter's hair stand on end.

The witnesses reported it to the local police, who said the driver was quite upset, and was worried people might think he was a "bit of a nut."

Nullarbor Station (SA), 9 September 1989

The following report came from K. Basterfield and J. Johnston of UFORA.

It was a clear starry night and the Hennessy family were about 35 kilometres west of Nullarbor Station driving home to Perth in West Australia. At about 10.30 p.m. Mr. Hennessy, who was driving their station wagon, could see about a dozen lights to their right, through the windscreen. At first they were 10-15 degrees above the north- west horizon, but soon came much closer to their vehicle.

Mr. Hennessy thought that it was a plane, about to crash. His wife thought it was a UFO. The craft was silent – a metallic, rectangular shape, with a large number of dull yellow lights around. They pulled up, and he took a photograph. (Unfortunately the negative came back blank.) There were no adverse effects on the witnesses or their vehicle.

It passed them, at a distance of about 70 metres, parallel to the road, and moved quickly out of sight into the north-east.

Cocklebiddy (WA), 7 August 1994

Lisa and Morton Waltham were driving across the Nullarbor in a B-train, of 3x18 wheeler trucks, transporting goods from Melbourne to Perth. At about 8.30 p.m. (West Australian time) they were between Cocklebiddy and Norseman (WA) when an object came down and sat with the trucks.

"It was a white, solid teardrop-shape, with a red light at the bottom," Lisa said. "It was totally silent, and didn't hurt my eyes to look at it. It is hard to say how far it was away from us. It was just above eye level at about a 45 degree angle to the driver's seat. I was in the army for six years, and don't scare easily, but this time I was really frightened, so I got out of the passenger seat and into the driver's bunk at the back! From that position I was able to calculate its size, movements, changes, etc. in relation to the sun-visor and full windscreen. Three times I can recall it going up, hovering, then turning upside-down. Maybe it was an optical illusion, but it seemed to change shape at times."

Although they were travelling at 105 kilometres per hour, the object stayed with them for about 30 minutes. Lisa seemed a little confused when asked about the object's departure, saying, "It just disappeared – like it 'went out'. It was there for about two hours. I must have had a sleep in the bunk, a terrible nightmare! I was paralysed and screaming. After I woke up I asked Morton, 'Why didn't you help me?' And he didn't know what I was talking about."

Lisa said she didn't have any side-effects, and didn't seem to realise or acknowledge the time-duration discrepancies in her statement. She then commented that she was glad their two children were not with them, and I wondered why, if nothing untoward had happened. It would have been really helpful to any further investigation to at least talk to Morton, however, whatever happened he wasn't saying.

Apparently, one of the other truck drivers took photographs, but Lisa was unable to contact him to get copies. (Drivers – not necessarily connected, often cross the desert together for security.)

Campfire tales

Sometimes we hear tantalizing details of what could be a landmark case, and cannot investigate further as to the authenticity of the incident. In 1998 one such case was reported at a get-together of motor-home nomads in the outback. One of the Central Coast witnesses was present and mentioned *The Gosford Files*.

Two of the guests were an ex-helicopter pilot and an interstate truck driver who said years ago they were on the Nullarbor Plain when they saw a round craft in the sky. They followed until it landed on tripod-type legs. Despite being a little scared and unsure, they got up close, until the military arrived. There were also local police present and a few onlookers. (The truck driver was part Aboriginal, and his people had told him of other objects seen before.)

A few black unmarked helicopters were seen, and a crane arrived. The craft was put onto a low loader, and taken away. The two men were told, in no uncertain terms, to "keep quiet about this." They were both under the impression this was an extraterrestrial craft, however it may just as well have been a test run of one of our own secret prototypes.

Balladonia (WA), 1 July 1992

Garry Travers was a shearer and he and his brother were camping out at Balladonia on the Nullarbor:

"At about midday we saw a very large white light hovering over a road on a hilly area about ten kilometres away. We were curious, but dismissed it from our minds after it disappeared. Later that night, I suddenly awoke. I was still in my swag, but something was dragging me out by my feet. I thought I could hear breathing, and screamed out to my brother: 'Dingo! Dingo!' Bruce woke up, and whatever it was disappeared in the dark, and I could hear the sound of something taking off. We were driving down the road the next day, and saw what looked like a flying saucer.

I thought it was just some reflection in the windscreen, but when we stuck our heads out the window, we could see it hovering over the town four kilometres away. It took off soon after.

"After that incident I had insomnia, terrible trouble sleeping. I don't know if it is connected but I started to get ill. I was unwell for two to three years and the doctors couldn't diagnose what was wrong. At one stage I developed a bad fever which nearly killed me. In the end they told me it must be chronic fatigue syndrome.

"My brother is now shearing in New Zealand. He came home for Christmas, and still recalls what happened over twelve years ago."

"I often wondered if it was just a case of coincidence until a friend told me of an experience which changed his outlook. He was a farm worker at Southern Cross, a town near Kalgoorlie and had a similar experience. He was on the tractor in the paddock one night, when a bright light came down and hovered overhead. He jumped off and ran. He went back after the light had gone, and the tractor was undamaged. That night he had the same sensation. He was indoors, with the window open, and suddenly woke up to hear heavy breathing. He was screaming and fighting back, and whatever it was went away."

Garry commented that the local Aboriginals in West Australia, who often sleep out at night, will not go south of the railway line in the dark. They speak of "bad spirits" accompanied by lights.

Norseman (WA), 22 February 1999

Doug Trefford and his co-driver Bill rang me regarding a memorable incident when they were driving their Pioneer-Greyhound coach and three passengers, from Ceduna back to Norseman. It was about 2 a.m., and they were halfway between Norseman and the South Australian border.

"We were about 45 kilometres inland from the coast, and that part of the road actually heads south. It was a great summer night, clear skies and no wind. Everyone was relaxed – passengers a little drowsy, but we were having the odd joke and sing-along.

"The first thing Bill and I noticed were some very bright white headlights coming towards us. The trouble was they weren't on the road. I'd guess at an altitude of no more than six or seven hundred feet. At first we thought it was an exceptionally low aircraft, and stopped the bus.

"Everybody got out to have a look, and this weird 'plane' passed very slowly overhead to the side of the coach, about 600 metres away. It was at an odd 45 degree angle, and totally silent. We all just stood and stared. It was like nothing we had seen before. It was short, about half the length of a Boeing, but very bulky. The moon reflected off the silver-white fuselage, which was much bigger than that of a normal plane.

"As it passed by, we could see three orange-red glows at the back and Bob insisted he could see something like portholes in the middle. A little way down the road it changed its northerly direction by turning right and heading east. Everyone started babbling at once: What was it? 'It wasn't like any plane I've seen,' said one passenger, 'it didn't have any wings.' There were murmurs of agreement from everyone else."

"Bob suggested a new type of rocket, as he had noticed a little smoke and glow from the back as it moved away. We all got back in the bus, still debating the matter. Who had ever heard of a rocket that moved slowly, with windows and obviously under intelligent control?"

Who indeed?

Woomera (SA)

Woomera is situated in the desert to the north of Port Augusta.

The Woomera Base was once a top secret facility where the military tested rockets, missiles, bombs and all kinds of classified "goodies." On 3 February 1997, the *Daily Telegraph* reported that a United States company was proposing a 15 to 18-year-program which involved launching a series of low-cost, low-earth orbit, reusable communication satellites. The plan included stages of the rocket falling back to earth cushioned by airbags.

There are many reports of 'bogies' (unauthorised air traffic) and it is intended to only mention a few here. Needless to say, the official explanations were nearly always conventional, no matter how improbable.

Obviously, in the past, personnel and civilians associated with the Woomera Base were not satisfied with the government's whitewash. What was most significant was that a Woomera UFO group had been formed in the 1960s called the *Scientific, Technical and Astronomical Research Society* (STARS). The authorities were not happy when they received reports completed on STARS forms, rather than official documentation. Senior personnel actively discouraged the "UFO Club", and its activities had gradually faded away altogether by 1974.

Early May 1954

At 4.45 p.m. a Ranger was watching trials through binoculars and spotted a dark-grey, circular object with a translucent appearance. It seemed to be travelling directly across the path of an approaching Canberra Bomber aircraft, then turned right and went in the opposite direction. It slowed above the Canberra craft, and appeared to be hovering over its flight path. The object looked to be about the same size as the plane, but travelled three times as fast. (Further reports estimated its speed as approximately 3,600 miles per hour at an altitude of 60,000 feet.)

Of interest is Bill Chalker's research reported in *UFOs – Sub Rosa Down Under*, where he detailed a May 1954 report as originally being classified SECRET. The event was also witnessed by an English Electric Company's Guided Weapons Division scientist (this was not James Stern, as he was not at Woomera at that time – see below).

6 October 1954

Five months later, Gunner Willis was operating a cinetheodolite (a camera device for collecting and recording trajectory data) when he observed and photographed an unauthorised aerial craft. He was tracking a *Jindivik* target drone plane, in a very clear sky, when he saw a half-moon-shaped, silver-white object at 40,000 feet, travelling at medium speed. The sighting only lasted a short time, and the Department of Air "gave the film negative to the Director."

Late 1950s

Ken Llewelyn (author of *Flight into the Ages*), detailed another disturbing event. The Group Captain in charge of range operations, and the recovery officer saw an unusual bright white-green light coming in from the north-west, about 85 miles away. It was at about 5,000 feet, and travelling very fast. It silently orbited the range buildings, about five miles to the south, and then climbed away to the north-east at a steep angle.

James Stern

In the late 1950s (between mid-1957 to mid-1958), James Stern was Telemetry Chief for the Australian Branch of the English Electric Company's Guided Weapons Division.

"I was sitting in my car in Salisbury South Australia, when I got an urgent message: the Red Shoe trial team had a fully guided round (a missile), on the launcher at Range E, near Koolymilka. The *Jindivik* target drone plane was on the back track, prior to coming round on the firing leg, when radar reported a bogey in the intercept area. On instructions from the Range E Controller, the nearest cinetheodolite made visual contact, and then filmed it."

"The object had appeared at 50,000 feet as a three-to-four-metre diameter disc. It remained stationary for several minutes, before ascending to 100,000 feet in four or five seconds. The 100,000 foot level is where our radar van lost it. I don't know how far the range theodolite and radar vans tracked it.

"When the film was developed, the official assessment was: 'Film blank – radar fault'! There was an outcry from several of the radar operators and the girls on the theodolite. The assessment was changed to: 'Clear turbulence, causing visual and radar effect, not shown on film'."

James said, "Comprehensive records of every minute and step of the trials were meticulously kept, and I would expect the Guidance team to mention a radar bogey in their section. After each firing the trials teams were given the opportunity to view a screening of all the films taken. This time the alleged blank film was not included.

"We all thought that Base Security was in a flap and had put a lid on it. The other side of the Iron Curtain might have got something we didn't know about, and I bet the theodolite film, if it still exists, is probably in some security file."

This information from James certainly confirmed my suspicions about the evasive answers and vague explanations officially given by Woomera with regards to UFO reports.

James gave me further details which I cannot disclose. He was neutral in his attitude to UFOs, and to whether they were extraterrestrial or not. He did believe our ancient ancestors had advanced knowledge. He had studied ancient ruins, and had completed complex calculations and equations. His expertise in physics was amazing, especially relating to cloaking, particle screening and inter-dimensional theories. (When I read his findings, I found myself saying, "Of course, of course!")

He hoped to complete his research one day, perhaps back in the United Kingdom, and asked me to keep the details confidential. He hoped to make some money out of any resultant discoveries. If his theories were correct, I'm sure they are now with the Ministry of Defence, or some large corporation.

1966–1967

While some sightings by locals near Woomera could be linked to the test range itself, some are most definitely intruders. UFOR(SA) reported that one poor man was walking home when he saw 'three lots of objects' in the sky. There was no wind or dust, and one broke away from the rest and hovered low overhead. He said it was "as big as a football field", and he felt as if he were "standing on air, but his feet were on the ground."

After a while it took off at great speed. He couldn't remember much, and when he arrived home he was taken to hospital, suffering from shock.

1968

Peter Moyle, a workers from a camp four kilometres out of Woomera, told *People* magazine, that he was walking home one night after a meal in town. A light moved swiftly from the horizon, and hovered overhead for a few seconds. As the man the year before had claimed, Peter said it was "bigger than a football field." He described it as being like two saucers, inverted towards each other, with a protrusion underneath, bathed in yellowish light. He saw brightly lit windows around the middle join, and three or four shadowy figures moving around. It soon did a right-angle turn and took off at incredible speed.

Mysterious spheres

In the late 1950s there was some speculation regarding mysterious metal spheres found in the vast Australian desert. It is possible that they were of earthly design, however it is just as possible they originated elsewhere.

Keith Basterfield wrote of information he obtained in the AURA-based *Disclosure Project*, regarding the retrieval of downed fragments of space vehicles. Keith estimated at least nine such pieces were found over New South Wales, Queensland, South Australia and West Australia, between 1963 and 1988. His research unearthed several records of spheres being recovered. All were determined to be of American origin and returned to the United States.

Jerome Clark wrote in *The UFO Encyclopaedia, Volume 3*: "In 1961 the United States Air Force established the classified *Project Moon Dust* to 'locate, recover and deliver descended foreign space vehicles'." I personally consider this was a normal and reasonable reaction of any government who not only wants to know the technology of other-earthly or more alien powers, but also needs to retrieve its own.

Flying Saucer Review reported three objects were found in 1963 and Mr. Allan Fairhall, UK Minister of Supply, stated that inquiries to the relevant American and Russian space agencies had failed to determine the origin of these spheres, raising speculation in some quarters. There was some mention and discussion of this and the mysterious spheres in the Australian media at the time, but the issue was basically downplayed.

In later years, my own career involved the possible scenario of my being first on the scene if something crashed into my local area. I was given strict instructions that no matter whom or what it fell on, if it was any part of any space vehicle or satellite, my primary duty was to guard it until the appropriate authorities arrived.

One of INUFOR's researchers discussed in a recent article how Timothy Good, in his book *Alien Liaison*, interviewed a witness who was employed in a workshop in the Woomera facility.

An unusual object ended up in the workshop after being found by a helicopter searching for a missing girl. The mid-grey, metallic sphere was about two foot, nine inches in diameter, and somewhat darkened, perhaps by extreme heat. It was lightweight for its size, and a perfect sphere – no bumps, rivets, welds or signs of being polished.

They tried everything to cut into it – saws, drills, hammers, chisels and even an oxy-torch, which didn't even heat the surface. Nothing they tried could raise it to oxidising heat, and it did not register any radiation, not even the background level.

The witness initially assumed that it came from a *Black Knight*, the only missile in existence that could have contained something that size, but they denied it had anything to do with the *Black Knight*. He also realised we didn't have the technology to produce that object. Before they could do further investigations, Range Security took the object for the United States Wright-Patterson Air Force Base, as "space debris."

Australian newspapers reported later finds in South Australia and Queensland, and our witness's work colleague suggested the safest approach was that this object "never existed."

Military sightings

Military personnel also reported seeing unauthorised craft in the sky. Often their senior officers actively attempted to dissuade or discredit their reports. I would never have known of the following incident had I not been at a government training college in the 1980s, and one of the witnesses, a fellow student, confided in me:

"I was with another army serviceman, on patrol duty at Woomera in the 1960s. As we drove along the perimeters, making a routine security check, we spotted a large cigar-shaped object, hovering over the electrical cables. It was making a strange noise, and I got the impression it was drawing power from the lines. My hair stood on end, as if there was a strange magnetism in the air. In fact, as I am talking to you, the hair on the back of my neck is standing on end, just like it did that day."

Upon return to base, they were subjected to three days of interrogation, and less than subtle intimidation. "At first they suggested we had been drinking, but once we proved our sobriety, they changed their tactics and said we must have been mistaken, and should withdraw our reports. We remained adamant in our testimony until eventually the base commander released us back to normal duty. He warned us never to discuss the matter with anyone again."

Maralinga (SA)

The Maralinga nuclear testing range is located in South Australia, half-way across the Nullarbor Plain, but further north. Much of this is still a Commonwealth-controlled area with limited or no access, due to long-term nuclear contamination created during the 1950s and 1960s.

There is a report that a RAF corporal, stationed at Maralinga sighted an unidentified craft hovering over the airfield for 15 minutes, following a nuclear test detonation. It was a metallic silver-blue colour, with a line of windows or portholes along the edge. Given the tight security around such projects, I don't think we will ever know full details or official analysis of this event.

Chapter Eleven

Western Australia

Southern Western Australia

Margaret River

Margaret River is a small township, 280 kilometres south of Perth. It is situated near the coast, at the side of the river, and has a mild climate suitable for its fruit orchards, vineyards and Mediterranean type agriculture. It boasts wonderful coastal scenery and beaches, and is located near a cave system noted for its prehistoric fossils.

Ruth is a recognised writer, published in Australia and overseas. However, she cannot divulge her own incredible true life story, for fear it may discredit her and affect her career. It took a long time for Ruth to gain enough trust to confide the bewildering and distressing experiences which she had confronted in her life. When we did meet, some segments were still too painful and difficult to recount:

"The first contact I can recall was in 1966, when I was eight years old. I don't really want to talk about that – it was so long ago. After that I started writing poetry and developing literary talents. I got married, much too young, in 1974, when I was only sixteen. My husband and I soon separated, and I, along with my 18-month-old son, moved into a small remote house, in the hills of southwest Western Australia.

"Not long afterwards I wasn't feeling so well. I couldn't believe it when the doctor told me that I was definitely about two and a half months pregnant! It wasn't possible!

"A short time later there were very bad storms – my son and I were isolated, flooded in. I cannot remember very much of those three days, except that I woke up and had lost the baby. It's all very hazy. There was no evidence of a baby, a miscarriage, or that I had ever been pregnant in the first place." Ruth went back to the specialist, who did another ultrasound, and confirmed the child had "gone" – something the medical profession could neither explain nor understand.

Ruth and her son continued to live in the same area, both enjoying the peace and tranquillity of the environment. In 1992, some 17 years later, there was a knock on the door.

"It was a pleasant woman, a stranger to us, who said she was a geologist, conducting fieldwork nearby. What she said next left me speechless. She claimed she had been in contact with UFOs and had a message for me! 'They' had my missing child and further, in the past, they had inserted an implant in my head! I was to go to a local landmark for further communication."

Ruth was flabbergasted, and didn't know what to make of this. Who was this strange woman, and how did she know about her previous experiences, which she had kept so private? Besides her natural misgivings, it was raining, and inconvenient at the time, so she said, "No, she wasn't going." Two hours later the strange female geologist returned and insisted that Ruth go to the designated spot. Her 18-year-old son was still living at home, so for safety, she took him with her and went to the mountain.

"I didn't see anything, and was frightened. I could feel and sense a tremendous source of energy. It was like a spiral of electricity surrounding me, creating a sort of encompassing humming sound. Then I heard a noise, like a bird – just three notes in repetition. I could feel a strange sensation in the bottom of my neck and skull and found myself returning the call. I had no control or will over it. I don't think I could voluntarily make those weird noises if I tried.

"The whole time I was clutching onto a necklace of nautiloid fossil in lava, which was around my neck. My son was just staring in amazement, and when he heard the bird calls, said 'That was real cool Mum'."

The next three nights Ruth was beset by vivid dreams. She felt as if she were an energy, rather than a body, and she was outside something, and going in and down, into some caverns. There were lanterns of fire all around. Suddenly, they heard the sound of feet – it was soldiers coming to get them. She started running into a tunnel, clutching a scroll in her hand. Somehow she knew she had to keep hold of the scroll.

"The first night I woke up at the beginning of the tunnel, and the second night I got further down. On the third I progressed even more until it caved in on me, and I was crushed by the pyramid. I woke up screaming: 'The scroll, the scroll!' Everything was so real and vivid. What was happening to me? What was the reason and meaning of these strange visions, and where were they coming from?"

About three months later, Ruth was in bed, reading a book. She blew out the candle and lay down to sleep. Suddenly, she saw two energy beams on the ceiling, which became two forms. Ruth got the impression they were male, one about the size of a six-year-old, and the other about twelve. They had grey skins or suits, "sort of all one-piece." Their eyes were big and shiny – "black like the colour of iron ore."

"There seemed to be energy all around. The smaller one extended his hand to me. I looked into his eyes and sensed a familiarity, and had the strangest psychic impression that he may have been my son." Since then she has often found herself drawing pictures of these two beings.

Ruth doesn't remember any more, but when she woke up she had a terrible headache, and a sore spot on top of her head, where there was blood and a lump. (I have met other experiencers who have presented with a similar lump after a follow-up encounter in adulthood.)

One night, about a year later, Ruth came home from a party, and went straight to bed. She had only been asleep a short while when she woke up feeling thirsty. As she was getting a drink of water she looked out the window.

"I saw the moon, coming up between the trees. No, it wasn't the moon; it was moving too fast! I started to feel nervous and sweaty, the way I always do before these strange encounters. When I got a better look, it seemed to be similar to those conventional flying saucers people talk about."

She tried to get a better view, but could only see the bottom. It moved over a paddock, and then the driveway, where it shone a beam of gold-white light onto the ground. At a distance it had appeared to be about the size of the moon, but close up it was "like looking at the underside of a huge balloon." Ruth was so frightened she hid under the blankets and prayed, and was relieved when the object seemed to take off and leave.

"After a while I heard a noise – the sound of feet on the stairs, coming from the studio door. I could see the light of a torch. Perhaps it was my neighbour, Jack, who had also seen the strange object. I put some clothes on and opened the bedroom door to see a complete stranger standing there. It was not Jack. How had he got in when the front door was still locked?

"He was a tubby man, bearded and slightly balding, with soft eyes. I felt paralysed, then suddenly his eyes changed to resemble the previous beings, and his tubby form just seemed to dissolve! As if in a trance I followed this being through the door, out to the paddock and into the craft, which hadn't left after all."

It took off, and after flying directly above a highway, shot up into space. Later the craft landed, and she doesn't know if it was somewhere else on earth or not, but she was able to breathe normally, as did everyone else. She noticed some "amazing architectural structures", and then followed some people going in line into one. She thought it may be some form of factory. After walking along the top of rafters, they looked down on people of all nationalities, dressed in grey body suits, who were making things on conveyor belts. The next thing she remembers she was back home.

On 25 September, 1994, Ruth had another strange feeling, and a little later she and several friends saw two bright, white cylindrical lights slowly descending to the ground nearby. It was during the investigation of this sighting that INUFOR researchers interviewed Ruth, and the details of her disturbing abductions began to slowly unfold.

"This is the first time I have told anyone what happened. I was afraid people would laugh, or think I was insane. Because my mountain home is so remote, I had no radio or television up until a few weeks ago, and had no idea that others around the world had experienced similar phenomena. While I think some of these entities may be evil, the ones who communicated with me seemed essentially good in nature."

Ruth admitted there were many blank parts in her memory, but she didn't want hypnotherapy, or to remember. The previous experiences had left her very stressed in the past, and she now has recovered, and is managing well. She feels she has some beneficial mission to perform, but doesn't know what it is. She has developed psychic and psychokinetic abilities and her talents have improved out of proportion. She just wants to "get on with her life."

Outer Perth, 18 January 2013

On the 20 January 2013, I received a phone call from Sophie Gardner who lived in a rural area, outside of Perth – due to the necessity of witness anonymity I cannot divulge the exact location. Over several months Bryan Dickeson and I liaised with the family, and investigations have not really reached a final conclusion.

At 9.30 p.m. on Friday 18 January, Tony (17) was giving his friend Greg (15, Sophie's son) a lift home. Tony recalled "As I turned into Greg's driveway, and stopped the car, I noticed the area around us was unusually light for a dark night. At first I looked northward, to the left of the car, but couldn't what was creating the light. I looked to the other side, and in the east, saw a very brightly lit object up in the sky."

"It had a central, intensely bright, bluish core, almost ultra-violet – about the size of a basketball, with a spherical outer zone producing strong pinkish-white light some two to four metres across. It was spinning slightly, giving a varied mottled surface, and almost seemed to be floating or hovering. It was actually flying from the north to the west, towards us, and had a fast steady speed parallel to the ground.

"Eventually it was only about 60 metres away, about 40 metres above the ground. It seemed to turn our way and projected a beam of light at us. My car lit up so brightly inside, like daylight. All around the vehicle it was still the same white light as before. We were both scared stiff, but I managed to get my iPhone and tried to get some video of it."

My colleague Bryan Dickeson has reviewed the pictures, which show a small white object but little detail. The background dialogue is informative, reflecting the agitated and hysterical state of the boys.

"Then it seemed to resume its original course northwards, and disappeared in the distance. As it moved away the colour changed, becoming less of a bright white and more orange, then red, and finally a less intense red until it disappeared from view.

"I guess the whole thing only took a few minutes. We rushed inside, and when four more family and friends arrived home soon after we told them all about it. They were quite excited when at 10.40 p.m. we saw another white light, identical to the first, up in the northern sky. It was actually heading away from us, going east to north, but everyone rushed out to see.

"Some of us were on the back upstairs balcony, and a braver couple had gone 80 metres down into the back paddock, where they were only about 700 metres away from it. We took videos at the same time – from the house the footage showed a small purplish-white sphere, but closer, from the paddock, it appears orangey-violet and triangular or conical. We were lucky with the videos, as the weather was fine and clear, with stars visible in a moonless sky.

"The Gardner's dog, which had originally been locked in the house when we first arrived, was now very excited, and ran across the paddock towards the object, barking. He continued barking and carrying on for some time after the object disappeared." The Gardners allow a neighbour to graze a few sheep in their large back paddock.

They did not get much sleep that night, but think it was partly due to the excitement. All six witnesses experienced severe migraines for four or five hours after their sightings, and when Greg took Panadol it had no effect. Tony had a sore left shoulder for the next three to four days, and both he and Greg had sore eyes for some time after, (in particular, Greg's left eye).

When my colleague Bryan Dickeson spoke to Tony four days later, his sight was still sensitive. If he looked at something bright or white, his visual response showed some colour retention when he closed his eyes. (As a red, blue or green after-image or rainbow of the item, which then faded away.) Bryan considered that this may suggest the object was emitting significant amounts of higher-frequency, ultra-violet light as Tony had reported. Also of significance was the reason Sophie had first rung me – she was very concerned as the boys' faces were reddened as if they had been severely sunburnt. There were also some discrepancies in the reports. While the boys had indicated they stayed in the vehicle, when they spoke to Greg's mother about their red faces they had admitted getting out of the car, to get a better look, before the object came down close to them.

The property has a series of sophisticated security cameras, which operate in normal light during the day and in infra-red light mode at night. Night footage recorded from the camera at the back of the house, examined the following Thursday, showed a series of seven unexpected light sources which were not seen by the witnesses on the previous Friday night. In infra-red, the light sources, hovered over the back paddock, turned off and on in several sequences for some minutes, and may explain some of the family dog's continued excitement at the time.

This was not the end of Sophie's problems on a property which has some unusual features. The family had occasionally noticed an unusual, faint pink glow in their back paddock at night, but had never bothered to investigate this further. It did not seem to affect the sheep at all.

Greg was able to access a high-resolution, satellite imagery database on the internet to see, from above, where their mysterious object might have come from and gone to. This database did not record his particular ball of light, but Greg found a night-time image of their property which showed a pink, luminous plume of light hovering just above ground level in their back paddock, in among their sleeping sheep! Greg also found several dozen identical pink plumes scattered over other properties in the area, and downloaded a plume image.

I referred the matter and plume image to Bryan Dickeson who has a science degree: He describes the plume as having a vertical core – a cylinder of bright white light some ten centimetres across and one metre high. This cylinder has hemispherical ends and a spherical white bulb, twenty centimetres in diameter, just above the base. The central, white core is completely enveloped by a pear-shaped zone of paler pink light.

We could not access the same satellite imagery database ourselves (the company concerned now charges heavily for their service – it's mostly used by wealthy mining companies). However, given the apparent extent of these plumes, we decided to see if there was any interesting geology common to the known plume area. (Ufologists in the northern hemisphere often refer to "earth-light phenomena" and "earthquake lights" as a potential source of UFOs, or as UFO-attractants.)

Sophie's property is situated within an unusual and extensive 'Archon zone', containing Australia's oldest rock formations; a geological relic billions of years old. This extremely ancient shield zone, has a few counterparts in Sweden, Labrador and South Africa. However, the stable Darling Fault runs north-south along the western edge of this shield zone, and close to Sophie's property. The rocks are highly mineralised, at various times a very wide range of rare and unusual minerals have been taken from this area, and prospecting continues today.

It is possible the pink plumes are part of this geophysical complexity. These ancient deposits of basic and ultrabasic deposits such as serpentine and olivine, may also contain perovskites – minerals with highly unusual and exotic electromagnetic properties that may give rise to the pink plumes. Unfortunately, we do not have the resources to investigate this further.

Perovskites are greatly prized high-tech materials, now finding the newest applications throughout our lives. Was Greg's strange object connected with a search – terrestrial or extraterrestrial – for rare and valuable minerals near Sophie's property? Sophie told me that there had been a conference, fairly low-key, in a local town which she thought was related to mining.

That was not her main problem. Her electricity bill was a ridiculous $2,800 a month, when she had used very little power. The supplier had been difficult, finding no fault with the lines or equipment which came over the property from the main road. Further, neighbours told her they also had been periodically plagued by lights, as had the previous owner, who also had exorbitant power bills – that is why she had been sold the property at a bargain price!

(The matter of the soaring power bill got my attention. There was a case in England – reported by the *Telegraph* in 1997 of a woman, who claimed multiple paranormal experiences. Despite the electricity board checking her meter, she had received astronomical power bills ever since an alleged abduction experience the previous year.)

Sophie was obviously traumatised by the events. Sometimes she would want to talk to us, and at others become distressed as if she wanted to psychologically hide from the whole episode, which made investigations difficult.

On 23 August 2013 she contacted us again in a very distressed state.

"I allow my neighbour (who is in his eighties), to graze some of his sheep on my property, and early this morning he found four of the animals dead, and their eyes had been removed. To the best of my knowledge their bodies were intact and there was no blood. One other was blinded but still alive. He had removed four carcasses, still warm to the touch, and left the injured one. He accused my dogs of being responsible, but I know this is not possible – both had been inside all night, and they have never attacked another animal. My little shitzu-cross, (only two kilograms), has gone missing from this morning."

"I raced up to the paddock and found the fifth sheep, now dead, but still warm. It was lying on one side. Its legs had been hobbled with twine, presumably by the farmer – and both eyes were missing, but there was no blood on the facial fleece. There was no sign of any other injuries, the carcass was intact." Sophie and the family were extremely agitated, and sent us distressing facial photos of the poor creature.

Bryan phoned Sophie on 3 September, and she gave the following update; "My dog came back after three days, distressed, hungry and very tired. She won't go outside at all, and hides in my bedroom whenever I go out. I don't know what has scared her so much."

"I've tried to contact the neighbours for confirmation that only the eyes were removed from the other four sheep he took away, and any further details that might help, but they are very elderly and distressed, and won't talk to me at all. My electricity company can still find no reason for the high-usage electricity bills and have agreed to halve it. No-one can figure out who or what is taking my power somewhere between the road and my home." The power company has a local substation on Sylvie's property, and Bryan had suggested to Sophie that she ask them to remove it, as "it was obviously faulty" – in an attempt to get a better, more sympathetic response from the company.

On our advice, Sophie then contacted the RSPCA and local Department of Agriculture (we insisted she did not mention the possibility of UFOs or animal mutilations!). Two teams visited separately, one from the Department and another from a Perth University. To inspect the remaining dead sheep on her land. Both were surprised that despite lying around in the heat in warm weather, there was no sign of flystrike or maggots. It was unusual that they did not take tissue samples or propose further tests. They said that there were no signs of dog attack and could offer no explanation for the sheep's injuries – except to say that the sheep was probably still alive when its eyes were removed.

Sophie was somewhat spooked by this, and together with strange lights that affected her son, some unknown entity draining her electricity, horribly mutilated animals and a strange "pink plume" in the back paddock, I got the impression she would like to sell up and move somewhere else as soon as possible.

As fascinating as this case is, we have still not reached any who or why conclusions in this complex series of events and factors.

Central Western Australia

Central Western Australia which encompasses the Pilbara region, is one of the world's most heavily mineralised areas. It is a vast, open landscape of massive, eroded red mountains, sand, spinifex and mulga scrub. Recently it has experienced a massive boom in iron ore mining, creating much mineral wealth. Stretching through the Pilbara is the Hamersley Range, with spectacular gorges and water features fed by springs from an underground basin.

Port Hedland, 2 May 2001

Port Hedland is a new port with streamlined facilities for exporting massive amounts of iron ore mined inland at Tom Price, Mount Newman and Paraburdoo.

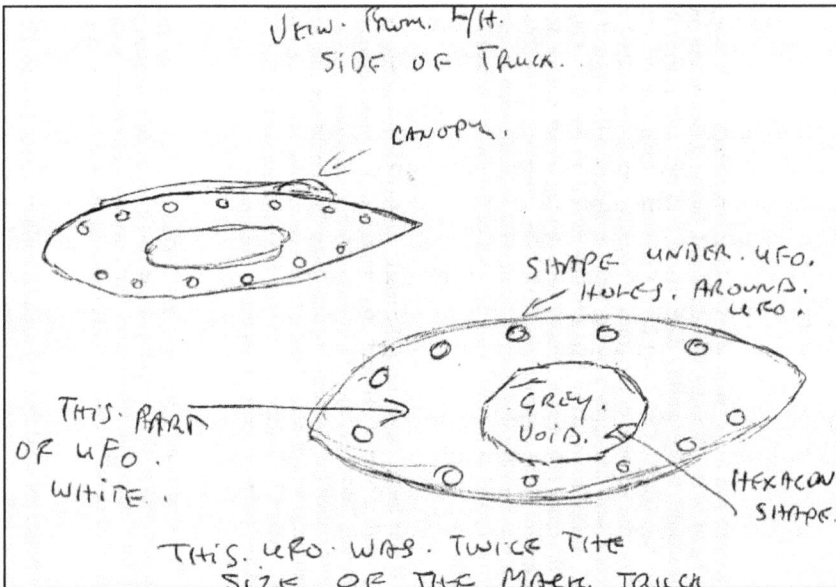

It was a clear day, about 6.15 p.m., and Roger Woods was driving east in a road train truck, with his offsider Chris Hanlon. They were on the Woodie Woodie Road, heading to the mine site, which is 400 kilometres east of Port Hedland. At the time they were about 340 kilometres from Port Hedland:

"I did not see anything until we were going downhill and the bull-lights on the front bar lit up the object, which stood out like a white stencil in the sky. I drove and Chris kept watching the approaching craft, which seemed to be tracking up the river. At that time we were about to cross over the river, and I noticed this shape on the left side of our vehicle. Next thing, this object came over the top of us, and seemed to stay there for a short time. It was only about 100 feet above us, and was solid – twice the size of a *Mack* truck. It was travelling very slowly, about 50 kilometres per hour, and after a while it turned left and then banked to the right, just above the treetops."

Chris told me he was able to get a better look, as Roger was concentrating on the road ahead. "It was shaped like a flounder fish, with a white under-body, holes around the underneath edge, and a grey hexagonal shape void in the middle."

The top, or "canopy", was a brown "turtle-shell type pattern, with several moving flaps on the edge of either side. I could see some seams and windows."

It was travelling southwest towards Tom Price and Mount Newman and they subsequently lost sight of the craft, as they were in an isolated area, and not prepared to stop.

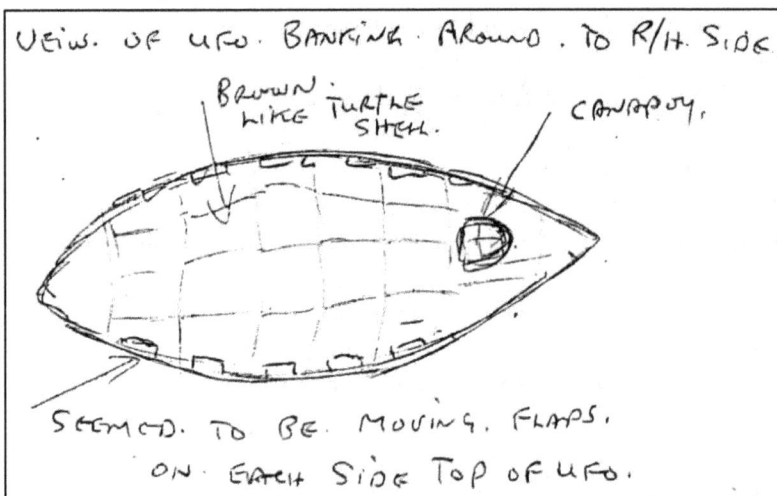

Dongara, Sunday, late September 1973

Dongara is on the West Australian coast, about 240 miles north of Perth, and 45 miles south of Geraldton. It is essentially a small coastal holiday and fishing spot.

It was about 5.30 p.m., and James Murphy and his wife Gwen were walking along the footpath in Port Denison, a fishing village near Dongara:

"I could see a large cloud just above the northern horizon. It had a small black spot in the middle, and I pointed to it with my fishing rod. Gwen said, 'It must be a plane'. But it wasn't. It kept getting bigger and bigger as it came nearer. After a couple of minutes it was getting much closer and we started to get a little alarmed, as there was no-one else around.

"It was certainly no plane! It moved steadily towards us at treetop level, over Dongara, then over the river and the sand hills along the shore. It was about 250 metres away when it slowed down and hovered behind the dance hall, just above the water line on the beach.

"The dance hall, a one storey building, about 30 feet wide and 60 feet long, was on a lawn just over the road. As the object passed along the shore I estimated that it would have been much higher, and at least three times wider.

"Gwen and I clung on to each other and stared for about five minutes in a mixture of fear and wonderment. It was clearly outlined – a huge, dark grey spherical or round ball, about 75 feet in diameter, with a cone shape on the top. About two-thirds the way up, maybe 20 feet from the top, was another smaller, cone shape protruding from the side.

"The main body seemed to be covered with a dark grey mesh, so I cannot be sure what lay underneath. There were no lights on it, and I couldn't see any doors or windows. It just silently hovered. There was no indication of what powered its movement. At no time did it appear to rotate.

"It then slowly, smoothly and steadily moved back along the exact identical route until it entered the same white cloud in the north. I was a police officer for 38 years, but have never seen anything like this before or since. I must admit to a sense of wonderment, there was no indication

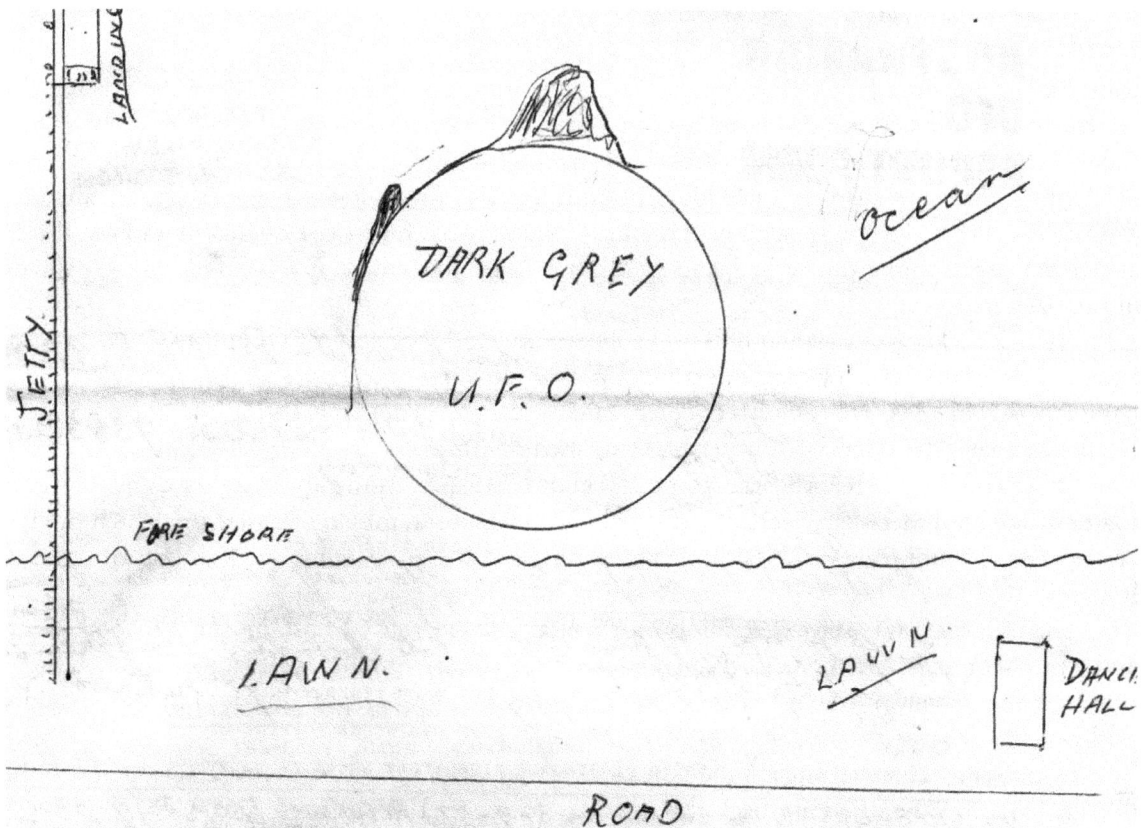

of what powered it, and I assumed it must have been controlled from inside the sphere. I was bursting with the logical questions: Who? How? What? Why?

"Gwen and I raced back to our van and turned on the television, but there was no mention of what we had seen. We checked all the newspapers for the next fortnight – nothing! I tried to make a report, but it was difficult in my position, and I kept getting fobbed off."

Unfortunately I had no answers for James either.

Exmouth, North West Cape, and other Defence Bases

Exmouth, on the sheltered waters of the Exmouth Gulf, is a modern town, built by the Commonwealth and West Australian Governments as a service centre for the United States Navy radio communications base on North West Cape. There have been sightings of unidentified craft over the Base from time to time, mostly witnessed by Base personnel, and as such not generally publicised. There are also Defence Signals Directorate (DSD) bases near Geraldton, at Kojarena, at Pearce near Perth (and in the far, far north at Shoal Bay, in the Northern Territory).

In the case of unusual craft over bases such as these, there is usually insufficient data to ascertain whether an object is maybe a prototype, one of our own or from a foreign agency, or something a little more exotic from further afield. Since one cannot interview Base personnel or conduct a thorough investigation, such reports should ethically be withheld, and not published accompanied by wild speculation, as has sometimes been the case.

In 1997 the *Sun Herald* (August 17) announced the United States was to test four *Terrier* missiles which would be launched, over a two-week period, from a station in the Kimberleys. After travelling 140 kilometres into the sky, they would land 100 kilometres at sea, between Port Hedland and Broome. Peace activists warned this might not be the only experimental launches, but many sightings of unidentified craft do not equate with this explanation.

In the first chapter of this book, in the section headed *Great Balls of Fire*, there is an account of massive balls of orange light seen over Tom Price. It is not known if these were in any way associated with nearby Exmouth or the base at North West Cape, though it is possible.

Denbarker, May 1981

John Pinkney reported on an incident at Denbarker, one night in May 1981. "Harry was watching television when the screen displayed serious static, so he decided to go to bed. On the way to the toilet at the rear of the house, he heard an enormous humming, "like a transformer substation."

"An enormous shadow filled our moonlit yard – and I looked up to see an absolutely monstrous oval-shaped craft with yellow-blue lights around the base. I rushed in and got the wife and my eldest daughter out of bed, and by the time they got outside it was hovering over the dam in the back paddock.

"It was making a crackling noise, like electricity, and was about two metres over the water. Blue and yellow bright light streamers were pouring from it, and the next day we went down to have a look. The grass around the edges was singed and the water level had dropped by 1.5 metres. I estimate that 120,000 litres of water had vanished overnight.

"I rang the Pearce RAAF Base, some 350 kilometres away, and although they didn't comment, I later discovered there had been lots of reports. They had scrambled a Mirage jet, which the UFO eluded for 15 minutes. We certainly heard something like a jet going back and forth over our house."

Then Harry's wife started acting out of character, and started flashing the outside lights on, and almost immediately the craft flashed back. After about 15 minutes of signalling, they heard a noise on the driveway, like a "rush of tiny feet, similar to a herd of sheep", but they could see nothing.

Harry rang Pearce again, and the duty officer told him to stay calm, and remember everything that happened. When he rang back the next day to report the missing water, he was told to say nothing to the media.

"From after about the second time we rang Pearce, there is a gap in our memories. The next morning we discussed the experience, and realised that none of us could recall going to bed. In fact everything went blank until we woke at around 6 a.m."

It wasn't until then that Harry started wondering if any unusual events in the previous six months had any connection. There had been tapping on the walls, and strange faces at the windows. At one stage the police were called, but could find nothing. Their neighbour had found deep holes in his paddock, as if made by some kind of object with tripod legs.

"I then remembered the previous owner of our property had been chased by a bright light while in his Land Rover one night. His son had fired at it with a .303 rifle, and at that stage, both their memories went blank, just as ours had."

Northern Western Australia

Kununurra

Kununurra, an indigenous name for *big water*, is northeast of Broome and southeast of Wyndham. It lies at the heart of the Ord River Irrigation Scheme at the top of Western Australia. It is remote, bordered by vast deserts to the southeast, lush green irrigated fields to the north, and the spectacular, varied landscapes of the Kimberleys to the south. There are many reports of strange craft and phenomena. However, as is often the case, locals prefer to avoid any publicity. Hapless motorists and truck drivers are often the focus of these intruders.

The Aboriginal people have long been aware of inexplicable visiting lights. Often a sentry will sit on a rock on a desert hill, scanning the skies. They tell of "big white lights" coming down and hovering, referring to them as "bad spirits." I have yet to hear of any friendly interaction between Aboriginals and aliens, although it might well exist. Sometimes there are hushed whispers of times gone by, when strange craft from the sky would land and sometimes steal their women and children.

Just over the Northern Territory border, hidden in a mountain range, are very old cave paintings. This rock art appears to depict strange beings which resemble spacemen or astronauts. We wonder about their secret knowledge and mythology. Many tribal elders worry that this is being forgotten as the younger generation are not so interested in the old ways. Stories from the Dreamtime refers to people coming down from the stars. Some tribes have the same word, *umbi*, to describe circular dish-craft – a typical flying saucer, by western definition.

14 August 1966

The *Sun Herald* (27 November 1966) reported that due to the daytime heat, Philip Johnston was working late on his bulldozer. He had stopped for a break at midnight, and spotted a bright white light which descended, stopped, and went behind a hill. He felt a little apprehensive and drove the bulldozer as far away as he could, switched off its lights, and started eating his supper.

"Then I saw the light come slowly back up over the hill. It seemed to focus on me, and got brighter and brighter, like a welding light until I couldn't look at it anymore. It covered the area all around the 'dozer and me with a sort of moonlight glow, but it wasn't the moon. I was so scared I thought of hiding under my bulldozer.

"The light went out, and all I could see were four red-coloured sort of pilot-lights, 40 feet apart. They came closer and then turned towards the neighbouring farm. The white light came back on, so bright it illuminated the whole field. For four or five minutes it hovered about 200 yards away, then rose, banked, and straightened out. At that stage I got a better view of it. I was about 120 to 160 feet long, but no more than six to eight feet high, when side on. It slowly moved away and disappeared.

"About half an hour later it returned, about 600 feet up, a vague ghostly shape with three red lights. It moved slowly around the valley, and settled in the mountains about six or seven miles away.

"The following night at about 11.45 p.m., I was driving back home fairly slowly, as I had cut my finger, and torn the nail off on the harrow. I saw that white light, about a quarter of a mile away, coming towards me. I got quite a fright, and thought it might be the same craft. I stopped the car, but decided to play it safe, and didn't get out.

"It was about 100 yards away, and travelling very low, parallel to the road. I shone my torch in that direction, and it was the same dimensions as the one the previous night. My torch reflected off its shiny metal surface. The rear light went out, there was a slight swish as it sped up to about five miles per hour. I kept pace with it for some time, still shining my torch along its side. There seemed to be a sort of windscreen on the front, and two doors and many windows along the side.

"After about three or four minutes, the rear light brightened, it gave another swish, sped up to about fifteen miles per hour and moved out of sight. I raced home and woke the family, who brought their cameras, and came back to the spot with me. Mum was patching up my finger as we raced along. While we saw a bright white light through the bush on the way, we did not see the craft again. Other locals told me they had also seen something similar, but as is the case in the country, did not say anything for fear of ridicule."

February 1987

The *Sunday Territorian* and other papers reported that Monty Barr, Brett Rogers and Wayne Trembath had a close encounter in a notorious area for unsolved mysteries. Later Wayne, who was a journalist with the *Northern Star*, contacted me regarding his experience and those of others in the vicinity.

Wayne and two colleagues were driving two trucks on the Great Sandy Desert, after delivering a portable home to an Aboriginal settlement, near Lake Gregory Station. "At first we noticed an object about 200 metres to the right of the dirt road," Wayne told me. "It was shaped like a large bus with glowing interior lights. There appeared to be amber-coloured triangular objects, three on the left-hand-side and five on the right. We spoke on the radio, at first speculating why a bus would be parked in an inaccessible sandy area.

"Initially, we had some concern, as in the 1970s one man near Golden Gate Creek disappeared without trace from his vehicle. Two years later another motorist, who had broken down, vanished after refusing help from a passing motorist. In 1990 two blokes went missing overnight from near Lake Argyle. Another fellow found the Range Rover the next morning. It had driven off the bitumen, done a U-turn, and come to a halt. The ground around was quite damp, but had no sign of footprints or tyre tracks anywhere around. The vehicle was in perfect working order, and there was no sign of foul play.

"Monty stopped to take photos. As soon as he snapped the first, the object lifted into the air, and he took two more shots before it flew out of sight. We drove another 25 kilomeetres before stopping on a hilltop for something to eat. We lit a campfire, and during our meal heard a rumbling sound, like a vehicle travelling over corrugations, but we couldn't see anything to account for it.

"Not long afterwards, we spotted a hazy silver object above and behind Monty's truck. He was brave enough to venture into the cabin to get his camera and take another photo. Nobody said a word. We just packed up and got on our way. I couldn't see the light anymore, but Monty in the semi-trailer behind, could see the object following our convoy until the Wolf Creek Crater turnoff, when it disappeared. During all that time we lost radio contact, which resumed without problem for the rest of the journey."

The colour photographs, taken on the two occasions, were authenticated as being the same object, and the blueness attributed to gamma-ray radioactivity.

Wyndham, early 1980s

Wayne Trembath also told me of an earlier experience related by a local who wanted anonymity. He and a friend had gone fishing about one hour by boat from Wyndham wharf. Not having a boat, or maybe wary of crocodiles, they were in their vehicle driving the long way around – a twelve-hour road trip.

"We were driving towards the river, looking for a particular turnoff, when my mate noticed an amber-coloured light ahead, above the waters of the gulf. It was pitch black, and as we were checking our location on the compass, right on course, we suddenly ploughed into mud. We had problems keeping the vehicle moving, and not getting bogged, as water was getting in. We eventually got back onto dry land, and checked the compass again. We were way off-course, but how could that be?

"We used the compass to work our way back to the turnoff. My friend intended camping until dawn, and we could see where we were going. He asked me about the light, which had still been evident in the distance, the whole time. I looked out the window and saw this thing coming at us "at a great rate of knots."

"He had not shown any concern about it before, but suddenly put his foot on the accelerator, asking, 'Where is it now?' At first I couldn't see it, and realised it was directly overhead – a big, elongated ball full of red smoke. My mate was driving so fast and wouldn't slow down – -it was like he was fixed to the seat. I was scared he would roll the vehicle, and leaned over, switched the engine off, and got out once we had stopped.

"That thing was still there, a bright red glow, pulsating stronger in red, and a smoky-amber colour when dimming. I grabbed my gun from the car, which made me feel a little better. My friend, safely in the driver's seat, kept insisting I shoot at it. I got him to pass me my camera, and tried to take a couple of photos instead. The flash wouldn't go off and the shutter jammed, so I jumped back in the car.

"We slowly moved away, and the object followed us, keeping pace whatever our speed. We were exhausted and stopped and lit a fire. No sleep, we just sat and kept an eye on that thing until dawn when it moved higher and disappeared.

"The next day I spoke to a station owner in the vicinity who said, 'Oh! Take no notice of that, they are here all the time. Sometimes when we are out in a stock camp, those lights are all around us. Don't look at them, don't talk about them, and they will go away.'"

Missing time

An experienced truck driver friend of Wayne Trembath's had a very disturbing experience when he was returning from Queensland to Kununurra. He pulled over to have a nap, and woke up stark naked in the cabin, with a pungent cyanide smell, like bitter almonds, all around.

About four hours later he met a car coming the other way, and was astounded to discover three days had elapsed – three days he could not account for! When he returned to the depot his boss said another truck driver, on the same route later, claimed he never passed him, and neither he nor his truck were on the dirt lay-by. It was as if he and his truck had just disappeared.

Planes and UFOs, 1992–93

A local lawyer and his colleague on their way to the airport, were followed by a bright white light which did unusual manoeuvres and right angle turns in the sky. At the same time a small Ansett plane was nearby, and came in to land to pick up passengers.

During the flight back to Perth, the lawyer wandered up to the cockpit, and asked the captain if he had seen an object or light.

At first he denied seeing anything, but the co-pilot admitted to watching it for some time. He added that he had seen inexplicable things on previous occasions, but it was not a wise career move to report such objects officially.

Chapter Twelve

Northern Territory

UFO researchers in the Northern Territory are a rare breed. They must tirelessly travel vast distances to interview witnesses about strange phenomena and unidentified craft, and I wish to commend Keith Douglass and Max Pearce who have forwarded some of their findings to INUFOR.

Darwin area

February 1943

W. Wyatt detailed an interesting report from World War 2, when he was an RAAF pilot. All witnesses were trained to identify aerial craft and objects:

"On a clear Darwin February night in 1943, RAAF squadron aircraft were doing 'circuits and bumps' – practice training for pilots in using flare-path landing strips on night flying. We had just received in the last aircraft for the night, and were preparing to refuel and get ready to return to camp, when the warning was given: 'Better hit the ground!'

"The alarm was caused by a bright light coming in like another plane, it was soon near us, and went off over the trees. There was no sound whatsoever and steady movement, but much slower than a plane. Our fear came because we knew of a Luftwaffe trick of trying to join up to the tail of Allied aircraft landings in Europe, then strafing and bombing the area as they sped off.

"But this was no plane, Japanese or Allied, and we had never seen a parachute flare, or Very flare, ever move under control. Our commanding officer immediately put planes back on readiness but nothing at all happened. To me it was just a large bright light moving over the landing strip, but I have no explanation. Later, our guards company said they had seen similar lights around our area, on other nights."

Those Orange Lights again!

In 2003, there was a flood of reports of orange lights in the sky over the Northern Territory. Most were the usual pranks, with one culprit publicly coming forward and apologising.

This wasn't the first time this had happened. In 1995 an article widely publicised in Northern Territory criticised material in the ABC's science magazine, *Double Helix*. This had printed instructions on how its young readers could construct these pranks as a bit of fun.

The Territory Fire Service warned of the danger these airborne Molotov cocktails presented, both as a fire-hazard in arid areas and as a risk to small aircraft. On one occasion then, local authorities had to temporarily close Darwin airport and warned that if they caught any further offenders, they would be prosecuted to the full extent of the law.

This warning was sweet music to the ears of ufologists, we were always having to explain to insistent members of the public that they had NOT witnessed an extraterrestrial visitation. It also put us in the difficult position of having to disregard some reports as pranks, when they were possibly something else entirely.

Alien technology?

While our research does not concentrate on paranormal events, there appears to be a more than casual connection between such phenomena and UFOs – possibly by inter-dimensional or other mechanisms. Colin Norris, editor of *Australian International UFO Research*, reported an interesting episode which occurred to a Northern Territory colleague who had some previous experience with unidentified objects:

Roger (pseudonym), was highly intelligent with a background in Mechanical Engineering, Science, Technology and Psychology. He had not been feeling well for a couple of days, and although he went to bed early, could not sleep.

"At first it was this horrible headache, like my brain was exploding with an energy or force rays which penetrated through my head, and then my whole body. It lasted for about an hour or two and then subsided. Believe me, I was awake the whole time.

"Suddenly, I could picture a large movie screen in my mind, a large movie screen, with writing projected onto it. It looked like a complicated formula, the letters like some kind of numbers and brackets, and so on. I exclaimed out loud, 'What the hell is that?' I heard a male voice saying that it was a formula for a very special material used to make certain parts and components, used to build spacecraft, flying saucers and advanced technology.

"Hearing that, I asked out loud, 'What does it look like?' The screen showed a large, round, oval object. It was some kind of component part of a sub-assembly, a grey-metallic colour. It had a very smooth, glossy surface, like metal – melted together, with no visible signs of screws, bolts or welding.

"The screen and voice disappeared along with my headache. I lay in the dark with the picture of that space component and material remaining in my mind. It occurred to me that whoever was showing me all this and giving me the formulae must be very advanced in their technology, perhaps more advanced and intelligent than we earth people.

"Some things still bother me today. My head hurt so much, and felt so heavy. Was it caused by energy or rays of some sort projected into my head by some genius, aliens, or something or someone else? Why would someone pick me up to be a messenger for a specific material? I do not know, but I do believe it was not human from the planet earth.

"Anything in this world or universe can be questioned, and for most things there would be logical answers – but not all."

Roper River, Katherine, 1956

Max Cooper, now 87, and his partner had owned a cattle station in the tropical north of the Territory. In those days it was very remote. No proper roads, and their homestead was built of large bush timber and stringy bark. In his book, *Territory Tales*, he wrote of an unusual sighting one night, and later completed a *UFO Sighting Report Form*.

He detailed life in the tropical north, especially what old-timers called the "knock 'em downs", when the dry season begins, and the wet season ends with a series of heavy, gusty storms and a lot of thunder and lightning.

During the humid weather, children would sleep on the cool veranda, in special cots, protected from snakes, mosquitoes and other dangers.

If a bad storm came, they would move the kiddies to safety, inside the house. This particular night they had already brought the children inside, but couldn't sleep due to the thunder and heavy rain on the roof. Max got up to check the radio transceiver on the inner edge of the front veranda.

"I heard a high-frequency scream from above the homestead roof." The rest of the family heard it from inside.

Sketches of object/s.

BRIGHT INCANDESCENT YELLOWISH/WHITE LIGHT FROM OVAL WINDOWS

SLOWLY MOVING.

"Looking up from the outer edge of the roof line I saw a longish, dark object, (a bit longer than a semi-trailer truck), floating a short distance above our home. It was emitting a bright yellowish-white incandescent light from regularly spaced, oval style portholes. It moved forward quite slowly, eventually disappearing towards the north."

Nhulunbuy, 1982

Rosalind Cooper is a nurse, who was working in Nhulunbuy, on the Gove Peninsula, in the Northern Territory. The area was a closed mining town in Arnhem Land, with an Aboriginal settlement:

On several summer afternoons in 1982, many witnesses saw groups of three to five objects fly in from the west. "They swooped around the sky, defying the laws of physics, and went into the water. The bottom of the bay is just sand, and each time the navy turned up with depth sounders, looked, and said they could find nothing. Nobody talked about it outside of the town, and it was never reported in the papers.

"I was nursing an Aboriginal elder, and he told me these sightings had been occurring for a very long time. They always landed in the water, and only once did the sequence of events alter, when two ships landed in a valley, on the other side of a hill. The tribe selected a delegation of elders to go and investigate the nature and intent of the visitors. They never returned from the valley, and it was subsequently declared a sacred site."

Tennant Creek, 28 August 1995

Territory roads are usually long and dark. Truck driver Kevin was a little alarmed when, for some time, on the road south from Tennant Creek, his cabin was flooded with a bluish-white light.

"As it started to fade I could see a white light, with a bluish hazy outline, to the southwest. I realised it must have initially been hovering over my truck, before one of us moved, and it came into my line of vision. It was hovering low in the sky for about five minutes. I kept a wary eye on it, until it slowly moved straight up at a 90 degree angle, then at a high rate of speed, shot off to the west. It was a dark, cloudless night, with no ice formations, which ruled out a lot of conventional explanations for what I saw. I don't know what it was, but it made me feel very uneasy."

The Devil's Marbles, early January 1995

The Devil's Marbles are a random pile of huge boulders, sitting in the middle of the Tanami Desert, 96 kilometres south of Tennant Creek along the road to Alice Springs. Some are almost perfect spheres, and the Aboriginal legend is that they are eggs from their mythical Rainbow Serpent.

The Australian summer holiday season starts just before Christmas and runs into most of January, and it is then that many workers and tourists take to the road.

178

One Victorian tourist travelling through the Northern Territory, parked his vehicle at about 2 p.m. and walked up to the Devil's Marbles. (A must-see stop for all visitors.)

"Initially, I did not take too much notice of a flash in the sky, thinking it may be a reflection from a car mirror. When I looked back there was a huge, round grey circular object, hovering about 45 metres away. It was only about 100 metres up, and had strange markings which seemed to be formed or engraved on the outer rim.

"For ten minutes I watched the object descend, three separate times, as if trying to land. Each time, when it was about five metres off the ground, a circular opening in the centre would appear, from which a red vapour would flow and rise into the air. Simultaneously there would be an ear-splitting shrill noise, which made me feel as if I was going to faint.

"I wonder if I hadn't been there, would it have actually landed. However, it gave a really bright flash and shot off up into the sky at a tremendous speed. I had been transfixed and frozen with fear the whole time. While I never believed in UFOs before, I have not been back to the Devil's Marbles since, and would not recommend it when no-one else is around."

The vast Outback

West of the main Alice Springs–Darwin Highway is a vast arid zone, comprising in part, the Tanami Desert. Except for a few, scattered settlements, it is uninhabited and unexplored. At Kurundi, 350 kilometres north of Alice Springs, there are unusual Aboriginal carvings depicting what resembles an oval craft, with four legs, and windows around the middle. There is also a figure wearing what looks like a full space-helmet.

Piccaninny Bore

Huge craft have been reported north of the bore. These are different to anything depicted on television documentaries or movies. For years they have been reported taking on spring water at Talbot Well:

At times, in the afternoon, a mist is seen to form into a cloud with a bright light, like a glow inside. The cloud comes down, and touches the spring well (a small dam). It sits there for some time, then slowly goes back up into the sky. This happens quite often, and after it has gone the Aboriginal people find the water has gone – the well is dry. Because there is an underground spring, it refills within a few days.

The people of the Chilla Well Aboriginal settlement do not trust strangers easily. However, in 1999 one elder confided the following: "One day a craft came down; it was just sitting above the ground. It looked like two plates with about four feet between, and there was a silvery blue light in the middle. Then these people got out of it, and they only had three fingers on each hand. (In 1988 there were several reports of people with webbed feet and hands seen in the area.) They spoke our native language, and went towards our people, who started to run away. The craft-people said, in our language, 'Don't be afraid', so we asked them if they needed diesel fuel.

"The craft people said they were looking for a 'blue crystal' for their craft, and the kids told them to go 'over there'. The craft then went away. It was as big as a service station, and was not on the ground – it had no landing legs.

"One Aboriginal man confided that north of Chilla Well the 'other ones' land. 'Look out for the ones that take our babies. They hurt you – they take our wives.'"

The Aboriginals also tell about a bus which was stranded at a flooded river, at the "Jump Ups" near Hooker Creek, and how it was mysteriously lifted up over the other side.

Pinja and Parnta

Situated way to the northeast of Piccaninny Bore and southwest of Hooker Creek are Pinja and Parnta. The local Aboriginals are very wary of the West Track, which connects the two settlements, and speak of a "landing spot" to the east of the track, where a lot of their people have gone missing.

At the Tanami Road to Hooker Creek (Lajamanu) they saw 92 vehicles travelling along the track, and were ordered not to take photos. Another time they saw a car being taken up into a craft which was "an army green and blue colour type of the Star Lifter."

At Yuendumu there have been many reports of unusual craft, all flying slowly from west to east. Some are three times larger than the local airstrip. They often see a cigar-shaped one, and also a huge box-type object.

Hooker Creek (Lajamanu)

Hooker Creek is an Aboriginal Reserve situated south of Wave Hill (Gurindji). Keith Douglass reported that, the Tanami Mines seem to mark an invisible border-line. The usual type craft appear in the south, but they are different to the north. They have been described as being like aluminium dishes with a brilliant blue band in the middle, two metres high and domed over the top, and standing a metre off the ground. At night, workers often see lights to the north, and in the distance, lights "like darts" going from the ground into the sky.

Nearby, there is a two-kilometre long runway in the middle of the desert; the Delamere Range Facility Airport, which is part of an extensive air-weapons testing facility used by the RAAF, and long enough for any known military air freighter. Whenever anyone tries to take photos within a 10 kilometre area of it, they always turn out blue, but are perfectly normal outside that boundary. One witness flew over the area, and saw a large airfield, some sort of runways with clear areas on the end, and a triangle on the ground.

West of Tanami a huge crater was found. A scientist who went to investigate, determined that it was caused by an explosion, and not a meteorite as previously thought. It was reported that he was later found dead in his car, with all his papers missing!

In 1998 a police employee, Mark, was with some colleagues, including an Aboriginal friend, Ian, when they saw a four-wheel drive pass through Lajamanu. It was very dirty, and there was one woman and several men inside. That afternoon Ian and his friends set up camp, outside of town, and were sitting around a campfire at about 4 p.m.:

"We noticed the same vehicle again, but now it was all clean and shiny. A huge green-coloured object suddenly appeared in the sky, over the four-wheel drive. It was long, round and flat, with a belly underneath. As we watched the bottom of the craft opened up, the car was gently lifted up inside, and the craft took off!"

Ian said, "This was not an army-type car, but one of the other ones. There are army ones, like army colours; friendly and not so friendly types."

Mark believes that "There is a base out there, somewhere.

"Sometimes, around 1999, I would get telephone calls from the kids at the Mount Theo Outstation, who were terrified and would scatter into the bushes, saying a UFO had come into their camp. They would tell me 'they' came to hurt them and take our uncles, and some of the girls got pregnant."

Victoria River Downs

Travelling north from Hooker Creek to Katherine, via Victoria River Downs, is normally a five-hour trip. However, a carload of people on their way to Katherine, spotted a light in the sky. They pulled over to the side of the road to get a better look. As they watched a huge craft came over the top of their car.

It literally put down on its light beams, which looked like glass tubes with coloured lights inside. A white light came down and they found they could not start their car. The craft itself was so huge it covered the width of the road, and they were relieved when a truck came the other way, and the object took off.

They restarted the car, glad to be on their way with whatever it was, now gone – but it wasn't. A bit further along the road it came back, just as before. None of them could remember what happened after that.

They finally arrived in Katherine, nearly three hours later than expected, and immediately reported the incident to the police station. Their car had used far less petrol than usual and they were all "totally wrecked", drained of energy with pains in their bodies. All the women had "pains in the abdomen."

Later, one of the women gave birth, without any problems, and the baby seemed normal.

Uluru (Ayers Rock)

Uluru, "the Rock", is 470 kilometres southwest of Alice Springs. The world's biggest monolith, it is 9 kilometres in circumference, and rises 350 metres above the surrounding plain. It has always been held sacred by Aboriginals, who consider it has spiritual properties.

Yulara, May 1999

This small town, is about 25km from Uluru, and used mainly to accommodate the tourists visiting the Rock and the nearby Olgas.

On 5 May 1999 the Yulara power station experienced a power surge at 5.15 a.m., which was totally out of the ordinary, and had never happened before. The generator stopped. After a short time, staff were able to start the motors again. Later investigation showed there seemed to be nothing wrong with the generator engine. At the same time several witnesses reported seeing strange lights moving in the sky:

Carol Logan and two friends were in the town square when the power went. She looked up into the sky at about 5.30 a.m. and saw two flashing red lights on a triangular object about 1,000 feet overhead. It was seen zigzagging at medium speed for about two minutes when it disappeared "into thin air."

Anna Baker estimated she was in the town square of Ayres Rock Resort at approximately 5.40 a.m. during the blackout. She noticed an extremely bright light to the southeast above Uluru. It was bigger than a star, and flashing in one spot. She watched it for about six minutes and suddenly, just before the power and lights were restored, she saw two objects zig-zag very fast and move out of sight.

Five weeks later on 11 June 1999, a local resident reported that at 5.55 a.m., two white stars were seen moving together, in a jiggling downward movement, across the sky. Suddenly they shot off in opposite directions. The witness commented "Stars don't move like that!"

A month afterwards, in July 1999, again early – at 5.45 a.m., Candy Neil saw an incredibly bright light travelling from west to east across the sky. It was a perfectly-defined, glowing white oval sphere, about the size of a small car. It disappeared over the horizon within 30 seconds. Candy said it was travelling exceptionally fast; she had never seen anything move at that speed.

All these sightings occurred before the Australian Defence Force began a six-week trial, in the Northern Territory, of a one million dollar, remotely controlled, pilotless surveillance vehicle. Described as an "unmanned helicopter-like craft", this was 1.8 metres tall and had a rotor diameter of four metres. It had vertical take-off and landing capability, but a Defence Force spokesman said at that time, that "there were no aircraft of its kind in use elsewhere in Australia." The drone's flight path could be pre-programmed or remotely controlled, and could travel up to 200 kilometres from its ground control station.

This vehicle was primarily used for surveillance. It had photographic capability, and it is unlikely to have been responsible for the blackout or sightings before its publicised test runs.

Alice Springs area

Keith Douglass of UFORAS has told me he is often puzzled by many reports of craft landing for a short time, then taking off again. He wondered if they were picking up or dropping off something, because such landings were followed by the appearance of army helicopters. He mentioned an Aboriginal woman out west, who said when she was a young girl, about 18-years-old, she and her friends saw a craft land and take off again a short time later. They went over and saw three burn marks. On the ground was a metal ball and some "square pieces", which they picked up. They got a "tingly feeling", dropped them, and never went back.

Hermannsburg (west of Alice Springs), 1980s

The Hermannsburg Mission settlement is situated north of Palm Valley, well off the beaten track. Keith Douglass, of UFORAS (and later our representative in Alice Springs), investigated a report by Jack, a police aid and indigenous tracker. Jack had been helping to search for a missing person in an isolated area, with a few scattered small trees and bush:

"It was a dark, clear night, about 11 p.m., and we were travelling at about 65 kilometres per hour, along a dirt road. I was sitting in the passenger seat, with the window open, when I noticed this round, dark metallic object following alongside our vehicle, some 70 metres to the right, at treetop level. It was as big as a car, shaped like those flying saucers people talk about, and had windows, like portholes, around the bottom of the dome. I was surprised at first, but then a little scared (see 1 below).

"This went on for a few minutes. Then it moved forward, crossed over in front of us to the left-hand-side of the road and out of sight (see 2 below). A few minutes later we spotted it way out in front, hovering above the road. As we drove closer, it moved away again. Soon afterwards, it reappeared to our right, and started pacing us, as before. "By this time we were wondering what to do, and one of the officers reached into the glovebox, got out a handgun, and rested it on his lap. Before we had decided what action to take, it flew off again.

"Further down the road there it was; this time resting on a small sand hill. Our officer in charge, a bit braver than some of us, drove up to it, stopping some 50 metres away. We watched it for several minutes, taking in all the details, until it took off (see 3 below).

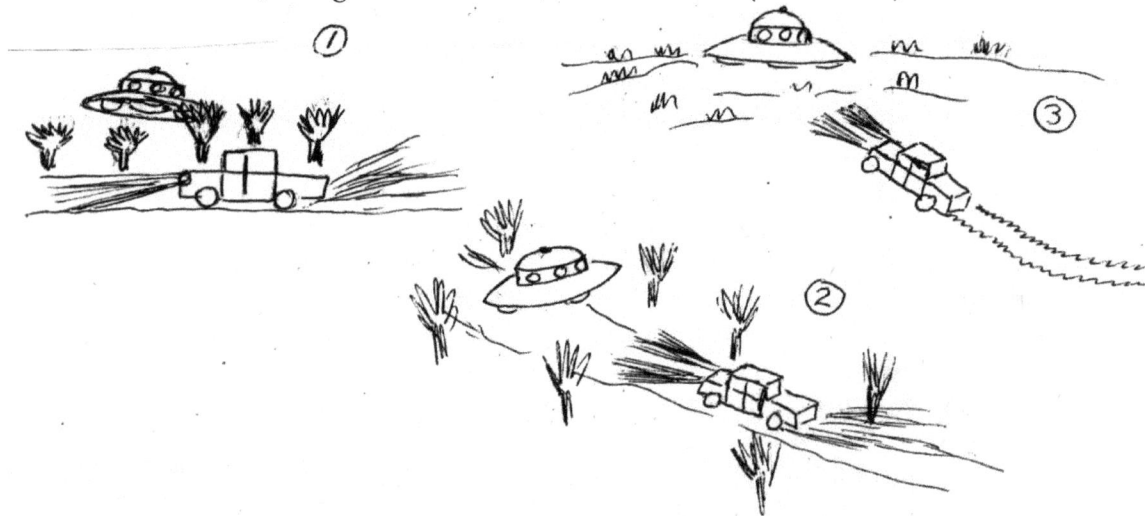

"We decided not to proceed. We turned around to return to the police station at Hermannsburg, and it followed us all the way back. We rushed inside, but by the time we convinced the staff there really was something 'up there', it had vanished."

While we have the witness statement and report forms from that sighting, it appears that the police force in Hermannsburg have more than their fair share of frustrating objects flying around their outback skies:

Gilbert Spring, 1984

The Alice Springs *Centralian Advocate* of March 1986 published a similar, but different instance, just after midnight on 1 January 1984.

A police officer, I'll call him Tony, was called on duty to help with the search for a stolen car. He and a tracker set out for Gilbert Spring, an outstation past Areyonga. They had travelled about 25 kilometres when the tracker pointed out lights to the south of the road, near the Haasts Bluff turnoff. They stopped, and thinking it might be the stolen vehicle, drove off the road towards the unidentified lights which were moving in their direction. Despite sometimes losing sight of these lights, they set off on a 45-minute pursuit across rough scrub country.

"They appeared to be changing position, on and off the ground, vanishing from view and reappearing somewhere else. Generally we could see two lights, but sometimes only one and at other times there were three. They were bright, light and rectangular in shape. In hindsight, we didn't notice any beam like a car headlight.

"We still thought we were pursuing the stolen vehicle, but after an hour or so thought that something funny was going on. We saw those lights sitting on top of a sand dune, and because even our four-wheel drive had problems travelling up it, we drove around the side. The lights and any vehicle, had simply disappeared.

"We found an old track to Gilbert Spring, and on the way noticed an unusual glow over the hills. After checking out two camps and finding nothing out of the ordinary, we decided to return to Hermannsburg. About 500 metres from the Areyonga Road, those lights returned, much closer to our vehicle than before. We couldn't make out the shape of the craft, or whatever they were on. There were two red lights on top, four large square white ones in the middle, and two long grey lights at the bottom.

"They travelled parallel to us until just before we reached Hermannsburg. Then they just switched off. My tracker told me his people at Gilbert Spring had seen them before, calling them "the car that never comes.""

Wycliffe Well, 21 July 1988

Keith Douglass, interviewed Mark Strong on our behalf. Mark was an experienced pilot – he had to be, as his job required him to travel thousands of kilometres across Australia's remote outback. Along with an excellent report, Mark provided a copy of his official logbook, with the corresponding entry noting the strange object.

It was a clear morning, good visibility with no clouds or wind, and Mark had started his flight just after daybreak. After about 35 minutes in the air, he was travelling south to southwest at 5,500 feet, and passed over Wycliffe Well, 400 kilometres north of Alice Springs, about 25 nautical miles to the south. He looked down at the ranges and noticed a slight movement at a 45 degree angle away from him.

"I could see a dull frosty-silver, round disc-shaped object. It was travelling quite slowly, and cast an elongated shadow on the ground. At first I thought it might be a balloon because of the oblong shape of the shadow in the early morning light.

"I contacted Alice Springs Flight Service and asked if there was any known traffic in the area. Their response was a little different to normal. They requested the sighting and position of the other aircraft. At this stage my plane caught up with the unusual object, and as I passed above, it suddenly accelerated and headed towards the ranges some ten kilometres away.

"I could see it was quite large, and travelling quite close to the ground. I would estimate it to be three times bigger than the average house, but flattish with no visible markings. It increased its speed, and curved to the right, as if to fly parallel to the hills. Suddenly it turned on its side, and seemed to vanish into thin air!

"I was stunned to see my non-directional beacon (NDB) arrow had swung to the right, in the direction of the object. It did not come back on track until five minutes after the object had vanished. Normally the NDB needle only goes awry during a tropical storm, when it points to the storm, but this was a totally clear morning. I have flown over this area many times before with no problem."

ON SIDE AND VANISHED.

SHADOW

WENT ON SIDE

D.G.H.

WYCLIFFE WELL

10 KLM

CURVED RIGHT

RANGES

N
W — E
S

STUART HWY.

400 KLM

A/S

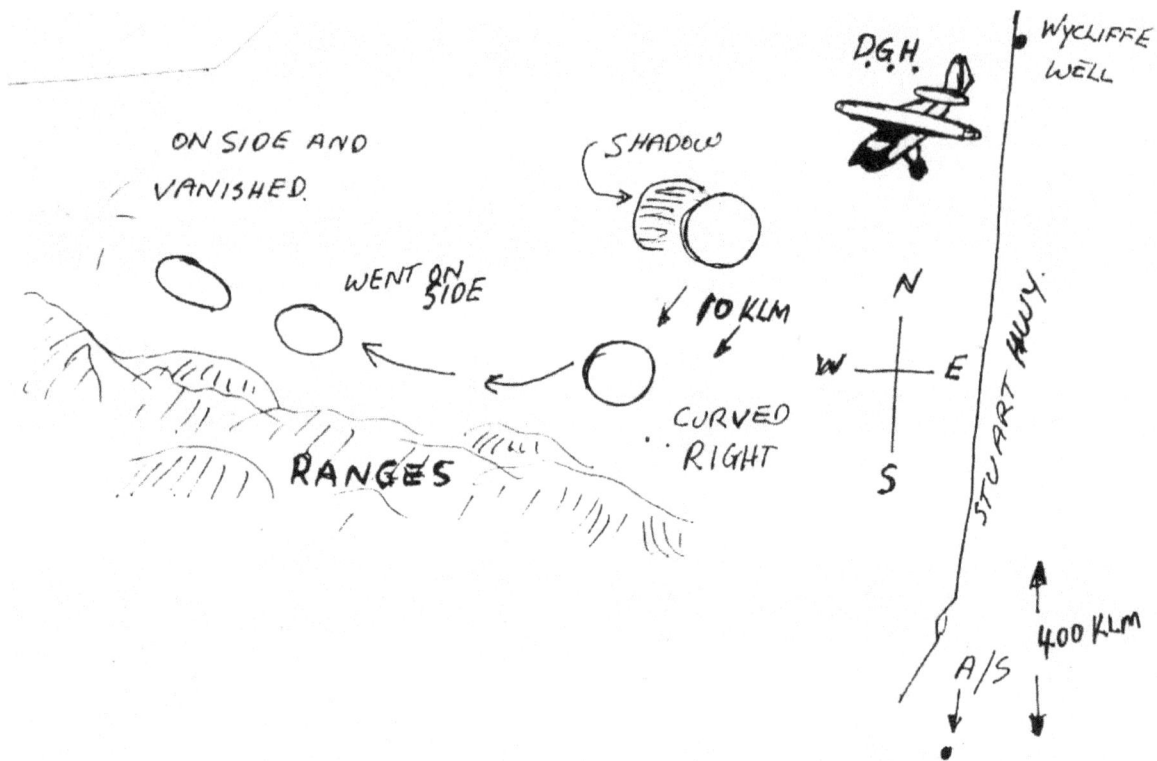

Flight Control were still trying to contact Mark for further details, and later told him that his transmissions were difficult to read during the sighting. (Unusual for that area, and his radio was not faulty). He wondered if the craft had been monitoring his transmissions; once he reported it the object shot away "in seconds." Mark decided discretion was the better part of valour, and told Alice Springs to disregard his report. He admits to being sceptical up until then, and says it is not advisable for pilots to report UFOs.

Honeymoon Gap, November 1996

Honeymoon Gap is about ten kilometres west of Alice Springs. It was about 11.20 p.m. and Mary was driving home (from west to east), when her passenger noticed a blue glow, to the right, at the foot of a large hill.

"At first it seemed to be among the trees, possibly on the ground, about half a kilometre away. Then it rose, almost floated up and came towards me. It followed above my car for about five minutes, and was making a whirly sound."

It was a solid, bright glowing blue, round object, about 40 metres in diameter – the size of a semi-trailer. The bottom had lines around and was flat. The top was round with a sort of "blue halo" above.

Mary's diagram shows a mesh pattern over the dome. Suddenly it took off and went back over the mountains, towards Pine Gap, and out of sight.

This may not be relevant to Mary's experience, but on 18 April 1999, an Alice Springs resident was watching strange lights in the sky through a pair of powerful binoculars.

They described the object in the sky as looking "like a headlight from a low-flying plane." Magnified it had a blue top with a yellow bottom, and resembled the previous craft, if seen on an angle.

Sketches of object/s.

CRAFT IS
ALL
SOLID
—
BRIGHT
BLUE
HALO

BRIGHT
BLUE
LIGHT

WHIRLY NOISE

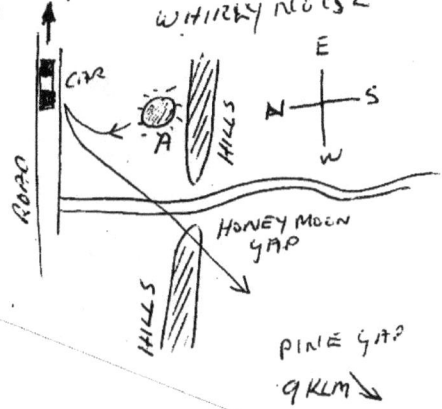

Honeymoon Gap, November 1996 (Mary's sketch)

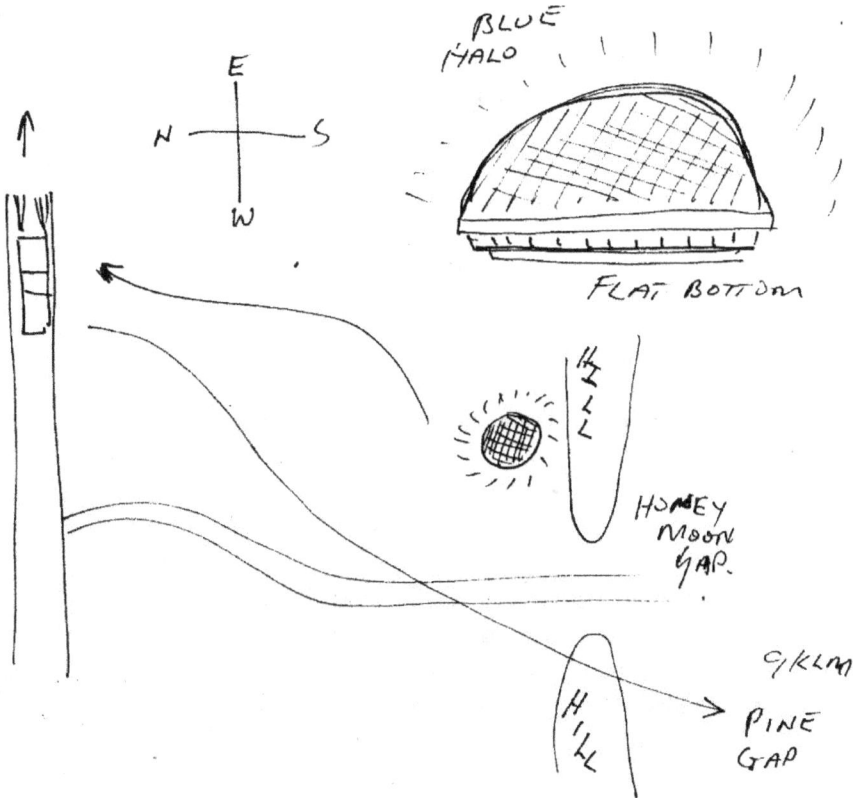

BLUE
HALO

FLAT BOTTOM

Honeymoon Gap, November 1996 (Passenger's sketch)

Santa Teresa 1997, and Alice Springs, 1998

There were two separate sightings of an unusual object in the same area – I can only liken it to a flying exclamation mark!

In November 1997, at about 7 p.m., a police assistant in Saint Teresa saw what looked like a long, thin flying cigar in a perpendicular position, moving across the sky. He estimated it as being about 100 metres long, and had a white fluorescent glow. It was noiseless, and stood on end the whole way as it slowly traversed the sky from west to east.

He commented that this object had been seen on various occasions by different witnesses: On 11 August 1998, an Alice Springs resident arrived home at 6.30 p.m. and saw an identical object crossing the sky. However this object had a large white fluorescent ball positioned below it which travelled with it, at a slow to medium speed.

He suggested that Pine Gap was only 15 kilometres away, which may be significant.

Pine Gap

Pine Gap, Australia's best-known and most-secretive military bases, lies 18 kilometres southwest of Alice Springs in foothills on the southern slopes of the MacDonnell Range. This joint United States–Australian facility is so secretive, it no longer appears in any of our maps or atlases, although everyone knows it's there. It is only 143 miles from the geographical centre of Australia:

Pine Gap is surrounded by a large buffer zone, and has security fences and 24/7 patrols. There is a no-fly aircraft zone over the area, and agreements with local station owners not to allow visitors onto their properties. The base itself comprises six silvery-white domes (at last count), a large solid 30-metre-high square tower, a powerful communications antenna and many single-storey, solid buildings, and purportedly laboratories, storage facilities, office blocks and accommodation, which are linked by underground tunnels. Regardless of the power source, there is no doubt in my mind that the entire base, and all its functions, would be totally self-sufficient.

Construction began around 1967, when a top secret facility to house (amongst other things), extensive computer facilities, initially designed as part of the *Rhyolite* program (fully operational by 1973), to process a vast amount of communications intercepted by satellites positioned over the Equator. It also provided a system for covert communications and formed part of a world-wide system with sister US bases in California, and CIA headquarters in Virginia. Various researchers and authors have claimed that its facilities are also linked to the United States base at North-West Cape and similar bases in Guam, Krugersdorp (South Africa), Menwith Hill (Britain), and even the Amundsen-Scott Base in the Antarctic.

It was fully funded by the United States Government and is officially listed as a Joint Defense Space Research Facility. While it was supposed to be a joint military intelligence project between the US and Australia, private contractors such as E-Systems and TRW (with expertise in aerospace and electronics), have had crucial roles from its inception. This caused a lot of controversy later. (An informative article, *Sabotaging Pine Gap – One Man's Story*, appeared in *The National Times*, 6 September, 1981.)

Of course, with rapid advances in technology, it is likely the capabilities and role of Pine Gap have significantly increased since the early days. Nearly forty years ago, in 1977, *Australian Financial Review* journalist Brian Toohey published an article calling for enhanced security capabilities to help detect and defend Australia from missile launches, nuclear capabilities, and laser technology.

Pine Gap would be a primary target for an enemy during any conflict. During the Cold War era, Russia's official newspaper *Pravda* pointed out that North West Cape, Nurrungar, Pine Gap and Darriman in East Gippsland are all targets for any Soviet first missile strike, and this will probably apply to any conflict today or in the future.

In the 1980s US President Carter approved a multi-million dollar expenditure to update Pine Gap. In October 1999 the Joint Facility base Nurrungar, near Woomera in South Australia was closed, and facilities transferred to Pine Gap.

There is much speculation about the nature and role of Pine Gap today. There is no doubt in my mind that it plays an enormous part in controlling satellites and all their operations, which are far more extensive than Pine Gap's founders could ever have imagined. I often wonder if the powers that be have a contingency plan if solar flares or an alien intelligence take out their key satellites and technically-advanced toys?

There have long been rumours in the conspiracy-sphere from 'reliable sources' that Pine Gap includes an enormous multi-levelled facility underground. This feature is connected with secret weapon experiments, advanced electronic warfare and weapons control. With input from the UFO-savvy, it now includes systems to detect alien intrusion into earth's skies, a secret alien base, and research facilities back-engineering recovered alien craft. There is little Pine Gap cannot do, apparently.

Personally, while saying I would avoid giving any opinions without evidence, I doubt these rumours are correct. Some projects probably do take place – in a massive continent the size of Australia, there are vast areas fairly free from curious inhabitants, journalists, conspiracy theorists, activists and enemy agents, which would encourage such covert activities. And the strange events witnessed by a very few people living in the remote tracts of Northern Territory and Western Australia, do provide some food for thought.

Of course, allowing and even encouraging a little speculation, diverts public attention elsewhere. I attended a UFO meeting a few years ago, where the guest speaker was an American who purportedly had worked for Pine Gap in the past. He was in his late thirties, very personable and good-looking – the typical poster boy. In fact, a few younger women in the audience were busy, gazing dreamy-eyed; I think he could have convinced them of anything. He was intelligent and articulate, and assured the entire audience that Pine Gap was no more than it purported to be. It was some very clever reverse psychology. He was too good to be true, so many there thought it was just another attempt to cover-up.

So, what are these unidentified lights and craft being seen around Central Australia? It is only logical to assume some must have a connection to Pine Gap, given their proximity. Furthermore, a British *UFO Magazine* article by Warren Aston reported that on 26 November 1996, there had been reports of fast-moving-lights over Alice Springs. Witnesses included local policemen, one of whom took a video. While following up the original sightings, the police spotted nuisance hot-air balloons over the town, and apprehended two suspects on an isolated back road. Their station wagon was full of the illicit objects, one in the process of being sent aloft. To evade prosecution, they eventually proffered their ID cards from Pine Gap. Warren Aston rightfully asked why? Was it to detract from a genuine UFO sighting earlier that evening?

There are many possible explanations, including extraterrestrial ones, for the many sightings, but I am surprised so few consider foreign countries or agents. I wonder how many may have been highly technical, remote-controlled, local or foreign drones? Given Pine Gap's importance to Australia and her allies' military capabilities, it seems logical that less-friendly powers would wish to obtain as much data as possible.

Planes and UFOs

9 December 1977

UFORA (Vol. 1, number 1, 1984) detailed a case on 9 December 1977, when Lindsay Smith and his wife Helen were flying their Cessna 206 light aircraft from Legune to Victoria Downs. It was about 4.30 p.m. and they were about 300 kilometres east of Kununurra (WA), travelling at 1,675 metres above extremely rugged and isolated terrain.

Helen pointed out what she thought was another plane, some five kilometres away, coming towards them. It passed at about 300 metres below and behind their plane, and they realised it was not a conventional aircraft. Lindsay said "I saw the object for about 30 to 40 seconds. It had well-defined edges but gave no depth perception, the size and height were hard to estimate. It had a dull metallic, non-reflective surface, an oval or lenticular shape, and from a 300 metres distance appeared to be nine metres long by three metres wide and probably one metre thick."

About five minutes later, they tried to make a routine radio check, but could not transmit on VHF or HF for the following 20 to 30 minutes, eventually raising Darwin shortly before landing at Victoria Downs.

Chapter Thirteen

New Zealand

Christchurch, August 1944 (*Mrs. Church Case*)

I have always been interested in reports of modern-style unidentified objects before the alleged Roswell UFO crash of 1947:

Researcher Bruce Harding received a call from Mrs. Church in 1973, after a radio interview with Bryan Dickeson. Bruce investigated the details at length, and found no discrepancies in her testimony or disposition:

Mrs. Church, a senior theatre nursing sister at the local tuberculosis sanitorium, was sure it was August, because the Industries Fair was being held at the King Edward Barracks. She had the day off, and went instead for a walk around the Port Hills, east of the city and away from the crowds. She cut her walk short, as cloud was coming in fast, and didn't want to get lost.

"I decided to head back down through the low hilly slopes and scrub, to get the 4.30 p.m. tram home. There, sitting on a gentle slope, hidden from the road, was this upturned saucer.

"I was really curious, thinking 'What will they invent next?' I walked closer and stood staring for about 8 to 10 minutes. At first I thought it was some gimmick from the Industries Fair, but after I saw the 'little men' inside, (only four feet tall), I thought this must be some kind of Japanese device.

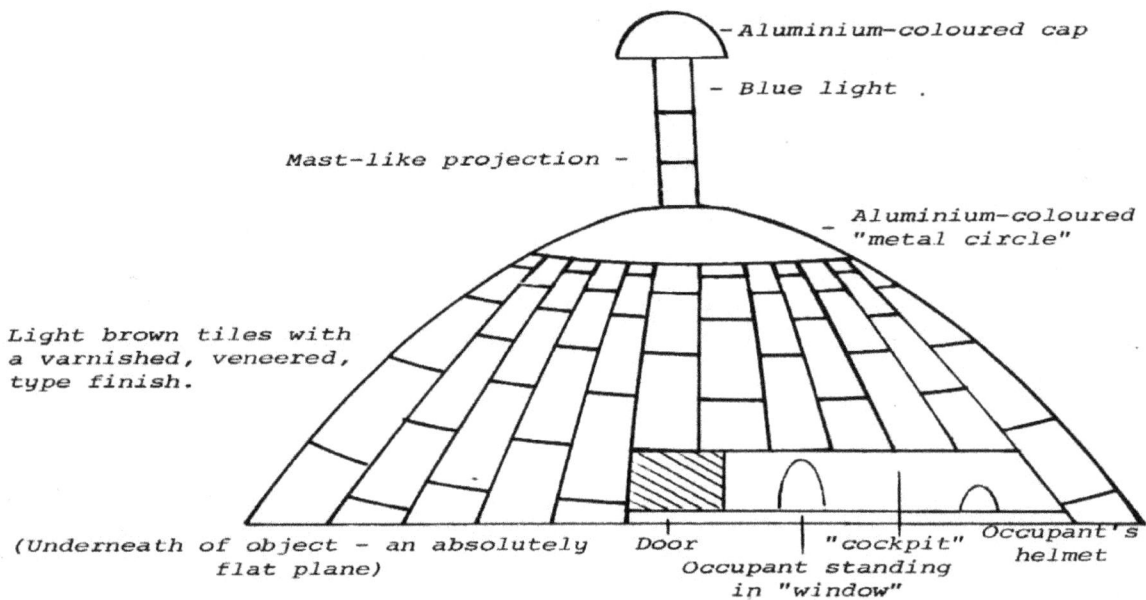

- Aluminium-coloured cap
- Blue light .
Mast-like projection –
- Aluminium-coloured "metal circle"
Light brown tiles with a varnished, veneered, type finish.
(Underneath of object – an absolutely flat plane)   Door   "cockpit"   Occupant's helmet
Occupant standing in "window"

"The object was about 18–20 feet across and 8–9 feet high, covered with light brown (almost wood grain-like) closely fitted vertical tiles, each about 13 inches by 10 inches. The base was dark brown and absolutely flat, with no lights and markings. There was a metal circle, (like dull aluminium) on top, somewhat like a protective cover, that fitted like a glove.

"On top was a two-foot high cylindrical projection, similar to a piece of four-inch pipe, with a mushroom shape aluminium colour cap.

"There were two little fellas, each inside a transparent casing, with a helmet on top. One was standing in the doorway–window, and I could see the top of another helmet in another window. A third was standing outside without a helmet, just a green-coloured being encased in a see-through oblong. He had quite a big head in proportion to his body; it would have been half his body height. The brief idea of fairies crossed my mind, but I thought 'Don't be silly, they must be Japanese.' We hadn't even contemplated extraterrestrials in those days.

"The one outside was just standing there – I thought they were just watching the fair and the city below. The cloud came down and enveloped us, and I moved closer to talk to those people. I didn't even feel afraid. And hoped I might get a ride in their strange vehicle. I got quite close to him, only about 20ft away, when I stood on something and made a slight noise.

"He saw me, and his helmet seemed to flip back on automatically. He drifted into the open doorway, which slid shut, and it looked like he was going into a cockpit.

"A blue light, started to shine steadily halfway up the mast on top, and I could hear a whirring noise, like a fan. The strange object rose vertically into the cloud, and I could see it climbing for a couple of minutes. "I know this sounds silly, but as it took off, I wished I could have gone with it. I felt a sense of loss as it disappeared."

It appears that Mrs. Church caught her tram, so there was little missing time, if any. When she got back she asked one of the nursing sisters 'if there was a thing at the fair to take you for rides?' and she said "No." Mrs. Church described an inexplicable sense of peace for the next week, and felt that there was an unseen presence in her room.

Kaponga, late 1956

On 5 September, Mr. Thomson, a Kaponga farmer had been treating a sick animal, and at 1.30 a.m. went out to check that the injections he had administered earlier that night were taking effect. As he was walking down the property, he heard a hissing noise, increasing in intensity.

Above him was a white light, followed by a blue one.

He could make out a huge white aircraft, unlike anything he had seen before, travelling across the sky at a surprising speed, perhaps 300-400 miles per hour, and an altitude of about 1,500 feet.

He estimated it was about 60 feet long and 30 feet wide, with a glass-type dome, from which a blue light emanated.

It had a smaller turret-like glass nose, which bulged out in front and from which the white light came.

It had delta-like rounded wings, and a tapering tail which he could not see very well.

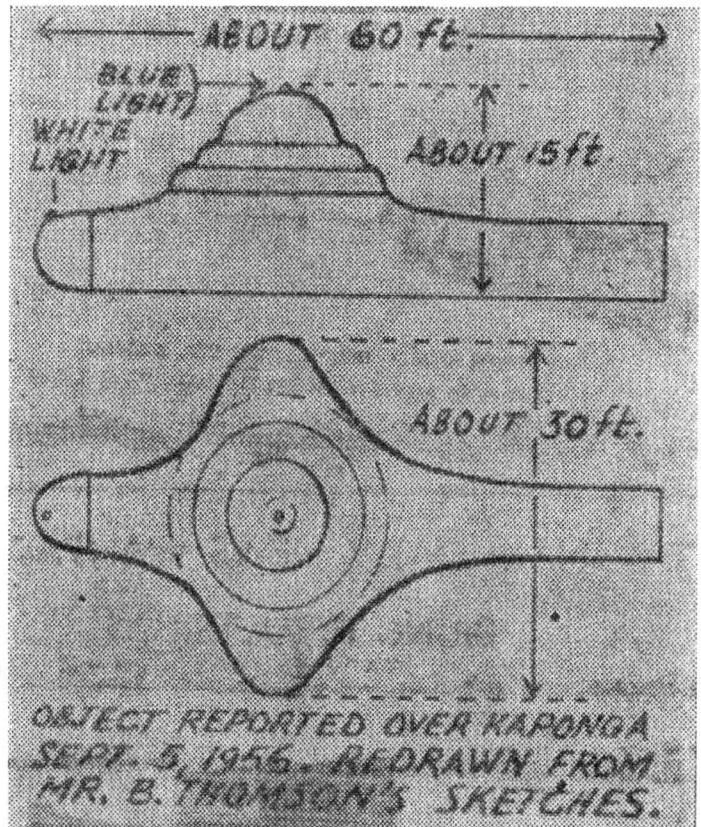

Waipukurau, 26–27 November 1956

On the night of 26-27 November residents reported unusual activity in the skies above.

At Hatuma, twelve miles from Waipukurau, local farmer Mr. Kibblewhite, woke at 2.10 a.m. on the 27 November, with a cramp in his knee, and got out of bed to walk around and ease off the pain. He was about to get back into bed, when a flash of light reflected on the mirror in front of him. He turned around, thinking someone was outside shining a torch through the open window.

As he looked out he saw a very bright bluish- silver colour beam, coming from a round object, high in the sky. The beam was round, like a pipe, about 12 to 18 inches through, with clear cut edges. There was no diffusion of light from it, and it was so dense he could not see through it. It cut out after a few seconds. The object remained for a few seconds more, before making a sideways-rotating movement and vanishing.

Mr. Kibblewhite's report was initially met with scepticism. However, another resident, Mr. Reehal of Puketapu (75 kilometres northeast of Hatuma) saw exactly the same sort of beam two hours forty minutes earlier at 11.30 p.m. on 26 November. It had woken him when it shone into his room. He had gone out onto the veranda, and watched as it shone down through poplar trees.

Blenheim, 13th July 1959 (*Mrs. Moreland Case*)

One of the most-reported close encounter cases from New Zealand is the sighting by Eileen Moreland, and I thank Bryan Dickeson for his research notes on this case.

Eileen Moreland managed a small dairy farm just outside Blenheim, and her husband worked at the nearby RNZAF Base at Woodbourne. It was dark, cold and still when Eileen went out at 5.30 a.m. to milk the cows. (As I, and everybody else who has lived on a dairy farm knows, the cows have to be milked every morning regardless of weather, and any other impediment!)

She went some distance behind the house, turned the milking shed light on, and with torch in hand, started off across the paddock to bring the cows into the shed. Halfway across, she noticed a green light bathing her, the cows and the ground all around. There seemed to be a green glow coming from the cloud layer above, and as she looked up, she saw two large green oval lights, surrounded by a band of orange lights, descending through the clouds.

She raced in panic for the shelter of the pine trees which bordered the paddock, and once in safety, watched the slow, smooth descent of a flattish, cylindrical object which she estimated at being about 2.3 metres high and 6.7 metres across. It hovered about five metres over some peach trees in the centre of the paddock, which placed it about 40 metres away and 8-10 metres above the ground.

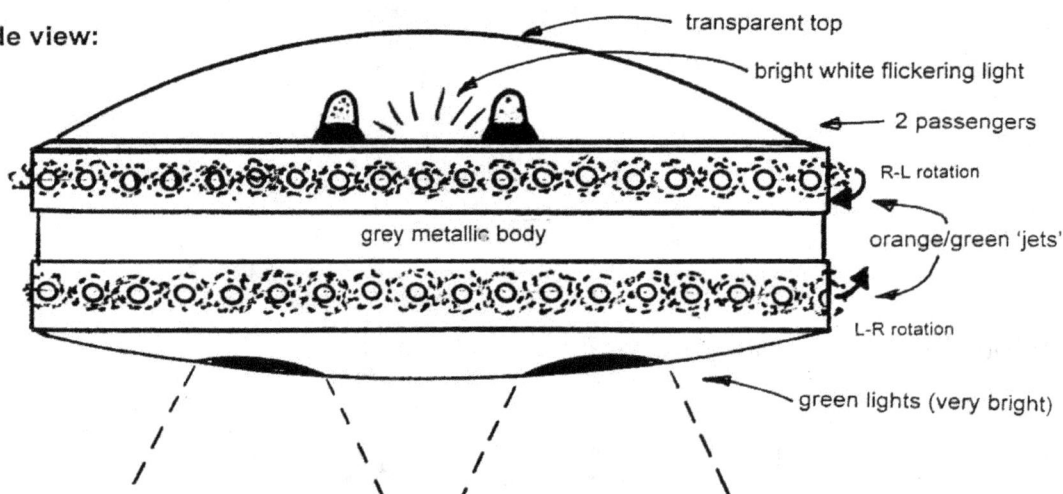

Side view: transparent top / bright white flickering light / 2 passengers / R-L rotation / grey metallic body / orange/green 'jets' / L-R rotation / green lights (very bright)

Set into the top and bottom of the metal cylindrical body were two encircling bands of orange-green jets – brilliant orange with greenish centres – which made a slight hissing noise.

When the object came to a halt, the jets shut off. After reappearing at a slight angle they began to rotate in opposite directions, the top band from right to left, and the bottom from left to right – the speed increasing until the bands of light looked like a continuous haloes. She could hear the jets hissing and a loud humming.

190

On top of the craft was a clear, dome-like structure, which was brightly lit with flickering white light. She could see two seated figures, dressed in skin-tight metallic suits, which reflected the flickering lights and seemed to "crinkle" with every movement. She thought they were a little over 1.5m in height (about five feet), but could not see their faces as they had their backs to her, and were wearing large silvered helmets which covered from one shoulder to the other.

The object tilted slightly, and the bands of jets stopped rotating and went out. The jets turned back on again, and with a loud "whoosh" of air, still tilted, the craft rose vertically and vanished back up into the cloud. During this time the cows seemed totally unaffected, and Eileen pulled herself together and rounded them up for milking.

It wasn't until she'd finished, that she went back into the house and told her family. Her husband told her to notify the police, and he reported the matter to Woodbourne base personnel when he went to work.

Several days after Eileen's hands became swollen, and she developed brown pigmented areas on her face. The row of peach trees died, however the grass in the area around grew much greener and faster than that in the rest of the paddock.

Air Force personnel visited Eileen and the farm. They conducted several tests, and said that they found higher than normal levels of background radiation where she had seen the object.

The case attracted so much publicity that Mrs. Moreland vowed if ever she saw another UFO she would prefer just to shut-up about it.

Plan view:

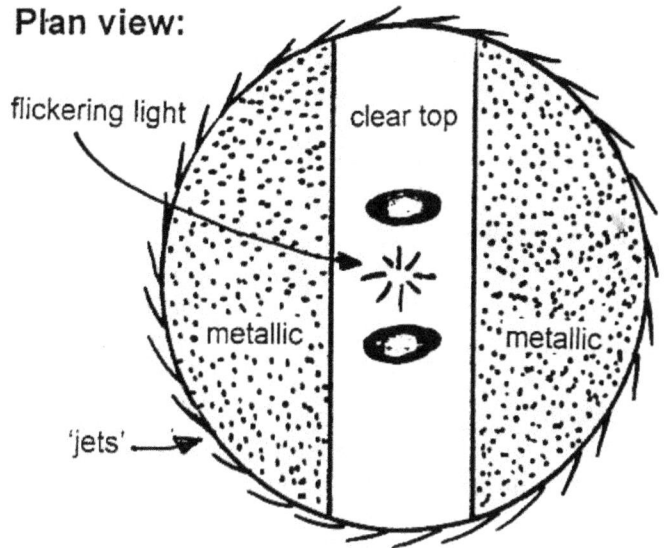

Entity detail:

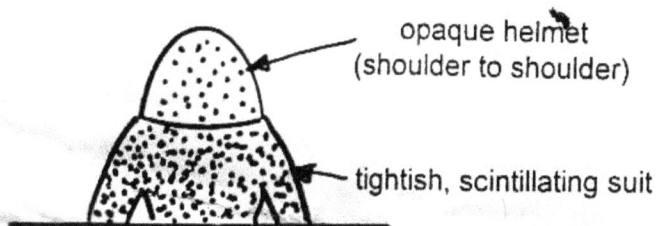

Back view:

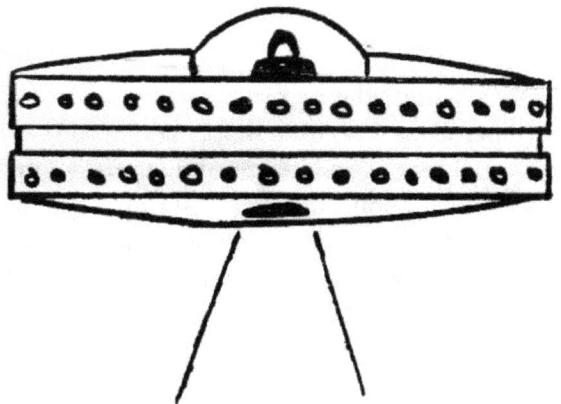

Of planes and UFOs

There have been several instances in the past when unidentified craft have been sighted by flight crews in New Zealand, and tracked on radar. Pilots are perhaps the most expert and reliable of all witnesses, and it is hard to dispute the radar evidence:

Tasman Sea, 1 May 1965

Witnesses in both Wellington and Christchurch, including from Civil Aviation, reported seeing unusual craft flying out over the Tasman. At the same time seven unidentified objects were sighted over the Tasman by an aircraft crew and both the New Zealand and Australian Air Forces.

Cook Strait, 4 September 1969

The pilot, Captain Cullum, and co-pilot of a Straits Air-Freight Express were above Cook Strait and saw a blue light travelling at 3,000 feet and an estimated speed of 25 knots. He countered sceptics by stating that the only known object capable of staying aloft at that speed was a helicopter, "and choppers don't give off a blue light." His credibility was supported by Wellington Radar station who confirmed tracking a blue pulsating light over Cook Strait.

2nd February 1974

Captain Telling was flying between Auckland and Wellington, at an altitude of 10,000 feet, in a Grand Commander. When he was over the area of Ohura Beacon, he thought his starboard engine was on fire. He realised that what had caused the illusion was a large blue ball of light, it was about 30 feet across, and the colour of a welding arc.

It was only about 30 yards from his plane, and flew alongside for about 25 seconds. During this time his instruments went haywire, including his automatic direction-finding compass, and his gyroscopic and magnetic compasses, which were spinning at twelve revs per minute.

These abnormalities continued long after he lost sight of the object, and did not normalise until somewhere around Wanganui. The original investigator suggested this may have been because the UFO was still in the vicinity of the plane.

Later, in April 1975 Captain Telling saw a high-flying UFO, changing colours, in the same vicinity.

In 1970 the Christchurch radar station was tracking a meteorological balloon when they encountered a second unexpected signal coming from an object way beyond the capabilities of any known craft. It was climbing at a rate of 7,000 feet per minute, its speed increasing with altitude. The radar station could no longer continue tracking it when it reached over 63,000 feet.

Plane pacing

1 July 1977

Xenolog printed a report by an experienced pilot and traffic officer Aronsen who was in a PA 28 (Piper Cherokee) on a short flight in the vicinity of Temuka, South Canterbury:

"I was at an altitude of 7,500 feet, and was aware of an inbound F27 Transport plane, and sighted it, about one mile west of my position.

"It was at 2,000 feet, and on long finals about five miles northwest of Temuka. What caught my attention was the close proximity of a black cigar-shaped object, enveloped in a heat haze, which appeared to be following the F27.

"It was about fifteen metres in length, positioned slightly above the starboard rear of the transport plane, and was maintaining its position at a distance of approximately 400 metres.

"I turned towards the object and commenced a dive in its direction, reaching maximum airframe speed in an effort to intercept it. The UFO stopped dead, hovered for two seconds, then accelerated sharply away on a heading of about 290 degrees magnetic.

"The rate of climb and acceleration was far in excess of anything I have seen before; it was lost to sight within five seconds. In thirteen years of flying I have never seen a craft to compare with that object."

The Kaikoura lights – a major incident

Kaikoura–Wellington, Christmas–New Year 1978–79

This is one of the most discussed and investigated events in ufology. It is a complex series of events, which I will sequence in chronological order. I have used the witness's and participants' real names due to the prior massive publicity these sightings received:

20 December 1978

Just before midnight air traffic controllers John Cordy and Andy Herd reported "unknown returns" on their radar.

At the same time, at Woodbourne RNZAF Base, Warrant Officer Ian Uffindell saw three bright lights in the southeast sky, near Cape Campbell and the Kaikoura coast. Bill Frame, in the control tower also sighted the white lights – one large, and two smaller, dimmer lights. Bill rang John Cordy, who advised there was no known air traffic to account for them.

During the next hour they moved up and down the coast, hovering at times, with occasional beams of light coming from them at a 45 degree angle. The two smaller objects seemed to move and stop in unison. The police in Blenheim received several calls from the public, and all reports corresponded with the others.

21 December 1978

At 12.50 a.m. Air Traffic picked up a second target – giving a return "the size of a large passenger plane", on radar. It was 30 miles off the coast, southeast of Wellington, and tracked for 30 miles, at about 120 knots, to a point 60 miles east of the mouth of the Clarence River. It then stopped moving for 45 minutes, and although it has been argued that radar should not pick-up stationary objects, this may not apply to something rotating or spinning. During the night of 20 December, and early the next morning the Air Traffic Control centre also received a number of calls, reporting strange lights and "weird high-pitched noises" in the area.

At 1.10 a.m. Captain John Randle and First Officer Keith Heine took off from Woodbourne in their four-engine turbo-prop *Argosy* freighter, (SAE – Sierra Alpha Echo), for their regular trip south over Cook Strait, to Christchurch, then back north over Cook Strait and on to Auckland. Air traffic controllers Cordy and Herd asked them to keep a lookout for the objects causing the inexplicable returns.

When they were over Cook Strait, 15 to 20 miles southwest of Wellington Harbour, the large object was detected moving, at 120 knots some 20 miles towards the *Argosy* track, and stopping again about 20 miles to the east. At the same time the crew, who kept heading south, noted a number of small white lights, close to shore, moving randomly over a considerable distance, occasionally shining down. Their weather radar showed a number of returns of very large objects, the only remote conventional explanation could have been illicit ships, but they would have been dangerously close to shore.

At 3.10 a.m. they left Christchurch for Auckland, and decided to deviate up the coast for another look at the unidentified objects and lights. During their trip up the South Island they saw the smaller lights were over the sea, and not the land, as previously thought. They considered helicopters or boats, but thought it unlikely. When they reached Cape Campbell, five strong targets faded – then reappeared behind the plane. At the same time, another target was moving in from the east on the same track. At 4.06 a.m., they did an orbit and spotted white lights, with an amber tint, randomly beaming downwards. (There are some differences in the details of witness observations at this time.) The plane proceeded on to Auckland without further incidence.

Simultaneously, at 3.10 a.m., a second *Argosy* plane (SAF – Sierra Alpha Foxtrot) took off from Woodbourne for Christchurch, with Captain Vern Powell and First Officer Ian Pirie in the cockpit. Wellington Radar asked them to also keep a lookout for the radar returns, especially the stationary object to the east of Cape Campbell. When the strange return was 50 miles from SAF, Wellington Radar advised it had moved 20 miles to the west, and halted 30 miles away from the plane, as it had done with the previous SAE flight. Powell could see a bright, glowing white light, tinged with red, but reported it as being a bright red glowing light, about 2,000-3,000 feet above the aircraft. It had been stationary for about 45 minutes, but then started to move parallel to SAF.

Shortly after 4 a.m. SAF was approaching Christchurch, and another target was detected on the weather radar. It moved one mile closer, now only 40 miles away. It put on a burst of incredible speed, heading straight for the plane, before veering left and disappearing off radar. The crew saw very little of this, just a few flashing lights to the front.

Quentin Fogarty, a television journalist in Australia, had returned to New Zealand for the Christmas break, and he was told of the events with the *Argosy* planes by a New Zealand journalist colleague, who asked him to check it out. The recent disappearance of Valentich and his plane over the Bass Strait was still fresh in Fogarty's mind.

He was very interested in the basic scenario that a large target had tracked out from Wellington at 120 knots, moving rapidly towards flight SAE and then made a similar approach to flight SAF, pacing it closely for twelve miles. There were radar, ground and pilot observations, and it was arranged for him to make a news presentation-type documentary.

He contacted David Crockett, a freelance cameraman, and his wife Ngaire, a freelance sound recordist, and together they started interviewing Cordy, Herd, Powell and other witnesses. Powell had commented that he wasn't scared, just excited. He had come to the conclusion that UFOs existed, and if they were going to harm anyone, they would have done so a long time ago.

Quentin wanted to include a re-enactment to complete their footage, and arranged to travel, one way, on a regular *Argosy* newspaper delivery run from Wellington to Christchurch, which covered the same route where both previous planes had encountered the large object.

30 December 1978
At 9.30 p.m. Fogarty's team boarded *Argosy* SAE, with Captain Bill Startup and Flying Officer Bob Guard, and set off on an identical route. It was only intended to be a re-enactment, and Quentin had already recorded the voice-over, "We had no luck in sighting anything mysterious", when the captain called them up to the cockpit.

There was a row of bright pulsating lights hovering over Kaikoura. They contacted Geoff Causer at Wellington Radar, who advised them he had been viewing anomalous targets off the Kaikoura coast for 30 minutes. Due to their erratic nature he had not considered them to be solid. As before, the lights were white to orange pulsating globes, with a red tinge.

31 December 1978
At 12.30 a.m. a second target appeared one mile to their left. It disappeared and then the same, or a third target, with a flashing light, reappeared and hovered, possibly in the same spot, but now three miles away, due to the plane's movement. Wellington Radar was showing a number of targets, which doubled in size for 47 seconds, a mile behind and following the plane.

Bill Startup twice performed 360 degree turns, in an attempt to see what was on his tail. The object following them was about four miles away, and looked like a star emitting bright green and white light. Wellington Radar had said the object, on their tail for ten minutes, had now been joined by two others. As they neared Christchurch the target following them, veered away, and headed inland to the southeast.

The film crew had only intended to make a one-way trip to Christchurch, but knew something was going on up there, and since they had obtained very little footage, Bill Startup invited them to make the return journey to Blenheim. New Zealand Television journalist Dennis Grant took Ngaire Crockett's place.

Only two minutes after take-off, while they were still climbing through the cloud, they saw a bright light, just within twenty miles on radar, keeping track with them. They cleared the cloud ten miles out of Christchurch, and observed a very bright, round yellowish-white light above, which was lighting up the surrounding clouds.

As they were going up the coast they could see a "great big" target at 3 o'clock and an altitude of 11,500 feet. David Crockett was in the cockpit filming as much as possible. Through his lens he could detect a definite structure through the light. It looked like a traditional flying saucer, with a brightly lit bottom and a transparent sphere on top.

Christchurch Radar was turned off, and Wellington Radar advised the *Argosy* that were out of range, but they did have lots of targets off Clarence, north of Kaikoura. The object had been following them for about 10-12 minutes. They were 35 miles out of Christchurch, at 13,000 feet, when Startup took the plane off autopilot and made a 90-degree turn towards the target, putting it in front of the plane. The object moved to the right, indicating some form of intelligent control.

It now moved to the front and below the plane, and then picked up speed and came back straight up towards the plane. In the footage it looked like a grey-white oval shape craft with rings of light going around.

Before they landed back in Blenheim at 3.30 a.m. on the 31 December, there was a lot more activity recorded visually and on radar. Going towards the North Island the aircraft picked up radar returns consistent with Wellington Radar and visual sightings.

Heading towards Kaikoura East Startup thought he saw a second object ahead and above the aircraft. Flying into Cape Campbell a huge bright light – orange with a red tinge, came into view high above Blenheim. The plane banked for landing, and they lost sight of it.

There was much excitement all round. Quentin Fogarty and the footage were raced back to Melbourne and Channel 0 late on 31 December. He had to work on getting it ready to go to air, and there were problems over copyright and use of the film. Eventually, after nearly three days without sleep, he was close to physical and mental collapse, and had to take three days off, returning to work on 5 January 1979.

For a long time afterwards Quentin Fogarty was exposed to extreme harassment, from sceptics, lunatics and even his own employers. A lot of inaccurate and incomplete data was publicised in the media. (I met Quentin while in Melbourne, and found him to be a quiet, modest, intelligent and very honourable man. In 1982 he wrote the book *Let's Hope They're Friendly!* I can recommend it as an exceptionally good example of the unpleasant and unethical practices that permeate the entire ufology scene, and victimise honest witnesses such as Quentin.)

About two days after the story made headlines, the New Zealand Air Force sent up an Orion with sophisticated monitoring equipment. They said they didn't find anything and suggested some unspecified, unusual natural phenomena. Their conclusion was couched in slightly ambiguous terms as it said it was not a craft from an unfriendly nation and of no defence significance.

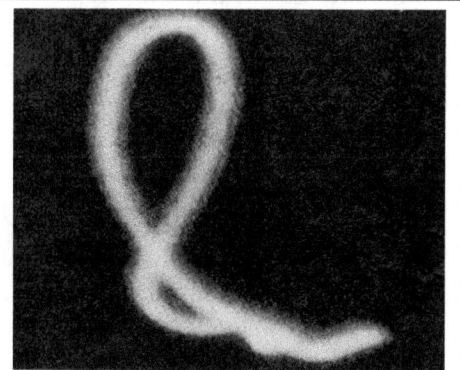

This famous frame from the film may show a UFO travelling at 18,000 metres per second

The film footage and details of the encounters were sent to the USA by Channel 0. They were examined by over twenty scientists, and experts in radar, optics and physics, and included:

- Bruce Maccabee, US Navy Surface Weapons Centre
- John Acuff, President NICAP
- Professor Allen Hynek, Director CUFOS
- Dr. Gilbert Levin, Biophysicist
- Dr. Peter Sturrock, Plasma Physicist, Stanford
- Dr. Richard Haines, Optical Physiologist, NASA

They commented that it was the only UFO sighting at the time, which had radar, visual and photographic evidence, and couldn't be identified by conventional means. They all ruled out the explanations proffered by authorities, sceptics, armchair critics, and other self-proclaimed experts.

The phenomenon was not – Venus, Jupiter, stars, meteorites, ball lightning, aeroplanes, ground lights, fishing boats, cabin light reflections, migrating mutton birds, reflections off cabbage patches, and certainly not a hoax or any of the other explanations which attempted to sweep the whole matter under the carpet.

They commented that no conventional object behaved that way, and while they had ruled out all other explanations and reasons, they couldn't totally eliminate Russian or American secret flying machines. They noted that Nazi Germany had plans for such craft as early as 1941, and the United States' *flying flapjack* which had never reached fruition.

In New Zealand, one pilot suggested they were experiments in holographic target decoys or interferometry by the Australian and New Zealand Navies. Another man claimed he had worked with top secret Air Force projects – *Hookdown* and *Sidescan*, involving controlled drones, and that the Americans had been testing advanced drones on Civil Aviation radar.

Bruce Cathie, a New Zealand airline pilot and ufologist, believed the objects were both man-made and extraterrestrial drawing their energy source from a world-wide grid system. He claimed a world-wide group of scientists had combined their research into one major experiment, based on re-engineering craft from outer space.

Quentin Fogarty does not hold an extraterrestrial theory, and felt that while they were intelligent, they may be something other than physical reality as we understand it.

Hamilton, March 1978

John had been having dinner at his friend's house, and afterwards Murray drove him home. Brian, Murray's 8-year-old son, had insisted on coming, and was seated in the back of the car.

"It was Brian who drew our attention to a large yellow pulsating light hovering, at treetop level, over some nearby houses. At first it was a little obscured, and as we got closer we could see it was an elliptical shape, very large, like a "hot dog on end." While it was pulsating, it did not illuminate the surrounding area.

"After a short time it moved silently away to the northwest. One aspect of this incident had me intrigued. Over dinner, Brian had asked me if I believed in UFOs, and I told him about something I had seen in Noumea in 1967. A couple of hours later we sight one! Coincidence, or what?"

Aliens to the rescue, June 1994

John Pinkney wrote about the unexpected help received by rescue crews during some violent storms at sea. The incidents were also highlighted in a New Zealand TV3 documentary, *Rescue South Pacific*. New Zealand and French ships had sailed to the South Pacific to help rescue yachts in serious peril in mountainous waves.

The survey ship, *Monowai*, was fighting 48-degree rolls, in the pitch dark and driving rain, unable to locate stricken vessels in such conditions. Dozens of witnesses saw what happened next. Midshipman Tracey Kaio, and Sub-Lieutenant Andrew Saunderson said, "Everything changed – the sky lit up, we were surrounded by a green light, and we could see for miles. The ocean seemed suddenly calm, at first we thought it was a flare, but the whole sky was blazing in bright emerald colours."

The yacht *Ramtha*, was one of the rescued vessels and crewman Bill Forbes was convinced a UFO intervened. "We all saw it quite clearly. It was floating above us in a low cloud – a big ball of white light, with a tinge of orange."

An American family, in their catamaran *Heart Light*, had an even more extraordinary experience. Their boat was starting to break up in the high seas, and things were not looking good for the couple and their two children. Darryl Wheeler was convinced a flying saucer stopped by to help: "The light speared right down on us," Darryl said. "We felt certain we'd be lifted up in some kind of tractor beam, but then it moved on."

Who knows – maybe it was. They survived the storm! Not all vessels were so fortunate. The yacht *Quartermaster* vanished with three people on board.

Christchurch, 1982

A reader wrote to the Australian *Ufologist* magazine, in 2002, about an interesting second-hand report from a 32-year-old man who had lived in Christchurch as a child. At 7 p.m. he and his mother had just returned home when they saw what they thought were several small fires in the hills to the south. They noticed a light moving very quickly towards them from that direction. Eventually it was overhead, where it stopped and silently hovered. Other neighbours were also staring.

It was a huge oval shape, "the size of two football fields" and a sort of a buff colour. They could not see any portholes, just lights coming from the bottom. After about five minutes it moved and took off at high speed. When they went inside and turned on the radio, the announcer said they didn't want any more people calling in about the UFO. They had been instructed to "say nothing."

Hawkes Bay area

Due to some confusion in the date of this next incident, my colleague Bryan Dickeson kindly provided me with the original report produced by Wynn Craven, who interviewed the witness twelve days after the event:

Waipukurau Aerodrome, 30 October 1969

Mr. J. Cudby, of Central Hawkes Bay Security Services, was making his regular security patrol at 3.10 a.m. with his 6-year-old Alsatian dog. The first thing he noticed was that the flock of young sheep, which grazed on the Aero Club's ground, were all bunched up in one corner, as if something had frightened them. He parked his station wagon, switched off the headlights, and let the dog out for a run.

As he walked to the clubhouse door he heard a noise, which he initially assumed came from a train on the nearby railway track. As he tried the lock he noticed three "out of place" lights reflected high in the glass door panel. He could hear his dog growling from the station wagon, and when he looked back, he was amazed to see the three lights, two green and one red, in the sky, just above and to the right of his vehicle. The lights were alternating – white, green, red, green, and beaming down to the ground, illuminating a 50-foot area below. They were at about telephone pole-height and he could see that they were actually attached to the turret portion of a big, saucer-shaped object.

The dog was now whimpering, racing round and round the station wagon. Cudby, who admitted to being frightened, hurried back to the vehicle and brought his centre mounted spotlight to bear on the object, about 300 feet away. He could see the object, about 60 feet long and 12 feet high, with a perfectly smooth surface like stainless steel. There appeared to be no joints, rivets or hatches in the metallic surface. It was moving sideways, to-and-fro, over a seven to eight foot span, and it was still emitting a constant, loud pitched, humming noise.

Mr. Cudby then reported, "As if alerted by the spotlight, several things happened. The light beams underneath suddenly brightened to the same intensity as the turret lights. Within about one second the to-and-fro motion stopped, and the noise built up to a high pitch. The whole craft tilted down at the right hand side, and it made off at high speed, its leading edge slightly down, and climbing at about a 15 degree angle to the southwest.

"The dog was still madly racing around the car, and I walked to the corner of the hanger, where a windsock was rotating wildly before it returned to its normal limp position for the windless night. I walked across the wet grass and noticed that the area underneath where the object was hovering was very warm and dry."

While some were sceptical, a Mr. Grant was travelling through Hawkes Bay to Gisborne at about the same time when he saw a circular object about 100 feet above the ground. It had gradually gained height and abruptly took off to the south. Two other residents who lived close to the airport reported hearing the noise, and that their sheep were very disturbed.

Gisborne, June 1976

One Sunday, at 2.30 p.m., a retired couple was driving northwest along the highway towards Frasertown. There was far less traffic than normal, for such a clear, sunny day.

Mrs. A was driving, and about 250 metres directly in front of the car, she saw an object which swooped down just above their vehicle. It quickly sped directly towards the car, and suddenly stopped about 100 metres ahead, on the right hand side of the road. Mrs. A slowed the car to a halt, hesitant to go closer.

It was bright silver, 20 to 30 metres across, and looked like "an inverted dinner plate, with a cupola dome on top." There were no obvious markings, except a line of small, evenly spaced dark apertures on the side. Neither she nor her husband noticed any noise or smell.

For five or six minutes the craft proceeded to tumble, roll and speed around in a tight circle, before speeding off to the hills in the northeast.

The Gisborne Flap, 1977–1978

My colleague Bryan Dickeson, was living in Wellington at the time, close to ground zero. He was able to visit Hamish McLean of the Gisborne APRG, several times during this memorable and much-publicised UFO flap which occurred between November 1977 and March 1978. Bryan conducted a very thorough investigation into the entire phenomena.

"When I flew to Gisborne", Bryan said, "I did not expect to find anything quite so startling. I found the local group had carefully recorded as much detail of the different events as it could, and had taken steps to authenticate the material it had collected."

Hamish himself witnessed an unidentified craft at 10.20 a.m. on 29 November, 1977. He had received a call from a farmer in the Waimata Valley, 16 kilometres from Gisborne: a flying saucer had landed in a nearby paddock. Hamish immediately set out to see for himself. At first he saw nothing, but as he drove around a bend in the valley, he saw the flying saucer 150 metres to his left, 100 metres above the road slightly above a hill. He stopped his car, and got out.

The craft sped downhill towards him, then stopped and hovered 60 metres away. He described it as being shaped like a large bowler hat; a fluorescent pink-red dome with a boomerang shaped frieze across the middle and five dark grey, rectangular line markings on the surface underneath.

The boomerang frieze itself was white with purple characters across it, like foreign-written symbols. There was a deep bright metallic blue rim below the dome. Underneath the rim were four dull grey square pads or feet, and four hazy green cylinders of light, with a slightly denser green light spiralling within.

Hamish watched the stationary object for about three minutes. Suddenly a bright beam of blue light shot out of a small square aperture on its lower left side. It focussed on a dead tree, some 15 metres away, which lit up like a Christmas tree. The beam lasted about seven seconds, during which time each tree branch radiated fluorescent-coloured light of different hues. Sheep in the paddock near the tree, immediately started bleating and ran away down the hill, where they milled about in small groups. (Later examination of the tree showed no apparent damage, even the resident spiders seemed unaffected.)

The craft moved fifteen metres to the right, hovered for two minutes, then swept back behind the hillside. It re-emerged back to its original place above the hillside where Hamish first saw it. It

McLean Object

Fluorescent 'dayglo' pink-red

Purple chars
on white
'Frieze'
(also ⑤)

5
tres

Metallic deep
bright blue

Dark grey
rectangular
markings

dull grey 'feet'
(squared pods)

rotating helices in
hazy green
cylinders of
light

(square blue beam of light

10 metres

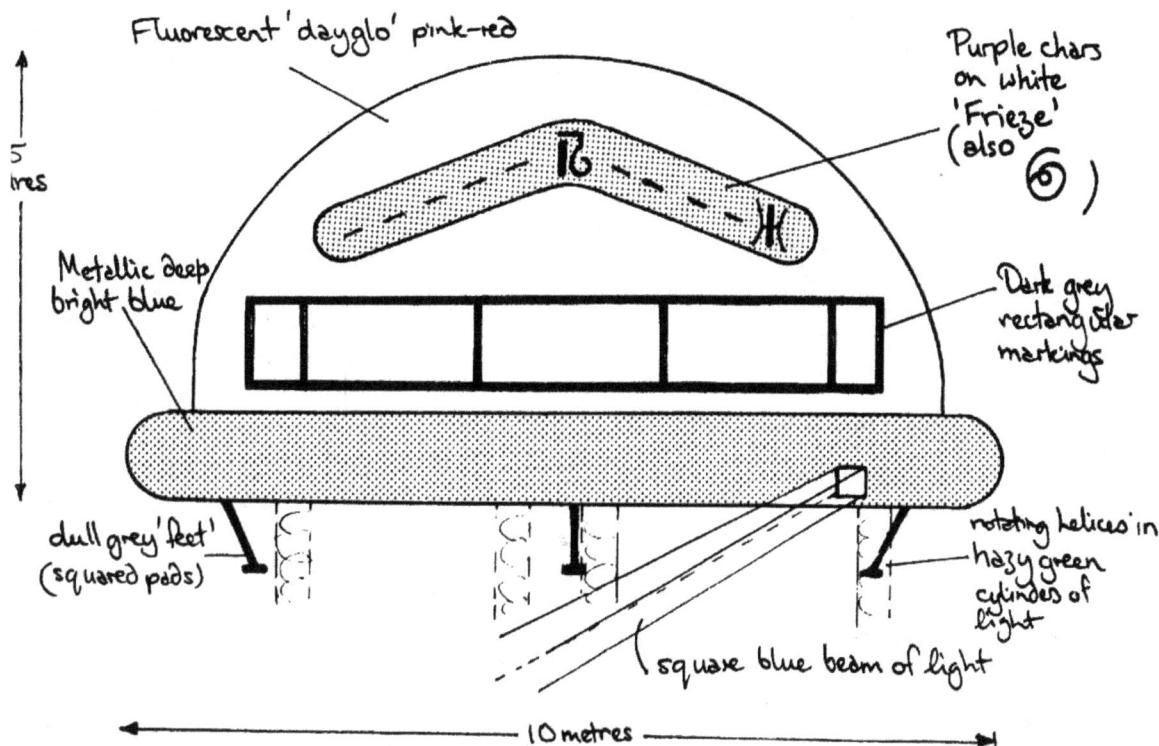

hovered there for a few minutes, so Hamish raced to the nearest farmhouse to ring another researcher.

Hamish was working part-time as a cadet reporter for the local newspaper. There had been many bogus calls, and when this witness called him, he had not expected to see anything. Now he wanted corroboration, and drove back to town to fetch a colleague. Unfortunately, by the time they returned, the object was nowhere to be seen.

The next week more unusual events were reported, which were difficult for Bryan and Hamish to confirm. However the witnesses were country people, not connected, and seemed genuine. Some of the details they gave corroborated previously-undisclosed data.

23 December 1977

A Waimata Valley farmer was woken by his dogs barking. He raced out the back door with his rifle, and was stunned to see a landed flying saucer to his right.

His description was similar to the 'bowler hat' craft Hamish had seen the previous week. It was 30 to 40 feet across, with a metallic outer shell, which glowed bright blue, and had an unusual boomerang shape drawing on the outside.

He also saw open rectangular doors, with an intensely bright red interior. To the left of the object he saw two humanoid figures, about 4 foot, 8 inches tall, wearing close-fitting metallic silver overalls, cuffed at the bottom over red, glowing boots.

They had white opaque helmets, extended across their shoulders, and their hands were covered with flared gauntlets extending halfway up their forearms.

Location 1:

Gisborne, NZ

Latitude 38° 40' South
Longitude 178° 01' East

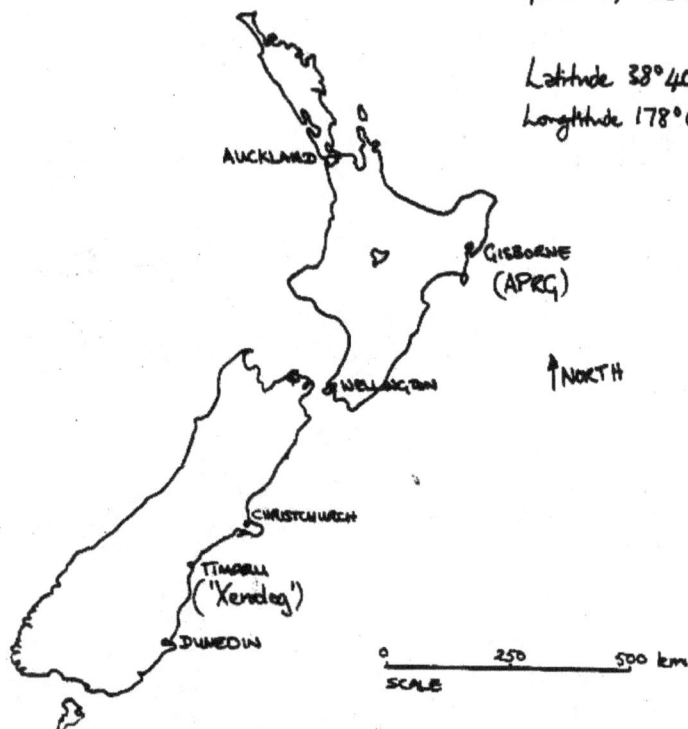

Between them they were carrying the limp, upside-down body of one of his sheep dogs. The farmer shot at the beings, winging one. He dropped the dog and ran into nearby bushes. The second being ran for the craft, which took off vertically, at great speed, after the doors closed behind him. The dog got up, rather groggy and started jumping around and barking.

There was an interesting turn of events: Six days later, at 7 p.m. on 8 December, a man driving down the Waimata Valley Road saw a "small man" trying to flag him down on the left-hand side of the road. Initially he slowed down, but had second thoughts and sped up and headed to town.

He described the hitchhiker as being 4 foot, 9 inches tall, wearing a silver suit and red boots. He was not wearing a helmet, and was jumping up and down and frantically waving. Was this the being left behind after the failed dog-napping attempt?

Although this is speculation on my part, I wonder if several sightings, in the Waimata Valley, after 2 December were the visitors searching for their missing comrade.

Location 2:

Waimata Valley, Gisborne N.Z.

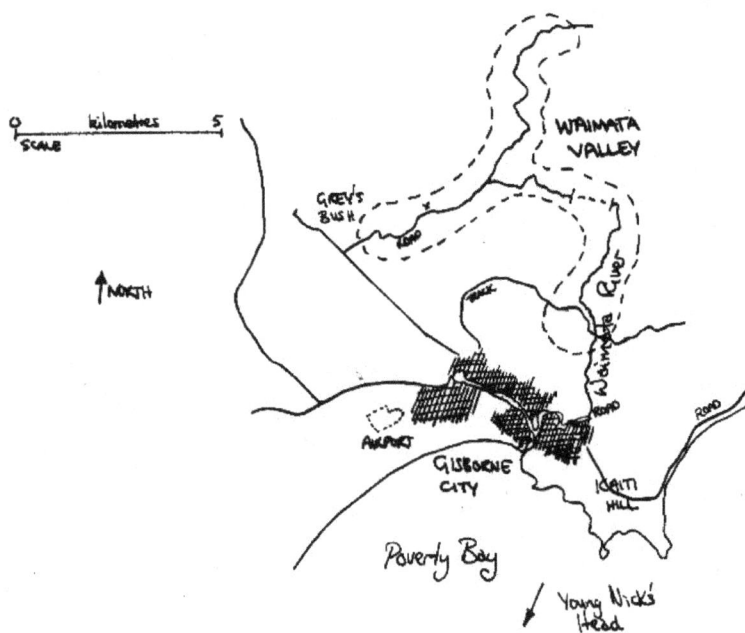

3 December 1977

One researcher was turning his car round, while a colleague waited at the roadside. A huge green object, about 100 foot across, came from behind a hill, just above the road, to the left and about 35 metres in front of him. It only hovered for a few seconds before moving back behind the hill.

6 December 1977

At 11.45 a.m. a man reported being paced for half a mile, by a bright object, about 100 metres away.

At 6.40 p.m. five people in a car were paced, for two km, by an object about 125 metres away and only six metres above the ground. It sped up until 375

200

metres ahead, and started zig-zagging across the road, causing an oncoming vehicle to nearly run off the road (a truck driver also witnessed this event). An hour later at 7.30 p.m. three women had a similar experience, when an object followed them for about a mile, 60 metres away from their car. All the witnesses that day described a bowler-hat shaped craft.

9 December 1977

A small bright red light was seen at 7.30 p.m., and later at 10.40 p.m., a bright, fast-moving red object, shaped like an "upside-down frying pan", was hovering behind a hill where it had joined a similar blue object. For several minutes they hovered side by side, moved back and forth, and then took off up into the valley at high speed.

During January and February many reports of unidentified lights and craft intrigued the local media and researchers. It was referred to as the "Gisborne Flap", with most sightings centred on the Waimata Valley. (The valley itself has a significant, though overlooked history. During the Maori Land Wars of the 19th century, European farmer-settlers were massacred there. Many Maori still consider it to be a sad and haunted place.)

Many Gisborne people hoped to see one of these strange objects for themselves. It was a great opportunity to take a picnic, or midnight snack, and go out to the valley on a warm summer night.

Gisborne "close encounters"

2nd February 1978

Three friends, Bronwyn Pauls, Ida Bishop and Sally Jones made occasional overnight trips to the valley, for stargazing and gossip as a break from shift-work and family responsibilities. Hubby would mind the kids while they had a giggle and reminisced on days gone by. At 5.10 a.m. while parked on the Waimata Valley Road near its junction with Manders Road, their girl talk was interrupted by a continuous buzzing noise:

"At first we thought it was someone driving down the road, but there was no sound of gear change or engine variation. A huge, dark shadowy shape passed very low, about 10 or 12 feet above our car, which started to shake. It was twice the size of a car, and emanating orange spotlights. It would have been travelling at about 20-30 miles per hour, and we could hear the continuous roar as it proceeded up the valley.

"We had seen a few odd lights a bit earlier, but nothing like this. We were determined to have another night out in the near future, to see what else we could observe."

Two months later, my colleague Bryan Dickeson conducted an in-depth investigation into this and subsequent incidents, and wryly commented that they might have heeded the old adage: "Be careful what you wish for!"

11–12 March 1978

It was nice, mild Saturday evening and Bronwyn, Ida and Sally thought it would be fun to go back to the valley and camp out overnight. Winter was coming and there would be few opportunities left for more 'girls nights' out.

Bronwyn detailed the events that evening: "We arrived about 10 p.m., parked the car just off the side of the road, out of sight, and walked up a steep hill nearby. We had a great view of the lower Waimata Valley, and could still watch our vehicle parked below. Last time, inside the car, our view of any object was restricted. This time, if anything turned up, we could see it a lot better. We snuggled into our sleeping bags; I positioned myself between Ida and Sally, it felt a bit safer!"

The UFO "fever" had one unpleasant aspect: groups of youths, a few armed with guns, had sometimes taken to cruising the road at night hoping to get a pot-shot at something. At about 11 p.m. a carload of people came down the road with headlights on full-beam and radio blaring. The women covered anything light-coloured which might attract attention in the dark, and settled down to wait for the hoons to go.

"A little later we heard a distinct noise, like tin cans buckling. This lasted about 20 minutes. We kept chatting for about another 30 minutes, and must have dozed off before midnight. I woke with a start at about 1 a.m. Ida and Sally were still asleep, but there was someone I could not see entirely, standing over me. I reached out behind and touched a cool, metallic calf length boot. I just turned over, snuggled up to Ida, and went back to sleep!

"The next thing I remember is kicking Sally with my foot and whispering, 'Did you see that? Let's get out of here, it's cold.' There was nothing in sight, but somehow we were all starting to panic. It was now 4 a.m. Sunday morning. We grabbed our sleeping bags, rushed down the hill to the car and headed home."

The women were all convinced that "something had happened", but couldn't remember what. They obviously had a total blank for the time period from just after 1 a.m. to 4 a.m. They now felt strangely attracted to that part of the valley and had returned to the spot several times since. Other people had accompanied them on some of these trips, and had also seen luminous objects.

The three women felt uneasy about the two lost hours, and wanted to know if anything odd had happened. However, only the nurse, Bronwyn, was prepared to undergo hypnotherapy:

After they had fallen asleep, Bronwyn recalled waking up on the hillside, shielding her eyes from a bright white light shining down from above. A large disc-shaped object was hovering directly out from where they lay, above the trees just beyond their car. It was hard-edged, with a dome on top. It was a bright white colour, and had yellow lights on the dome and underneath. She also recalled there were a few small red lights.

"It moved closer, and Sally and I were drawn up off the ground and along the bright white light beam towards the craft. The beam held us firmly, but didn't appear to be solid. We could see Ida below, still asleep in her sleeping bag. Sally was struggling and I called out to her: 'It's not meant to happen like this!'"

Bronwyn's next memory was of being inside a small round room. "I don't know how we got in there. I was lying on a raised horizontal slab of white material, and Sally was on another. There was a panel of coloured lights, and the whole room was a milky white colour. I could see doors, with round lintels, and a faceted column of some sort.

"Sally was looking over at me. There was a male being, average height and fairish appearance dressed in an off-white coverall or uniform, with white boots. (Not *metallic* as she had first thought.) He was talking to me, but his lips weren't moving; it was a long and fairly pleasant conversation."

Bronwyn said he had told her not to divulge what he had told her, and she became extremely angry when the hypnotherapist tried to press her for details. There was no indication of any kind of physical examination. (Many years later an implant was found, which another colleague of mine was arranging to have removed and examined.)

Bronwyn then remembered being returned to the hillside: "The same light beam seemed to push us back down until we were back on the ground again. For a few moments it bore down on me like a heavy weight. The craft quickly disappeared, and I came to and kicked Sally: 'Are you awake?' – 'Of course I'm bloody awake!' It was then we woke Ida and headed for the car."

At that time the women had very little knowledge of ufology, which prevented any preconceived ideas or fantasy regarding abductions. Further, the hypnotic regression was undertaken soon after the experience, when details were still fresh in their minds. When told of the results both found it rather unbelievable, and declined any further sessions.

The experience did haunt Bronwyn, who started reading a lot more about the subject. In 1989, after moving to Australia, she contacted several other researchers and UFO groups, and agreed to further hypnotherapy with other researchers.

They produced an entirely different report, consisting of a disjointed scenario containing of lots of 'oohs', 'aahs', and 'go away'-type comments, with few extra meaningful details. This was written up, some eleven years after the encounter, with disparaging remarks regarding the original hypnotherapy. I found Bryan's notes to be excellent, and the procedures definitely in keeping with the highest ethics and protocols. I have no idea whether Bronwyn had further experiences during the next 11 years, or of her later involvement with UFO research or abduction support groups.

Eventually Bronwyn received further assistance from a colleague in Queensland. Two chip implants were located. One, of an unknown metal substance, was removed from her chin, and the other, still in situ is visible in a foot X-ray.

Generation next?

In early 2008, some thirty years later, I received a call from Sonja, and realised she was the daughter of one of the three women involved in the 1978 Waimata Valley incident. She was now 34 years old, and had lived in Australia since leaving New Zealand when she was 13. She was now in Hawkes Nest, one hour north of Newcastle in New South Wales.

"Despite my mother's experiences, I don't recall seeing anything until 30 October 2007, when I was camping at Barrington Tops, and saw lots of inexplicable craft in the sky. I haven't seen any actual large traditional UFOs before or since.

"Across the road from where I live, is a large patch of grass about the size of two football fields, leading to a small bay and inlet of water. I used to see lots of white and orange lights, all about twice the size of a planet, on the other side of the water. I know it was silly, but I used to flash my torch, to try and communicate with them. Sometimes there would be a red light over the water – I felt like it was watching me. It wasn't a boat or something conventional as it would levitate up and down in a wobbly fashion. On these occasions I felt some weird sensations, and I would go home with my hair standing on end, and a feeling of heightened senses.

"On 11 January 2008, Melinda, a girlfriend from Brisbane was staying with me. She showed me a light in the sky one night. I thought it was a star, but then it moved. We went back outside after midnight, and took photos of lights zooming in. Just after dawn, on the morning of the 12 January 2008 we could still see something strange, and took more photos of what looked like sparkler trailers, or serpents-gone-wrong."

That night my 16-year-old daughter, Trudy saw lights in the sky, and took some more pictures. A bit later Melinda thought she saw something else:

"We got the camera, and the three of us went outside. There was a red orb of light over the water. At first we thought it was a boat, but then it split in two, and both objects zig-zagged up and down, and from side to side over a small area.

"We went closer for a better look. The red light was blinking, and we noticed a larger orb of white light, with another white light behind, to the side. It looked like a searchlight, and we could see reflections of a lot of people, both short and tall, and shadows of them scurrying about. We tried to take more photos, but the camera wouldn't work properly, except to give out a big flash, at which time the white light moved to the side of the trees.

"In its full beam we saw very tall, seven to eight-foot beings, with long arms and legs, and oblong almond-shaped heads. They walked, or almost floated, across the grass towards us. I was terrified, and the three of us ran back to the house. After we got through the front door, to the side, in the hallway, I could see an almond-head watching. The baby woke up and was crying; the two children were scared. 'It' stopped moving, stood up watching, and seemed to get taller. Melinda, Trudy and I all felt the same overwhelming weird sensations inside."

When Sonja rang me she was nervous, upset and a little confused. She told me of taking several series of photographs during that period. It seemed they had become abnormally obsessed over a 36-hour timeframe. Her report after this became very disjointed and out of sequence.

"My three-year-old, who was inside all the time, now won't sleep in her room. She talks of a nice, beautiful princess, who has a small 'ogre' companion. Trudy had marks on her body – small oblong red welts from her shoulder blade to her waist. These can fade, and reappear in a minute. She spoke of dreaming of a tall, elegant female with dark black almond eyes, which didn't blink, and looked like a camera lens with an oily effect. A few weeks later she told me she had been on a spaceship one night. "They've lost something and are running out of time." She saw pictures of "wormholes and DNA structures."

"Melinda is a different matter. She had psychological problems before and used to 'hear' radio waves. She had a strong feeling to come to Hawkes Nest at that time. Now she also dreams of a 'tall, elegant woman', and the doctor says it goes a lot deeper than bi-polar disorder."

Given her mother's experiences with the other two women in New Zealand, I referred the matter to a competent colleague, as I thought these latest events may well be related.

More "missing time" from Gisborne

March 1978

About a month after the three women's experience in the Waimata Valley, there was another disturbing event an hour out of Gisborne, in the Tokomaru Bay area. Suzanne Hansen, the lead New Zealand researcher from UFOCUS, documented this incident in great detail:

A husband and wife, I shall call them David and Joan, had been shopping and visiting friends in Gisborne. At 10.30 p.m. they started out on their nearly three-hour journey home to East Cape. About an hour later, they reached a high point in the hills and saw a huge area of bright white light, coming up from the paddocks on the valley floor below.

"It was such a shock; we skidded to a halt, and the car stalled. There were a couple of small rises in the landscape which partly obscured our view, but the sides of the valley were bathed in this intense, dense, silvery-white light. It was brighter than daylight, and seemed to permeate every nook and cranny; frightening in its intensity and awesome in its magnitude."

They were both in shock and disbelief, and scared because it was a very remote area, with no telephone or traffic on the road. David tried to reassure Joan with some rational explanation, but Joan wasn't having any of it, and would have preferred to go back to Gisborne rather than drive any further as long as that light was there.

"After a relatively short space of time I started to feel numb and tingly in my arms and legs," Joan said. "My body suddenly felt tired and heavy and all around me became quiet, distant and vague. I became slightly dizzy and faint, and could hear a deep increasing buzzing sound. I tried to tell David, but don't remember if I did as I couldn't move."

The next thing Joan could recall was just sitting in the car, in darkness. The light had gone, she felt totally drained, and David was almost unresponsive at first. They drove home in silence. (I would note that a loss of conversation after an encounter is frequently reported.)

Over the next few days Joan experienced painful, sensitive hearing, several nosebleeds, and extreme fear at any unexpected noises. David refused to discuss anything about the light or the night trip. That left her feeling very alone with her fears, as she could recall a similar experience in 1975 on a rural road near Hastings.

It took many years, and more unusual experiences before Joan could really come to terms with this and other incidents which had a huge impact on her life and relationship. As in many cases, it was some years before some suppressed memories surfaced from her subconscious.

"Eventually I began to have flashbacks and dream-like recall, culminating in later years in conscious recall of on-board craft experiences, and communications with extraterrestrial entities."

Mount Cook (Aoraki)

In the 1970s Jason was a porter at the Hermitage Hotel below Mount Cook (Aoraki). During one evening he noticed a green, red and orange ball of bright light down in the valley below, near Lake Pukaki. He had a look with his binoculars, as it seemed unusual and was pulsating. He went on with his work, and checked half an hour later, at about 10 p.m. It was still in the same position.

"I lost interest and retired to the staff quarters. The following week I had a couple of days off. I finished work at about 5 p.m. and was about to head to my parents' home in Timaru, a four-hour drive. I was in a hurry, as it was mid-winter and it got dark early. I was halfway there, at about 7 p.m., and between Lake Tekapo and the township of Fairlie when my 1951 Ford V8 Twin Spinner started missing and surging. I was worried, because I had just had a new fuel pump installed, and I thought it was failing.

"I was looking at the car's gauges, when out of the corner of my eye, through the passenger window, I saw that same ball of light. At the same time my engine cut out, and I put my foot on the clutch so that it would coast along down the hill. Luckily my headlights still worked.

"The light was now a huge sphere, the size of a basketball, with red, green, orange and yellow colours mingling and merging, quite brilliant in the clear, dark starry sky. It seemed to be following me, keeping pace with my car, like it was playing with me. I thought, 'shall I pull over and stop? No, better to coast along.' At this stage it silently passed behind my car, and I was getting very nervous as this seemed to go on for a very long time.

"Suddenly it picked up speed, turned gracefully in front of my car, and sped back off high into the southeast sky at phenomenal speed. I breathed a sigh of relief, and let out the clutch. The engine started again. It ran trouble free for the rest of my journey – at a fast pace, I might add!"

Jason has tried to think of more conventional explanation, noting that the McKenzie Basin area is full of hydro-electric dams and long lines of power pylons, supplying the national grid.

He also noted that there is an Astronomical Observatory at Mt. John, next to Lake Tekapo. This is run by Canterbury University Physics Department in Christchurch, in association with the Lick Observatory (University of California, United Sates). Besides the usual range of astronomical functions, the observatory conducts sky-mapping and satellite tracking for the United States Air Force, via the University of California.

Chapter Fourteen

Out in the Pacific

Papua New Guinea

Papua New Guinea (PNG) spans Australia's tropical north – the eastern half of a large island with rugged mountains and dense rainforest. Its difficult terrain means western influence has made few inroads into local cultures there over the last two centuries. While German colonists developed plans to explore the island's interior using zeppelin balloons, these ideas were abandoned when Australia took over political control at the start of World War 1.

While it was an Australian territory, attempts to spread European influence relied mainly on a network of Christian missionary schools, accessed mostly by coastal steamships and Highland jungle tracks. Road and rail developments have always been limited by the rugged terrain.

One friend, stationed in New Guinea before independence from Australia, tells me that UFO sightings were frequent there. The locals usually found them frightening. They had encountered them before, and would run up the hill to shelter in the mission from the "evil spirits".

Although common, UFO sightings are hard to investigate fully as reports only become known much later. Many reports have been unearthed from official records by Bill Chalker and the team working on the *UFO Disclosure* project.

Startling events in 1959 (*Father Gill case*)

Reverend Father William Gill is a highly respected UFO witness of the utmost integrity. Educated in Australia and ordained a priest of the Anglican Church, he spent more than eight years as a missionary in New Guinea.

He admitted that although a man of the church, he did not place any religious interpretation on the UFO events he witnessed, and would not commit himself to any particular theory. He was merely an observer and recorder of events. (He did wryly comment on overhearing colleagues discussing the possibility of people living on other planets, and how their mission work could be extended! As a researcher, I find the thought of "converting aliens" an intriguing one.)

Goodenough Bay is a remote, thinly-populated area, mountainous and covered with thick, tropical rainforest. One of the larger towns there, Dogura, has a cathedral, various government buildings and a large Base Hospital. In November, 1958, at about 8 p.m., Dr. Ken Houston was called out by villagers in Waimera, a mile from the hospital, who claimed a green light had swept across the sky from southwest to northeast. Dr. Houston couldn't see anything so went back into the house. A short time afterwards more people came, claiming there was something in the sky, but again he saw nothing. At about 2 a.m. he was attending to a patient, and went outside to the dispensary. He saw a bright green light cross the sky, and called his wife outside to watch, and she also observed it.

In 1959, Father Gill was stationed in Goodenough Bay, at Boianai. During May 1959 and on 13th June 1959, local schoolboys reported seeing green elliptical objects moving across the sky.

21 June 1959

On 21 June Stephen Moi Gill, head teacher at a local school, was outside his house when he saw a Very light – a bright, white light, in the sky. (A Very light is an aerial flare fired from a pistol, sometimes coloured, used as a distress signal.)

This light did not descend and go out as expected, but moved horizontally across the sky. He said that when close up, the light's outline was "an upturned-saucer shape" with four round spots, like little black balls, underneath. It hovered about 300 feet away in the sky, and after about 30 seconds it silently ascended and disappeared. There had been other reports of strange lights made over the previous few months.

26 June 1959

At 6.45 p.m. on 26 June, Father Gill was outside and noticed a bright white light in the northwest sky, which began descending towards him. He called out Eric Langford and Stephen Moi Gill, who confirmed it was similar to the light seen the previous Sunday. Within ten minutes it was hovering about 350 feet over the sea a very short distance away.

They called more people out to have a look. The craft was solid, about 35 feet in diameter, with a top deck measuring about 25 feet across. It was a dull yellow to pale orange colour, and at first they could see a man-like object moving around the flat top of the object.

Over the next few hours Father Gill and at least thirty-seven neighbours (medical assistants, school teachers, villagers and children), watched as up to four glowing figures at a time, came and went. They moved above the upper deck and were obviously busy "doing something." Although they were illuminated by the object itself, both the figures and the craft had a sparkling effect around them, like a child's sparkler. There was a gap separating the outline and the "shimmering sparkle."

Everyone was getting quite excited, pointing out and commenting on the various comings and goings on top of the craft. Father Gill commented, "The thing that interested us was the display, or ejection, of a blue light from the top of the craft every now and then – a rather thin, powerful blue light, rather like a very, very bright torch light (possibly a laser light?). The beam shot straight into the air at an angle. It went on and then off several times – a few seconds on, and then off. Perhaps five or ten minutes later it was on for another few seconds. Then it hovered, went very, very high and disappeared behind a cloud. After ten minutes or so of waiting, we didn't see it any more. I had been taking notes all the time, and I called everyone in and told them there was nothing to be frightened of."

Father Gill got Stephen and Aranias Rarata (another teacher) to draw sketches of what they saw, separately. All three sets of witness details matched.

27 June 1959

On Saturday 27 June the visitors returned. At 6 p.m. Annie Borewa, a medical assistant, saw a large object in a similar position as the one the previous night. She ran down to Father Gill calling out: 'It's back, it's back!' He immediately came out, soon to be followed by many more locals, and they all watched from a nearby open playing field.

On the Friday they had also seen four smaller discs in the sky, this night there were seven, and Father Gill felt they were definitely companion discs to the larger craft, although they never saw them going in or out of it.

"They were quite easy to see – their outline was quite distinct. They were not the shape of the big one, and I should think quite a lot smaller. Unless they were very, very high up, but they didn't appear to be. One disc was overhead, and as it slanted towards us, it clearly showed five panels on the side, they could have been windows, but they formed duller or brighter parts of the object. It was hard to distinguish on the others, but all of them had four legs – like two sets of bipods. And unlike the four balls on the object seen by Stephen the previous Sunday.

"We stood there as the larger craft descended over the playing field. We all thought it was going to land. We hoped it was going to land, and were in a state of anticipation. They came down, and then stopped. The figures were so near and so close, although we still couldn't discern very much of their appearance, I have calculated their height to be about 5 feet 8 inches.

"We spontaneously waved, and they waved back, which was a surprise. It occurred to me that although it was a form of acknowledgement, they copied us. When we used one hand, they waved with one hand; when with two hands they waved with two hands, and when we waved with my hand above my head, so did they – they copied us.

"We were still hoping it would land, so I got one of the boys to bring my torch. I began to flash things – dots and dashes, and things, and then we got the answer by movement. We couldn't see any figures on deck but the whole thing swung across the sky, like a pendulum, three or four times before coming back to its original position. I flashed a number of times, and every time it answered, until the man came back on deck and seemed to lose interest in us. Despite the interaction, at no time, during any incidents did we hear any noise from the craft or its occupants.

"They seemed to be adjusting something, and then this blue light came up again, and lasted for some time before it flashed off. The craft moved off across the sky, hovered and disappeared over the hill, only to come back then shoot 30 miles across the bay in less than a second."

28 June 1959

"The third night we only saw the larger craft very high up, and a few of the smaller discs around at a lower altitude. We saw no more after the Sunday. If I'd been rich enough to afford a camera, of course I would have taken photographs, but at least we had the signed statements of multiple witnesses."

Father Gill talked about a colleague, Reverend Norman Crutwell, who lived thirty miles away across the bay at Menapi. He was miffed that he was the only European in the area who had not seen a UFO. He even went to bed each night with a portable telescope and camera – hoping to strike it lucky.

"In August 1959, his school – he's got a school over there with about 200 children in it, and a dozen Papuan teachers. That school is the only place on record in the area, in New Guinea, I think, that's had a daylight sighting. It was a great silver disc which sped, faster than a plane, over the school yard, at about 9 a.m. All the kids were lined up to go into the classrooms, so they, and all the teachers saw it. A couple of teachers and children ran to the house, but by the time the unfortunate Reverend raced out, it had gone."

Reverend Crutwell later went on to conduct investigations into unidentified objects over New Guinea, producing excellent reports for London and Brisbane societies.

Father Gill also told researchers that a lot of uneducated locals from the mountains, who are completely untouched by western civilisation, had reported unidentified objects to himself and the other clergy or the Assistant District Officer. They described various shapes and referred to them as "boats in the sky" or "sky balls", which ascended or descended, getting larger or diminishing into pinpoints. Patrol Officer Bob Smith had also witnessed these "ball things" in the sky. Often they would walk for three days to ask what it was and where it had come from – was it from the government, and should they be frightened of it?

Bases under the sea?

The *Australian Ufologist* (Volume 8, number 4) carried an overview of documents obtained from the government in the Australian UFO Research Association (AURA), and *Disclosure* research projects. It noted there were a large number of sightings in the islands and seas off the Milne Bay area, on the eastern tip of Papua. The author believed there may well be an underwater base located on the deep sea floor, littered with uncharted caverns.

Reverend Crutwell, later elevated to Reverend Canon Crutwell, detailed the following incident in a 45-page report on New Guinea UFOs:

> "Unidentified objects that emerge from the ocean are frequently reported in Australia and Papua New Guinea waters. Frightened PNG fishermen have been offering near-identical descriptions of one mystery craft for more than 50 years. They say it is a huge light-spangled object which suddenly surfaces near their boats.
>
> "A remarkable submarine object was seen on Goodenough Bay by Mr. Albert Robins, store manager of Rabaraba. He was travelling at about 2 a.m. in a small coastal

boat. The sea was reasonably calm, and the five crew members on board also witnessed the object.

"A light appeared beneath the sea on the starboard side, and a huge, brilliantly lit object, about 25 metres long, rose slowly from the water. It was cigar-shaped, with both ends pointed, and seemed to be completely silent. The object was self-luminous, dazzlingly bright, so it hurt the eyes –and paced the boat for four minutes. When they tried to take evasive action the object followed, and eventually they turned two complete circles in the water before the object finally submerged.

While this may have been some form of new submarine, its behaviour and self-luminosity convinced the witnesses that it was not a conventional man-made object.

Pilot reports

28 May 1963

Colin Phillip investigated a case which happened off Bougainville Reef at 3.25 a.m., when the pilot, co-pilot and stewardess on a charter flight from Brisbane to Port Moresby, reported to Townsville Ground Control that they were being "buzzed by a flying saucer." They described the object, which paced the plane for ten minutes, as being a "round ball with exhaust gases coming from it."

He also advised that he had taken photographs of the object, however when the plane arrived in New Guinea, the pilot was told not to get the photos developed. When they returned to Australia the pilot was met in Brisbane and the film and flight tapes were flown to Canberra. The crew and DCA officials were told they would lose their jobs if they ever discussed the matter.

In his book *The Jarrold Listings*, Phillip Frola has published copies of several contradictory official letters received in response to various enquiries by researchers at the time. While there was an official denial of the incident, confidential testimonies received tend to confirm the sighting and surrounding circumstances.

1965

Paul Norman investigated a case where the pilot of an Ansett-ANA plane took several photographs of an unidentified craft while flying from Brisbane to Port Moresby. He naturally reported the encounter, and was instructed not to get the photos developed until he returned to Canberra. As soon as he landed back in Australia the film was confiscated, and he and the crew were warned not to discuss the matter.

Mount Hagen, 1974

Some years ago I was talking to a Dutch man, Wilhelm, who had lived in Indonesia and then New Guinea, and worked as an engineer on oil rigs and the Northwest Shelf. He was living in Mount Hagen in 1974, and was astounded to see an unbelievable sight in the sky outside his home, at dusk one evening:

"It was a huge saucer-shaped object, the size of a football field. But what was amazing, was a bloke standing on top of the dome. He wasn't anything like the beings Father Gill described all those years ago. This one looked very human – six feet with hair, but his skin did look rather greyish. However, it might have been the half-light. He had no helmet, and was wearing, of all things, a grey suit!

"I assumed it must have been something of ours. It hovered for a short while and then I couldn't see him. I got a shock when the craft oscillated, then shot off at an unbelievable speed. I knew an English bloke at one of my jobs, who had walked for three days, with the locals, through the jungle from West New Guinea to Port Moresby. He said that during the trip, near the Fly River, they had stopped to eat fruit, and saw several UFOs in the sky overhead."

Madang, 1985

On 26 February 1985, the *Papua New Guinea Post Courier* reported that on the previous Thursday night, twelve unidentified flying saucers flew, in a wedge-shaped formation, low through the gorge of Wara Simbu, towards Madang.

A medical worker and the Kimbr villagers, six kilometres outside Kundiawa, described the objects as being circular, with lights like "car brake lights."

4 November 1999

In November 1999, New Guinea media reported many sightings of an unusual object on Thursday 4 November. Reports came from far and wide, including the north coast of Rabaul, the Gazelle Peninsula and Baining Mountains of New Britain, and Palipal, the Duke of York Island.

Because we have to rely on second-hand reports, and cannot interview witnesses, it is difficult o obtain details. However, the sheer number of sightings indicate something significant occurred.

It was variously described as being "huge", and an oblong shape – somewhere between 200 metres to 300 metres long and 50 metres wide. Some thought it had "huge lumps" on the side, and others described a "pyramid type" top. All reported bright white lights around it, either around the craft or on the back or top. It lit up the area below "like daylight." It hovered, and moved at a very slow pace, over both land and sea.

It was always at an extremely low altitude, "just above the mango trees", or "metres above the sea." Most did not detect any noise, although some reported "quite a puffing noise."

What was it? Where did it originate? Who or what controlled this craft, and what was its purpose? Did anyone's military investigate?

I don't know, and probably never will.

Solomon Islands

In the mid-1990s my phone rang very late one night, and half asleep, I stumbled out of bed to answer it. A very distressed and agitated man on the other end was trying to tell me there were some very nasty aliens in the Solomon Islands, and I must organise a military expedition to go there and "get rid of them."

I asked him why he thought they were aliens, and he assured me they came in "spaceships" and terrorised the villagers. I must admit to making the mistake of assuming he was more than a little deranged, and not seeking further details. Rather than argue with him, I patiently explained that I was only an investigator, and in no position to order out the military. Further, I asked him to consider the implications of such an Australian incursion into the sovereign territory of an independent country.

Having finally humoured him, and sent him on his way, I went back to bed and dismissed the entire matter from my mind. I was wrong, and should have followed up on the report. I guess we can all be wise in hindsight.

It was many years later, I mentioned the call to a colleague. "He was genuine," she said. "At first, when he also rang me, I thought he was drunk. It turned out he was a local chief, and in a high position in Solomon Island society. His English was a little different to ours, and he was quite stressed.

"He told me that there were very tall human-looking beings, coming from caves up in the mountains, who abducted their women, and now there were 'half-breed' children. There were unusual craft coming in and out of one cave and flying down the valley before taking to the sky over the sea. He mentioned the area was rich in gold and oil, and said one lake used to 'bubble black'. He was looking for help, and even offered to pay my fares to go there and investigate."

In 2003 *Nexus* magazine printed an article, *The Dragon Snake, a Solomon Islands UFO Mystery*, by Marius Boirayon, a former RAAF engineer, who grew up in the Mount Hagen area of Papua New Guinea. If true, his report confirms the claims of our mystery caller:

In 1996, after Marius moved to a small village 70 kilometres west of Honiara, the locals warned him to be careful of the Dragon Snake that was in the area. He was fishing with friends one night when they pointed out a very bright white luminous craft, which was about 60 feet round. It was over the sea, about one kilometre away, and they watched for a couple of minutes until it silently went under the water. About ten minutes later it re-emerged, twice as bright as before, and flew back in the direction it had come from.

Over the next seven months Marius saw this, or a similar object, on more than sixty occasions, and wondered what was under that part of the sea where they were submerging. He taught the locals a little bit about astronomy, and they began to realise that this was a real physical object, rather than a fearful phenomenon and superstition.

During that time he witnessed one local with a damaged boat and serious burns to most of his body. He claimed that he had been out fishing at 3 a.m. one morning when the Dragon Snake came flying along. He flashed his torch at it, and it moved overhead, hovered, and while he was trying to get away, hit him with some form of light beam. Marius learned that the Dragon Snake had been terrorising them for over one hundred years, and received independent verification of their reports of deaths and abductions all over the area.

The locals had also reported how the Dragon Snake could vanish in an instant, and when he witnessed this himself, he felt certain the craft possessed some form of cloaking device.

When he became accepted by the local community, he asked a couple of chiefs where the Dragon Snake's house was located. They pointed out an 800-foot mountain, about eight kilometres inland, which had a lake and a waterfall, where the Dragon Snake lived. Marius also located a five kilometre long valley, which would be ideal for a craft to travel through without detection.

Having seen one take this route early one morning, he decided to visit the lake and waterfall, and confirmed his belief that there was indeed an entrance, in fact three entrances, to a base in the mountain.

Marius also started asking questions, especially of another westerner married to a local girl. He said there is a very rare type of gemstone under this kimberlite rock volcanic island. Between 1958 and 1960 a geologist, Mr. Gropher conducted a few expeditions and saw the UFOs. In 1961 a white man, claiming to be from NASA, arrived and got some of the locals to take him to the entrances of the subterranean base.

The description of the entities controlling these craft varies. Marius found depictions of mythical beings in the museum, and these were similar to the four-foot tall aliens with big heads and big eyes which we see in our own literature and documentaries. Other Islanders have told him of flat stingray-type humming craft, with big round lights underneath, which fly over the jungle and sometimes land near villages. They have seen people, both black and white, get out of them, wearing strange grey uniforms, the like of which they haven't seen before.

An elderly friend of mine first brought Marius's article, and the situation in the Solomon Islands to my attention. Her brother was working in the Solomon Islands as a senior administrator, and her son was also working there on a temporary contract.

I don't know if she had specifically been asked to contact me, but it was a long time since the phone call made to me by the concerned chief. I wondered if it had been Marius who rang me back in the mid-90s, but it was unlikely, as his RAAF service would have led him to approach military intelligence or similar. When a colleague, also an investigator rang Marius for further details, he said that he didn't want to discuss it anymore, and feared persecution from paranoid government officials.

Fiji

An alien visitor – we will never know?

Sammy a young Fijian taxi driver had an unusual and mystifying encounter with a strange passenger on 5 May, 1976. He was subsequently investigated, much more thoroughly than would be expected, by Christopher Carden and Jope Rokotuibau, both Fiji government employees.

It is interesting that they concentrated on every minute detail of the stranger's behaviour and appearance, and followed up with comprehensive inquiries with residents and the police.

Sammy was driving from Suva to Tamavua. Just after 11 a.m., before he completed the six-mile trip, he was hailed by a man leaning against a lamp-post next to the roundabout turnoff to Edinburgh Drive:

"He wanted to go to Serea. I told him it cost $20 and took an hour and a half, and he asked me to make it in one hour. He looked and appeared unusual, about 30 to 35-years-old, 5 feet 9 inches and 190 pounds. He looked solid and fit and had a very pale complexion and smooth skin. A round, normal-sized face but I couldn't see his ears as they were covered by sideburns and long, straight shoulder-length black hair. He had slightly sunken dark wide eyes, a straight, pointed nose (nostrils not prominent), long bushy eyebrows and a short, neat moustache.

"He spoke English badly and smelt of the wet clothes he was wearing, despite it being a fine, hot day. His clothes were a little strange; long greyish denim, slightly flared trousers and a long-sleeved woollen shirt, not in keeping with the tropical weather. There were a lot of pockets with flaps and snap fastenings, and all appeared to be full.

"He sat in the front seat, but would not participate in any conversation I tried to initiate. When we reached Sawani Village he asked if there were any shops. He got me to stop, went into an Indian store, and came out, putting something in his pocket. He looked at his watch and told me to go quickly. After a while, at about 11.45am, before we reached Serea, he asked me if I could point out a long, flat stretch of road, about a quarter of a mile long. About midday, just beyond Naqali Health Centre I pointed out such a spot.

Then things became rather inexplicable. After ensuring there were no houses around, he got Sammy to stop. They both got out of the cab, and when Sammy asked him if he knew someone there he said: "No, I've just come here to meet someone to give him a message."

He asked Sammy if he knew him, and when Sammy said no, the stranger said he couldn't explain himself, and told him to take a good look "in case we meet again."

"He told me not to be afraid, and gave me five wet $20 Fijian notes, saying 'Here is your fare and eighty dollars tip.' He opened an airline type bag, and got a damp envelope out. 'Please take this letter with you. Don't read it on the way. As soon as you reach Suva you can read it.'

"When I reached out with two hands to take it, he pulled back, as if suddenly afraid. When I asked him who I should give it to he said, 'You or somebody. Don't be afraid of me or the letter. Just go.'

"I offered to take him the five miles to Serea, as there were only a few farms between, but he said No, that this was the place he wanted to come. While we were talking behind the cab, the only vehicle I saw was a Public Works Department Van which passed, going in the direction of Serea."

Sammy got back in the taxi and turned around, but he was both curious and frightened. He stopped about a mile up the road, and threw the letter in the grass, worried it might be a bomb. He locked the cab and walked back a way, to where he could see the man from the bushes, along-side the road.

"I could see him, apparently speaking into what looked like a black walkie-talkie, rather like those used by the police. I watched for about fifteen minutes, but could not hear what he was saying. Then I became a little afraid of him if he saw me, and hurried back to my car. I picked up the letter and put it in the boot with my hundred dollars. I drove to Nausori and took the letter into the police station and told my story to the duty officer.

"An Inspector opened the letter away from me, but still in view. He said nothing other than to tell the duty officer to record my statement. I then returned to Suva, gave my boss $20, and banked the $80 myself. I have no idea where the man might have come from or gone to, nor did anybody make any suggestions to me regarding this man."

Christopher Carden, who was still waiting for a promised photocopy from the police, reported that the letter purportedly said: "I'm waiting between Sawani and Serea with 'MG' between 12 noon and 3 p.m., yours truly, a friend of Bruce Lee."

This is interesting as Bruce Lee had died the year before. (Sometimes the visitors' information is a little out of date.)

The subsequent investigations were unusually comprehensive, and indicated Sammy was telling the truth. The Police Superintendant wondered if he may have jumped ship, due to the wet clothes, but this theory was discounted.

Considering no crime had been committed, it is unusual that they actually discussed the matter with the Assistant Police Commissioner, who strangely enough mentioned a case of Lautoka school children reporting "little men" appearing out of the ground some fourteen months earlier.

Christopher Carden speculated in his report that the local roads are narrow and winding, hardly safe or sensible for a spacecraft to land, and that many reports of landings were straight, open stretches of road, with only slight slopes. (Carden felt this was of particular significance as it was the topography requested by the stranger who was obviously not familiar with the area.)

He pointed out that it was clear that he had a prearranged rendezvous with someone or something in the vicinity of Sawani at midday. He went on to mention the *Edwin case*, related by Dr. Carl van Vlierden of South Africa, which contained many similar points, including the calling up of a spaceship with a walkie-talkie from a particular spot.

So who was the mysterious stranger? I guess we will never know, and if somebody does, they aren't telling.

Over the ocean

Like most Pacific Islands surrounded by the sea, a lot of unusual craft are seen over the ocean:

8 October 1957

A year before the sightings by Reverend Gill and the Papua New Guinea mission, the *New Zealand Herald* (Auckland) reported that two Fiji couples in a boat saw a white object descending vertically from the sky. Thinking the object might be an aircraft in difficulty they went to investigate. When they got nearer they found the object was hovering about 20 feet above the sea. It appeared to be revolving over one spot.

As they got closer, they saw a figure of a man standing on the outside of the object. This figure shone a very bright light on their boat – a light so powerful that they were dazzled and felt weak. When the boat was just over half a mile from the rotating object, the figure disappeared and the object rose straight up vertically and was soon out of sight.

October 1977

Twenty years later in October 1977, the cruise ship *SS Arcadia* had just left port in Lautoka, Fiji. It was a hot evening, just before dusk, and crew and passengers were up on deck when someone noticed a really large mass of bright red lights in the clouds.

Suddenly an immense saucer-shaped disc, nearly as long as two jumbo-jets, silently descended and hovered. It was metallic, with a dome and red lights all around. Most of the witnesses froze in fright and amazement. It then moved to the shore, inland and over the hills.

Chapter Fifteen

More Unusual and Perplexing

The 'well' that wasn't there, Mosman (Sydney) 1990

It was 7.15 p.m. one Saturday night and Andy was stretched out on the lounge watching his favourite television program:

"I don't know what possessed me," he recalled. "I wouldn't have missed that show for anything, I always taped it if I was out. I just got this inexplicable impulse to get up, jump in the car, and go for a drive. I never go for a drive at night. Maybe on a sunny day, when I have nothing to do, but certainly not after dark, when I'm enjoying the television.

"I was drawn to a spot, only five minutes away, on the Mosman shoreline nearly opposite to the Heads of Sydney Harbour. I don't even know why I went there. When I arrived at the end of the street, there were two vehicles already parked there; a fairly new white Commodore sedan, and parallel to that, a very unusual truck. I think it had a cabin, and was silver, like steel, with some red writing on it. There was an empty flat tray at the back. No sides, but six steel posts, about four feet high, sticking up in the air. I parked to the left of the truck, and got out.

"There was a rock overlooking the water. It seemed a long way down at the time. Down below there was a well of light, like a floodlight or spotlight. It was triangular-shaped, coming from the ground. In hindsight, it could have been penetrating the ground, perhaps there was sand it had gone down into, I'm not sure.

"I could see two or three people down there, on a rock ledge at water level, and I thought, although they were probably fishing, something didn't look right. There was a male, wearing white jeans and a red top, and what looked like a female in some kind of dress – it was all a bit wafty. I got the impression there could have been a third person in the shadows.

"I could see a torch being held by someone, and just after I arrived it was shone upwards, towards me, straight into my eyes. It was blinding, but they moved it after a couple of moments. It was strange, no beam of light seemed to come from that torch when it was turned away. It was dark and I was a little nervous, so I didn't walk down any further.

"Several times the male went down into the well of light, which looked about 100 feet deep, and I thought I saw a couple of steps in the shadow. He seemed to be walking down steps, by his movements when he descended. Sometimes he and the female would hand things to one another. I was quite fascinated and curious. What were they doing? It looked like they had dug down, deep into the ground. Were they burying or retrieving something?

"I had speculated it might be a film set, but there was no camera or crew, and every so often, the spotlight would turn on and off. I never heard any sound, but perhaps I was too high up to hear any quiet talking.

"I noticed a fluorescent green light, a short distance away, like a buoy bobbing up and down in the water. The male raised his arm up, like a signal, and the green light rose up in the air, like it was remote-controlled. It was bigger than a soccer ball, and flew straight towards the man. It looked like it zoomed straight into his chest!

"I didn't see what happened next. I just ran, must have got in my car. When I got back home, I was still scared. The television shows were over. I hadn't even thought to start the video recorder before I left. I had to talk to someone. My adult son was in his bedroom. I thought of ringing you then, but changed my mind.

"I drove back the following morning. The truck was gone and the white car, which was perfect the night before, was burnt out. There was charcoal and rust, the tyres were gone, and the boot off. I couldn't understand it. I had just assumed the truck belonged to the man, and the car was the woman's, as they were the only people there."

One of our investigators had known Andy for many years, and assured me of his sincerity. In fact, he presented as a very mature, intelligent professional man. He was also concerned we might think he had gone crazy, and didn't want us to divulge his name.

I have reviewed the tapes, made when we interviewed him less than two weeks later, and I am convinced he was sane and honest. He was vague and unsure of how long he had been at the scene, and when he actually got home. We could not, as ethical researchers, suggest there had been "missing time", or hint there was more to his sudden impulse than he realised. He did, however, mention being frustrated that there was something else he couldn't remember.

When he was taken back to the site, in daylight, he realised that he had not been standing as high above the mysterious people as he had thought – certainly nowhere near the 100 feet he reported. Underneath was dead-flat, solid rock, nowhere for the well of light to go, or the man to climb into, and no trace of any activity.

Poor Andy was really lost for words, and we all wished he could recall that "something" he couldn't remember.

Where did they go?

Andy's experience brought to mind some similarities with a Welsh case from 30 October 1977, documented by Randall Jones Pugh, who was a fellow member of BUFORA at the time. There was a spate of mysterious events in Dyfed, of which this was just one:

A round, flat white disc was seen moving low across the sky, at a speed of about 25mph. It headed towards a 90 foot high rocky cliff on the seashore, and without slowing down, literally crashed into it. There was no sound, no debris. It was as if it completely disappeared into the rock.

The witnesses scurried over to the water's edge, and could see two figures which looked quite human except for their heads, which looked larger than average, and more of an oblong shape. On part of the craggy rock face, there seemed to be a door, the same size as an "ordinary household door." It had a shimmering haze around it, and when, on several occasions, it quickly slid open and shut, the interior was "quite black."

One silvery-clad humanoid, seemed to be walking up and down steps, when there were no steps there. The witness insisted "the motion of the figure was such that first the head, shoulders and the chest would appear, up to about waist high, when the motion would cease and the figure would descend again." After a while the door closed, and the "energetic humanoid abruptly vanished." The cliff, on later inspection, looked quite normal.

Lithgow, NSW, 17 September 1976

A similar event was told me in the 1980s in Australia. A colleague, Martin, who was a no-nonsense army officer, claimed he was rabbit shooting (which I doubt in that area), near Lithgow, west of the Blue Mountains. Having served in the Citizens Military Force (CMF) for a short time myself, and due to his terminology, I actually suspect it may have been a night Reserve Army Exercise. However, I will reproduce his own words in his report:

"The following report was written up from fragmentary notes, and recollections of the people involved in the sighting, three years after the fact.

"The background of the people involved is military. We all served in specialist roles in the fields of intelligence, long-range reconnaissance patrols, specialist missions, ground controllers. Our training involved all forms of combat, demolitions (constructive and destructive), small arms, intelligence gathering and evaluation, Command and Control, Communications, and a host of others. Upon discharge, we joined our local CMF unit as we were still on the active list for a further five years.

"Observers involved; Sunray, Sunray Minor, Section Command 1, Section Command 2. At no time prior, during, or after the event did any of us drink alcohol, take prescribed or unprescribed drugs, nor any hallucinogenics; this is against all our training and our personal responsibilities to others.

"On the evening of 17 September we met at my place to go spotlighting for rabbits on a property at Lidsdale, near Lithgow. (This was routine procedure for us – it had several purposes, and we had permission to shoot on this property, of which the Lithgow Police were aware.) We left at 1800hrs and arrived at 1900hrs, by which time it was already dark. After assembling our weapons and loading them up, we proceeded to drive around the property on the Mini-Moke to check for likely target areas.

"As was our normal practice, we drove at low speed with only the spotlight for illumination, so when we reached a hill, and turned the spotlight on it, we were somewhat at a loss to explain a sudden increase in general illumination. It was obvious from the shadows cast that this illumination was coming from behind us.

"On turning around, we looked east, and directly above the escarpment behind us, at an altitude of about 200 metres, was a ball of light that was increasing in intensity as it moved towards us. The escarpment was about 1,600 metres in a direct line from our position. From this range it appeared to be the size of a golf ball, travelling at the speed of a light aircraft – a velocity of about 100kph. It was round, and appeared to be on fire, with flames trailing behind. The angle of descent was approximately 20 degrees and dropping, which indicated that it would impact with the top of the hill directly behind us, only 50 metres away'.

"At this point I yelled: 'Cover!' whereupon we all grabbed our bum packs and weapons, then hurriedly found depressions in the ground to take cover (abandoning the vehicle as lost). We would still be able to observe events and hopefully survive, as we expected a reasonably violent explosion.

"From our positions we had a full view of the event as it unfolded. The illumination became very bright, with a reddish-orange tinge to it, and it was absolutely silent! No sound was emitted by the object, and even though on fire, there was no whooshing of air to indicate passage, nor was there any odour as would be expected from something burning.

"Our initial estimation was correct, and the object continued on its downward course towards the hill that was now 50 metres in front of us. The hill was about 60 to 65 metres to the crown, and when close to impact, we calculated the object to have a diameter of six to eight metres.

"We observed this ball of flame impact into the hill five metres below the crown, and we stood up, dumbfounded. When we had abandoned the vehicle for cover, it was with the assumption that we would be exceptionally lucky to survive the blast from impact, let alone ancillary effects of such an event. However the object influenced the hill or vice versa, and the expected did not happen; it appeared to literally enter into the hill, as if there was an invisible doorway for it to go through.

"We got back together and began writing up what we had just seen and experienced, in the notebooks that lived in our bum packs. After ensuring no salient points had been missed, we spent the next four hours combing that hill for anything that was out of place or unusual."

"Nothing was found to indicate that anything had happened, let alone an impact of a fiery object, there was no scorched vegetation, broken trees or branches (which there should have been), no rocks disturbed or moved. Absolutely no indication that anything had transpired weeks ago, let alone very recently.

"Having come up with nothing to verify what we saw, we discussed our next course of action. It was agreed that this should be reported, so we packed up and went to Lithgow police station to report the incident. They took our details and a brief synopsis of the event, after which we left.

"The following morning I rang MI (Military Intelligence) at Holsworthy as we had discussed, and we were requested to come in immediately for debriefing. This we did, and the rest is classified.

216

"The MI at Holsworthy (Army base) in co-operation with the RAAF confiscated ALL notebooks from us, took our statements, and conducted full individual debriefs about the incident. Psychological evaluations were also conducted, after which we were instructed that nothing had happened.

"This event occurred within a six-month period of another incident at the Canungra Jungle Training Centre, Queensland (in which we were all also involved) which has been classified under National Security, hence the Official Secrets Act. This incident was also fully documented, and all evidence, drawings and notebooks were confiscated by MI."

He didn't say too much more – and I realised any further details constituted a 'don't ask – don't tell' type situation.

North Queensland

Are these disappearing objects related to military exercises? In 1994 *People* magazine published an article about a similar event. Unfortunately they did not give the date of the occurrence, so it is not known if this is the same incident Martin referred to, or a separate event:

Four Army Reserve instructors were on exercise in Northern Queensland. Their combined training and experience certainly qualifying them as accurate and reliable witnesses.

"We were using a spotlight, but turned it off when we were suddenly bathed in a ruddy glow. We turned around and saw a huge red ball, engulfed in flames, hurtling towards us, at the speed of a light aircraft. The flames left no smoke or vapour trail, and it was headed for a 200 metre cliff escarpment above the river.

"We automatically expected a sizeable blast on impact and dived for cover. There was no explosion – nothing. It seemed to enter the hill, without disturbing anything. We couldn't believe how this enormous object could simply vanish, as if it had been swallowed up by the cliff."

They were concerned about the incident starting a fire in the surrounding forest, and spent three hours searching the impact area. There was nothing, no smell or scrapes, no burnt or broken trees. In fact, no signs of any crash, or the mysterious object.

Singleton, Northern Territory, 1938-1946

These reports go back to over 70 years ago, when army personnel would move up and down the road about 50 kilometres north of Alice Springs.

They often saw green lights travelling south. They would turn on their edge, go red, and head towards the ground at some speed. They would literally appear to go into the ground. Everyone would wait for the crash, but nothing was seen or heard.

Inchbonnie–Lake Brunner, New Zealand, 25 December 1977

When I was discussing the mysterious objects that get swallowed up by the cliffs, my colleague Bryan Dickeson recalled another incident investigated in New Zealand, and kindly made his research data available:

It was just after 9 p.m. Christmas Day's evening. Mrs. Baker heard her dogs barking, and remembered she still had to refill their water dishes for the night.

"Halfway down to the kennels the dogs suddenly stopped barking, which was most unusual. The dozen or so cows in our paddock were all standing and looking at Mount Te Kinga. It was then I heard a strange humming noise.

"I looked back and upwards towards the mountains and saw these two objects approach. They swept overhead at incredible speed, (later calculated at 1,500 mph), much faster than the Wigram jets which frequently fly through the valley. They were about 2,500 feet up and descending, then vanished into the blackness of Mount Te Kinga, which is over 4,000 feet high. They did not go over or around the mountain, they just appeared to go into it.

black   white
black   white

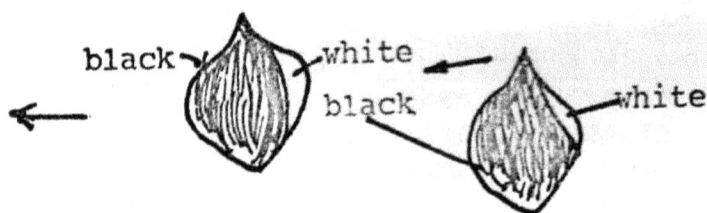

"I couldn't call my husband, as I was too dumbfounded. I could only stand and gape. I didn't mention this to anyone outside of the family for fear of ridicule, but we visited some friends two miles away the next day. They told us they were woken at 2 a.m. that morning (26 December) by a loud humming noise above their house. When they went outside the humming diminished, and gradually faded away. It was only then that I told them what I had seen the previous evening. It was too uncanny or eerie. Whatever they were, they were not of this world."

As with the previous cases, Mrs. Baker did not report any noise or indication of an impact. As this occurred during the Christmas holiday season, some locals began an in-depth investigation a few days later. There was an unlikely possibility the objects could have gone into Brums Creek, a valley not visible from the ground, and they felt it even more unlikely that the RNZAF would send a helicopter into this area.

Blueprints for a UFO? Oberon, NSW, 28 June 1992

In 1996 I received a call from a 52-year-old Polish immigrant, Wład, who stated that he was a metal polisher by occupation, and had been for the last 30 years. Before that he had been a farm worker outside of a village east of Bodzechów in Poland.

His reason for calling me was to advise of what he had seen in Oberon, New South Wales, on 28 June 1992. "I was driving to the paper shop at 9.30 a.m. one very cold winter's morning, when I noticed a huge object, about the size of a jumbo jet, but it was moving more like a kite. It was like it was trying to lose altitude, backwards. It shook sideways and up and down like a fish going up-water. I stopped the car, switched off the engine, and stopped next to my vehicle to watch.

"For a long time the aircraft went up and down before losing altitude. It then flew very close to the ground, behind the Fibron factory. It was lower than the hills, and while it changed direction in a split second, it flew directly towards me at no more than about 20kph. It passed me about 100 feet away, so low it was nearly touching the power lines and houses. At this point I can only quote what he wrote in his report, as it was rather confusing:

"It was white, black and burgundy red, and I was able to see all the details. At one time, when the engine went off, the white plates separated from the tubes, tangled on the side, making at least three big bangs on metal plates. After about 20 seconds the power went off, the plate and tubes joined together. I don't know how they joined, I didn't see any screws or pins, but the aircraft shook more when tangled.

"Dome on top of aircraft, can't see bottom or top – more like a rainbow. Some kind of pattern between nothing about three inches thick, like a three-dimensional movie in motion. The three cabin windows were coloured like lead had been added to glass – he can see you, but you can't see inside.

"It went blurry and very low before it disappeared over the houses. The day after seeing this, my short vision was damaged. I don't know if this was a coincidence or something to do with the aircraft. I enclose twelve sketches of the aircraft."

This is where his case became highly unusual and most interesting. Wład's sighting report form was in slightly messy handwriting with several spelling mistakes. His sketches were entirely different.

They were immaculate, in small block printing, and appeared to have been drawn in Indian ink. They literally detailed each nut, rivet, screw and bolt, their measurements to a fraction of an inch, and their purpose.

The blueprints estimated the craft to be 298 feet long, 19 feet high, and 100 feet across.

These sketches were so good that a skilled aircraft engineer or draftsman would have trouble emulating them. Ten sheets had been joined together to complete plans for the sides and underneath of the craft. One sheet had detailed diagrams of thirty-seven movements the object made during Wład's sighting.

It certainly did not equate with any conventional craft, unless it was some unknown test prototype.

How did Wład, in a sighting he claims lasted only 15 minutes, get all these details? It would have taken our best experts hours to measure and document them all.

Except for a couple of minor spelling mistakes, and given the vast difference between his writing style on the report form compared to these blueprints, I thought he might not have compiled them at all.

If he did, how did an itinerant worker have this skill and knowledge? And if he didn't, then who did, how, and why? Did it have any connection with the "six suns" he saw in 1960? I guess we will never know.

Wład told me of the day, in 1960, when he saw six suns:

"It was 11.30 a.m., a clear day, with no wind. I saw another sun in the west, and 30 seconds later another in the south, then one over my head. I was still trying to comprehend what was happening when three more appeared, in the east, southeast and northeast. They were all the same size as the real sun. For 15 minutes, in the clear cloudless sky, the six extra suns had an aura around them. They looked to me like powder and light, changing colours to match the surroundings.

"The air all around changed, and I got a strange feeling like 'God had come from heaven.' At midday, about 10 seconds apart, they all began to disappear like 'switched off lights'. The air was still strange and took about 30 minutes to get back to normal.

I was mystified, had he seen unidentified flying objects? Given the area was part of the old Soviet Union, was it some Russian experiment? Was that all that happened to Wład that day, or was there more he didn't remember?

Flying submarines: Tairua, New Zealand, January 1972

It was just after dawn, and a motel owner and deep sea fisherman was out in his launch with a companion, about six miles east of Great Barrier Island in the Hauraki Gulf.

The ocean is about 600 feet deep in this area, and some distance ahead of them a disc-shaped object rose out of the sea. After ascending a little way up it moved in the direction of their boat, and then sped away at about 2,000 mph.

Balmoral, Sydney 1974–75

Samuel Copper, an American engineer, had lived in Mosman, a suburb on Sydney's North Shore, for most of his life. The suburb overlooks the Balmoral Naval Base and Georges Heights Army Barracks. Shortly after an inexplicable blackout a kilometre or so to the north in Seaforth, his excited neighbours drew his attention to unusual events in the waters of Sydney Harbour, just off the naval base:

"We could see a vertical shaft of white light penetrating the water from above," he said. "We looked up, but could see nothing – was it coming from below? The light was big, about 150 feet in diameter. It moved slowly back and forth under the water for the duration of the blackout. It was different to the things that the navy usually messes with.

"My wife, Fiona, was very jittery. A short time before she had been driving north, from the Hawkesbury to Toronto in Newcastle, and had been harassed by a strange ball of lights. They had followed her, in a rolling motion, for over 60 miles – over, behind, beside and in front of the car. The locals were quite nonplussed, and said it was a regular occurrence.

"This harbour light had her convinced the aliens were still there.

"On this occasion our socialite neighbours settled Fiona's nerves with an astonishing conventional explanation. They had been invited to a party for some Russians who were visiting Sydney in a secret submarine! At first this was a little hard to believe, it was the height of the Cold War. On reflection, they must still have held meetings or negotiations. What better way to arrive and depart, undetected, than underwater!

"I was a little uncomfortable myself as I had previously seen a strange craft coming into the area. It was lower than 500 feet (under radar) and big, soundless – with a large rim of little lights around it. What was weird was I could see no body to it! My imagination jumped to some kind of cloaking device – ours or theirs?"

While other strange phenomena have been reported in the vicinity over the years, we cannot dismiss advanced military technology as being a possible explanation. Another instant is worth mentioning.

Len, a fellow researcher, had been visiting a friend on a headland near Balmoral. They had wondered about late night moving lights, muffled voices and some activity on the shore. Without warning a large craft of some kind emerged from under the water and shot up "into the sky and away", at a very fast pace. Could it be a "flying submarine"? I guess we will never know!

(Only a few years later, in 1978, an off-duty policeman and two mates were going fishing off the coast of Western Australia. They had left Rockingham and were headed for Rottnest Island. They noticed the water nearby was lit from underneath by a powerful light with a circumference of about 40 feet. The water started to foam, and there was a hissing sound. A grey-black object surfaced, rose silently above the ocean, hovered for several seconds, and took off at unbelievable speed into the northeast sky. It was described as being like two saucers, joined at the lip, with a green glow at the base.)

White death

Most of us are aware of the frantic transmissions by Frederick Valentich in 1978, when he claimed contact with a UFO before he and his plane mysteriously disappeared over Bass Strait. In late 1979 an Air New Zealand DC-10 tragically crashed into Mt Erebus during a sightseeing flight to the Antarctic.

A few days later I received a long-distance call from John Pinkney, a Victorian researcher and journalist. He claimed he had information from several ham radio operators, in Australia and New Zealand, that just before the plane crashed they had picked up a distress message stating it was being buzzed by a craft of unknown shape and origin.

I am still not sure if John was seeking further information, or just wanted my opinion. My thoughts immediately turned to a case in Madrid, a couple of weeks before. Several UFOs had pursued a passenger plane, which had made an emergency landing at the airport. My initial comment was, "They missed the Madrid plane, but grabbed one over the Antarctic instead!"

I revised that opinion later, when the official investigation determined that the plane was on the wrong course and headed straight for the mountain. I wondered if the UFO had disrupted the plane's instruments. Perhaps the unidentified craft was trying to warn them they were on the wrong course? We will never know.

I advised John he would never be able to publish this information, and felt sure the authorities would prevent it one way or another, if only for the tired old reason of "not frightening the public." John was so convinced of the accuracy of the reports that he swore he would publish and be damned. He did and probably was.

In December, 1979, the *Melbourne Truth* published his article where he stated his informants were senior RAAF officers and public servants, and the UFO messages were received in both Auckland and Sydney. Air traffic controllers and RAAF personnel were ordered to keep the UFO report top secret. The RAAF and NZAF were placed on full alert following the crash.

The Department of Transport denied any radio transmissions about unusual objects. John commented, "If any UFO evidence is found in the DC10's flight deck recording or in the black box, you can be sure it will never be publicly released."

In February 1980, John wrote in the *Daily Mirror* that two contacts had premonitions of the crash. However, they had said nothing because they did not have enough accurate details, and thought they would be ridiculed and ignored:

One Sydney woman had a dream that she was floating alongside a plane which took off from an airport. She saw it descend rapidly into a big white mass and explode. She woke in fright, feeling somehow it was more than a dream.

Another gentleman described a "vision", after he got an enormous pain in his nose, while changing his car tyre. He thought he'd been hit by something, "but then realised the pain was in my mind. It didn't stop me seeing stars, but then something else – a vivid vision of a plane hitting a steep white wall. The vision was so intense I had no trouble recognising the crash mountain when it appeared on television several days later."

Reminiscences of World War 2

One elderly gentleman wrote to us with a fascinating report of how a UFO directed him to migrate to Australia.

It was 9 July 1945, (perhaps a coincidence, around the time of our first use of atomic warfare). Jarrard was in Northern Transylvania, Hungary. It was a summer day, and there were a lot of Russian troops on the move, clogging the roads and highways. At about 5 p.m. a huge UFO flew over northern Europe.

"It was so big that it was reported as being seen in a circumference bordering Tokyo, Canada, Iceland, Finland and Italy. I swear it was 30 miles in diameter and 600,000 feet up in the ionosphere. Its vapour trail was still visible the next morning. The authorities played it down as being a close shave. It was a perfectly round, tiered cake shape."

"I was getting telepathic messages, 'You must go to Australia'. Despite the hot weather, I kept shivering and getting goose-bumps from head to toe. It was a bizarre sight to see those communist troops dropping to their knees and praying, 'Borge-moi, Borge-moi' – 'My God, My God'."

Was it a UFO or a more natural or cosmological phenomenon? We may never know. Jarrard did migrate to Australia, and his experience led him to an ongoing interest in UFOs.

Korea

Many years ago I knew two Australian ex-Korean POWs. They were always very quiet and tight-lipped when it came to the subject of UFOs.

Even earlier than the Vietnam War, some Korean War veterans reported unidentified aerial objects, which had capabilities far beyond our own airpower. In his book *Advanced Aerial Devices Reported during the Korean War*, author Dr. Richard Haines discusses the electromagnetic effects on United States Air Force and Navy planes. The description of these strange craft did not correspond with anything Soviet or American, and they were certainly not the tired, old official excuse; "a lighted enemy balloon." One GI reported a huge luminous disc hovering over his unit, which emitted an intense ray at him and his fellow soldiers.

There is now a great deal of information now available about the damnable nuisance to the United States military in particular of countless radar plots and metallic discs hurtling and hovering over the ocean.

Vietnam

An anonymous report was made in the January 2013 edition of *The Ufologist*. In the spring of 1969, a 20-year-old Australian soldier in 62nd Maintenance Battalion, was manning a 30-foot gun-tower in Plieku, South Vietnam. For five minutes he watched a yellowish glowing object about three miles away over the rice paddies. Within a split second it moved from that location to within 300 feet of his position, and hovered at a very low altitude.

It appeared to be a thick cloud, with a yellow glow coming from inside. Over the next five minutes he watched as the mist got thicker and thicker. Three or four orbs were around the perimeter, just floating at different heights and locations to the razor wire. He did not hear any noise, and did manage to take a photograph before they all "simply disappeared."

Phuoc Tuy

I knew Walter Morgan for several years, and assumed his psychological problems were post-traumatic stress caused by war service. After he confided in me, I wondered if there was more.

"I was serving with the Australian Army in 1968-69. I was on patrol with D-Company in Phuoc Tuy Province early one morning. It was a clear night, with a full moon on the horizon. We came to a clearing in the jungle, where there was a building and a bizarre object outside, about 100 metres away. It was quite clear, but kind of fuzzy at the same time. It was silent and had steady lights shining from it. It was hard to say if it was actually on the ground or hovering just above.

"Our nerves were already on edge, so this made us quite jittery. We were ordered to withdraw to consider the situation. The officer in charge broke us into two sections, and we tentatively advanced, not really knowing what to expect. As we edged closer we could see it was round, like an egg, and about the size of a double-decker bus.

"I felt weird, we all did. Maybe it was something coming from this craft or just our own fear. Every hair on my head was standing on end. It started sending out tremendous vibrations and humming and disappeared, I assume straight up. There were burn marks on the ground where it had been.

"There was no explanation forthcoming from HQ – there never was. Strange objects were often seen in Vietnam, especially during battles, and they were not known aircraft."

HMAS Hobart, 1968

Researcher Jon Wyatt wrote in the *Australasian Ufologist* that in 1968 the *HMAS Hobart* had been hit by friendly fire in Vietnam. It was claimed that it occurred during a night operation against enemy helicopters, but Wyatt suggests it was in reality a UFO story.

He relates how, on 15 June 1968, after seeing strange lights in the sky over the Demilitarised Zone, the Allied Command, assumed they were North Vietnamese helicopters. They feared another Tet-Offensive style build-up, and placed forces on stand-by, including the *HMAS Hobart*.

More lights appeared in the sky, and air, sea and land forces sprang into action, firing at the "enemy helicopters" which moved down the coast and out to sea. That is when things went wrong. Just after midnight United States Navy swift boat, PCF-19, was sunk by friendly fire – three air-to-air missiles. There was great military activity over the next few hours, and at about 3.30 a.m. the *HMAS Hobart* (blacked out and maintaining radio silence), was struck by a *Sparrow* air-to-air missile on the starboard, and then by two more missiles.

There were many subsequent enquiries. It appears that there was no evidence of enemy helicopters being present or shot down. The lights were sighted for some weeks afterwards, but were left unchallenged. Wyatt quotes the US Commander in Vietnam at the time, General George Brown, as saying, "UFOs plagued us in Vietnam. They weren't called UFOs, they were called "enemy helicopters", and were seen up around the Demilitarised Zone in the early summer of 1968. This resulted in quite a battle, and an Australian destroyer took a hit. There was no enemy involved, but we always reacted after dark."

Wyatt also quoted another retired US serviceman who claimed that upon the first friendly fire the target disappeared in a flash of light. This corresponded to a report I received from a retired navy colleague who told me: "My mate was on the *HMAS Hobart* that night. He said heat-seeking missiles were being fired at a UFO, but they deviated and hit the *Hobart* instead."

A young boy remembers: Sydney's Northwest suburbs

When she was six years old Mary was scared "something was coming to get her," and several times in her life she saw strange craft from a distance. She often felt people were trying to do psychic harm to her, and at one stage had a bit of a breakdown and was taking anti-depressants.

In 1989 the dogs were behaving strangely, and Mary and her neighbour heard a humming noise outside their houses at about 8 p.m. one night, but neither looked out.

Around Christmas 1994, Mary had an out-of-body experience, where she saw herself walking out the back door and down to the summer house. "There was an old school friend there, who persuaded me to go in, but when I did, she disappeared. I was hit with a blue beam which paralysed me. Next thing I was lying on a slab, in a big round silvery-coloured room, with red and green lights coming from the walls.

"There were five beings surrounding me. They were about four feet tall, with tan coloured skin. They had large oval black eyes, a vertical split for a nose, and a horizontal split for a mouth. They appeared to have three fingers and a thumb – all very long.

"At one stage I got angry, and when they backed off, it was with a type of rubbery movement. There was one human-looking person, about six feet tall, of ethnic appearance, brown to black hair, short back and sides, and a small, thick moustache. One time when I was trying to fight back, I remember silver discs, about the size of a dinner-plate, like little drones coming out. They weren't nice – like small robotic guards.

"None of them communicated with me in any way. While I was lying down a white sheet was placed over me. It sort of clung. I found it suffocating. Next thing I was on my side, and a needle was inserted in my lower spine – it was agonising. I had triangular tiny red marks, in a triangular shape, on that spot, for the next couple of weeks.

"It is a bit hazy, I had got up and gone out at just after midnight, but I was back in the house and the clock said 5.30 a.m. Things didn't seem the same, it was confusing."

"One night, in June 1996, I woke to the sound of Muffy, our dog, running around the lounge room, barking like crazy. All the dogs in the street were barking, I felt really weird, and even though I didn't want to, went back to sleep again.

"The next morning, when my 5-year-old son John woke, he was quite excited and said 'Oh! The aliens were here last night. Me and Gran were awake and knew something was going on because the dog was barking and shaking and was really scared'. I asked him what they looked like, and he said, 'It was a baby, a baby one. It was really little, and it had round eyes, slit nose and a slit mouth. We could hear him, but his mouth didn't move.

"When I questioned him about the skin colour he said, 'The usual colour – a sort of tan, and he had dirty-like ripped clothes on. Don't you remember; you opened the front door for him and they came in. His mother was behind him, and he sat on the lounge next to us. You were cuddling it, and it put its hands around us.' He was also saying something about 'little silver discs'. I was in shock, and didn't remember any of this."

When interviewed by investigators, young John remembered everything, and drew childish pictures of a typical "saucer" with a beam shining to the ground. One person was caught, halfway up in the beam, and another seemed to be falling out. Apparently this confirmed a 1994 incident. He claimed that his Gran was also beamed up towards the disc, but the beings threw her to the ground before taking his mother. Mary was not aware of this, but said at that time her mother had suffered a couple of fractures. The doctor said she must have fallen out of bed, but her mother had strongly denied this.

This entire sequence of events was investigated by a colleague of mine, and it presented many problems. The grandmother, a European migrant, was not prepared to be interviewed. (This is not unusual, some are steeped in superstition and religious beliefs.) Often people, especially under psychiatric care, can suffer fantasies or hallucinations. Other abductees report instances where they are in "another dimension", and psychic phenomena play a part. Many witnesses have memory blocks where it appears their recall of the experience can be erased from their conscious mind. All of these factors could have applied in Mary's case, and the X-rays of her lower spine did not show any implant or abnormalities.

The most interesting aspect, from a researcher's viewpoint, was the conscious recall of John, a young boy, whose statements and childish drawings confirmed, in part, the abduction reports of Mary, his mother, who was more worried about his wellbeing than her own. He did not appear to have been coached, and was most matter of fact in his testimony. There was nothing he said that indicated he had ever been inside a craft – mostly he talked of watching from the garden, or interacting with the beings inside their own home.

We were left with the possibility that, in erasing Mary's memories of the events, her abductors had forgotten about what young John had seen, and left his memory intact. (This is reminiscent of the 1997 Portland, New South Wales, case, when young Lucy and Peter had conscious recall of all the events which had been blocked from the memory of their mother Linda.)

Often witnesses will go from one researcher to another, seeking answers. I hoped that Mary did not – she needed professional help, regardless of the cause of her trauma.

A very confused Doctor, Southern Sydney, 1989

Sometimes we are contacted by people claiming UFO abduction experiences and we cannot in all honesty make an ethical or definitive judgement:

In 1989 I was contacted by a Sydney doctor, held in high regard by the local community. I will call him Dr. Damon Harrison (pseudonym). He was intelligent, articulate, and married with three children.

His problems began around 1970 when he was 45. At that time he worked as a government medical officer, and was accused by his workmates of being an ASIO plant (Australian Security Intelligence Organisation). In those days the security agencies did have informers in government departments. Despite his denials the continued hostility made him psychologically disturbed.

He was very interested in the moon landings as his elder brother had been a Squadron Leader pilot in World War 2. He could easily identify aircraft flying in and out of nearby Mascot International Airport, but suddenly started seeing unidentified objects in the sky.

He confided in me, "Before going to sleep, I had visions of bee-type insect beings, with fluorescent eyes and green-black striped heads. One night, in a local park, a UFO was overhead, and a blurred image appeared in front of me. While I feel I stayed away from it, I suffered a severe cough for the next two weeks."

What Damon did not know was that I had received a separate UFO report over that very park the same night. He then added that three weeks later an unidentified craft flew ahead of him, above the power lines to the old Bunnerong Power House. Partly due to this, his family committed him to a psychiatric hospital. One night he was on the patio with a nurse, and they both saw a UFO. She started to wonder about his claims, and wrote a statement for him. Later, his exasperated son tore it up, and ensured Damon received further psychiatric treatment several times after that.

Damon claimed he was suffering post-traumatic stress due to the UFOs-aliens, and admitted his psychiatric treatment.

"My family don't understand. I have telepathic communication with these bee-type aliens. Many times I have been teleported. Sometimes in my surgery I am terrified by a full feeling in my ears, and being lifted up onto my toes."

My colleague, Bryan Dickeson, insisted he interview the good doctor, as his psychological state was an unknown. He found Damon in a very agitated, hyperactive state, and had been given the classic "messages from aliens" regarding care for the planet, peace among humans, etc. The doctor showed only very similar traits to most experiencers that Bryan had encountered. However, his situation had been vastly exacerbated and worsened by the high expectations of his family.

We agreed that due to so many conflicting aspects of this, and several similar cases, it was difficult and unfair, to arbitrarily dismiss this case. We could not formulate any definite conclusion as to what really did or didn't occur. In cases such as this, I often wonder which came first – the UFO experience, or the psychological discomfort?

Do aliens have a sense of humour?

During the mid-1970s, when employed as a Commonwealth public servant, I often worked with military personnel, a few of whom were aware of my interest in ufology. One serviceman, based at Glenbrook HQ Command related how, when the RAAF had classified documents, they often used to deliver them to Richmond Air Base by hand. A motorcycle dispatch rider, would usually take the back road across the lower mountain area, between Glenbrook and Richmond.

On a couple of occasions different riders had arrived in a dishevelled state, claiming they had been "buzzed by a UFO." The craft had continued to harass them until they fell off their bikes into a ditch at the side of the road. The object then shot off and away. The RAAF had hushed up the incidents and treated them as a joke; an attitude not shared by the victims, who my informant felt were genuine and honest.

We will never know if it was aliens with a sense of humour, or more human airmen piloting prototype craft not even known to their Air Force colleagues. Due to the repeat incidents the latter explanation seems unlikely.

Time and space distortions

During our research we have uncovered some fascinating cases which involve apparent distortions of time and space. These phenomena may be associated with UFO activity, or totally unrelated:

Newell Highway – near Temora, NSW

A Melbourne couple were returning from their Gold Coast honeymoon on 30 May 1969. It was about 9 p.m. and they were driving south down the Newell Highway, heading towards Temora in western New South Wales.

Weather conditions were bad. It had been raining heavily for three days, and Gordon was driving quite slowly. Suddenly, "in a split second", he found himself off the tarmac and driving on a narrow dirt track. He followed this for a short while, looking for a place to turn.

"At this stage we thought we must have missed a detour or side track sign, as the road we were on was definitely not the highway."

After turning he headed back the way they had come. They drove about half a mile, and just as suddenly, were back on the main highway again, this time heading north. Gordon made a U-turn, retracing their route south, ensuring they stayed on the correct road.

"At precisely the same spot as before, we were suddenly back on the old dirt track! I said to Lily, 'I can't understand this – it's like we're passing in and out of some kind of time warp.' I decided to keep going as I could see two sets of wheel tracks left by other cars. The narrow road wound its way around trees and bushes and we often had to slow down to a walking pace.

"After a mile or so we reached a ford across a small creek. We stopped and checked the depth of the water – only about six inches – easy for us to drive through. We followed the other wheel tracks up the opposite bank, and as we reached the other side the rain stopped. We could see cows lying in the grass nearby, and continued slowly on, as we thought we must be near a farmhouse or property where we could get help or directions.

"There was a strange glow around the car, but I didn't pay too much notice to it at the time. I thought it was just normal mist as my headlights were on full beam, there was bad weather, rain and humidity, with trees and bushes very close. A bit further on we spotted a few kangaroos and rabbits sitting close to the track. I was amazed, I was driving only a few feet away from them, yet it was like they didn't know we were there. There was no panic to move out of the way!"

After about a mile of this strange environment, they came to another small creek without sighting any homestead, but decided to keep going. Once they crossed the second creek the strange glow around the car dissipated, and the rain started again. They followed the track for about another mile and in a "split second" again passed through "a time warp or whatever it was" and were back on the tarmac of the main highway.

"By now we were both really shaken, not sure what had happened. It was like we had been passing in and out of another dimension. We decided to call it a day, and stop at the first motel we came to. As we were registering at the office, the manager asked where we had come from. When I told him from the north he gave us a very strange look, and said he'd heard the highway to the north had been cut by heavy rain."

They settled in their room and turned on the news – astounded to hear an announcement that rain had washed away the bridge on the Newell Highway. A few cars had driven off and into the river, with two fatalities. Gordon and his wife have discussed this incident many times, and have come to the conclusion they must have bypassed the bridge when they passed in and out of some "dimension." This still did not explain how they reached the motel without crossing the river. The two creeks had been only six inches deep, something totally inconsistent with the heavy rain in the area at the time. Gordon has trouble rationalising the event.

"It may be that we were being cared for by some guardian angel or something," he mused. "I have always been puzzled at how so many thousands of people disappear every year or are never seen or heard of again in Australia. There must be a valid explanation for most, but in some cases they vanish altogether with their cars, and never use their bank accounts or credit cards again.

"I wonder if they had a similar experience to what we had, and during their passing have had an accident – hitting a tree or getting bogged down, which prevented them from getting back to the present time. I guess we will never know."

Bundaberg, Queensland

When discussing the Newell Highway case with Gosford colleagues, one recalled a similar incident that she and a friend experienced in the late 1980s at Bundaberg in Queensland. It occurred when driving back from a friend's home to the centre of town – a trip they had made many times before:

As they passed through a suburban housing estate, they turned a corner to find themselves on a dirt track, surrounded by bush.

"We stopped the car dead, and looked at each other exclaiming simultaneously: 'Where are we?' We had travelled some distance. I tentatively reversed the car all the way back down the track until we were suddenly back on the main road, surrounded by houses and bitumen once more.

"We slowly made our way home feeling quite spooked. The next day we went back and retraced our route, hoping to find a rational explanation. There was neither a dirt track nor any bush in the area. It was almost like one of those time slips people talk about, as if we'd been instantly transported back in time to when the suburb was still undeveloped."

Encounter near Grafton, NSW

In April 1996, a retired Victorian couple were returning from a "Gemfest" in Toowoomba. They had stopped near Grafton and intended camping at Minnie Waters. Both the caravan park and the lake foreshores were full-up, so they went back to the main road. Taking a side track into the bush, they found a clearing and set up camp, about four to five kilometres away.

William woke up in the early hours of the morning and left the tent to go to the toilet.

"When I got outside I was surprised to see an eerie blue light about 200 yards away. It seemed to beam down from above and covered an area of 50 feet or more in diameter over the scrub. I was puzzled. I couldn't see any object in the sky and there was no noise. On the perimeter of the whitish-blue glow there seemed to be people moving about. I counted about five figures, one was standing as if directing things, and four seemed to be gathering something. At first I thought they might be druggies gathering a crop."

William went back to the tent and woke his wife. They both watched for about 20 minutes and agreed the figures were strange. They were about 5 feet 9 inches tall, had thin bodies and large heads, with thin arms and legs. "Everything was so silent, and all sort of bluish. I felt the hair on the back of my neck rising."

They felt a little scared and retreated to the dubious safety of their tent. A couple of hours later William crept out again, but there was no sign of the strange light or mysterious figures. He was sure there must be a conventional explanation so the next morning he went to investigate the area where the light had been.

"The area was covered with very thick scrub and there was no way a vehicle could have driven in. The only marks on the track were those made by our own vehicle. We are still mystified. It was not a dream or hallucination, we both stood there and watched it for so long. There appeared to be nothing but thick vegetation over the area and no evidence or traces of activity from the night before. What had we been watching?"

What indeed!

The missing moon slides

Before my dear friend, Australian researcher Paul Norman died, he sent me copies of some amazing correspondence, dated 1971, between NSW researcher Bill Moser (deceased) and a colleague in the United States. It related to three sets of slides showing some unexplained items on the moon:

SLIDE Z6/78 FW: Taken by the *Apollo 10* crew, showing crater IAU No. 302. A very bright blue object, height estimated at over 20 feet, showing clear against background and looking a bit thicker on top.

SLIDE Z20/96 MD: Taken by *Apollo 11* crew, showing south-west part of Mare Tranquillitatus (Sea of Tranquility) with crater Maskelyne. Again, a bluish-looking globule was noticed, shaped "like an orb."

Bill had shown the slides to an Australian radio-astronomer, a government astronomer and a Deputy Director of the CSIRO, and all had suggested a proper research investigation could be done much easier in the United States than anywhere else.

He requested his colleague forward the slides to Professors Hynek and McDonald, noting he could make more copies available for any other scientists, as required.

In 1995 Paul Norman wrote to Bill Moser's colleague in the United States, who subsequently contacted seven different investigators in America trying to locate these slides and the final appraisal by the two professors.

He replied to Paul in rather mysterious terms, asking how Bill had come by the slides. Who had initiated his request to on-forward them to Hynek and McDonald, and why hadn't he sent them direct? He wanted to know the involvement of the Australian scientists and went on to say he had enjoyed meeting and talking to Dr. Lindtner and 'his death was a most unfortunate thing.'

Paul Norman wrote to me later in 1995 asking me to follow-up the slides and publicise it at a later date. However given the circumstances, there was a real possibility this may have been considered a sensitive matter. I did not pursue the slides, as obviously someone 'on-high', did not want them released or scrutinised.

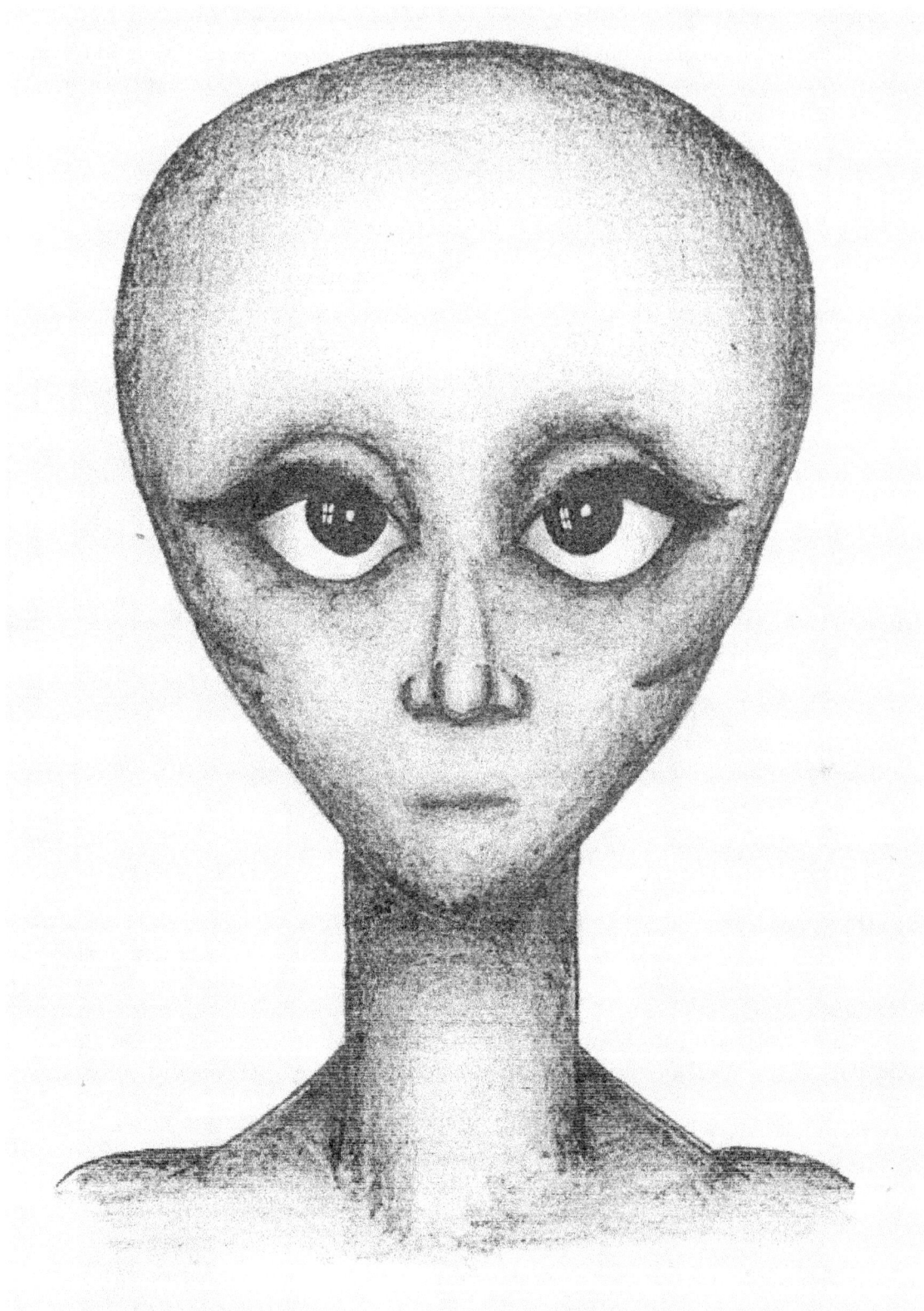

(One abductee's sketch of an alien visitor.)

Chapter Sixteen

The agony of the Abductee

This is probably the most contentious topic in the field of UFO research.

Some UFO abductees hold professional positions in the community, and it is of the utmost importance and priority to them that their confidentiality and anonymity are guaranteed. These witnesses have everything to lose and little to gain from publicity, and are often the most credible.

Some witness support structures provide a high-confidentiality buddy system whereby individual investigators share resources to provide a range of support options for abductees (hypnotherapists, psychologists, medical practitioners for implants or physical symptoms, for example), where applicable. They may also liaise with other experiencers and researchers.

Is there a role for hypnotherapy?

Sooner or later, all ufologists come across a case where the witness has apparently interacted with alien beings. More often than not there are conscious memories, interspersed with blank or fuzzy periods. Many years ago BUFORA published a paper I wrote explaining the time lapse it takes for short-term memory to transfer information to long-term memory. If this process is interrupted or blocked, data may still remain and can sometimes be accessed. (Our own scientists have been able to manipulate it for some time.) Of course, retrieving lost memory is more complex than this.

A recent problem which has cropped-up, is the increasing number of cases where there is unspoken mental communication, or telepathy, between an experiencer and the visitors, whoever they might be. In my experience this is a very real occurrence, yet I come across investigators who pronounce that it is all a personality disorder. Rubbish! I have seen enough proof that this phenomenon really exists.

In the *UFO Reporter* (Vol. 5, number 4) Bryan Dickeson wrote an excellent article, *UFO Abduction Research in NSW*. He outlined the complex psychological and evidentiary problems which exist when researching this type of incident, and interviewing a traumatised witness. Many papers have been written by professionals regarding the hypnotherapy approach, however these findings can be affected by the practitioner's own personal beliefs regarding extraterrestrials. The problems encountered during regressive hypnotherapy are many and varied, and it must be remembered that many abductees are already suffering from post-traumatic stress.

Personally, it is my preferred approach to allow plenty of time to let the experiencer recover, and allow subconscious or repressed memories to surface. Sometimes they need to relax, and talk it through until they are ready. Often memories return as disjointed flashbacks, and the investigator has to be patient. One qualified hypnotherapist tells me the majority of witnesses display conscious recall of most of their experience without the need for regressive hypnosis, however I guess this will always be a contentious issue.

It is postulated these entities can change molecular structures and use light to transport an experiencer. Once captured, their ability to not only manipulate the abductee's mind, but also to communicate telepathically and create memory blocks is extremely advanced – a superiority in mind control I am sure our own powers-that-be would love to be able to accomplish – if they haven't already mastered the technique.

Induced amnesia, while effective short-term, does not guarantee forgetfulness. Experiencers often show great mental flexibility and adaptation. They experience flashbacks and dreams, and develop great determination to regain control of their memory.

Abduction of and interference with a human being is a criminal offence in our society. However we must be careful not to infringe the sometimes fuzzy boundaries of human rights when we attempt to not only assist the abductee, but also to gain more precious details and information about the visitors and their technology.

While I was a member of BUFORA the committee decided to place a moratorium on the use of regressive hypnosis. Gloria Dixon wrote a very good summary:

"...this can be a totally unreliable method of eliciting further information about the event, not necessarily eliciting the objective truth, but the truth as the witness was able to perceive or understand it with the imagery available to them. Conscious memories, fragmented though they may be, are far more significant than those recovered under regressive hypnosis."

There were other reasons of a legal nature and possible consequences, which were outlined by the UK group MARA:

"We feel the investigations behind 'abductions' may have reached a dangerous level with regard to the effects hypnotic regression may have upon the mental health of the witness, the subjectivity of the research and the ever-increasing legal consequences if things go wrong."

This decision was reached for several reasons. There were the obvious problems of false memories planted by the abductors, suggestions made by inexperienced practitioners coupled with a subconscious wish by the witness to give the required answers, fantasy-prone subjects, reality distortions, and in some cases recall of disturbing events in the witness's personal life, such as sexual abuse etc. One of the main reasons for the stance by BUFORA and MARA were recent court cases where the plaintiffs won substantial damages payouts – claiming the effects of their recovered memories had seriously damaged their mental health.

Often it was not the person themselves, but their families who initiated the legal claim for damages. Some researchers use consent forms, but from a legal point of view these may well not stand up in court. It can be claimed that the witness was not in the state of mind to understand or that they were already delusional, and didn't have the legal capacity to give consent. A sceptical court may well consider someone claiming alien abduction is automatically delusional – and the belief of the hypnotherapist as to the client's mental capacity will probably be of no consequence.

The wise recommendation is to always utilise a recognised, qualified professional, whom the witness contacts and consults independently. (There seems to be a vast difference in the interpretation of a qualified professional – ideally he/she should be recognised by the medical fraternity and/or the court system.)

Not all agree with these opinions. Some researchers use hypnotic regression because their experiencers insist on it. I have usually followed BUFORA's practice and advised the witness of the pitfalls of hypnotic regression. I advise they must arrange this for themselves, independently of the official INUFOR investigation, and usually recommend a couple of ethical and experienced practitioners. This also guarantees them complete confidentiality. Even I cannot know the results without their permission.

Some witnesses, desperate for answers will attempt multiple sessions, with more than one researcher or support group. Bryan Dickeson and other colleagues have emphasised that usually the most accurate and valuable information comes out raw in the first two or three interviews or regressions. There are often memories, locked so deep in the subconscious, that it takes some form of often innocuous trigger to release them, and bring them to the surface. It can be many things – often a traumatic event later in life. I have investigated several cases where all the witnesses to a specific incident suddenly and simultaneously recalled it many years later, as if there had been a time-lock put into their minds.

The late Ken Phillips of BUFORA had an excellent witness support buddy system. After careful scrutiny he would match experiencers into various groups and sub-groups, and it was not only of great psychological benefit to the participants in coming to grips with their encounter, it also assisted them with greater clarity of memory. I know of a couple of cases where he actually rescued victims from well-meaning investigators who had utilised aggressive techniques and hypnotherapy to obtain as many details as possible.

Roma, Queensland, 1963

Penny Taylor rang me in 1999, still haunted by an incident which 36 years earlier in 1963, when she was twelve years old. Initially, she was very clear and concise, and I did not realise the profound effect of her experience on her subconscious.

"My father worked on outback properties, and we lived and travelled with him, sometimes doing it rough. We were driving through Queensland and had problems with our vehicle. Dad got a temporary job in town, but it would take about two weeks to earn enough money to pay for the motor repairs. We had to camp about ten miles out of Roma. There was a railway line fairly close by, at its nearest point about 200 yards away. The line crossed a bridge over a small creek.

"I didn't mind, it was an unexpected adventure. It was summer, and the weather was quite warm. One evening, just on sunset, we had finished tea and were all sitting around a blazing campfire. We first saw an approaching beam of white light, which my father thought was a train. It moved very slowly, and we could hear no noise at all. As it neared the bridge it suddenly went up in the air, just above the trees. At first it looked like a low-flying plane, and started moving towards our campsite. Dad shouted 'It's a plane, about to crash! Turn off the radio.' As I leant over the table, to reach the radio, our whole area lit up like day. The dog was cringing."

"The bright light was in fact two separate oval objects – sort of stretched out. Each was about the size of a small bus, but they had no wings. They had a bright white searchlight at the front, and an orange-blue jet, like an exhaust, at the back. There was a green lighted top, like a cockpit, and the green light seemed to ooze around the object. I felt someone was watching us from that cockpit.

"The whole area was brightly illuminated by this hovering craft. My father was a very practical bushman, and I had never seen him frightened before. He kept a 22-calibre in the tent, and was running towards us crying out: 'They've seen us! Don't move! Where's my gun?' Our fearless blue cattle dog raced for the camp, not to get the rifle but to crawl, whimpering under the groundsheet. I remember my mother screaming, 'No John', and holding my two youngest siblings close.

"That green light had an effect on me, like a vibration which made me sick with fear. I was terrified and felt like that intense white light was piercing my soul. I remember running; through a fence, and hiding under a bush. That beam of light followed me, there was no escape. It lit up my foot, and travelled up my leg. It felt warm – and was pulling at me, like some strange magnetic force. (I can't remember what happened after that, but once I had a flashback memory of telepathically talking to a bright light, which asked me about the older ones.) Next thing I was standing next to the campfire, now burnt out and dead, watching the two objects depart."

"My father came out of the tent where he and my mother were sleeping and put Roger and me to bed in the car. We were too scared to sleep, even the moon terrified us. The next morning Dad went into Roma, and while he didn't officially report the incident, the police advised there had been other reports of strange lights. The national newspapers contained articles of strange objects over Melbourne the same night. Back at our campsite the tops of all the trees were wilted.

"My father threatened us kids if we told anyone what happened, but from the start I had the feeling I wasn't supposed to say anything, not even to discuss it with the family. I did talk to my brother Roger, and we both drew what we saw. We both had conscious memories of the craft itself. I have a vague recollection of him outlining figures of little guys with big eyes, although I can't consciously remember any similar beings myself.

"He was only a year younger than me, and we were very close, like twins. We both used to be afraid of the moon, and thought 'they' were coming back. He used to scream at night the 'little people' were coming through the wall. 'Don't let them take me.' For the rest of his life Roger was frightened, always slept with a light on, wouldn't travel alone or even go out of the front door after dark.

"Except for a telepathic connection with my daughter, I never felt I had any psychic abilities except for the occasional precognition. Two days after the incident in Roma, Roger and I were watching the road outside our camp, when a car came speeding past. I pointed my finger saying 'He's going too fast', and suddenly the car rolled over. I didn't understand why he blamed me for pointing my finger.

"I have other memories from my childhood which were not important at the time, but make me wonder now if they have any significance. I had a sheltered life as a child, and lived on remote cattle or sheep properties. I couldn't read or write and was eight before I went to school. My mother never read stories to me. When I was younger, I had little friends – small chubby round mice, wearing clothes, who used to come and visit. They would take me away, outside in the air where I could see the tops of the trees below. I just thought this was my imagination.

"I remember picking flowers on the way to catch the school bus, and Roger and I saw a young boy sitting on a log near the scrub. We felt compelled to go over, but it was not a boy – it was a little man in a blue suit."

(As a researcher, my interest was immediately aroused by two important factors. Firstly, her father's reaction "They've found us!" How did he know what the object was, who "they" were, and what "they" wanted? Further, whatever had happened to Penny had also happened to her brother Roger, and yet she never seemed to remember him being present during her interactions with the "visitors." She had also made the comment that after what happened at Roma she needed to talk to someone, but her mother backed away. Her parents seemed different, and she had this weird thought that they were strange new people, and not her parents.)

Penny was now a respectable grandmother, living a quiet life in an Australian country town. For 36 years she had been haunted by the memory of that strange night. She couldn't ask her family. Her father died four years later in a mining accident, and a car crash claimed her brother. Her two other siblings were too young to remember and her 78-year-old mother was adamant that the two lights just passed overhead and kept going.

"The incident is still etched vividly in my mind," she said. "For years I was too scared to sleep in the dark. My overreaction to some normal events puzzles me. Certain noises, especially a low-pitched, pulsating drone can trigger a total personality change in me. The sound of a particular car engine in the garage beneath my flat used to make my sick and nauseous. Sometimes I suffer a combination of frantic, desperate fear and irrational anger."

Other events and flashes of memory had now prompted Penny to come forward and request assistance and possible hypnotherapy. I tried to counsel her regarding the downside of hypnosis, however she was insistent that she wanted answers as to what happened that night in Roma, and how it may have affected her family then and now. In keeping with my policy, I recommended a couple of qualified practitioners, and Penny booked the appointment herself, with Thomas – who generously agreed to see her without charge.

Penny obviously retained a lot of her lost memories that surfaced during her hypnosis session. She rang me after the first to discuss these recollections.

The encounter at Roma continued from when she was hiding under the bush, and the light was pulling at her leg. "A tubular green laser hit my forehead, and I couldn't pull away. I was in a dark room and could see little people – lights, then a time lapse. I was in a lit cockpit, with pilots moving around. They had tiny feet and shuffled rather than walked.

"They put me in this chair, and gave me this full glass of yellow stuff that they made me drink. It was like cordial gone wrong – kind of salty, horrible. It made me vomit. They made me wait, and this little man came up and stared at me. His eyes seemed to penetrate me and I get this message that I'm 'theirs' and it's just me they want.

"I could hear them talking, but couldn't understand. They held me down and put a probe in the back of my head, connected to a wall panel with dials which they adjusted. It really hurt at first, and I felt like being sick again. I started to understand in my mind what they were saying: They wanted me to learn. I should understand, they cared for the earth. They asked if I believed in God,

I must believe as our God is their God. Visual things started flashing through my mind, my brain felt like a merry-go-round. Disease, animals and people dying, fish dead in the ocean, and an explosion, like a bomb. Images flashing through my brain. There was this cable in my head, and I could read alien writing, one word was 'Peace', but I got the impression they didn't like us, we were a threat to them. If we didn't stop being evil, they would destroy us, the whole world."

What Penny told me next was nothing short of a familiar horror story. "It's a bit disjointed but I can remember the lady. She was very nice and her skin was so soft. I was lying on some sort of table and she kept telling me I was their little girl, and they pricked my finger with something sharp. I can remember tests. Something being put on my nose, sticky stuff, and a horrible smell, like gas. Then something smooth, like a drill going in or out of my nose. It hurt! A bit was taken out of the top of my leg, (I still have a scoop mark). A probe or something was put in the left-hand side back of my head. It was very painful when they took it out.

"The 'nurse' took off my pants from under my dress, and the doctor was looking into me. He was doing something. It hurt. After a few minutes they told me they had taken my eggs, but at twelve years old, I didn't understand about ova, and thought they were talking about chooks. (There was a round bowl with gunk and blood in it, and it was only after my periods started three years later, doctors realised I was missing one ovary and had fallopian tube problems.)

"There was a little female making a swishing noise as she went in and out of the room, talking to the little 'doctor', about equipment I think. She put my clothes back on and prodded my forehead, and then said she was my mother, and the last time she saw me I was a small baby. I couldn't believe this little lady was my mother. She wanted me to stay and go with them. I didn't know and started crying.

"The little pilot took me over to the cockpit to show me how the craft flew. I was taken on a trip as a treat. For a long time. From darkness into daylight, where I could see trees and the ocean, and forests and snow-capped mountains. While we were travelling I could feel a vibration and hear a noise. He said it was the motor. During the trip I was offered a little round wafer biscuit – some sticky brown-black substance which tasted fishy, and a glass of something which looked like milk, but tasted like water. They asked me again to stay with them, but all I wanted to do was go home, especially to my brothers.

"The little lady said she loved me, and while her heart was broken, she could understand my love for my brothers. I was only a little girl, and when I was ready they would come for me. I can remember starting to cry at that time, and being torn two ways.

"The doctor put some form of light in the right-hand side of my head, and told me I was clever, smart. This was so I would remember, and know when they were coming. They flicked a switch on the box and I felt sick, oozy and emotional – like I could read their minds."

When asked, Penny said that she has seen them three times since. She considers the little alien may well be her mother, and almost feels like she is abandoning her when it is time to go.

"I still wanted to go back to my family, and became excited when I looked out of the front windscreen and saw the light on our camp below. We stopped; the little 'doctor' said 'Go to sleep', and the next thing I remembered was being next to the dead campfire and the two objects leaving.

Initially Penny sent me several drawings of the craft and beings as she remembered. She later asked me to return those pictures, which I did. They were her property, and ethics prevent me from reproducing them. However I can describe them as best as possible:

The Beings

They appeared to be short, about four and a half feet tall, bald with a high, broad forehead, tapering from the eye bone to a pointed chin, totally black round eyes, tiny nose, slit mouth, and no teeth. They had pale white skin and their hands were slim, with only four fingers (no thumb). The middle finger was longer, the little finger smaller, and they had black nails, like a monkey.

There were two drawings of pilots, both "males" wearing a type of blue metallic overalls – no front opening. The insignia, embroidered on both their shoulders differed. One was a gold eagle, with the feathers in detail. The other was a bull, with a red, brown and black bar across the face. A third picture was of a "male doctor" in blue overalls with no insignia. The last sketch was of a female "nurse" wearing rusty metallic overalls, with three white birds in flight on each shoulder.

The craft was a typical rusty-coloured flying saucer: a wide, flat circular base with rounded dome top. Oblong windows surround the base where it meets the dome. Above them, at the bottom of the dome, some larger windows, with two figures standing, as if it is the equivalent of a cockpit.

Inside the Craft

The interior appeared to be circular, with a lead-coloured dome ceiling, with what looked like vents, which tapered, meeting the wall at about five feet in height at the lowest point. The floor was a dull colour, and part of the walls looked like finely-grooved lead. She drew herself sitting in a chair on one side of the round room, with a cable, attached to her head, plugged in to the wall behind. In front of her on the other side was a door, next to what seemed to be a control centre, with four chairs in front of consoles, which looked out on large windows where she could see the dark sky and stars outside.

There was one very interesting sketch of a device placed on her lap, which looked like a computer or iPad screen and was attached to a cable. She had noted that the screen rolled from left to right. (The characters on-screen were very similar to those written by contactee Trevor Hare, from the Northern Territory.) In the two final sketches, one showed four little figures with the caption: "They came at me with little torches; the room was dark." The other was a scene of a grassy plain in front of snow-capped mountains, presumably a destination in her "trip."

Penny had several children. One daughter, Clara, who looks very much like her, and they have a telepathic communication. "We are so close, we went to two separate libraries one day, and came back with identical books. She is also scared to look up at night, and says: 'They'll come.'

"In 1990, when Clara was twelve, we were staying at Lightning Ridge. Clara had said she had a 'terribly annoying night', and it was only recently I asked her about it:

"She had 'woken up at about 3 a.m., and heard a noise from the porch, and lay in bed wondering what it was. I went to get up, but there was a blue light, coming from the roof and filtering all through the house. I felt doped and went back to sleep, but when I woke up in the morning, I didn't remember sleeping.'

"Clara said she had run out the front and thought she saw the police outside with flashing lights. This was unlikely, as the town only had two policemen on duty, and one car. When I asked further questions, Clara said she wanted to distance herself from what happened back then."

(Penny's case was unusual. Many female abductees whose reproductive system has been 'interfered with', claim they have mothered hybrid children. Here was a witness claiming she was an alien-human hybrid. She is not the only female abductee who has mysteriously had one ovary removed or severely interfered with at or before puberty.)

Sometime after the hypnosis Penny wrote to me. She regretted the hypnosis and said, "If I could have it over again, I would want to live with the questions of what happened that night in Roma."

Following the hypnotic regressions with Thomas, Penny was very traumatised and see-sawed between confiding in me and becoming hostile. In March 1999 she requested I give back her copies of the tapes. She wouldn't accept my explanation that I didn't have them, as she had made her own appointment with Thomas, and I was not party to that. It was a matter of confidentiality between Thomas and herself; he could not allow anyone access without her consent. Further if, as in her case, the session revealed distressing details, Thomas was ethically bound to go through the tape with her, and provide the necessary counselling before releasing them, or gaining permission from her for me to have a copy.

Thomas told me he considered her case very genuine but also traumatic, and the details she had given me corresponded with the hypnotic regression. He noted she had reverted to an immature 12-year-old during the session: crying for her Daddy, or giggling when the aliens felt her teeth, and tried to copy her smile with their little mouths, and crying when they hurt her. Even her voice had changed to that of someone much younger.

Penny was refusing to return for the counselling visit, and therefore I could not have access to the tapes I was not able to adequately assist her without knowing if Thomas recommended professional counselling, or the 'buddy system'.

She became so hostile and abusive that Thomas refused to co-operate with any more hypnosis for abductees. I had been prepared to assist Penny, as I knew other women who had endured similar experiences, including losing ova at a young age, and being left with permanent reproductive damage. They would have assisted with confidential support, provided I could guarantee their own privacy and security. This was inadvisable as Penny, in addition to her hostile attitude, had contacted other researchers and made several defamatory remarks. I decided discretion was the better part of valour, and withdrew from the case altogether.

About six months later a letter was published in a UFO magazine, which I assume was from Penny, as the details were very similar. There was no mention of the more distressing details, and I don't know if they were deliberately omitted or she had blocked them from her mind. Unfortunately, she made no mention of getting any professional help or counselling.

Trevor Hare

Trevor first rang me in 1995, by which time he was not only a respected geologist, he had a commercial pilot's license and trained air cadets for the RAAF.

He was originally from Washington State in the United States (near the Canadian border). In 1982, when he was fifteen, he and many other witnesses, observed a round football-shaped craft, at treetop level in the east, doing aerobatics and making erratic movements in the sky. It was about 11 p.m. one week night during the June-July summer holidays. He and his mother watched the big reddish-bronze object from their garden.

"It had a fluorescent glow, and after a few minutes darted off to the south-east, at incredible speed. Mum reported it to Allen Hynek, at CUFOS I think. Apparently it had also been reported by two families returning from a camping trip to some cabins in the mountains. It was only many years later I wondered if my mother had any previous knowledge or experience of UFOs that she had never mentioned. How did she know about CUFOS or Allen Hynek?"

In 1988 Trevor was working as a recently-qualified geologist at the Roxby Downs, Olympic Dam Uranium Mining Project, some 250 kilometres north of Woomera in South Australia. His main job was analysing ore samples, and he worked rotating shifts. He and his pregnant wife had their own home in town, 15 to 20 minutes' drive away.

"This particular October night I was rostered to work midnight to 8 a.m. I had been lying down and at 11 p.m. got up to get ready for work, leaving Lynn asleep. I left about 11.15 p.m. to arrive at about 11.30 p.m., giving me a chance to have my regular coffee and chat with colleagues before starting my shift. I also liked to get there early, to show off my new RX7 white sports car, the only one in the district and the envy of all.

"It was a very clear, starry night, a bit hotter than usual. Everything was the same as any other trip for the first ten minutes. Nearly halfway to the mine gates I caught sight of a very bright, white, solid light on the right-hand side of the road. It was pretty close, moving slowly west to east over the desert scrub. I was really puzzled as to what it was, as there were never any helicopters around there. I pulled up the car, and the object also stopped and hovered for about a minute. Suddenly it darted straight up in the air at incredible speed, paused, then shot back to the west very fast.

"I drove off again, wondering what it could have been. About two minutes later I reached a small rise, and was astounded to see a similar (or the same) light, much closer than before, on the ground in the bush. It looked bigger but the same brilliant white, about 40 feet across. It was metallic, saucer-shaped with a dome on top, and a blue fluorescent haze at the bottom. It was hard to see what lay under the light, but I could detect a slight shadow underneath."

Trevor seemed confused. "I have vague recollection of getting out of the car to see if there were any other witnesses coming up or down the road. I don't recall any, and my immediate memory is of proceeding along the road to work."

When Trevor arrived, he couldn't understand why the place looked so deserted and thought something must be wrong with the mine. "I wasn't wearing a watch, but estimated it must be about 11.45 p.m., even allowing for the time I pulled up at the side of the road. The place should have been buzzing with the shift change-over. I went into the Geo-Room, and then down to the underground Cribb room for a cup of coffee. I was surprised to find my supervisor there, worried as to what had happened to me – it was 1 a.m.!

"A couple of days later I was shopping in town, when a colleague from the machinery section asked if I had managed to get my car repaired. I didn't know what he was talking about. He explained that on the night of the sighting he and a friend were also driving to the mine for the midnight shift. He said, 'We saw your white sports car at the side of the road at about 11.45 p.m. We thought you must have broken down and pulled up to see if we could help. You weren't in the car or anywhere around, so we thought someone else must have given you a lift'.

Trevor asked, but they hadn't seen anything else – not the UFO or anything unusual. He didn't have the courage to raise the matter with other workmates.

Since that time Trevor started to be plagued by sometimes frightening, strange dreams, and mysterious occurrences which disrupted his previously stable life and marriage. He told no-one, not his mother, or even his wife from whom he separated soon after. His main reaction to everything was one of denial, trying to explain everything in conventional terms. He moved from place to place, trying to escape the dreams and phenomena.

Trevor first rang me in 1997, not quite knowing where to turn, or who to trust. The only person he had confided in was his current girlfriend Doreen. He was having bad dreams once or twice a week, often only remembering just after he awoke, but not later. He had recollections of faces and black eyes like in movies etc. but wondered if exposure to the media had affected his thinking. He was Catholic, and having trouble coming to grips with this problem.

In September 1994 he had a girlfriend, Tracey, and while they didn't live together she often stayed the night. "One night I was experiencing that same dream-like state I had become used to, when something told me to move my arm up, which I did, only to deflect a blow from Tracey. I woke to find Tracey sitting up in bed, throwing blows in all directions. She seemed to be freaked out, petrified with a blank stare. She wouldn't say what was wrong, or what she had seen.

"The next morning she was still traumatised, but later described waking and seeing five people, or beings. Two of them were holding her down, and three were holding me. She had started hitting out at them in terror. Tracey was so devastated she ended our relationship."

In January 1995, Trevor moved to Katherine in the Northern Territory. He rented a caravan, down a dark road on a secluded vacant block of land. There was an industrial property next door, with a lot of barbed wire fence around. By this time he had started a relationship with his new girlfriend, Doreen – a sane, intelligent woman who held a senior administration position at work.

"It was only two days after I had moved in, and Doreen and I went to bed before midnight. Suddenly I woke to the same sensation. I felt strange, and just lay there thinking, 'No, they couldn't have found me already.' The curtains on the windows blocked out nearly all light, but the van was flooded with a bright white light. I wasn't scared, and the light was soft. It didn't hurt my eyes. I couldn't move, but I didn't really want to.

"Two months later, in March, I woke up, but my eyes were still shut. I felt a bump on the van, like someone was shaking it, and heard the sound of running steps – it was a human sound. I got up and went outside. It was a clear night, no-one was in sight. Not even a kangaroo could have got over the barbed wire fence.

"I looked around for Oscar, Doreen's blue heeler dog. He was normally very boisterous, barked a lot and chased kangaroos. He is also very protective, and will attack anyone who threatens his 'people'. He was not in sight, which was very out of character. Eventually he came out from

236

under the van. His behaviour was weird, he was really placid and kept trying to push his way into the van with us.

"I thought Doreen was asleep when I came back into the van, and left it to the next morning to discuss it. She remembered the noise and waking up, but then couldn't move. She didn't recall my going outside, and said she seemed to lose time, like someone had thrown a switch."

"The next day Doreen was on an evening shift and had gone to work. I was alone in the caravan, and went to bed. I vaguely remember more light, and woke at 4 a.m., totally disorientated, and lying the wrong way around in bed. I put the light on and found my pillow, standing on end, at the other end of the van. I tried to rationalise that I might have been sleepwalking, but due to the positioning of the furniture in the narrow van, I couldn't have even thrown the pillow there."

The next night Trevor dreamt that he was sitting at a desk writing symbols. At 8 a.m. he woke, got up, and found a pen and paper on the table. He hadn't put it there. The pad was covered with strange symbols, which he feels must have some connection with his dream the night before. He also realised that this time his memory wasn't totally blocked, as it had been on previous occasions.

"My mind kept thinking of words to which I would immediately write down a symbol I wouldn't even understand. It would even happen when I was driving the car, like my mind was possessed or being controlled. Things kept flooding into my head and I kept jotting them down. I went to the State Library. The nearest language I could find was Arabic, but it wasn't the same. I tried to copy the original symbols written on the pad, but could not duplicate the actual style. I assumed I had written them in my sleep that night. If I didn't write them, who did?"

Trevor and Doreen got a flat together in Darwin, and we became friends and kept contact for several years. He did have more visitations, less traumatic, and only when he was alone.

Without warning he just disappeared, without a trace. I wondered if he was still running, as many experiencers do, and can only hope that he is still alive and well.

Casino, NSW, 16 March 1996

In 1996 I received a verbal report from "Stan and Wanda Langer", intelligent, educated business owners, who showed great courage in coming forward with their disturbing encounter. They had a great deal to lose, and nothing to gain. Colleagues Bryan Dickeson and Barry Taylor conducted extensive investigations into this complex case. Although the witnesses were extremely honest and genuine, I am not going to take advantage of their permission to use their real names, and will adhere to my policy of pseudonyms.

Sometime after 7 p.m. on Saturday 16 March, 38-year-old Stan, his wife Wanda, and their two children Steve and Bella, were driving south on a 130 kilometre trip from Lismore to Grafton. They were five kilometres north of Casino when Stan saw two bright yellow lights with white haloes (which later merged into one), in the rear vision mirror. At the same time, Wanda noticed, about 100 metres to the front left of the vehicle, a large spherical cluster of some 200 small white and bright green fairy lights.

They were sure these events lasted less than a minute, but when they arrived home realised their journey had taken over 75 minutes longer than normal. Despite the long trip, they both felt unusually alert and energised.

The next day the whole family developed severe cold symptoms. Stan had a blister on his right toe and a runny nose. Wanda had a sore throat and the left side of her abdomen hurt. Both had red marks on the back of their necks. Steve had mucus with traces of blood streaming from his nose and had trouble sleeping for the next fortnight.

Both Stan and Wanda were sent for separate hypnotic regressions, so their reports were independent, and initially unknown to each other. Wanda's regression was more vague and blurred than Stan's recall, which I will detail later.

Wanda found herself in "an unknown space somewhere", lying on her back on a table. There were eight to ten faces around her, which seemed to be wearing "ice-hockey" type masks. She could not see their bodies from her position. She recalled bright lights and a mechanical arm nearby. She couldn't remember any communication with the entities or any physical examination, although she recollected being "levitated from time-to-time."

"Then I was back on the ground, being carried by the beings back to the car on the other side of the road. They put me back in the seat. I got the impression they were after Stan, and that this time around I had been taken along as well.

Under the first of several hypnosis sessions Stan remembered that after they saw the lights, their car was stopped at the side of the road. Above the car, from "some point in space", he could see himself and his family "asleep."

"I could see two beings, each about seven feet tall, smoke-like skin colour, no nose as such (just two dots) with small pointy ears and mouth (no lips), and big black eyes. I helplessly watched as these aliens opened the car door and carried me out. Two more took Wanda out, and a smaller one took Bella from the back. They had trouble with Steve's baby-seat and he was still in the car.

"I looked down as they laid me on my stomach, on the ground, and pressed some form of staple-gun into the back of my neck and put something in my big right toe. At this stage I seemed to return to my body. I stood up and leaned against the boot of the car and could see Steve running around with two little aliens of his own size, at times they seemed to be laughing and talking to each other. Larger beings were putting Wanda and Bella back into the car and doing up their safety belts.

"Around that time I found I could communicate telepathically with them, and asked what they wanted. They told me they were a lost family and conveyed the impression they wanted samples. Suddenly I noticed about twenty-nine aliens in the paddock, and a spacecraft overhead. At first they said: 'We want you.' I indicated that I couldn't go with them as I had my family here on earth. Suddenly they were all gone from the paddock.

"Next thing I found myself naked, on a table somewhere, with different creatures looking at me. I started yelling I wanted to go home to my family – and all of a sudden I was calm and sitting up with a thick rubber blanket around my waist, and looked out the window, to see that while it was dark, there were tall, high rise buildings out there.

"The room around me had the table, with a mechanical arm with four claws at the end. A powerful set of lights were to my left, and three round lights overhead."

His next memory was of being back in the car, but the second hypnotherapy revealed many more details. It certainly appeared that these beings had the ability to levitate a person both bodily and as a type of astral projection.

(The experience of viewing one's body from above is a phenomenon experienced by a couple of my own acquaintances while involved in an accident or on a hospital operating table.)

Stan continued: "This time I went from being on the table, to looking down from above, separate from myself below. The beings were six to seven feet tall with a wrinkled appearance and long necks. They were inserting a rod into my right eye, which was uncomfortable – and then dabbed it with some form of tissue once the rod was removed. Something was drilled into my right toe, and I was levitated up into the air while a silvery rod was inserted into my rectum and I could feel it moving around inside me as it took bone samples from my spine and pelvis.

"After the examination I saw a pyramid-shaped glass object which was apparently a baby incubator. It contained two five centimetre long pink baby aliens, facing each other."

Stan's memory then was the same as before, when he was sitting on the table, but this time the aliens were all around him. Two very small ones were standing at his feet, and he was telepathically told that he was their father.

Some of Stan's recall came as a surprise to him and everybody else, and made sense of Wanda saying she thought the aliens had come for Stan, and not her. Stan's second regression revealed previous encounters at the age of four, eight, and fourteen.

"I was four years old and I could see myself standing in the backyard. There was an alien there who took me into the shed and physically examined me. He checked my toes, calves, biceps, fingers and chest. I called him 'Mr. Ant' as he had a rubbery body and large black eyes. I walked

238

around the side of the shed and saw an egg-shaped spacecraft floating just off the ground. One alien asked me if I would like to go for a ride, and I was levitated up into the craft. We went backwards and forwards before I was levitated back to the ground.

"At eight I watched as two craft landed; one in our backyard and one in a nearby paddock. I ran to the one alien as it walked down the ramp, and it patted me on the head as I walked back to the shed with it. The same physical examination was done, as we walked back to the craft I asked to go in.

"I was fourteen years old, when my father and I saw a UFO in the backyard. I was levitated up into it, while he seemed frozen in space. I was running around playing with aliens of my own age, and when I was told it was time to go, I wanted to stay with them. All of a sudden I was back with my father, who has always refused to discuss that UFO."

Stan's memory after the incident on 16 March 1996, was of suddenly being back in the car, as if he had been asleep. He patted Wanda on the knee, and both she and Bella woke up. Steve was already awake, and they drove back to Grafton. "Not long after we arrived I looked through the study window and saw a small craft just outside in the backyard. I asked what they wanted and they said they were making sure we got home safely."

It is also of interest that there were many sightings of yellowish lights, surrounded by a white haze, over Grafton after their encounter that night.

Stan did have another regression session where he remembered an alien who was not as pleasant or benign as he originally thought. This distressed him, and the session was terminated early.

John Auchettl of PRA (Victoria) who also greatly assisted with the investigations, flew to Lismore and then conducted a flyover of the landing and abduction site, but could not detect any unusual geomagnetic or gravity anomalies.

Gundiah, Queensland, 4 October 2001

This case attracted some publicity at the time. I have still given this abductee and the two witnesses pseudonyms, as they need to be able to get on with their own lives free from harassment. Investigated by two prominent researchers, and the subject of television coverage and an article in a prominent magazine, the case was contentious, but certain aspects indicate she was indeed telling the truth. Although some sceptics have suggested it was an elaborate hoax, I do not agree.

The basic facts are that Andrea Reynolds was taken from Gundiah, 250 kilometres northwest of Brisbane at 11 p.m., and found, two and a half hours later, at 1.30 a.m. in McKay, 800 kilometres away. The aviation records show that there were no private jets that night, the only known possible way to make that journey within the proven timeframe. Andrea, her husband Kevin and friend Paula were all intelligent enough to know that you do not involve the police if you are going to pull a stunt, and Kevin and Paula's actions were all consistent with the circumstances as reported. Their characters were attested to by local townspeople, and they suffered considerable financial loss by having to close their business for some time, due to the publicity.

Andrea and her husband, Kevin, along with their business partner Paula, were living in a caravan and annex on a property they were developing. At 11 p.m. that night Kevin had gone to bed, and Andrea had fallen asleep on the couch, in front of the television in their annex lounge room. Paula woke suddenly, and when she walked into the annex saw a rectangular beam of light being projected, through the open window, from a disc-shaped object hovering outside. Suspended in the beam was a sleeping Andrea and a few items off the coffee table which had been beside her.

Paula fainted for a few moments, and when she came to Andrea and the craft were gone. She screamed for Kevin, who came out to find the window flyscreen torn and open, and the contents of the coffee table strewn on the floor underneath. At first Kevin did not believe Paula, but Andrea was nowhere to be found.

At 11.40 p.m. Kevin called the very sceptical local police, who arrived about 1.10 a.m., to investigate what they thought might have been foul play or murder. They investigated the torn flyscreen and one bush outside, which seemed to have been affected by heat. While they were still searching the property, they took a call Kevin received from a woman in McKay, nearly 800 kilometres away, saying Andrea was in hospital there.

Andrea later recounted her memory of the events. She could remember falling asleep on the couch, and the next thing she was lying on a bed with a thin sheet up to the top of her legs. She got up and cautiously inspected her surroundings. The room was semi-lit, with the light appearing to come from the ceiling and walls. The floor was a dull grey and it was devoid of any furniture except the bed. It looked like it was an internal area as there were no windows or control panels.

She could not see or hear anybody, so she started screaming out asking where she was and why? A robotic voice told her to remain calm, and asked permission to enter the room, and her questions would be answered. It was such a strange monotone voice she asked what he looked like and he said "like a man, a humanoid." He said he would release her if she would at least talk to him. She agreed and got a shock when the wall seemed to move away and a six-foot tall "man-like" person entered the room.

He was wearing a grey bodysuit of fine, smooth fabric unlike anything she had seen before, and a face-fitting mask which looked like the pictures people draw of aliens. Before she left he revealed part of his face, and he had blue eyes, similar to a human!

He told her that he was a biologist from another planet far away, and he and a geologist companion were travelling through the galaxy, and hoping to gather information about earth and its inhabitants along the way. They were keeping to the "dark side" of our planet, and their scans had picked her up when searching for organic specimens. They wanted to carry out experiments without being witnessed, and it was too late when they had already taken her on-board.

A small shorter version of him then inserted a metal probe into her thigh, and put two circular discs in her heels. (Later photographs were taken of triangular marks on her right thigh and marks on each heel.) She consented to this as he told her it was merely to monitor her bodily functions

She asked about where he came from, what were they like? He told her there were many like him throughout the galaxy, but their bodies are all genetically engineered. Their planet is sterile; everything is made of miniature computer chips, and air, food and water are all manufactured. He told her they don't eat and have no emotions.

From an investigators point of view this made disturbing sense. Our own scientists have recently warned about the dangers of modern technology and robotics to the fate of mankind and our own humanity. Could previous contactee' be right when they say these aliens, so similar to us, are seeking to discover the secret of our souls, spirituality and emotions, qualities they have lost?

Before she was returned to earth he showed her his workstation which comprised some chairs and a big screen which looked holographic. He also assured her she would never see him again. She fell asleep on the bed before waking up in the bush near McKay.

Although reports have Andrea being located at 1.30 a.m., it may have been earlier, making her 800 kilometre transit-time even shorter. She had woken up "in the middle of nowhere", feeling alone, disorientated and confused. She was on the ground, with trees around, and she stumbled through the bush for some time before coming to a road. She saw a petrol station in the distance, walked to it. At first she didn't know who or where she was. A passing female motorist took a somewhat distressed and dehydrated Andrea to McKay hospital, and then rang Kevin. At that stage Gundiah police contacted their counterparts in McKay, to be incorporated into the investigation, making a total of three police stations in all. They went to the hospital, and later took her sworn statement at their police station.

Kevin and Paula both immediately went to McKay to be with Andrea. Over the next few days they moved to at least three different motels due to not only the publicity, but also a claim that they had experienced what could have been a men-in-black experience. They had been followed by a high powered, dark brown four-wheel truck, which frightened them.

They were also being contacted by well-meaning researchers, who were very frustrated by Kevin's attempts to protect a very fragile Andrea, by supervising all interviews by both the media and investigators.

The most intriguing aspect of this entire incident is a detail I have not seen any discussion about. Andrea's captor looked human, but was wearing a mask to resemble a typical alien. It therefore begs the question, are human-looking extraterrestrials wearing masks to detract from their true identity, or are terrestrial MI-LAB operators masquerading as aliens?

Many current debates are centred on human/military black-operations experimentations masquerading as extraterrestrial abductions. One interesting factor would suggest this encounter may not have been with someone terrestrial. The humanoid indicated he was aware people were looking for her. Our own technology would have ensured Andrea was left close to home, as he intended, not nearly 800 kilometres away.

While the original investigators consider this affair to be an "elaborate hoax", the Queensland police refused a Freedom of Information request to release any documents about the incident. Andrea, Kevin and Paula found the publicity prevented them, at great personal loss, from continuing their vineyard project on the Gundiah property and returned, or more likely fled to the United Kingdom. Perhaps they just wanted to get on with the rest of their lives.

Australian researchers were still trying to locate them overseas, although I don't know why when they had already publicly stated it was fraudulent!

Since there is no real proof of any hoax, and only the evidence as presented, it is up to your own judgement to decide about this case.

Greenhill, NSW, 8 April 1971

This was not the first reported case of someone being levitated through a window – in Andrea's case it was only a mesh flyscreen. In a similar incident, reported by the *Macleay Argus*, it did not quite go as our visitors planned:

On 8 April 1971 a man from Greenhill (northwest of Kempsey in NSW) had gone into his darkened kitchen to get a glass of water just after 10 p.m. As he tipped his head back to take a drink, he could see a strange face pressed against the window in front of the sink. It was like "a small saucer", with features but no hair. He got a shock, but could not run. Instead he found himself suddenly drawn head-first through the glass window as if he was "sucked out by some unknown force."

His wife heard the breaking water glass and rushed into the kitchen to see her husband's hips and legs disappearing horizontally through the window glass: "He was not struggling or thrashing about at all, just going through." Later investigation showed it would have been almost impossible for him to achieve this alone. However I suspect he may have already been immobilised.

His seven-foot fall onto his back on the steps and the ground below should have caused more injuries than a couple of minor cuts to one hand and arm. (However, if a body is totally relaxed it suffers far less injury than one which is rigid on impact.) His wife raced outside, and couldn't believe that instead of being at least stunned or injured, he jumped up and ran down the road very distressed.

This leads me to believe that whatever induced state he was in, once he hit the ground the link was broken. He could not remember much after he first saw the face at the window, and didn't recall going through the glass. He was found some distance away, crying and shaking, begging his wife not to leave him alone, as he was frightened.

Several Kempsey witnesses had reported unusual bright lights in the sky between 6.10 p.m. and 6.30 p.m., and had seen an "object come to ground" on a scrub covered reserve, just over one kilometre from our poor victim's residence. While he did not previously believe in ghosts or men from space the incident had terrified him so much he refused to live in the house again, and moved to Sydney, asking his wife to join him there.

Leura, NSW, 5 December 1993

More frequently these days we are told of incidents where abductees experience interactions with beings on an inter-dimensional or telepathic level, almost like an out-of-the-body scenario. In this case Maria Talbot was at least able to fight back, and consciously confront her abductors:

"The first time I saw a UFO was from the top of a building on 47 Street, Manhattan, New York in 1974. I was, alone, relaxing on the roof, looking up at the clear blue sky. A round white light, like a Frisbee, was rotating sideways in the middle of the sky. It went upwards at lightning speed and disappeared from view.

"For years since then I've experienced paralysis. Usually it starts with feeling a presence in the room, and then the paralysis and inability to think. The few times I'd tried to open my eyes I passed out. This was the first time that I had been able not only to open my eyes, but stayed conscious to see the space craft.

"On this Saturday night I went to bed in my son's room, because he had a habit of waking up crying in the middle of the night. I had noticed a weird humming, but didn't give it much thought. As soon as I lay down, my body was paralysed. I couldn't scream, open my eyes, or think. I struggled to create a thought, and finally succeeded by mentally saying. 'It is against the universal law to act against my will'. When that whole thought was formed, I was still paralysed, but able to open my eyes.

"Right above me was this space craft, hovering. It seemed as big as the room. It was a silver colour, with dark grey partitions and a grey spiky thing hanging underneath. (It looked like it hooked onto something else) I was terrified. It felt ominous, like it was there to collect me. I tried to scream, because I felt I was going to be pulled into the ship. Finally I was able to manage a yell for help to my husband Martin, and bolted for the door, where he met me. (At this time the craft disappeared.) I was still screaming, and eventually tried to tell him what had happened. He said he had heard the weird humming noise, but also hadn't given it much importance.

"I developed severe toothache, and the dentist said the tooth had split under the bridge, he didn't know how. When he did the extraction, there was a white thing in the tooth, partially sticking out."

Maria had been ignored by several investigators she tried to talk to, so we arranged for her to see a hypnotherapist, but this was only partially successful. She recalled lying on a table by herself. There were normal humans around, quite tall. It felt like these were people she knew before, but she was still afraid.

She had a couple of photos of what appeared to be UFOs in the sky. They had been on a roll of film, developed from their camera, but neither she nor Martin could remember even taking them, let alone where or when. Hopefully, by fighting back, and getting support and a possible implant removed, Maria will be free from what she describes as being "violated."

Alien sex

This is rather a taboo subject, and although I don't intend to dwell on it to any extent, it cannot be completely ignored. Some male, but very few female, abductees have reported encounters of a sexual kind. As a female researcher, I sometimes find other women will confide this type of experience when they would not tell their own partners, let alone a male investigator, and would never disclose it publically. I certainly respect their confidences, which I would never betray.

There are many cases of phantom or lost pregnancies reported, but it is not known whether they were caused by intercourse or artificial insemination. It must be understood that to the best of our scientific knowledge inter-breeding between different species is still prevented due to incompatibility in both chromosomes and DNA.

Whether an advanced technology could overcome such natural barriers is unknown. However, we do know that test-tube babies can be created using human sperm and ova.

If experiencers are being told the truth, then humanoid-looking extraterrestrials have so genetically engineered and computerised themselves, they are deprived of normal human spirituality and emotions. Our sexuality from birth to death affects every aspect of our society and family life, it is likely to be a major area of study for any alien culture. Perhaps they are seeking several differing experiences, in order to re-connect with their lost 'humanity'.

There are several cases reported out of Brazil, including the famous Antonio Villas Boas incident where he claimed he was forced to make love to a beautiful human-looking woman. Afterwards she pointed to her stomach and then to the stars, presumably indicating she would have a baby somewhere out there. According to some researchers he was not an itinerant farmer, but a lawyer in his local town.

At one MUFON conference I attended, a Chinese researcher discussed a case of a poor peasant, who had a similar experience. In every photo he had an enormous grin, I wonder why?

In 1995, actress Shelley Winters claimed on television that in 1945 she had sex with an alien, on a beach at Malibu. Despite shouts of disbelief from researchers, she claimed it was "one big orgasm" – lucky Shelley!

Australian Peter Khoury reported two intimate encounters with alien women, one of whom left two blond hairs under his foreskin. Researcher Bill Chalker had them analysed and DNA-tested. They did not belong to his wife. Testing revealed they contained unusual Asian-type genetic material, and had probably been genetically-manipulated – the hair was *chimeric*.

These intimate encounters are more prevalent than most people realise, but most participants never reveal them. The main reasons for their silence are fear of ridicule (or perhaps even being certified insane), or of what their partner, family and friends may think, and often not even wanting to admit to even themselves that they enjoyed the experience. One Tasmanian woman claims a long-term relationship with an alien; they are raising their three children between them. Another said her brief encounter in 1976, with an alien on-ship, was "the best sex (she) ever had."

Another contactee found herself on board a craft along with an unknown man, much younger than herself. She found herself having sex with him, with no thought of her husband and family, something she would "normally never do."

On 11 August 1966 a woman reported that when she was on her way to the local shop in rural Victoria she heard a humming sound. A silver disc, 50 feet across and 10 feet thick, landed in a paddock, about 30 feet away. A handsome man, wearing a metallic green tunic, stepped out from a sliding door. He touched her, and silently "willed" her to go into the craft with him, where he raped her. She found herself back in the paddock, with a burn on her ankle she said was caused by tripping over some kind of switch. The only other after-effects were a large indentation in the ground, and her subsequent pregnancy.

Long dissertations have been written regarding the possibility of inter-species breeding, our genetic heritage and other aspects of this subject, but there is a vast difference between the harvesting of human ova or sperm, where an abductee feels violated, and a full-on sexual encounter. It may be that they want to understand the most intimate of human experiences – or could it just be that our visitors are far from home and feeling rather lonely, and horny.

The effect of this kind of experience, especially on the female contactee's family and marriage, is more complex. The wife can develop an understandable aversion to sex, or even worse, dissatisfaction when comparing her own partner's performance. Her husband can feel angry that he cannot protect her, and jealous or betrayed that she has somehow been unfaithful, even against her will. Any publicity can further demoralise the husband and can contribute to an eventual breakdown of a marriage.

There have been more instances of this interaction than is generally realised, and each case is different, with different participants. The answers may be just as varied, especially given the belief that we have more than one species of visitor.

It has been correctly stated by psychologists that sex or the sexual urge begins in our brain, which tells us someone is desirable. Women have long known this secret inherently, hence the seductive use of make-up, clothing and especially perfume, to arouse the senses and the brain, which in turn instinctively communicate to the hormones and natural instincts of a male target. There are examples in the animal world, especially many species of male birds, who use plumage, song and dance try to attract the female. He appeals to her senses to tell her brain he is sexy.

How many people whose brains have been affected by drugs or alcohol, wake up in a strange bed, after the effects have worn off, and say, "What the hell was I thinking?" It has been clearly established that the use of implants, be they of human or alien origin, can affect mood, memory and the thinking processes of the recipient. It should prove no problem to the manipulators to create the required level of sexual attraction and desire in the mind of the hapless subject, which may explain the feeling of shame some experience later.

If the abductors require male sperm, then it may be easier and less invasive to excite him and collect it naturally. The female anatomy and reproductive process is much more complicated. We certainly have cases where ova, or the entire ovary are surgically removed, and in other cases of women being impregnated and foetuses removed early in their development. But what of the cases when it was just sex? Sometimes is it genuine romantic attraction, strange as that may seem?

Each situation is different. With different participants, motives, technology and emotional involvement. There is no all-encompassing explanation, and investigators cannot just wrap it up, and file it away in one neat little package. It is all much too complex and varied.

While there are several explanations being proffered at the moment, and many more we haven't even thought of yet, at this stage I am going to break my normal rule, and suggest one theory (among *many*) for *some* of these encounters – only suggest as I don't know the answers. In doing so, I will probably bring the wrath of my fellow researchers down upon my head with an enormous thump – but here goes!

Our own scientists have been very vocal in their belief that it is not possible for us to make inter-galactic voyages due to the time it would take to traverse the vast distances involved, but it might be possible to send robots. They have also voiced a concern that our new technology is such that one day we may find artificial intelligence virtually replacing us as humans, and some of the newest computers and robots are disturbingly intelligent.

In the past there were many reports of contact with humanoids who look like us, or vice versa. They usually re-iterated the same benign message of peace and love and how we must avoid our warlike ways and take care of the planet. The humanoid visitor in the Andrea Reynolds case told her that their bodies were genetically engineered, everything was miniature microchips, and they don't eat or have emotions. Is it possible that *some* of these human look-alike aliens are in fact extremely advanced biological robots? Androids, so advanced in fact, that as suggested in some sci-fi tales, they want to become truly alive and human and experience our full gamut of emotions, of which sex and reproduction are some of the strongest? Just a thought!

One aspect of human DNA and genetic material that UFO researchers completely overlook, is that it also provides a detailed chemical record of how life on planet earth has developed and *evolved* over the last 4000 million years! We have only just begun to appreciate some of the detail available ourselves, discovering we are related to ancient Neanderthals and Denisovians for example. Visiting aliens would consider that sort of detail about earth, its evolution and a dominant species with the potential for space travel, to be essential information.

While there is much witness data on aliens of varying bizarre shapes and descriptions, some visitors may be just as human as us, with the same needs and emotions, who maybe just fall in love, or more basically, aren't above using advanced intelligence, technology and mind control to get a bit on the side. Who knows? I don't have the answers!

Regardless of whether the experience is regarded by the victim as being pleasant or horrific – the plain simple fact is that it is a violation of their free will and physical, emotional and spiritual being, and no reason or excuse can justify it.

Epilogue

The mystery of the unidentified flying object will not go away. Over the last century alone, tens of thousands of reports have been made in Australia, and statistics tell us that this is only a small percentage of the actual incidents, most of which go unreported. If we consider the subject in the context of the world-wide scenario we are considering many millions of inexplicable events.

I have no doubt that the sceptics are right in that many can be identified as being of earthly origin, due to our own advancing technology. If one, only ONE, of these events or encounters is openly proven and accepted as being of an extraterrestrial origin, it will change mankind forever. Perhaps this is what the major powers mostly fear, and power, religion, greed, peer pressure and many other factors ensure the truth and its implications remain suppressed.

After Penny, who had her encounter as a child in Roma, had discussed the incident with us, as a mature adult, she took some time to reflect on her memories and thoughts. I have a feeling there was more she wasn't sharing, and part of a letter she later wrote to me was the following profound and thought-provoking statement.

"While scientists search for life on other planets and pose questions of whether we're down here alone or not, the alien has encroached on mankind in a very obscure and non-intrusive way. This form of invasion cannot be fought by our military. We are not equipped to defend ourselves.

"Invasion and adaptation go hand-in-hand. Genetic engineering is very high on the alien agenda. We hear about abductees seeing hybrids and having eggs taken from them, not to mention their embryos being removed. It is ignorant on our part to assume that they need us or our DNA to survive, or for that matter that they are the hybrids. Dipping into the human gene pool might give the alien the genetic make-up to adapt and multiply.

"In other words, you might say the alien has landed, genetically speaking. Who knows, maybe the microscope, and not the telescope, will be the first to discover the alien in all his glory and wonder. It is not a few of us who are chosen, it is all mankind. This would account for the elusive and insidious behaviour by the so-called greys. Most people would laugh at such an idea, but it is human nature to laugh at what we fear – the truth."

Penny made a very pertinent observation. With our current technology we cannot travel the galaxy ourselves due to the vast distances, however robots could go in our place. Perhaps the same applies to other intelligences way out there in the great beyond. Whether robotic or biological – or a combination of both – the visitors are taking tissue and genetic samples of most living organisms on earth. Are they also sharing their DNA with us?

Index

247

248

www.ingramcontent.com/pod-product-compliance
Lightning Source LLC
Chambersburg PA
CBHW080952050426
42334CB00057B/2601